Good Housekeeping

THE ILLUSTRATED BOOK OF
NEEDLECRAFTS

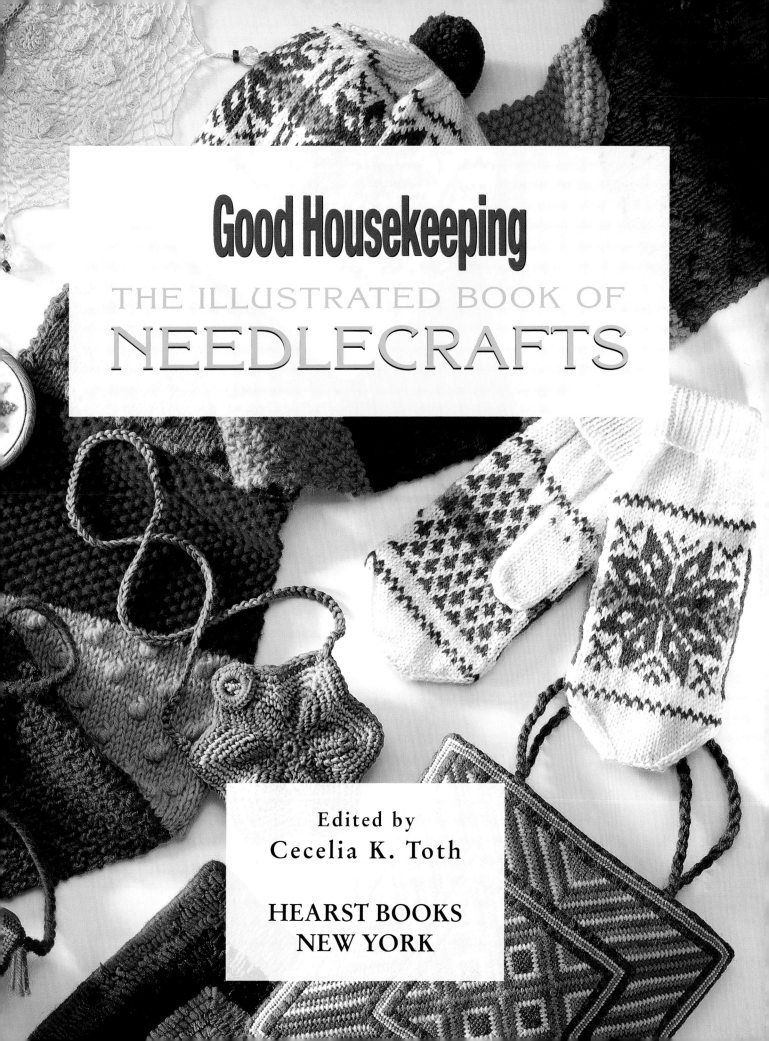

Good Housekeeping

THE ILLUSTRATED BOOK OF
NEEDLECRAFTS

Edited by
Cecelia K. Toth

HEARST BOOKS
NEW YORK

GOOD HOUSEKEEPING

Editor-in-Chief   Ellen Levine

The Good Housekeeping Illustrated Book of Needlecrafts
was created and produced by
CARROLL & BROWN LTD
20 Lonsdale Road, London NW6 6RD

Editor	Madeline Weston
Contributing Editor	Kate Poutney
Assistant Editor	Patricia Shine
Art Director	Denise Brown
Art Editor	Lisa V. Webb
Designer	James Arnold
Design Assistant	André-Scott Bamforth

Every effort has been made to ensure that all the information
in this book is accurate. However, due to differing conditions,
tools, and individual skills, the publisher cannot be responsible
for any injuries, losses, and other damages which may result
from the use of the information in this book.

1 3 5 7 9 10 8 6 4 2

Published by Hearst Books, a division of
Sterling Publishing Company, Inc.
387 Park Avenue South, New York, N.Y. 10016
Copyright © 1994
Carroll & Brown Limited and Hearst Communications, Inc.
Distributed in Canada by Sterling Publishing
c/o Canadian Manda Group, One Atlantic Avenue, Suite 105
Toronto, Ontario, Canada M6K 3E7

Printed in China
All rights reserved

ISBN 1-58816-035-1

CONTENTS

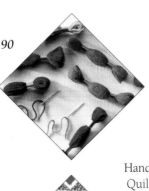

INTRODUCTION

We hope this book will help you discover the satisfaction of creating needlecrafts. There is something especially satisfying about making an item by hand. From the moment you embark on a project, you'll find tremendous pleasure in selecting quality materials, choosing a design that reflects your taste, and creating a piece that is uniquely yours.

In this book, we provide step-by-step instructions for learning knitting, crocheting, embroidery, needlepoint, quilting, and rugmaking. Each of these crafts has been around for generations, but all find honest uses on the contemporary scene. The techniques and patterns offered in the following pages represent the ingenuity of early needlecrafters, but the garments, accessories, and household items you'll see featured in the book are far from old-fashioned. The crafts may be ancient, but the effects you can achieve after learning a few basics are timeless. All it takes is a little time and a little imagination.

For each craft, **The Good Housekeeping Illustrated Book of Needlecrafts** describes and illustrates the necessary materials and equipment, how-to-techniques, and extensive stitch and pattern glossaries. In addition, the book offers an enticing selection of beautifully designed garments and accessories to make.

After you've entered the world of needlecrafts, you will find that the natural world around you – leaves, flowers, shadows, colors – will jump out as inspiration for your next project. After you've knitted your first sweater, stitched your first patchwork quilt or hooked your first rug, patterns, fabrics, and textures will strike you in completely new ways. For instance, you may glance on a pale green leaf, and suddenly imagine using it as the pattern for a knitted sweater or the border for a rug. Someone once described needlework as painting with a needle and we couldn't agree more!

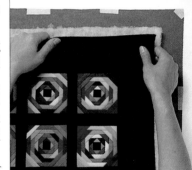

The Good Housekeeping Illustrated Book of Needlecrafts gives each reader the confidence to create completely new items or to personalize the projects that appear it is pages. You'll find items that can be worn, used in your home, or given as gifts, and the illustrated, step-by-step instructions and techniques give you all the information you need to start and *finish* these projects. Sweaters, hats, and mittens; pillows, quilts, and rugs; scarves, bags, and boxes – the book contains over 60 fabulous items to show off your skills.

Each technique in **The Good Housekeeping Illustrated Book of Needlecrafts** is presented in full color photographs that let you follow the action each step of the way. And the photos are so vivid, you can almost feel the texture of the yarn. It's like having an expert at your elbow. In the stitch and pattern glossaries, the large-size color samples are so bold that it is easy to see each individual stitch – a boon for beginners as well as experienced needleworkers.

In addition to the satisfaction of learning new skills, it is our wish that **The Good Housekeeping Illustrated Book of Needlecrafts** will open your eyes to the fine needlecrafts found in many homes and museums. We sincerely hope that you will use this book as a stepping stone to new skills and new interests – and to create heirlooms for the future.

The Editors of Good Housekeeping

KNITTING

*H*and knitting offers a lovely way of individualizing a wardrobe or a home. Today's knitters have a wide choice of colors and fibers to choose from, ranging from soft-colored wools, to jewel-toned silks, and versatile acrylics and cottons. In addition, knitting is quickly mastered, giving people of all ages creative satisfaction.

Knitting was around long before American settlers or Irish fishermen were bundling up in warm, woolly sweaters. In fact, it was practiced as far back as Biblical times. Over the years, the basic stitches have been joined with more complicated patterns, many of which have been used as a kind of signature to identify a particular village or clan. Each generation takes pleasure in rediscovering the satisfaction of creating hand-knit garments and accessories for themselves and their family. And today, with the wide range of exciting yarn colors and textures on the market, and the availability of fashionable patterns like those that appear in Good Housekeeping, there's even more reason to become adept at this exciting art.

EQUIPMENT & YARNS

STARTING A KNITTING project requires little more than enthusiasm, yarn, and a pair of standard straight knitting needles. These are made of aluminum, plastic, wood, or bamboo and come in a range of sizes. For large pieces, and for knitting in the round, circular needles are useful, while gloves call for double-pointed needles. A few simple accessories are also helpful.

TYPES OF NEEDLES

Special needles are used for cables, or for knitting in the round.

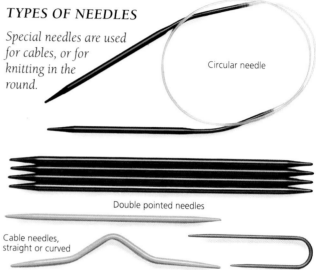

Circular needle

Double pointed needles

Cable needles,
straight or curved

KNITTING NEEDLE SIZES

Below is a table of approximately equivalent knitting needle sizes:

US	Metric (mm)
0	2.00
1	2.25
2	2.75
3	3.25
4	3.50
5	3.75
6	4.00
7	4.50
8	5.00
9	5.50
10	6.00
10½	6.50
11	8.00
13	9.00
15	10.00

OTHER USEFUL EQUIPMENT

These will help you hold or count your stitches, mark your place, or handle colors separately. Long pins and a blunt-pointed tapestry needle are needed for joining.

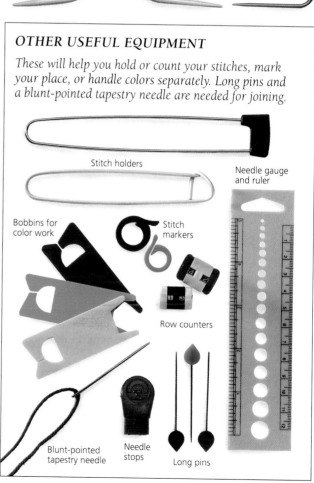

Stitch holders

Needle gauge and ruler

Bobbins for color work

Stitch markers

Row counters

Blunt-pointed tapestry needle

Needle stops

Long pins

YARN WEIGHT AND PLY

Yarns come in a range of standard weights, and the most popular knitting yarns relate approximately to one another: Knitting worsted is twice the weight of sport weight, with fisherman (Aran) being roughly equal to three strands of sport weight. Bulky is approximately equal to four strands of sport weight or two strands of knitting worsted.

The term ply refers to the number of strands which, when twisted together, make up the yarn, i.e. 2-, 3- and 4-ply are made up of that number of strands. Ply does not define weight – a thicker yarn may have fewer strands than a thinner one.

YARN CONTENT

Popular knitting yarns come in natural or synthetic materials. Natural yarns can be of animal or vegetable fibers, the former include wool, mohair, angora, cashmere, alpaca, and silk, while vegetable fibers produce cotton or linen yarns. Synthetic yarns include polyesters and acrylics; these are easier to wash and can be worn by people sensitive to wool. Yarns are often made of blends of two different types of fiber – mohair and nylon, or wool and silk are popular combinations.

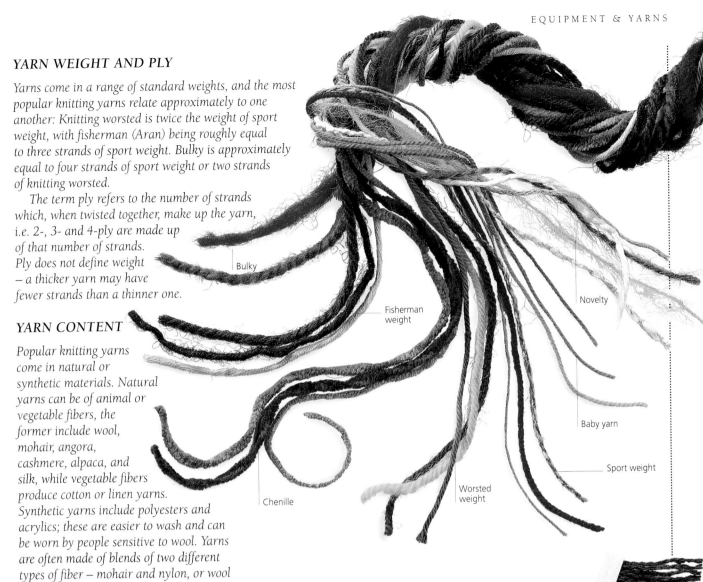

Bulky

Fisherman weight

Novelty

Baby yarn

Sport weight

Worsted weight

Chenille

BUYING YARN

Knitting yarns are most often sold in ready-to-use balls and skeins.

Some yarns are sold in hanks or cones which are best wound into balls before use.

SHADE CARDS

Popular yarns usually come in a wide range of colors.

CASTING ON

THE FIRST STEP in knitting any article is to place the required number of stitches on the needles – this is called casting on. These stitches will form one edge of the finished article, usually the bottom. If you want the edge to be even, it is important that the stitches all be the same size. It is also necessary for the stitches to

be moderately loose so you can easily work them off the needle. We recommend the one-needle cast on method for beginners, as it is easy to master, but if your resulting stitches are too snug on the needle, try the two-needle cast on. The first stitch in both methods is formed by making a slip knot.

Making a slip knot

About 6 inches from the yarn end, make a loop and insert needle under the short length (*left*). Draw the thread through loop and pull both ends to tighten the knot on the needle (*right*).

ONE-NEEDLE CAST-ON EDGE

This should be made at a measured distance from the end of the yarn. Allow 1 inch per stitch for heavyweight yarn and ¹/₂ inch per stitch for lightweight. For example, start 24 inches from the slip knot to cast on 24 stitches in knitting worsted. The cast-on stitches will form a firm, yet elastic, foundation for all subsequent stitches, which is suitable for all patterns except those with a delicate edge.

TWO-NEEDLE CAST-ON EDGE

With this method, each new stitch is formed as a knit stitch (see page 14) and transferred to the left needle. If you work through the loop fronts on the first row, it produces a soft, loose edge, suitable for fine lace stitches. If you work through the loop backs on the first row, a firmer edge will be produced. Casting on with this method is useful when increasing stitches at one side (see page 18) or when completing a buttonhole (see page 62).

LEFT-HANDED KNITTERS

Reverse the instructions for left and right hands if you are left-handed. To cast on, hold the needle in your left hand and manipulate the working yarn with your right hand. When knitting, hold the needle bearing the stitches in your right hand and insert the left needle through the stitches. If you find it helpful, place this book in front of a mirror to follow the correct hand positions.

One-needle cast on

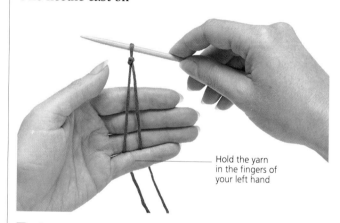

Hold the yarn in the fingers of your left hand

1 Allowing sufficient yarn for the number of stitches you want to cast on, form the slip knot; hold the needle in the right hand. Using the ring and little fingers of your left hand, hold the strands of yarn securely.

2 Slip your left forefinger and thumb between the strands so that the strand from the skein is at the back, and the working yarn is at the front.

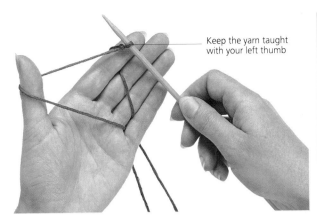

Keep the yarn taught with your left thumb

3 Bring your left thumb up and spread your other fingers still holding on to the yarn ends.

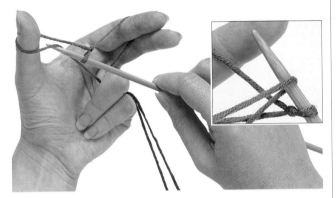

4 Take the needle under the yarn held across your thumb (*left*) and then up to the yarn on your left forefinger (*right*).

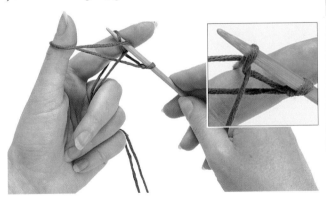

5 Putting the point of the needle behind the yarn on your left forefinger (*left*), draw the needle and yarn through the loop on your thumb to make the stitch (*right*).

6 Let the loop slip from your thumb and pull both ends to secure the new stitch. Repeat steps 1 through 6 for each required stitch.

Two-needle cast on

1 Make the slip knot and hold the needle in your left hand. Insert right needle through front of loop and pass the working yarn under and over its tip.

2 Draw yarn through the slip knot to form a new stitch.

3 Leaving the slip knot on the left needle, place the new stitch next to it.

4 Insert needle through front of loop of new stitch and pass the working yarn under and over its tip. Continue to form a new stitch as in steps 2 and 3 above.

Soft edge
Knit through the front of the stitch on the first row.

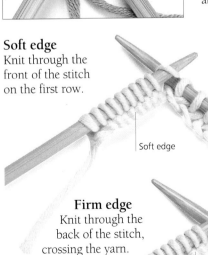

Soft edge

Firm edge
Knit through the back of the stitch, crossing the yarn.

Firm edge

KNIT & PURL STITCHES

KNIT AND PURL are the two fundamental stitches which most people recognize as plain knitting. Although these stitches are basic, they can be used in endless combinations to create any desired effect, whether you are knitting the simplest scarf or the most elaborate sweater. The knit stitch forms a flat, vertical loop on the fabric face; the purl stitch forms a horizontal semicircle. The simplest knitted pieces are worked in garter stitch, where every row is knitted; both sides look identical. Knitting and purling alternate rows produces stockinette stitch – with a smooth knitted side and pebbly purled one.

The knit side of stockinette stitch is smooth and flat

The reverse shows all the ridges of the purl stitches

STOCKINETTE STITCH

This basic and versatile knitting pattern produces work that tends to curl if not blocked (see page 64). It stretches more widthwise than from top to bottom. The knit side is generally used as the right side.

REVERSE STOCKINETTE STITCH

This is knitted in the same way as stockinette stitch, but with the purl side used as the right side. It is often used as a background for cables and other raised patterns.

Reverse stockinette stitch, with its purl stitches, can be used as a right side

The back shows the plain, smooth texture of the knit stitches

GARTER STITCH

This stitch is most commonly formed by knitting every row, but the same effect is achieved by purling every row. The work formed stays flat and firm, resists curling, and is good for borders, buttonhole bands, and edgings. It has a loose structure with "give" in both directions.

Knitting every row produces work that is identical on both sides, with ridges and furrows

KNIT STITCH USING RIGHT HAND

In this method, use your right hand to draw the yarn around the right needle. The amount of yarn released with each stitch is controlled by wrapping the working yarn between your two end fingers. Your left hand propels the knitting forward while your right hand makes the stitch – raising the thread, placing it over the needle, and pulling it through the loop.

The forefinger keeps the yarn taught

1 Hold the needle with cast-on stitches in your left hand. Take yarn around the little finger of your right hand, under the next 2 fingers, and over the top of your forefinger.

2 Keeping the yarn behind the work, hold the 2nd needle in your right hand and insert it into the front of the first stitch.

3 With your right forefinger, take the yarn forward under and over the point of the right needle.

4 Draw yarn through the loop and push the resulting stitch toward the tip of the left needle so you can slip it onto your right needle.

KNIT STITCH USING LEFT HAND

In this method, often found to be faster than holding yarn in your right hand, you use the forefinger of your left hand to keep the yarn under tension and to scoop the yarn onto the right needle. The amount of yarn released is controlled partly by your last two fingers, and partly by your forefinger. Hold your left hand up slightly to help keep the yarn taut.

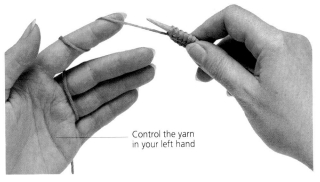

Control the yarn in your left hand

1 Hold the needle with the cast-on stitches in your right hand. Wrap the yarn over your left forefinger, let it fall across the palm and take up the slack between the last 2 fingers.

2 With work in left hand, extend your forefinger, pulling the yarn behind the needle. Using your thumb and middle finger, push the first stitch toward tip and insert right needle into front of stitch.

3 Twist the right needle and pull the tip under the working yarn to draw loop onto the right needle.

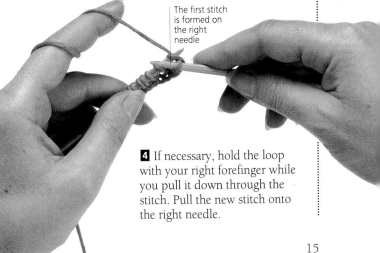

The first stitch is formed on the right needle

4 If necessary, hold the loop with your right forefinger while you pull it down through the stitch. Pull the new stitch onto the right needle.

PURL STITCH USING RIGHT HAND

The movements here are opposite those for knit stitch. The needle is put into the front of the stitch, then the yarn, which is held in the front, is thrown over the back of the needle. Purl stitches tend to be looser than knit ones, so keep your forefinger closer to the work to help make the stitches even.

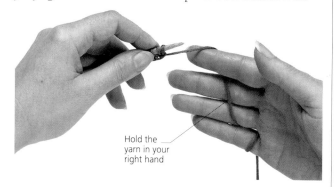

Hold the
yarn in your
right hand

1 Hold the needle with stitches (cast-on or knit) in your left hand. Wrap yarn around your little finger, under your next 2 fingers, and over the forefinger of your right hand.

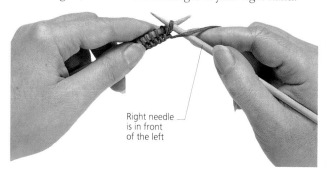

Right needle
is in front
of the left

2 Keeping the yarn in front of the work, pick up the needle in your right hand and insert the point into the front of the first stitch on the left needle.

3 With your right forefinger, take the yarn over the point of the right needle, and then under it.

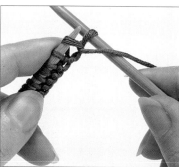

4 Draw the loop on the right needle through the stitch and push the new stitch toward the tip of the left needle so you can slip it onto your right needle.

PURL STITCH USING LEFT HAND

With this method, your left forefinger holds the working yarn taut while you scoop up a new loop with your right needle. This action is helped by twisting your left wrist forward to release the yarn and using your middle finger to push the yarn towards the tip of the needle.

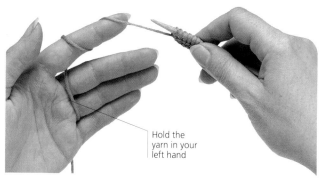

Hold the
yarn in your
left hand

1 Hold the needle with the stitches in your right hand. Wrap the yarn over your left forefinger, let it fall across your palm, and take up the slack between your last 2 fingers.

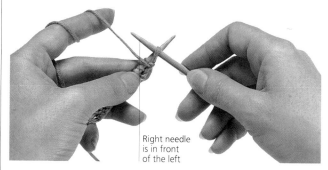

Right needle
is in front
of the left

2 With the work in your left hand, extend your forefinger slightly, pulling the working yarn in front of the needle. With your thumb and middle finger, push the first stitch toward the tip and insert the right needle into the front of the stitch. Hold stitch with your right forefinger.

3 Twisting your left wrist back slightly, use the forefinger of your left hand to wrap yarn around the right needle.

4 Push down and back with the right needle to draw the loop through the stitch and slip the new stitch onto the right needle. Straighten your left forefinger to tighten new stitch.

CORRECTING MISTAKES

THE SOONER YOU notice an error in your knitting the easier it is to correct. If a stitch has fallen off the needle one row down, you can retrieve it using your knitting needles. If you don't, it will ravel and form a run, and you will need a crochet hook to pick it up. If you knit a stitch incorrectly one or two rows down, you can unpick it and then correct it in the same way. If a mistake has occurred near the start of your piece, you will have to ravel your work to get close to it. If you are working in stockinette or ribbing, always pick up stitches with the knit side toward you, as this is easiest. Be careful not to twist any of the stitches.

Retrieving a dropped knit stitch

1 Insert your right needle into the front of the dropped stitch, picking up the loose yarn behind it.

2 Take your left needle into the back of the stitch and gently lift the stitch up and over the loose yarn and off the right needle.

3 To transfer the new stitch, insert the left needle into the front so that the stitch slips onto it in the correct working position.

Retrieving a dropped purl stitch

1 Insert your right needle into the back of the dropped stitch, picking up the loose yarn in front.

2 Take your left needle into the front of the stitch and gently lift the stitch up and over the loose yarn and off the needle.

3 Insert the left needle into the new stitch on the right needle and slip the new stitch onto it in the correct working position.

Correcting a run of dropped stitches

With knit side of work facing you, insert crochet hook into front of fallen stitch and pick up loose yarn behind. Draw yarn through stitch, forming a new stitch. Continue until you reach top of run. To work on purl side, insert hook into back of stitch and pick up yarn in front.

RAVELING YOUR WORK

*Mark the row in which your error occurred. Take the work off the needles and carefully pull the working thread, until you are **one row** above the error.*

To replace stitches on needle, hold yarn to back, and insert your left needle into front of first stitch below unpicked row. Pull on working yarn to remove top stitch.

INCREASING

IT IS NECESSARY to increase (add stitches), when you are shaping a garment. Increases are also necessary in creating certain stitch patterns, such as bobbles and laces (see pages 38 and 42). Where increases are made in garment shaping, they are often worked in pairs so that the item widens equally on both sides. Where increases are made in stitch patterns, they are combined with decreases (see page 21) so the total number of stitches remains constant.

There are several methods of producing increases. The yarn-over method (see page 20) is visible and is used for lace patterns. The other methods are called invisible. In reality, all increases can be seen but some are more obvious than others and different methods are used at different times.

Bar, raised, and lifted increases are all invisible increases, and are typically used in garment shaping. When you are creating a gradual shape, such as a sleeve, it is neater to make the increases two or three stitches in from the sides and to use one of the invisible increases. With a complicated pattern, you will find it easier to add the stitches at the edges.

BAR METHOD

This frequently used technique produces a small bump on the right side of the work, hence its name. It is commonly abbreviated as Inc 1. You knit (or purl) into the front and back of a stitch to make two stitches. This increase can be used near the edge of the work when shaping garments or when making bobbles, where the bump will not matter.

1 Knit a stitch in the usual way but do not remove it from the left-hand needle.

2 Insert right-hand needle into back of the same stitch and knit again.

3 Remove the stitch from the needle. The extra stitch formed by this method produces a small bump on the right side. This will not be noticeable at the edge of the work.

MAKE ONE

Here, you pick up the horizontal strand between two stitches and knit (or purl) it to make a new stitch. To make it virtually invisible, you have to work into the back of the strand so that it twists. It is effective for shaping darts on mitten or glove thumbs, and is commonly abbreviated M1. This increase is sometimes called the raised method.

1 Insert your left-hand needle from front to back under the horizontal strand between 2 stitches.

2 Knit (or purl) into the back of the strand on your left-hand needle.

3 Remove the stitch from the needle; the twist in the stitch prevents a gap from appearing.

LIFTED METHOD

This increase forms a slant, which needs to be paired with another to balance the work. You have to work both left-side and right-side increases from the center. This method is particularly suitable for raglan sleeves as the resulting arrows create a fully fashioned appearance. Knit it with a loose tension since this method tends to tighten the work. The increase is made by knitting (or purling) into the horizontal strand below the next stitch to be worked. It is abbreviated as K (or P) up 1.

Paired increases on either edge of a piece of knitting form slanting lines

Right-side increase

1 Insert your right-hand needle from front to back into the top of stitch below the next one to be knitted.

2 Knit the loop you have just picked up in the usual way.

3 Then knit the following stitch normally.

Left-side increase

1 Insert your left-hand needle from back to front into the top of stitch below the last completed stitch.

2 Pull stitch back gently and knit into the front of the loop.

DOUBLE AND MULTIPLE INCREASES

To make two increases in the same stitch (M2), knit, purl, and knit into the front of the stitch. To make more than two stitches, as in bobble and embossed patterns (see page 38), continue to knit and purl in the same stitch for the number of stitches that must be made. An increase of, say, five stitches is used to form a large bobble.

YARNOVER VISIBLE INCREASE

This is used for lace and other fancy patterns. This increase method produces a hole, which forms an openwork pattern. The basic technique is to wind the yarn once around the needle to form a loop, which is knitted or purled on the next row. The yarn is wound in different ways depending on where the new stitch falls (see below). This yarn over increase method is abbreviated as yo.

Yarn over in stockinette

1 To make a yarn over in stockinette, bring the yarn forward to the front of the work, loop it over your right-hand needle *(left)* and knit the next stitch *(right)*.

2 The loop and new stitch are on the right-hand needle; knit to the end of the row.

3 On the following row, and with the rest of the stitches, purl the loop in the usual way.

Between purl stitches in reverse stockinette

Purl stitch, then take yarn back over right needle then forward under it.

Between two knit stitches in garter stitch

Bring the yarn forward over the right-hand needle, then back under it again.

Between two purl stitches in garter stitch

Take yarn back over right needle, then forward under it.

Between knit and purl stitches in ribbing

After knitting a stitch, bring yarn forward between needles, then back over right-hand needle and forward under it.

Between purl and knit stitches in ribbing

After purling, take the yarn over the right-hand needle from front to back.

DOUBLE AND MULTIPLE INCREASES

Several stitches may be made by the yarn-over method. In stockinette stitch, to make a double increase, yo2, on a knit row, bring the yarn forward as for single yarn over but wrap it twice around the right needle before knitting the next stitch. On the next row, purl the first of the new stitches and knit the second.

When making multiple increases, yo3 (4, etc.), bring the yarn forward and then 3, (4, etc.) times around the needle. On the next row, purl and knit the new stitches alternately, always knitting the last new stitch.

DECREASING

BINDING OFF (see page 23) is the preferred method of decreasing when three or more stitches have to be lost, for example, at an underarm. However, if only one or two stitches have to be decreased, as when shaping a garment, any of the three methods described below may be used. Each method is visible and pulls stitches on a diagonal to the right or left. If you are decreasing randomly, or at the edge of the work, the direction of the slant is not important. In symmetrical shaping, however, such as with a raglan sleeve or V-neck, the decreases must be paired, to the right and left of the center, so that the decreases balance one another. Right and left slants are made by knitting (or purling) two stitches together in the fronts or backs of the stitches.

Slipstitch decreases slant in only one direction, so in the same row they are generally used in combination with knitting two stitches together.

KNITTING TWO STITCHES TOGETHER

Decreasing by knitting two stitches together creates a slightly tighter decrease than the slip-stitch method. It is abbreviated K2tog for a right slant; K2tog tbl for a left slant.

Right slant

Knit 2 stitches together through the front of both loops. A slant to the right is used at the left edge of the work.

Left slant

Knit 2 stitches together through the back of both loops. A slant to the left is used at the right edge of the work.

PURLING TWO STITCHES TOGETHER

Decreases to the right are made by purling two stitches together through the front of both loops. This is abbreviated P2tog. For a decrease which slants to the left, purl two stitches together through the back of both loops. This method is abbreviated P2tog tbl.

THE SLIP-STITCH DECREASE

This results in a slightly looser decrease than knitting two stitches together. When made on a knit row, it slants from right to left, and is abbreviated Sl 1, k1, psso. A similar decrease can be made on a purl row, when it slants from left to right. It is abbreviated Sl 1, p1, psso.

On a knit row

1 Slip one stitch knitwise from your left needle onto the right needle then knit the next stitch.

2 Insert your left needle into the front of the slipped stitch and pull it over the knitted one.

3 The right-to-left slant is used on the right side of the center of the work.

SELVAGES

THE CAST-ON and bound-off (see page 23) stitches usually form the top and bottom ends of the work, and often have another finish applied to them, such as a fringe or neckband. The sides, known as selvages, may be sewed into a seam or left exposed. If the sides are to be joined, use one of the simple edges since they are easier to sew. If you are knitting something with exposed edges, such as a scarf, tie, or blanket, use a border. This will be more attractive and help the finished piece lie flat.

Use the slip-stitch edge where there will be an edge-to-edge seam

SIMPLE SELVAGE

The edge in stockinette stitch, is formed by the work's alternate knit and purl rows. Beginning knitters often have trouble keeping this edge tight. Two variations can make this a more stable edge and one more suitable for seaming. The slip-stitch edge is suitable when you will be seaming edge-to-edge, the garter-stitch edge is effective for backstitched and overcast seams.

Slip-stitch selvage
On all right sides of work (knit rows): Slip the first stitch knitwise then knit the last stitch.
   On all wrong sides of work (purl rows): Slip the first stitch purlwise then purl the last stitch.

Garter-stitch selvage
Knit the right-side rows as usual, and knit the first and last stitches of every wrong-side (purl) row.

A garter-stitch edge can be used when there will be a backstitched seam

The double garter-stitch edge is firm and even

BORDERS

Most pattern instructions do not take special edges into account, so you may have to add two additional stitches on each side. The double garter-stitch edge is firm and even, and will not curl. The double chain edge is decorative as well as firm.

A double chain edge is a more decorative edge

Double garter-stitch edge
On every row: Slip the first stitch knitwise and knit the 2nd stitch; knit the last 2 stitches.

Double chain edge
On all right sides of work (knit rows): Slip the first stitch knitwise, purl the 2nd stitch. Knit to the last 2 stitches, then purl 1 and slip last stitch knitwise.

BINDING OFF

BINDING OFF PROVIDES a selvage (finished edge) at the end of your work. This technique is also used in armhole and buttonhole shaping. Plain binding off is the most common and easiest method.

Usually you bind off on the right side of the work and work the stitches in the same way as they were formed, knitting knit stitches and purling purl stitches. It is important that you bind off somewhat loosely, otherwise the edge may pull in and become distorted. If your stitches are too tight, try binding off with a needle one size larger than used for the work, or use the suspended bind off.

PLAIN BIND OFF

This produces a firm, plain edge that is suitable for seaming and armhole and buttonhole shaping.

1 Work your first 2 stitches in pattern. *Keeping the yarn to the back, insert the tip of your left-hand needle through the first stitch.

2 Lift the first stitch over the 2nd stitch and off your needle.

3 Work the next stitch in pattern.* Repeat sequence set out between the asterisks until the desired number of stitches are bound off. Secure yarn at end (*see box below*).

SUSPENDED BIND OFF

More flexible than the plain bind off, this method produces a looser edge and is preferable if your selvages tend to be tight.

1 Work first 2 stitches in pattern. *Keeping yarn to the back, insert the tip of your left needle through the first stitch. Lift the first stitch over the 2nd stitch off the right needle, and retain on left needle.

2 Work the next stitch and drop the held stitch when you complete a new stitch.*

3 Repeat the instructions between the asterisks until 2 stitches are left. Knit these 2 together. Secure yarn at end, (*see box below*).

SECURING YARN END

After binding off with either of the two methods above, you will have a single stitch left on your needle. Slip this off your needle, take the yarn end and slip it through the last stitch and pull firmly to tighten the loop.

Then, using a tapestry needle, weave the secured yarn end into the seam edge to a depth of two to three inches.

STITCH GAUGE

AT THE BEGINNING of every knitting pattern you will find the stitch gauge – the number of stitches and rows to the inch that should be obtained using the specified needles and yarn. This measure is very important to the size and fit of your garment and you must check that you are working to the given gauge. Before beginning a new project, make a swatch four inches square and measure the number of stitches and rows.

CHECKING THE GAUGE

Using the given gauge as a guide, and the needles and yarn designated, cast on four times the number of stitches that equal an inch. Then take your sample and pin it to a flat surface; do not stretch it. Use a ruler, plastic tape measure, or stitch gauge to measure both horizontally and vertically.

Use a tape measure to check the distance between the pins

MAKING ADJUSTMENTS

If your stitch gauge does not exactly equal that given, change needle size and knit another sample. One needle size makes a difference of about one stitch over two inches. If you have more stitches to the inch, your tension is too tight and you should change to larger needles. If you have fewer stitches, your tension is too loose so use smaller needles.

Measuring horizontally

In stockinette, it is easier to measure on the knit side, where each loop represents one stitch. In garter stitch, count the loops in one row only. Place 2 pins one inch apart and count the stitches between them.

Measuring vertically

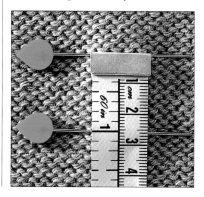

In stockinette, it is easier to measure on the purl side where 2 ridges equals one row. In garter stitch, a ridge is one row and a valley another. Place 2 pins an inch apart and count the number of rows between them.

THE EFFECT OF YARNS AND PATTERNS

Yarn and pattern also affect stitch gauge, so it is especially important to make a sample if you are changing either one from those called for in the instructions. Loosely spun or thick yarns, such as knitting worsted weight, will knit up with many fewer stitches and rows than firmly spun yarns, such as silk. Rib and other textured patterns produce much tighter work than do lacy patterns.

Sport weight is the finest of the three yarns and produces the smallest square

Knitting worsted, worked to the same number of stitches, makes a larger piece than sport weight

Fisherman (Aran) yarn is the bulkiest yarn of the three and has fewest stitches to the inch

KNITTING TERMINOLOGY

A SET OF standard abbreviations, terms, and symbols have been devised in order to reduce knitting instructions to their shortest possible length. Otherwise, the row-by-row instructions for even a simple garment could take several pages. Multiples and repeats are commonly found in patterns and a fuller explanation is offered below.

Pattern abbreviations

alt	alternate
beg	beginning
CC	contrasting color
cn	cable needle
dec(s)	decrease(s), (see page 21)
dp	double pointed
join	attach yarn
k	knit
k2tog	knit 2 stitches together
k-wise	insert needle as though to knit
inc(s)	increase(s), (see page 18)
lp	loop
M1	make 1, (see page 18)
MC	main color
p	purl
pat	pattern
psso	pass slipped stitch over the knitted one, (see page 21)
p2tog	purl 2 stitches together
p-wise	insert needle as though to purl
rem	remaining
rep	repeat
rnd(s)	rounds
sk	skip
sl	slip (always slip sts purlwise unless otherwise instructed)
sl st	slip stitch, (see page 21)
ssk	slip, slip, knit decrease (see page 43)
st(s)	stitch(es)
tbl	through back of loop (work into back of stitch)
tog	together
work even	to keep in pattern across the row
WS	wrong side
yb	yarn to back
yf	yarn forward
yo	yarn over needle, (see page 20)
*	Work instructions immediately following *, then repeat as directed, (see Repeats)
[ ]	Work or repeat all instructions enclosed in brackets as directed immediately after, (see Repeats)
–	The number of sts that should be on your needles or across a row is given after a dash at the end of the row. This serves as a check point, especially after a section of increasing or decreasing.

Repeats

Because a knitting pattern usually consists of sequences of stitches, two devices are used to express this in the shortest possible space. One is the asterisk*, which is placed before the instruction it relates to. For example, *P2, *k2, p2; rep from *, end k2,* means you purl the first two stitches, then for the rest of the row until you are two stitches from the end, you knit two, purl two. The last two stitches are knitted.

Brackets are also used to indicate repeats. For example, *P2 [k2, p2] ten times, k3* means that after purling your first two stitches you repeat the sequence of knitting two and purling two ten times (a total of 40 stitches) before knitting the last three.

Multiples

Preceding each stitch pattern is an instruction about the number of stitches required to complete the pattern across the row. This is expressed as a multiple of a number of stitches, for example, *multiple of 6 sts.* It may also include an additional number to balance the pattern or account for a diagonal, for example, *multiple of 6 sts plus 3.* The number of stitches on the needle must be divisible by the multiple, so for a multiple of 5 sts plus 2, you would need to cast on 5 + 2, 10 + 2, 15 + 2,.... 100 + 2, etc. In the pattern instructions, the multiple is expressed in the following ways:

Multiple of 8 sts plus 2
Row 1: *K4, p4*, k2.
Row 2: *P4, k4*, p2.
or
Row 1: *K4, p4, rep from *, end k2.
Row 2: *P4, k4, rep from *, end p2.

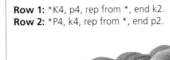

TEXTURED PATTERNS

WITH ONLY THE two basic stitches, a wide variety of patterns can be created. Though the techniques are simple, the results are often sophisticated, and lend themselves to use on a wide variety of garments. In combination, knit and purl stitches play off each other, creating texture. When they are worked vertically, the knit rows tend to stand out from the purl ones. When they are worked horizontally, in welt or ridge patterns, the purl rows stand away from the knit rows. In textured patterns, the stitches form subtle designs that alter the surface of the fabric.

Vertical rows of knit and purl are known as ribbing, and will stretch in a crosswise direction. This quality is ideal for use on garment edges, and for children's clothes because the garment will expand to accommodate the child. To be sure cuffs and waistbands are snug fitting, use a smaller needle than those used for the body of the garment.

KNIT AND PURL PILLOWS

Use up scrap yarns by working small squares or rectangles in some of your favorite textured stitches; then sew them together for these patchwork knit pillows. They will serve as samplers of different knitting stitches. (See page 225).

Combining different yarns with various stitches can make subtle texture changes

A three by three rib can be knitted in two-color stripes

Ladder stitch panels are interspersed with plain panels of stockinette stitch

LADDER ▲

Worked over 11 sts on a background of st st

Row 1 (right side): P2, k7, p2.
Row 2: K2, p7, k2.
Rows 3 and 4: as rows 1 and 2.
Row 5: P.
Row 6: as row 2.
Row 7: as row 1.
Rows 8 and 9: As rows 6 and 7.
Row 10: K.
Rows 1 to 10 form the pattern.

◄ THREE BY THREE RIB

Multiple of 6 sts plus 3

Row 1: *K3, p3; rep from * to last 3 sts, k3.
Row 2: P3, *k3, p3; rep from * to end.
Rows 1 to 2 form the pattern.

MOSS STITCH RIB ▼

Multiple of 11 sts plus 5

Row 1: K5, *[k1, p1] 3 times, k5; rep from * to end.
Row 2: *P5, [p1, k1] 3 times; rep from * to last 5 sts, p5.
Rows 1 to 2 form the pattern.

BROKEN RIB ▲

Multiple of 2 sts plus 1

Row 1 (right side): K.
Row 2: P1, *k1, p1; rep from * to end.
Rows 1 to 2 form the pattern.

MOCK FISHERMAN'S RIB ►

Multiple of 4 sts plus 3.

All rows: *K2, p2; rep from * to last 3 sts, k2, p1.

27

DIAMOND BROCADE ▲
Multiple of 8 sts plus 1
Row 1 (right side): K4, *p1, k7;
rep from * to last 5 sts, p1, k4.
Row 2: P3, *k1, p1, k1, p5; rep
from * to last 6 sts, k1, p1, k1, p3.
Row 3: K2, *p1, k3; rep from * to
last 3 sts, p1, k2.
Row 4: P1, *k1, p5, k1, p1; rep
from * to end.
Row 5: *P1, k7; rep from * to last
st, p1.
Row 6: as row 4.
Row 7: as row 3.
Row 8: as row 2.
Rows 1 to 8 form the pattern.

SEED STITCH ▲
Multiple of 4 sts
Row 1: *K3, p1; rep from * to end.
Row 2: P.
Row 3: K.
Row 4: P.
Row 5: K1, *p1, k3;* rep from * to last 3 sts,
p1, k2.
Row 6: P.
Row 7: K.
Rows 1 to 7 form the pattern.

SEEDED TEXTURE ▲
Multiple of 5 sts plus 2
Row 1 (right side): K2, *p3, k2; rep from
* to end.
Row 2: P.
Row 3: *P3, k2; rep from * to last 2 sts, p2.
Row 4: P.
Rows 1 to 4 form the pattern.

DOUBLE MOSS STITCH ▶
Multiple of 4 sts plus 2
Row 1: K2, *p2, k2; rep from * to end.
Row 2: P2, *k2, p2; rep from * to end.
Row 3: as row 2.
Row 4: as row 1.
Rows 1 to 4 form the pattern.

◀ MOSS STITCH
Multiple of 2 sts plus 1
All rows: K1, * p1, k1, rep from * to end.

CHEVRON RIB ▲
Multiple of 18 sts plus 1
Row 1 (right side): P1, *k1, p2, k2,
p2, k1, p1; rep from * to end.
Row 2: *K3, p2, k2, p2, k1,
[p2, k2] twice; rep from * to
last st, k1.
Row 3: *[P2, k2] twice, p3, k2, p2,
k2, p1; rep from * to last st, p1.
Row 4: *K1, p2, k2, p2, k5, p2,
k2, p2; rep from * to last st, k1.
Rows 1 to 4 form the pattern.

MARRIAGE LINES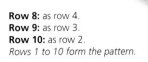

Worked over 17sts on a background of st st

Row 1 (right side): P3, k6, p1, k2, p1, k1, p3.
Row 2: K1, p1, [k1, p2] twice, k1, p5, k1, p1, k1.
Row 3: P3, k4, p1, k2, p1, k3, p3.
Row 4: K1, p1, k1, p4, k1, p2, k1, p3, k1, p1, k1.
Row 5: P3, [k2, p1] twice, k5, p3.
Row 6: K1, p1, k1, p6, k1, p2, [k1, p1] twice, k1.
Row 7: as row 5.

Row 8: as row 4.
Row 9: as row 3.
Row 10: as row 2.
Rows 1 to 10 form the pattern.

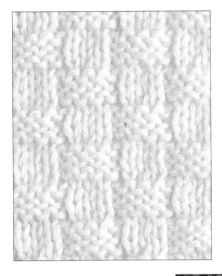

RIPPLE STRIPE

Multiple of 8 sts plus 1

Row 1 (right side): K4, *p1, k7; rep from * to last 5 sts, p1, k4.
Row 2: P3, *k3, p5; rep from * to last 6 sts, k3, p3.
Row 3: K2, *p2, k1, p2, k3; rep from * to last 2 sts, k2.
Row 4: P1, *k2, p3, k2, p1; rep from * to end.
Row 5: K1, *p1, k5, p1, k1; rep from * to end.
Row 6: P.
Rows 1 to 6 form the pattern.

BASKETWEAVE ▲

Multiple of 8 sts plus 3

Row 1 (right side): K.
Row 2: K4, p3, *k5, p3; rep from * to last 4 sts, k4.
Row 3: P4, k3, * p5, k3; rep from * to last 4 sts, p4.
Row 4: as row 2.
Row 5: K.
Row 6: P3, *k5, p3; rep from * to end.
Row 7: K3, *p5, k3; rep from * to end.
Row 8: as row 6.
Rows 1 to 8 form the pattern.

SQUARE LATTICE

Multiple of 14 sts plus 2

Row 1 (right side): K.
Rows 2, 4 and 6: P2, *[k1, p1] twice, k1, p2; rep from * to end.
Rows 3, 5, and 7: K3, *p1, k1, p1, k4; rep from * to last 3 sts, k3.
Row 8: P2, *k12, p2; rep from * to end.
Row 9: K2, *p12; rep from * to end.
Row 10: P.
Rows 11, 13, and 15: K2, *[p1, k1] twice, p1, k2; rep from * to end.
Rows 12, 14, and 16: P3, *k1, p1, k1, p4; rep from * to last 3 sts, p3.
Row 17: P7, *k2, p12; rep from * to last 9 sts, k2, p7.
Row 18: K7, *p2, k12; rep from * to last 9 sts, p2, k7.
Rows 1 to 18 form the pattern.

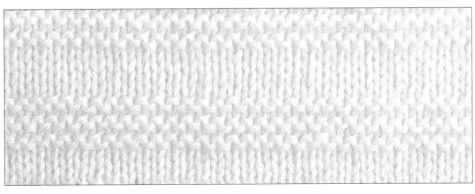

GARTER STITCH RIDGES

Any number of stitches

Row 1 (right side): K.
Row 2: P.
Rows 3 and 4: as rows 1 and 2.
Rows 5 to 10: P.
Rows 1 to 10 form the pattern.

CABLE KNITTING

CABLES CAN TRANSFORM an otherwise simple knitted garment into something really special. They can be used as single panels or combined into an allover pattern. Originally, fishermen's sweaters were often decorated with cables and patterns that served to identify a man's parish. Heavily textured patterns add to a sweater's warmth and durability. Learning to make cables is within the abilities of every knitter. If you are adding cable panels to a plain sweater pattern, you must remember that cables tend to decrease the overall width, so plan the pattern and yarn requirements accordingly.

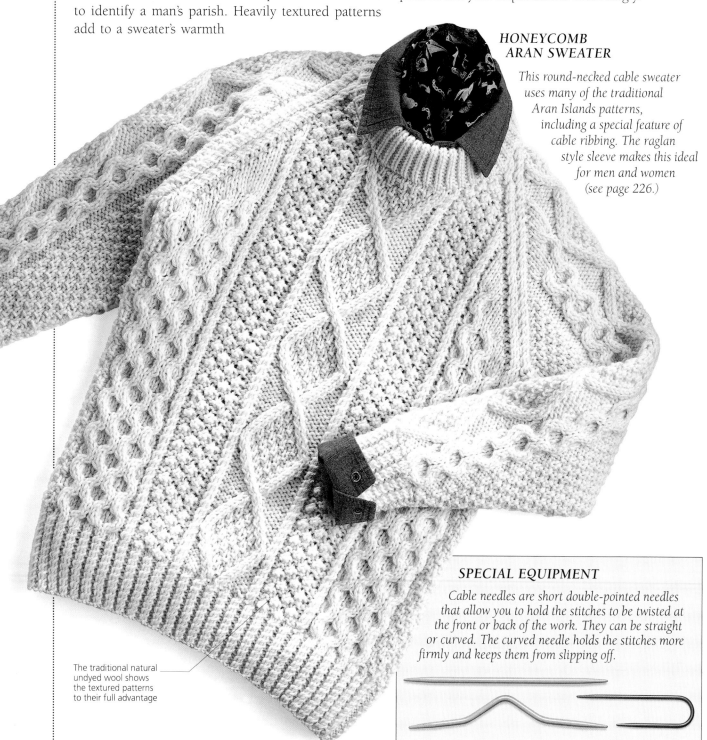

HONEYCOMB
ARAN SWEATER

This round-necked cable sweater uses many of the traditional Aran Islands patterns, including a special feature of cable ribbing. The raglan style sleeve makes this ideal for men and women (see page 226.)

The traditional natural undyed wool shows the textured patterns to their full advantage

SPECIAL EQUIPMENT

Cable needles are short double-pointed needles that allow you to hold the stitches to be twisted at the front or back of the work. They can be straight or curved. The curved needle holds the stitches more firmly and keeps them from slipping off.

CABLING BASICS

The basis of all cable patterns is a simple technique whereby stitches are crossed over another group of stitches in the same row. Some of the stitches making up the cable are held at the back (or front) of the work on a special cable needle, while the other stitches are knitted. Then the stitches on the cable needle are knitted, thereby creating a twist.

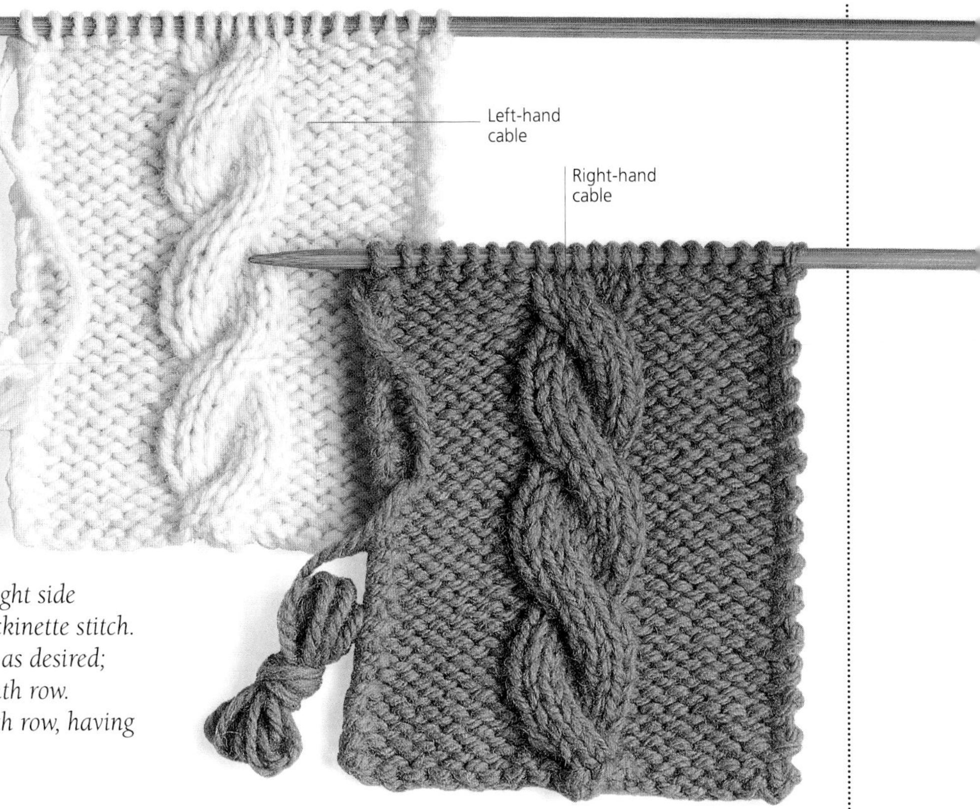

MAKING CABLES

The cables shown below are 6 stitches wide; these 6 stitches are knitted on the right side and purled on the wrong side.
The stitches on either side are purled on the right side and knitted on the wrong side, i.e. reverse stockinette stitch.
The length between the twists can be changed as desired; commonly they are crossed every sixth or eighth row.
The cables shown here are crossed at the eighth row, having started with a wrong-side row.

Left-hand cable

Right-hand cable

Left-hand cable

Holding the stitches at the back of the work always produces a left-over-right cable.

1 Slip the first 3 stitches onto a cable needle and hold at the back of the work.

2 Then knit the next 3 stitches on the main needle.

3 Finally, knit the 3 stitches held on the cable needle.

Right-hand cable

Holding the stitches at the front of the work always produces a right-over-left cable.

1 Slip the first 3 stitches onto a cable needle and hold at the front of the work.

2 Then knit the next 3 stitches on the main needle.

3 Finally, knit the 3 stitches held on the cable needle.

◀ **CABLE INSTRUCTIONS**

For the pattern instruction C4B (Cable 4 Back), C6B (Cable 6 Back), C4F (Cable 4 Front), C6F (Cable 6 Front) etc, where the number is even, work cables as follows: Slip two (or three etc) sts onto cable needle and hold at back or front of work, knit two (or three etc) sts from left needle then knit sts from cable needle.

◀ **LARGE DOUBLE CABLE**

Worked over 20 sts on a background of reverse st st

Row 1 (right side): K.
Row 2: P.
Row 3: C10B, C10F.
Row 4: P.
Rows 5 to 12: Rep rows 1 and 2 *four times.*
Rows 1 to 12 form the pattern.

MEDALLION MOSS CABLE ▲

Worked over 13 sts on a background of reverse st st

Row 1 (right side): K4, [p1, k1] 3 times, k3.
Row 2: P3, [k1, p1] 4 times, p2.
Rows 3 and 4: as rows 1 and 2.
Row 5: C6F, k1, C6B.
Row 6: P.
Row 7: K.
Rows 8 to 11: rep rows 6 and 7 twice.
Row 12: P.
Row 13: C6B, k1, C6F.
Row 14: as row 2.
Row 15: as row 1.
Row 16: as row 2.
Rows 1 to 16 form the pattern.

LITTLE WAVE ▲

Multiple of 7 sts plus 4

Row 1 (right side): K.
Row 2: P4, *k2, p5; rep from * to end.
Row 3: K4, *C2F, k5; rep from * to end.
Row 4: P4, *k1, p1, k1, p4; rep from * to end.

Row 5: *K5, C2F; rep from * to last 4 sts, k4.
Row 6: *P5, k2; rep from * to last 4 sts, p4.
Row 7: K.
Row 8: as row 6.
Row 9: *K5, C2B; rep from * to last 4 sts, k4.
Row 10: as row 4.
Row 11: K4, *C2B, k5; rep from * to end.
Row 12: as row 2.
Rows 1 to 12 form the pattern.

◀ **TELESCOPE LATTICE**

Worked over 12 sts on a background of st st

Row 1 and every alt row (wrong side): P.
Row 2: K.
Row 4: *C4B, k4, C4F; rep from * to end.
Row 6: K.
Row 8: *K2, C4F, C4B, k2; rep from * to end.
Rows 1 to 8 form the pattern.

◀ **CROSS RIB CABLE**

Multiple of 11 sts

Row 1 (wrong side): K2, [p1, k1] 4 times, k1.
Row 2: P2, [k1 tbl, p1] 4 times, p1.
Rows 3 to 6: rep rows 1 and 2 twice.
Row 7: as row 1.
Row 8: P2, slip next 4 sts to front on cable needle, [k1tbl, p1] twice from main needle, [k1tbl, p1] twice from cable needle, p1.
Rows 9 to 12: rep rows 1 and 2 twice.
Rows 1 to 12 form the pattern.

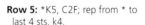

SMALL TWIST STITCH CABLE ▲

Multiple of 8 sts plus 3

Row 1 (right side): *K3, p1, k1tbl, p1, k1tbl, p1; rep from * to last 3 sts, k3.
Row 2: P3, *k1, p1tbl, k1, p1tbl, k1, p3; rep from * to end.
Rows 3 to 6: rep rows 1 and 2 twice.

Row 7: *K3, p1, slip next 2 sts to front on cn, k1tbl, p1, k1tbl from cn, p1; rep from * to last 3 sts, k3.
Row 8: as row 2.
Rows 1 to 8 form the pattern.

OPENWORK AND TWIST ▶
Multiple of 15 sts plus 12

Special abbreviation

T4LR (Twist 4 Left and Right): Slip next 3 sts onto cn and hold at back of work, knit next st from left needle then slip the first st on cn back to left needle, p2 from cn then k1 from left needle.

Row 1 (right side): P1, T4LR, p2, T4LR, p1, *k1, yo, sl 1, k1, psso, p1, T4LR, p2, T4LR, p1; rep from * to end.

Row 2: K1, p1, [k2, p1] 3 times, k1, *p3, k1, p1, [k2, p1] 3 times, k1; rep from * to end.

Row 3: P1, k1, p2, T4LR, p2, k1, p1, *k2tog, yo, k1, p1, k1, p2, T4LR, p2, k1, p1; rep from * to end.

Row 4: as row 2.

Rows 1 to 4 form the pattern.

BRAID CABLE ▲
Multiple of 8 (min. 16 sts) worked on a background of reverse st st. Shown worked over 24 sts

Row 1 (right side): K.
Row 2 and every alt row: P.
Row 3: K.
Row 5: *C8B; rep from * to end of panel.
Row 7: K.
Row 9: K.
Row 11: *C8F; rep from * to end of panel.
Row 12: P.
Rows 1 to 12 form the pattern.

Up   Down

Up   Down

◀ 9 STITCH PLAIT
Worked over 9 sts on a background of reverse st st.

Downwards plait
Row 1 (right side): K.
Row 2 and every alt row: P.
Row 3: C6F, k3.
Row 5: K.
Row 7: K3, C6B.
Row 8: P.
Upwards plait
Row 1 (right side): K.
Row 2 and every alt row: P.
Row 3: C6B, k3.
Row 5: K.
Row 7: K3, C6F.
Row 8: P.
Rows 1 to 8 form each pattern.

◀ CLAW PATTERN
Worked over 9 sts on a background of reverse st st

Special abbreviations

Cross 4L (Cross 4 Left): Slip next st onto cn and hold at front of work, knit next 3 sts from left needle then knit st from cn.

Cross 4R (Cross 4 Right): Slip next 3 sts onto cn and hold at back of work, knit next st from left needle then knit sts from cn.

Downwards claw
Row 1 (right side): K.
Row 2: P.
Row 3: Cross 4L, k1, Cross 4R.
Row 4: P.
Rows 1 to 4 form the pattern.

Upwards claw
Row 1 (right side): K.
Row 2: P.
Row 3: Cross 4R, k1, Cross 4L.
Row 4: P.
Rows 1 to 4 form the pattern.

Medallion moss cable

STRIPED MEDALLION CABLE ▶
Worked over 16 sts on a
background of reverse st st

Special abbreviations
T8B rib (Twist 8 Back rib): Slip next
4 sts onto cn and hold at back of
work, k1, p2, k1 from left-hand
needle, then k1, p2, k1 from cn.

T8F rib (Twist 8 Front rib): Slip next
4 sts onto cn and hold at front of
work, k1, p2, k1 from left-hand
needle, then k1, p2, k1 from cn.

Row 1 (right side): K1, p2, [k2, p2]
3 times, k1.

Row 2: P1, k2, [p2, k2] 3 times, p1.

Row 3: T8B rib, T8F rib.

Row 4: as row 2.

Rows 5 to 14: Rep rows 1 and 2
five times.

Row 15: T8F rib, T8B rib.

Row 16: as row 2.

Rows 17 to 24: Rep rows 1 and 2
four times.

Rows 1 to 24 form the pattern.

◀ ALTERNATING BRAID CABLE
Worked over 6 sts on a
background of reverse st st

Row 1 (wrong side): P.

Row 2: K.

Row 3: P.

Row 4: C4B, k2.

Row 5: P.

Row 6: K2, C4F.

Rows 3 to 6 form the pattern.

◀ CELTIC PLAIT
Multiple of 10 sts plus 5 (min. 25 sts) on a
background of reverse st st. Shown worked
over 25 sts

Special abbreviations
T5B (Twist 5 Back): Slip next 2 sts onto cn and
hold at back of work, knit next 3 sts from left
needle, then purl sts from cn.

T5F (Twist 5 Front): Slip next 3 sts onto cn and
hold at front of work, purl next 2 sts from left
needle, then knit sts from cn.

Row 1 (right side): K3, *p4, k6, rep from * to
last 2 sts, p2.

Row 2: K2, *p6, k4; rep from * to last 3 sts, p3.

Row 3: K3, *p4, C6F; rep from * to last 2 sts, p2.

Row 4: K2, *p6, k4; rep from * to last 3 sts, p 3.

Row 5: *T5F, T5B; rep from * to last 5 sts, T5F.

Row 6: P3, *k4, p6; rep from * to last 2 sts, k2.

Row 7: P2, *C6B, p4; rep from * to last 3 sts, k3.

Row 8: as row 6.

Row 9: *T5B, T5F; rep from * to last 5 sts, T5B.

Row 10: as row 4.

Rows 3 to 10 form the pattern.

DOUBLE CROSSOVER ▼
Worked over 16 sts on a background of reverse
st st

Special abbreviations
T3B (Twist 3 Back): Slip next st onto cn
and hold at back, k next 2 sts from left
needle, then p st from cn.

T3F (Twist 3 Front): Slip next 2 sts onto cn and
hold at front of work, purl next st from left
needle, then knit sts from cn.

Row 1 (right side): K2, p4, k4, p4, k2.

Row 2: P2, k4, p4, k4, p2.

Row 3: K2, p4, C4B, p4, k2.

Row 4: as row 2.

Row 5: [T3F, p2, T3B] twice.

Row 6: K1, p2, [k2, p2] 3 times, k1.

Row 7: P1, T3F, T3B, p2, T3F, T3B, p1.

Row 8: P2, k4, p4, k4, p2.

Row 9: P2, C4B, p4, C4B, p2.

Row 10: as row 8.

Row 11: P2, k4, p4, k4, p2.

Rows 12 and 13: as rows 8 and 9.

Row 14: as row 8.

Row 15: P1, T3B, T3F, p2, T3B, T3F, p1.

Row 16: as row 6.

Row 17: [T3B, p2, T3F] twice.

Rows 18 and 19: as rows 2 and 3.

Row 20: as row 2.

Rows 1 to 20 form the pattern.

◀ HONEYCOMB
Multiple of 8 sts

Row 1 (right side): *C4B, C4F; rep from * to
end of panel.

Row 2: P.

Row 3: K.

Row 4: P.

Row 5: *C4F, C4B; rep from * to end of panel.

Row 6: P.

Row 7: K.

Row 8: P.

Rows 1 to 8 form the pattern.

INTERLACED CABLES ▼
Multiple of 8 sts plus 10
Special abbreviations
T4B (Twist 4 Back): Slip next 2 sts onto cn and hold at back of work, knit next 2 sts from left needle, then purl sts from cn.
T4F (Twist 4 Front): Slip next 2 sts onto cn and hold at front of work, purl next 2 sts from left needle, then knit sts from cn.
Row 1 (right side): P3, k4, *p4, k4; rep from * to last 3 sts, p3.
Row 2: K3, p4, *k4, p4; rep from * to last 3 sts, k3.
Row 3: P3, C4B, *p4, C4B; rep from * to last 3 sts, p3.
Row 4: as row 2.
Rows 5 to 8: as rows 1 to 4.
Row 9: P1, *T4B, T4F; rep from * to last st, p1.
Row 10: K1, p2, k4, *p4, k4; rep from * to last 3 sts, p2, k1.
Row 11: P1, k2, p4, *C4F, p4; rep from * to last 3 sts, k2, p1.
Row 12: as row 10.
Row 13: P1, *T4F, T4B; rep from * to last st, p1.
Rows 14 and 15: as rows 2 and 3.
Row 16: as row 2.
Rows 1 to 16 form the pattern.

ALTERNATED CABLE ▲
Worked over 10 sts on a background of reverse st st
Special abbreviations
T3B (Twist 3 Back): Slip next st onto cn and hold at back of work, knit next 2 sts from left needle, then purl st from cn.
T3F (Twist 3 Front): Slip next 2 sts onto cn and hold at front of work, purl next st from left needle, then knit sts from cn.
Row 1 (right side): P1, k8, p1.
Row 2: K1, p8, k1.
Row 3: P1, C4B, C4F, p1.
Row 4: K1, p2, k4, p2, k1.
Row 5: T3B, p4, T3F.
Row 6: P2, k6, p2.
Row 7: K2, p6, k2.
Rows 8 and 9: as rows 6 and 7.
Row 10: as row 6.
Row 11: T3F, p4, T3B.
Row 12: as row 4.
Row 13: P1, C4F, C4B, p1.
Row 14: K1, p8, k1.
Row 15: P1, C4B, C4F, p1.
Row 16: K1, p8, k1.
Row 17: P1, k8, p1.
Rows 18 and 19: as rows 14 and 15.
Row 20: as row 16.
Rows 1 to 20 form the pattern.

CHAIN CABLE ▶
Worked over 8 sts on a background of reverse st st
Row 1 (right side): K.
Row 2: P.
Row 3: C4B, C4F.
Row 4: P.
Rows 5 and 6: as rows 1 and 2.
Row 7: C4F, C4B.
Row 8: P.
Rows 1 to 8 form the pattern.

SNAKE CABLE ▲
Worked over 8 sts on a background of reverse st st
Row 1 (right side): K8.
Row 2: P8.
Row 3: C8B.
Row 4: P8.
Rows 5 to 10: Rep rows 1 and 2 three times.
Row 11: C8F.
Row 12: P8.
Rows 13 to 16: Rep rows 1 and 2 twice.
Rows 1 to 16 form the pattern.

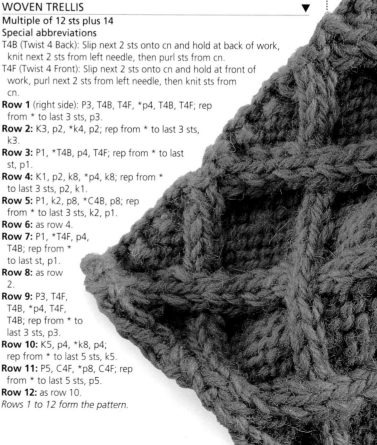

WOVEN TRELLIS ▼
Multiple of 12 sts plus 14
Special abbreviations
T4B (Twist 4 Back): Slip next 2 sts onto cn and hold at back of work, knit next 2 sts from left needle, then purl sts from cn.
T4F (Twist 4 Front): Slip next 2 sts onto cn and hold at front of work, purl next 2 sts from left needle, then knit sts from cn.
Row 1 (right side): P3, T4B, T4F, *p4, T4B, T4F; rep from * to last 3 sts, p3.
Row 2: K3, p2, *k4, p2; rep from * to last 3 sts, k3.
Row 3: P1, *T4B, p4, T4F; rep from * to last st, p1.
Row 4: K1, p2, k8, *p4, k8; rep from * to last 3 sts, p2, k1.
Row 5: P1, k2, p8, *C4B, p8; rep from * to last 3 sts, k2, p1.
Row 6: as row 4.
Row 7: P1, *T4F, p4, T4B; rep from * to last st, p1.
Row 8: as row 2.
Row 9: P3, T4F, T4B, *p4, T4F, T4B; rep from * to last 3 sts, p3.
Row 10: K5, p4, *k8, p4; rep from * to last 5 sts, k5.
Row 11: P5, C4F, *p8, C4F; rep from * to last 5 sts, p5.
Row 12: as row 10.
Rows 1 to 12 form the pattern.

SIMPLE PROJECTS

ONE COLOR PROJECTS are a good choice for beginners, but they need not be ordinary. The use of texture stitches can transform a simple garment into something special.

EMERALD ISLE VEST

This vest is worked in Irish tweed yarn, which enhances the cable pattern borrowed from Irish fishermen's sweaters. Because the back is plain, the vest knits up quickly. (See page 227.)

Cable panels liven up a stockinette stitch vest

Work edge and vest ties in crochet

HERRINGBONE SWEATER

This long sleeve boat neck sweater has a sporty appeal and is ideal for outdoor wear. Because it is worked in one color in a bulky yarn it is quick and easy to knit. The simple texture pattern is easily followed once a few rows have been worked.
(See page 225.)

A one-color sweater with simple texture pattern is a good choice for a beginner

A herringbone pattern of simple knit and purl stitches sets off a yoke knit in a single rib

RAISED PATTERNS

A VARIETY OF dramatic effects can be achieved by using stitches to create patterns that stand out from a ground fabric. These stitches are produced by increasing and decreasing techniques, sometimes combined with twist or cable stitches.

Raised stitches come in all sizes, and can be worked in rows or panels, or as allover textures. They can also be combined with lace patterns and cables. Bobbles, popcorns, buds, and clusters are some of the most common patterns. A garment that has many motifs will be much thicker and heavier than a plainly knitted one, and will use more yarn. For this reason traditional outdoor wear, such as fishermen's sweaters, is often heavily patterned. To make these stitches, you need only to master the technique of multiple increases in a single stitch. For an easy-to-work pattern that has a strong texture, Popcorn stitch is a popular choice. Instructions are on page 57.

BOBBLES

A bobble is a large cluster of stitches that is independent of the knitted ground; it can be worked in stockinette or reverse stockinette. It is formed by increasing into a single stitch so that three, (four, or five) additional stitches for a small, (medium, or large) bobble are made. Work backward and forward on these stitches only. Finally, decrease these extra stitches to the original one. The increases can be made in two ways – using the yarn-over method or working into the front and back of a stitch. The stitches on either side must be worked firmly. Bobbles will make the edge uneven, so start a few stitches in to make the sewing up easier.

Small, medium, and large bobbles

Yarn-over increases

Knit up to your chosen stitch then make a yarn over – insert your right-hand needle into the stitch and knit as usual but do not discard. To make 5 new stitches (a total of 6 stitches), yarn over and knit into the same stitch 3 more times; slip last stitch onto right needle. This may be abbreviated as *yo, k1; rep from * twice (3, 4 times, etc.).

Working into front and back of stitch

Knit up to your chosen stitch then insert your right-hand needle into it. Leave the stitch on the needle as you knit first into the front and then the back the appropriate number of times. To increase 4 times, making 4 new stitches (a total of 5 stitches), knit into the front and back of the stitch twice and then knit into the front again. Occasionally, the pattern instructions will ask you to increase by alternately knitting and purling into the stitch.

1 For a medium bobble, work up to the chosen stitch. Then increase 3 times into the stitch (4 sts altogether). [We've used the yarn-over method.]

2 Turn work and knit 4 stitches; turn work and purl 4 stitches; turn work and knit 4 stitches; turn work (3 rows of reverse stockinette).

3 Decrease 3 stitches in the row:
Sl 2, k2tog, p2sso. Continue in pattern.

4 The completed bobble on a stockinette stitch ground.

BUBBLE STITCH AND REVERSE BUBBLE STITCH ▶

Multiple of 8 sts plus 4

Note: Slip all sts p-wise.

Row 1 (right side): K.

Row 2: P.

Row 3: P1, yb, sl 2, yf, *p6, yb, sl 2, yf; rep from * to last st, p1.

Row 4: K1, yf, sl 2, yb, *k6, yf, sl 2, yb; rep from * to last st, k1.

Rows 5 to 8: rep rows 3 and 4 twice.

Row 9: K.

Row 10: P.

Row 11: P5, yb, sl 2, yf, *p6, yb, sl 2, yf; rep from * to last 5 sts, p5.

Row 12: K5, yf, sl 2, yb, *k6, yf, sl 2, yb; rep from * to last 5 sts, k5.

Rows 13 to 16: rep rows 11 and 12 twice.

Rows 1 to 16 form the pattern.

Bubble stitch

Use the reverse side of the bubble stitch as the right side

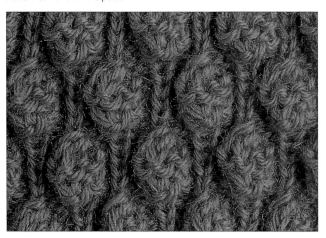

ORCHARD PATTERN ▲

Multiple of 6 sts plus 5

Note: Sts should only be counted after rows 6 or 12.

Row 1 (right side): P2, *k into front, back, front and back of next st, p2, k1, p2; rep from * to last 3 sts, k into front, back, front and back of next st, p2.

Row 2: *K2, [k1 winding yarn round needle twice] 4 times, k2, p1; rep from * to last 8 sts, k2, [k1 winding yarn round needle twice] 4 times, k2.

Row 3: P2, *k4 (dropping extra loops), p2, k1, p2; rep from * to last 6 sts, k4 (dropping extra loops), p2.

Rows 4 and 5: as rows 2 and 3.

Row 6: *K2, p4 tog, k2, p1; rep from * to last 8 sts, k2, p4tog, k2.

Row 7: P2, *k1, p2, k into front, back, front and back of next st, p2; rep from * to last 3 sts, k1, p2.

Row 8: *K2, p1, k2 [k1 winding yarn round needle twice] 4 times; rep from * to last 5 sts, k2, p1, k2.

Row 9: *P2, k1, p2, k4 (dropping extra loops); rep from * to last 5 sts, p2, k1, p2.

Rows 10 and 11: as rows 8 and 9.

Row 12: *K2, p1, k2, p4tog; rep from * to last 5 sts, k2, p1, k2.

Rows 1 to 12 form the pattern.

HONEYCOMB STITCH ▼

Multiple of 4 sts

Special abbreviation

C2B or C2F (Cross 2 Back or Front): K into back (or front) of 2nd st on needle, then k first st, slipping both sts off needle at same time.

Row 1 (right side): *C2F, C2B; rep from * to end.

Row 2: P.

Row 3: *C2B, C2F; rep from * to end.

Row 4: P.

Rows 1 to 4 form the pattern.

HAZEL NUT ▲

Multiple of 4 sts plus 3

Special abbreviation

HN (Make 1 Hazel Nut): K1 without slipping st off left needle, yo, then k1 once more into same st.

Note: Sts should only be counted after rows 4, 5, 6, 10, 11, or 12.

Row 1 (right side): P3, *HN, p3; rep from * to end.

Row 2: K3, *p3, k3; rep from * to end.

Row 3: P3, *k3, p3; rep from * to end.

Row 4: K3, *p3tog, k3; rep from * to end.

Row 5: P.

Row 6: K.

Row 7: P1, *HN, p3; rep from * to last 2 sts, HN, p1.

Row 8: K1, *p3, k3; rep from * to last 4 sts, p3, k1.

Row 9: P1, *k3, p3; rep from * to last 4 sts, k3, p1.

Row 10: K1, *p3tog, k3; rep from * to last 4 sts, p3tog, k1.

Row 11: P.

Row 12: K.

Rows 1 to 12 form the pattern.

GARTER STITCH CHEVRON ▶
Multiple of 11

Rows 1 to 5: K.
Row 6 (right side): *k2tog, k2, knit into front and back of each of the next 2 sts, k3, ssk; rep from * to end.
Row 7: P.
Rows 8 to 11: rep rows 6 and 7 twice.
Row 12: as row 6.
Rows 1 to 12 rows form the pattern.

BOBBLE FANS ▲
Worked over 11 sts on a background of reverse st st
Special abbreviations
MB (Make Bobble): [K1, p1] twice all into next st, turn and p4, turn and k4, turn and p4, turn and sl 2, k2tog, p2sso.
T2F (Twist 2 Front): Slip next st onto cn and hold at front of work, purl next st from left needle, then knit st from cn.
T2B (Twist 2 Back): Slip next st onto cn and hold at back of work, knit next st from left needle, then purl st from cn.
T2FW (Twist 2 Front on Wrong side): Slip next st onto cn and hold at front (wrong side) of work, purl next st from left needle, then knit st from cn.
T2BW (Twist 2 Back on Wrong side): Slip next st onto cn and hold at back (right side) of work, knit next st from left needle, then purl st from cn.
Row 1 (right side): P.
Row 2: K.
Row 3: P5, MB, p5.
Row 4: K5, p1tbl, k5.
Row 5: P2, MB, p2, k1tbl, p2, MB, p2.
Row 6: K2, [p1tbl, k2] 3 times.
Row 7: MB, p1, T2F, p1, k1tbl, p1, T2B, p1, MB.
Row 8: p1tbl, k2, p1tbl, [k1, p1tbl] twice, k2, p1tbl.
Row 9: T2F, p1, T2F, k1tbl, T2B, p1, T2B.
Row 10: K1, T2BW, k1, [p1tbl] 3 times, k1, T2FW, k1.
Row 11: P2, T2F, M1 p-wise, sl 1, k2tog, psso, M1 p-wise, T2B, p2.
Row 12: K3, T2BW, p1tbl, T2FW, k3.
Row 13: P4, M1 p-wise, sl 1, k2tog, psso, M1 p-wise, p4.
Row 14: K5, p1tbl, k5.
Row 15: P.
Row 16: K.
Rows 1 to 16 form the pattern.

SCATTERED BOBBLES ▼
Multiple of 10 sts plus 5 worked on a background of st st

Special abbreviation
MB (Make Bobble): Knit into front, back and front of next st, turn and p3, turn and k3, turn and p3, turn and sl 1, k2tog, psso.
Rows 1 and 3: K.
Rows 2 and 4: P.
Row 5: K7, *MB, k9; rep from * to last 8 sts, MB, k7.
Rows 6, 8 and 10: P.
Rows 7 and 9: K.
Row 11: K2, *MB, k9; rep from * to last 3 sts, MB, k2.
Row 12: P.
Rows 1 to 12 form the pattern.

◀ VERTICAL BOBBLE AND STRIPE
Multiple of 10 sts plus 5

Special abbreviation
MB (Make Bobble): Work [k1, p1, k1, p1, k1] into the next st, turn and k5, turn and k5tog.
Row 1 (right side): P2, k1, *p4, k1; rep from * to last 2 sts, p2.
Row 2: K2, p1, *k4, p1; rep from * to last 2 sts, k2.
Row 3: P2, *MB, p4, k1, p4; rep from * to last 3 sts, MB, p2.
Row 4: as row 2.
Rows 5 to 20: rep rows 1 to 4 four times.
Row 21: as row 1.
Row 22: as row 2.
Row 23: P2, *k1, p4, MB, p4; rep from * to last 3 sts, k1, p2.
Row 24: as row 2.
Rows 25 to 40: rep rows 21 to 24 four times.
Rows 1 to 40 form the pattern.

BUD STITCH ▲
Multiple of 6 sts plus 5

Note: Sts should only be counted after row 6 or 12.
Row 1 (right side): P5, *k1, yo, p5; rep from * to end.
Row 2: K5, *p2, k5; rep from * to end.
Row 3: P5, *k2, p5; rep from * to end.
Rows 4 and 5: as rows 2 and 3.
Row 6: K5, *p2tog, k5; rep from * to end.
Row 7: P2, *k1, yo, p5; rep from * to last 3 sts, k1, yo, p2.
Row 8: K2, *p2, k5; rep from * to last 4 sts, p2, k2.
Row 9: P2, *k2, p5; rep from * to last 4 sts, k2, p2.
Rows 10 and 11: as rows 8 and 9.
Row 12: K2, *p2tog, k5; rep from * to last 4 sts, p2tog, k2.
Rows 1 to 12 form the pattern.

TRINITY STITCH ▼

Multiple of 4 sts plus 2

Special abbreviation

M2 (Make 2 sts): K1, p1, k1 all into
next st.

Row 1 (right side): P.

Row 2: K1, *M2, p3tog; rep from * to
last st, k1.

Row 3: P.

Row 4: K1, *p3tog, M2; rep from * to last st, k1.

Rows 1 to 4 form the pattern.

MOCK CABLE ▲

Multiple of 5 sts plus 2

Row 1 (right side): P2, *sl 1, k2,
psso, p2; rep from * to end.

Row 2: K2, *p1, yo, p1, k2; rep
from * to end.

Row 3: P2, *k3, p2; rep from
* to end.

Row 4: K2, *p3, k2; rep from
* to end.

Rows 1 to 4 form the pattern.

SINGLE BELL EDGING ▲

Cast on multiple of 12 sts
plus 3

Note: Sts should only be counted
after rows 1 and 2.

Row 1 (right side): P3, *k9, p3; rep from
* to end.

Row 2: K3, *p9, k3; rep from * to end.

Row 3: P3, *yb, ssk, k5, k2tog, p3; rep from
* to end.

Row 4: K3, *p7, k3; rep from * to end.

Row 5: P3, *yb, ssk, k3, k2tog, p3; rep from
* to end.

Row 6: K3, *p5, k3; rep from * to end.

Row 7: P3, *yb, ssk, k1, k2tog, p3; rep from
* to end.

Row 8: K3, *p3, k3; rep from * to end.

Row 9: P3, *yb, sl 1, k2tog, psso, p3; rep
from * to end.

Row 10: K3, *p1, k3; rep from * to end.

Row 11: P3, *k1, p3; rep from * to end.

Row 12: as row 10.

Rows 1 to 12 form the edging.

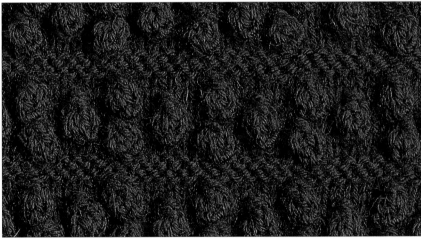

BOBBLE AND RIDGE ▲

Multiple of 6 sts plus 5

Special abbreviation

MB (Make Bobble): Knit into front, back and
front of next st, turn and p3, turn and k3,
turn and p3, turn and sl 1, k2tog, psso.

Row 1 (right side): K.

Row 2: P.

Row 3: K5, *MB, k5; rep from * to end.

Row 4: P.

Row 5: K2, MB, *k5, MB; rep from * to
last 2 sts, k2.

Rows 6, 7 and 8: as rows 2, 3 and 4.

Row 9: P.

Row 10: K.

Rows 1 to 10 form the pattern.

PUFF BALL EDGING ▶

Cast on 13 sts

Row 1 (right side): K2, k2tog, yo2, k2tog, k7.

Row 2: K9, p1, k3.

Rows 3 and 4: K.

Row 5: K2, k2tog, yo2, k2tog, k2, [yo2, k1]
3 times, yo2, k2 – 21 sts.

Row 6: K3, [p1, k2] 3 times, p1, k4, p1, k3.

Rows 7 and 8: K.

Row 9: K2, k2tog, yo2, k2tog, k15.

Row 10: K 12 sts wrapping yarn twice around
needle for each st, yo2, k5, p1, k3 – 23 sts
(each double wrapped st counts as 1 st).

Row 11: K10, [p1, k1] into next st, slip next
12 sts to right needle, dropping extra loops.
Return sts to left needle then k12tog –13 sts.

Row 12: K.

Rows 1 to 12 form the pattern.

OPENWORK PATTERNS

YARN-OVER INCREASES form some of the loveliest and most delicate stitches a knitter can create. Made with fine yarns and needles, openwork patterns are ideal for gossamer shawls, fancy sweaters, or dressy scarves. Where a more robust appearance, or a warmer fabric, is required, use medium-weight yarn to knit patterns with smaller openings.

There are two major categories of openwork pattern – lace and eyelet. Lace is truly openwork, unlike eyelet which is solid work punctuated by small openings. Lace, when combined with other stitches, lends itself to being used as panels. Knit the panels in or near the center and away from the sides, where they are difficult to shape.

Wool, synthetics, silks, cashmeres are among the many yarns that knit up beautifully in lace patterns. Cotton lace is often used for trimming curtains, place mats, bed linens, and other household items.

OPENWORK BASICS

Openings are formed by yarn-over increases, which are later offset by the same number of decreases so that the number of stitches remains constant. It is important that you work to the correct tension, and with appropriate needles and yarn. Openwork needs stretching before it is fully effective. Therefore, when you are substituting a lace pattern for stockinette, cast on less stitches than the width requirement – about three-quarters the number should suffice.

The shawl shown here is worked in a simple openwork pattern with a knitted border worked separately and then sewn onto the main piece.

(To make, see page 228.)

This triangular shawl features an attractive leaf pattern and a decorative border

LACE EDGINGS

These are marvelous for trimming bed and table linens. Use fine crochet cotton and sew finished edging to the cloth. When trimming knitting with a lace edge, first complete the main piece then pick up the required number of stitches for the lace edge (below).

Picking up stitches for an edge

Hold the working yarn behind the completed piece and insert your knitting needle through it, between the rows and between the last 2 stitches of each row, from front to back. Take the yarn over the needle as if knitting and draw a loop of the yarn through to form a stitch. Continue until the correct number of stitches have been formed.

EYELETS

There are two main types of eyelet: The chain and open. Made singly, eyelets can be used as tiny buttonholes or formed into a line for threading ribbon through. Used in combination with plain rows between, eyelets can be placed vertically, horizontally, or diagonally to form decorative motifs. Do not make eyelets at the beginning or end of a row; work them at least two stitches in from the edge.

A row of open eyelets

Chain eyelet

This is the simplest and most common type of eyelet. It can be combined with the open eyelet in more intricate stitches. It is abbreviated as *yo, k2tog.*

1 Make a yarn-over by bringing your yarn to the front, and then knitting the next 2 stitches together.

2 The yarn-over adds one stitch, but knitting 2 together reduces the stitches to the original number.

3 A chain eyelet has been made in the knitted work.

Open eyelet

To work a slightly larger opening, use this method. This is more suitable for threading ribbon. It is abbreviated as *yo, sl 1 k-wise, k1, psso.*

1 Make a yarn-over by bringing the yarn forward around the front of the needle. Slip the next stitch knitwise, knit the next stitch, and then pass the slipped stitch over.

2 The increase made by the yarn-over has been replaced by the slip stitch decrease. The number of stitches remains the same.

3 A finished open eyelet.

SLIP, SLIP, KNIT DECREASE

This decrease is especially useful for lace and openwork and leaves a smooth finish, abbreviated as ssk.

1 Slip the first and 2nd stitches knitwise, one at a time, onto the right needle.

2 Insert the left needle into the fronts of these 2 stitches from the left, and knit them together from this position.

3 The completed slip, slip, knit decrease is made.

DIAMOND AND WAVE EDGE ▶
Worked over 13 sts

Note: Sts should only be counted after rows 1 and 20.

Row 1 and every alt row (wrong side): K2, p to last 2 sts, k2.

Row 2: K7, yo, ssk, yo, k4.

Row 4: K6, [yo, ssk] twice, yo, k4.

Row 6: K5, [yo, ssk] 3 times, yo, k4.

Row 8: K4, [yo, ssk] 4 times, yo, k4.

Row 10: K3, [yo, ssk] 5 times, yo, k4.

Row 12: K4, [yo, ssk] 5 times, k2tog, k2.

Row 14: K5, [yo, ssk] 4 times, k2tog, k2.

Row 16: K6, [yo, ssk] 3 times, k2tog, k2.

Row 18: K7, [yo, ssk] twice, k2tog, k2.

Row 20: K8, yo, ssk, k2tog, k2.

Rows 1 to 20 form the pattern.

LEAF PATTERN ▲
Multiple of 10 sts plus 1

Row 1 and every alt row (wrong side): P.

Row 2: K3, *k2tog, yo, k1, yo, ssk, k5; rep from *, ending last rep k3.

Row 4: K2, *k2tog, [k1, yo] twice, k1, ssk, k3; rep from *, ending last rep k2.

Row 6: K1, *k2tog, k2, yo, k1, yo, k2, ssk, k1; rep from * to end.

Row 8: K2tog, *k3, yo, k1, yo, k3, sl 1, k2tog, psso; rep from * to last 9 sts, k3, yo, k1, yo, k3, ssk.

Row 10: K1, *yo, ssk, k5, k2tog, yo, k1; rep from * to end.

Row 12: K1, *yo, k1, ssk, k3, k2tog, k1, yo, k1; rep from * to end.

Row 14: K1, *yo, k2, ssk, k1, k2tog, k2, yo, k1; rep from * to end.

Row 16: K1, *yo, k3, sl 1, k2tog, psso, k3, yo, k1; rep from * to end.

Rows 1 to 16 form the pattern.

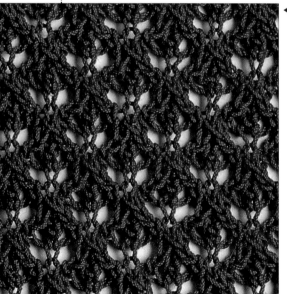

◀ ENGLISH LACE
Multiple of 6 sts plus 1

Row 1 and every alt row (wrong side): P.

Row 2: K1, *yo, ssk, k1, k2tog, yo, k1; rep from * to end.

Row 4: K1, *yo, k1 sl 1, k2tog, psso, k1, yo, k1; rep from * to end.

Row 6: K1, *k2tog, yo, k1, yo, ssk, k1; rep from * to end.

Row 8: K2tog, *[k1, yo] twice, k1, sl 1, k2tog, psso; rep from * to last 5 sts, [k1, yo] twice, k1, ssk.

Rows 1 to 8 form the pattern.

FEATHER PANEL ▶
Worked over 13 sts on a background of reverse st st

Special abbreviation

S4K (Slip 4 knit): Slip next 4 sts knitwise, one at a time, onto right needle, then insert left needle into fronts of these 4 sts from left, and knit them together from this position.

Row 1 (right side): K.

Row 2: P.

Row 3: K4tog, [yo, k1] 5 times, yo, S4K.

Row 4: P.

Rows 1 to 4 form the pattern.

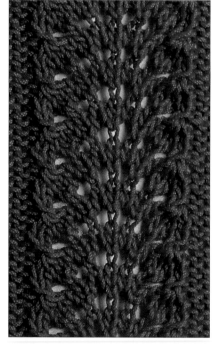

FLEURETTE ▶
Multiple of 6 sts plus 5

Note: Sts should only be counted after rows 1-3, 6-9, and 12.

Row 1 and every alt row (wrong side): P.

Row 2: K2, *k1, yo, ssk, k1, k2tog, yo; rep from *, ending k3.

Row 4: K4, *yo, k3; rep from *, ending k1.

Row 6: K2, k2tog, *yo, ssk, k1, k2tog, yo, sl 2 k-wise, k1, p2sso; rep from *, ending yo, ssk, k1, k2tog, yo, ssk, k2.

Row 8: K2, *k1, k2tog, yo, k1, yo, ssk; rep from *, ending k3.

Row 10: as row 4.

Row 12: K2, *k1, k2tog, yo, sl 2 k-wise, k1, p2sso, yo, ssk; rep from *, ending k3.

Rows 1 to 12 form the pattern.

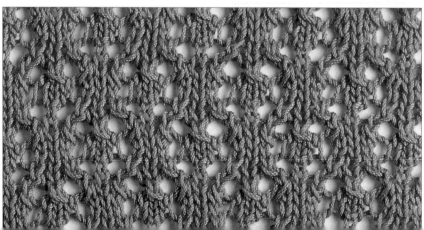

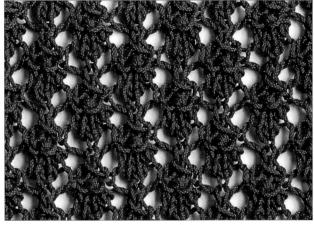

CAT'S PAW

Multiple of 16 sts plus 9

Row 1 and every alt row (wrong side)**:** P.

Row 2: K10, *k2tog, yo, k1, yo, ssk, k11; rep from *, ending last rep k10 instead of k11.

Row 4: K9, *k2tog, yo, k3, yo, ssk, k9; rep from * to end.

Row 6: K10, *yo, ssk, yo, k3tog, yo, k11; rep from *, ending last rep k10 instead of k11.

Row 8: K11, *yo, sl 1, k2tog, psso, yo, k13; rep from *, ending last rep k11 instead of k13.

Row 10: K2, *k2tog, yo, k1, yo, ssk, k11; rep from *, ending last rep k2 instead of k11.

Row 12: K1, *k2tog, yo, k3, yo, ssk, k9; rep from *, ending last rep k1 instead of k9.

Row 14: K2, *yo, ssk, yo, k3tog, yo, k11; rep from *, ending last rep k2 instead of k11.

Row 16: K3, *yo, sl 1, k2tog, psso, yo, k13; rep from *, ending last rep k3 instead of k13.

Rows 1 to 16 form the pattern.

LATTICE STITCH ▼

Multiple of 6 sts plus 1

Row 1 (right side)**:** K1, *yo, p1, p3tog, p1, yo, k1; rep from * to end.

Row 2 and every alt row: P.

Row 3: K2, yo, sl 1, k2tog, psso, yo, *k3, yo, sl 1, k2tog, psso, yo; rep from * to last 2 sts, k2.

Row 5: P2tog, p1, yo, k1, yo, p1, *p3tog, p1, yo, k1, yo, p1; rep from * to last 2 sts, p2tog.

Row 7: K2tog, yo, k3, yo, *sl 1, k2tog, psso, yo, k3, yf; rep from * to last 2 sts, ssk.

Row 8: P.

Rows 1 to 8 form the pattern.

OPENWORK EYELETS ▲

Multiple of 4 sts plus 3

Row 1 (right side)**:** K.

Row 2: P.

Row 3: *K2, k2tog, yo; rep from * to last 3 sts, k3.

Row 4: P.

Row 5: K.

Row 6: P.

Row 7: *K2tog, yo, k2; rep from * to last 3 sts, k2tog, yf, k1.

Row 8: P.

Rows 1 to 8 form the pattern.

WAVE EDGE ▶

Worked over 13 sts

Note: Sts should only be counted after rows 1, 4, 5 or 14.

Row 1 and every alt row (wrong side)**:** K2, p to last 2 sts, k2.

Row 2: Sl 1, k3, yo, k5, yo, k2tog, yo, k2.

Row 4: Sl 1, k4, sl 1, k2tog, psso, k2, [yo, k2tog] twice, k1.

Row 6: Sl 1, k3, ssk, k2, [yo, k2tog] twice, k1.

Row 8: Sl 1, k2, ssk, k2, [yo, k2tog] twice, k1.

Row 10: Sl 1, k1, ssk, k2, [yo, k2tog] twice, k1.

Row 12: K1, ssk, k2, yo, k1, yo, k2tog, yo, k2.

Row 14: Sl 1, [k3, yo] twice, k2tog, yo, k2.

Rows 1 to 14 form the pattern.

◀ FALLING LEAVES

Worked over 16 sts on a background of reverse st st

Row 1 (right side)**:** P1, k3, k2tog, k1, yo, p2, yo, k1, ssk, k3, p1.

Row 2 and every alt row: K1, p6, k2, p6, k1.

Row 3: P1, k2, k2tog, k1, yf, k1, p2, k1, yo, k1, ssk, k2, p1.

Row 5: P1, k1, k2tog, k1, yo, k2, p2, k2, yo, k1, ssk, k1, p1.

Row 7: P1, k2tog, k1, yo, k3, p2, k3, yo, k1, ssk, p1.

Row 8: K1, p6, k2, p6, k1.

Rows 1 to 8 form the pattern.

USING COLOR

COLOR IS ANOTHER way of transforming simple shapes. Its use may be subtle or dramatic, providing a mosaic of shades in a complex arrangement.

The simplest way of using color is to make horizontal stripes. Here, you introduce a new shade at the beginning of a row. To make vertical stripes, use a separate ball of yarn for each color and, when you get to the end of each block, pick up the new yarn in a way that prevents a hole from appearing. Another effective but easy way of adding color is to combine two different yarns, working them as one strand. Color also may be embroidered onto a stockinette background using duplicate stitch (see page 58).

Simple color patterns are often shown in chart form. Charts can be colored or printed in black and white with symbols representing the different colors.

SIMPLE COLOR PATTERNS

Simple color patterns may use only one color in any one row.

Fair Isle pattern

FAIR ISLE KNITTING

When working a pattern that uses two colors in a single row, you should carry the yarn not being used across the back.

Simple color pattern

INTARSIA

These intricate patterns have a motif contained within a plain color background.

Intarsia pattern

BOBBINS

When working with many different colors or when only small amounts of yarn are needed, use plastic or cardboard bobbins to help keep your work neat. If you choose cardboard, make a slit in the top to catch the yarn. If only a small amount of a color is needed, cut a short length of yarn for that part of the design.

ADDING NEW YARN AT START OF ROW

Use this method when knitting horizontal stripes. If you will be using the old color again, leave it at the side. Make sure any ends are woven neatly into the edge or back of the work.

1 Insert your right needle into the first stitch on the left needle and wrap both the old and new yarns over it. Knit the stitch with both yarns.

2 Drop the old yarn and knit the next 2 stitches with the doubled length of the new yarn.

3 Drop the short end of the new yarn and continue knitting in pattern. On the subsequent row, knit the 3 double stitches in the ordinary way.

ADDING NEW YARN AND WEAVING IN

If you are joining a color at the start of a row, use this method to weave in the ends of yarns on the wrong side of the work .

1 Cut the old color, leaving about 3 inches. With the new yarn, purl the first 2 stitches. Lay the short ends of both the old and new yarns over the top of the needle and purl the next stitch under the short ends.

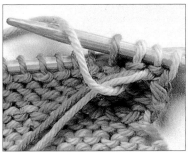

2 Leave the short ends hanging and purl the next stitch over them. Continue until the short ends are woven in.

ADDING NEW YARN WITHIN THE ROW

Use this method when you will be working the original yarn again in the same row. See page 48 for instructions for carrying the yarn along the back.

1 Leaving the old yarn in the back of the work, insert your right-hand needle into the stitch. Wrap the new yarn over the needle and use this to knit the stitch.

2 Knit the next 2 stitches with the doubled length of new yarn.

3 Drop the short end and continue knitting with the new yarn while carrying the old yarn across the back. On subsequent rows, knit the double stitches normally.

MAKING VERTICAL STRIPES OR DESIGNS

This method is known as intarsia and is suitable for knitting motifs. The pattern instructions are always in chart form.

To make vertical stripes or independent blocks of color, use a separate ball or bobbin of yarn for each color. Drop the old yarn and pick up the next one from underneath it so the yarns cross. By twisting the yarns in this way, you will prevent a gap appearing in the work. *(Top left.)* Work in the same way for the purl row *(bottom left).*

CARRYING COLORS ACROSS THE BACK

When working multicolor patterns, you must alternate between two or more balls of yarn. The yarn not in use has to be carried along the back until needed. There are two main methods, stranding and weaving. Stranding is suitable for short distances (5 stitches or less); weaving is better when the yarn is carried 6 stitches or more.

STRANDING

The strands, known as floats, can make knitting more difficult. Floats have to be carried along the back at the correct tension – not too loosely or tightly. With more than two yarns, you will have to drop and pick them up as needed.

If you have only 2 colors in a knit row, hold one in each hand using the methods shown on page 15. *(See above left)*. For the purl row *(below left)*, follow the instructions for holding the yarn given on page 16.

Do not make your floats longer than 5 stitches, and take care that your strands are the same tension as the knitting.

WEAVING

In this method, the carried yarn is brought alternately above and below each stitch made so that it is woven in. It is best worked using both hands. You can also use it in combination with stranding; for example, weaving in at every third stitch and stranding in between will create a more elastic fabric, which will have a smoother finish.

Yarn above the stitch

Holding one yarn in each hand, knit 1 *(left)* or purl 1 *(right)* with the first color, and, at the same time, bring the 2nd color over the tip of the right needle.

Yarn below the stitch

With one yarn in each hand, knit 1 *(left)* or purl 1 *(right)* with the first color, holding the 2nd color below the first.

Front of work using stranding method

Back of work

Weaving method showing the front of work

Back of work

WORKING FROM A CHART

COLOR PATTERNS ARE often charted on graph paper. Each square represents a stitch and each horizontal line of squares is a row of stitches. A colored-in chart, where the indicated colors fill the graphed squares, is the easiest to follow and has the added advantage of giving you a preview of what the finished work will look like.

Many knitting charts are printed in black and white, and different symbols are used to indicate the different colors. These charts usually come with a color key, and show only one pattern repeat. In the case of a large multicolored sweater, the chart may represent the whole garment.

Charts are read from bottom to top; they are usually based on stockinette stitch where the first and all odd-numbered rows are knitted from right to left and all even-numbered rows are purled from left to right. Therefore, the first stitch of a chart is the bottom one on the right. You may find placing a ruler under each row will help you keep track of where you are. When knitting in the round (see page 60), the right side always faces you so that, for every row, you always read every row of the chart from right to left.

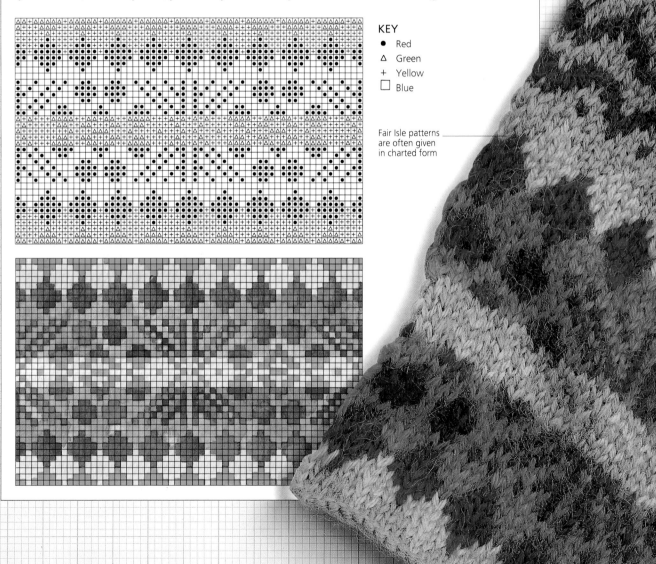

KEY
- ● Red
- △ Green
- + Yellow
- ☐ Blue

Fair Isle patterns are often given in charted form

FLEUR DE LIS ▶

Multiple of 6 sts plus 3

Rows 1 and 3: K3 MC, *k1 CC, k5 MC; rep from * to end, carrying the threads behind the work.

Row 2: P1 CC, *p3 MC, p3 CC; rep from * to last 2 sts, p2 MC.

Rows 4 and 6: P2 MC, *p1 CC, p5 MC; rep from * to last st, p1 CC.

Row 5: K2 CC, *k3 MC, k3 CC; rep from * to last st, k1 MC.

Rows 1 to 6 form the pattern.

◀ DOT AND SQUARE PATTERN

Multiple of 7 sts plus 4

Row 1 (right side): With MC, k.

Row 2: With MC, p.

Row 3: With CC, k1, sl 2, *k5, sl 2; rep from * to last st, k1.

Row 4: With CC, p1, sl 2, *p5, sl 2; rep from * to last st, p.

Row 5: With MC, k3, *sl 2, k1, sl 2, k2; rep from * to last st, k1.

Row 6: With MC, p3, *sl 2, k1, sl 2, p2; rep from * to last st, p1.

Row 7 and 8: as rows 3 and 4.

Rows 1 to 8 form the pattern.

TWO-COLOR RIBS ▼

Multiple of 4 sts

Row 1: *K2 MC, p2 CC; rep from * to end, carrying the threads behind the work.

Row 2: *P2 MC, k2 CC; rep from * to end.

Rows 1 to 2 form the pattern.

GREEK KEY PATTERN ▲

Multiple of 10 sts plus 2

Row 1 (right side): With MC, k.

Row 2: With MC, p.

Row 3: With CC, k1, *k8, sl 2; rep from * to last st, k1.

Row 4 and every alt row: Using the same color as previous row, purl, slipping all sts slipped on previous row.

Row 5: With MC, k1, *sl 2, k4, sl 2, k2; rep from * to last st, k1.

Row 7: With CC, k1, *k2, sl 2, k4, sl 2; rep from * to last st, k1.

Row 9: With MC, k1, *sl 2, k8; rep from * to last sk, k1.

Row 11: With CC, k.

Row 13: With MC, *k4, sl 2, k4; rep from * to last 2 sts, k2.

Row 15: With CC, k2, *sl 2, k2, sl 2, k4; rep from * to end.

Row 17: With MC, *k4, sl 2, k2, sl 2; rep from * to last 2 sts, k2.

Row 19: With CC, *k6, sl 2, k2; rep from * to last 2 sts, k2.

Row 20: as row 4.

Rows 1 to 20 form the pattern.

ZIGZAG ▼

Multiple of 12 sts plus 3

Cast on with MC and knit one row.

Row 1 (right side): With CC, k1, sl 1, k1, psso, *k9, sl 2, k1, p2sso; rep from * to last 12 sts, k9, k2tog, k1.

Row 2: With CC, k1, *p1, k4 (k1, yo, k1) in next st, k4; rep from * to last 2 sts, p1, k1.

Rows 3 and 4: With MC, rep rows 1 and 2.

Rows 1 to 4 form the pattern.

This easy-to-wear shape is knitted across from cuff to cuff

Two-color ribs are not very elastic but they make an attractive finish on a patterned garment. They are the traditional trim to Fair Isle knitting

KALEIDOSCOPE SWEATER

This multicolored sweater is knitted with asymmetric front patterns to make it even more individual and striking.

◀ FLORENTINE

Multiple of 24 sts plus 2

Cast on with MC and purl one row.

Row 1 (right side): With CC, k1, *sl 1, k2; rep from * to last st, k1.

Row 2: With CC, k1, *p2, sl 1; rep from * to last st, k1.

Row 3: With MC, k1, *k1, sl 1, [k2, sl 1] 3 times, k3, [sl 1, k2] 3 times, sl 1; rep from * to last st, k1.

Row 4: With MC, k1, *sl 1, [p2, sl 1] 3 times, p3, [sl 1, p2] 3 times, sl 1, p1; rep from * to last st, k1.

Row 5: With CC, k1, *k2, [sl 1, k2] 3 times, sl 1, k1, sl 1, [k2, sl 1] 3 times, k1; rep from * to last st, k1.

Row 6: With CC, k1, *p1, [sl 1, p2] 3 times, sl 1, p1, sl 1, [p2, sl 1] 3 times, p2; rep from * to last st, k1.

Rows 7 and 8: With MC, rep rows 1 and 2.

Rows 9 and 10: With CC, rep rows 3 and 4.

Rows 11 and 12: With MC, rep rows 5 and 6.

Rows 1 to 12 form the pattern.

COLOR MOTIFS

COLOR KNITTING CAN be as simple or as intricate as you wish. In theory, any pattern that can be drawn out on graph paper can be transferred to knitting, but the more colors you have in any one row, the more practice you will need to master the techniques of picking up and joining the new color, and carrying the unused color or colors behind the work. In more complicated color patterns, stranding and weaving can be combined with intarsia. An example of this is found in the Old Rose motif shown on page 55.

You can use most of these patterns to stand as single motifs, or arrange them in repeats in rows or diagonals. Plot them out on graph paper to fit the shape of the garment pieces you are knitting.

Big Bow
You can use a large single motif to work on a pocket, or a border around the hem of a sweater. Space the motifs as close or as far apart as you like. The colors you choose will affect the look of the pattern; avoid using too strong a background.

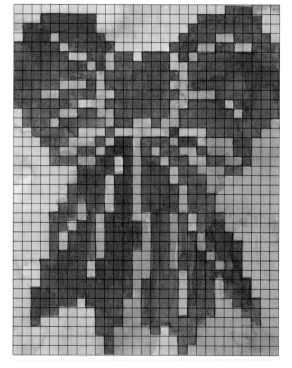

Little Bows
A row of small bows can be knitted in the same color, alternating colors, or a string of different colors, according to your mood. Use a small border like this around the sleeves and hem of a cardigan.

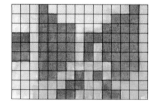

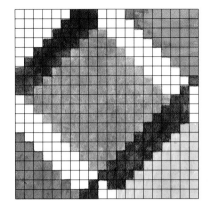

Harlequin

Interlaced black and white grid lines provide a framework for multicolored diamonds in this all-over pattern. Use it on vests, cardigans, and sweaters in bright or subdued tones – and create a garment that will be a modern classic. Note how the knitting elongates the pattern shape.

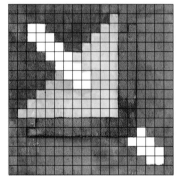

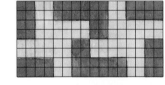

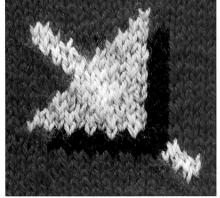

Big Arrow

A bold geometric shape (*right*) can be used as a scatter-pattern – combine the big and small arrows together in one pattern, or use motifs of all one size.

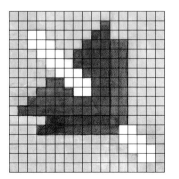

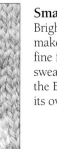

Small Arrow

Bright, paint-box colors make this pattern (*left*) fine for children's sweaters. Use it with the Big Arrow or on its own.

Houndstooth

A traditional pattern (*above*) used in tweeds is easily adapted to knitting. Use more heathery colors for classic men's vests and sweaters.

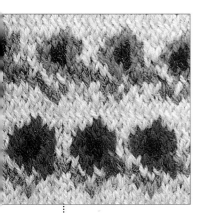

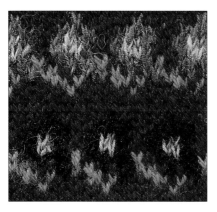

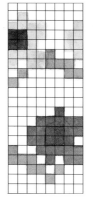

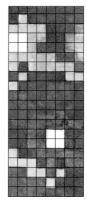

Bavarian Flowers

Small, neat rows of this flower repeat *(left)* would make an all-over pattern. Notice that the dark and light colorways create a completely different effect.

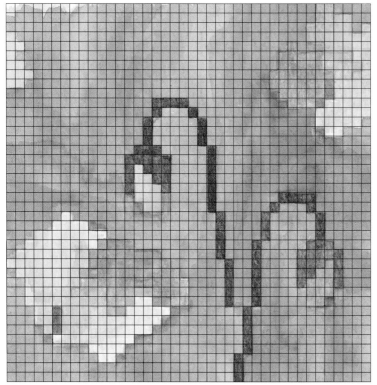

Welsh Poppies

For a hotter color variation, knit the flowers in bright reds. This motif *(below, left)* could be spaced wide apart on afghans or cardigans.

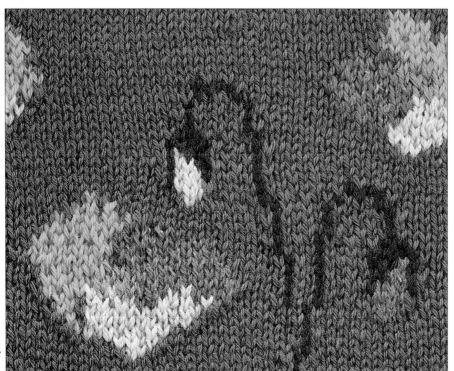

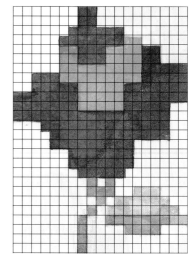

Purple Flower

The simple shape of this pretty flower *(above)* takes on a richness by the use of six colors.

Old Rose

A classic old rose pattern (*right*) reminiscent of upholstery chintzes, with carefully shaded petals and leaves. Use this as a single motif on a dressy cardigan.

Single Anemone

This flower and leaf motif (*below*) could be spaced over the back ground and set into diagonal lines. The edge of the motif must be carefully knitted.

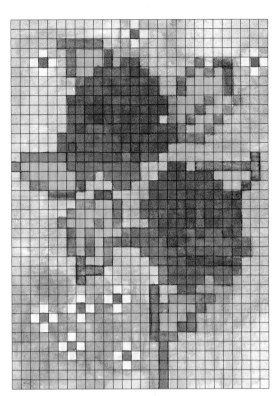

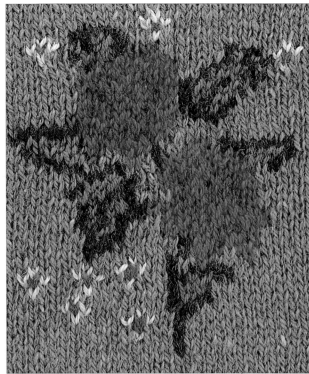

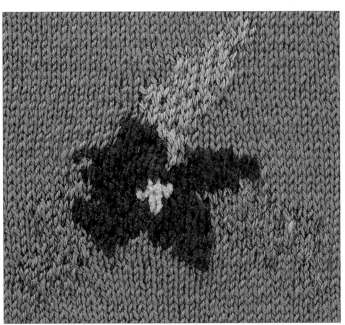

Anemone border

A flower border (*right*) with overlapping petals can be adapted into many different colorways; use it to set off the Single Anemone pattern as a hemline trim on a cardigan.

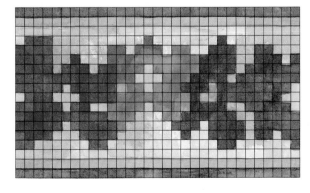

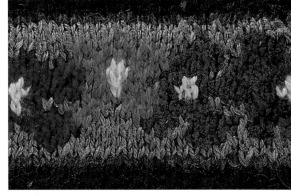

COLORFUL WINTER WEAR

MULTICOLOR KNITTING IS popular for scarves and sweaters, and can be done in a variety of ways. Here we show a sweater, cardigan, and scarf that all use different techniques. The Log Cabin pattern sweater consists of blocks of color, and uses the technique of intarsia. The cardigan is knitted in one background color with a contrasting dot, and the colorful embroidery added at the end. This scarf makes an excellent project for a beginner – it features Popcorn stitch on every other stripe, and is knitted in vivid bands of color.

LOG CABIN SWEATER

This turtle neck sweater in a tweed Fisherman weight will keep you warm and cozy in winter weather. The flecked tweed adds a dimension to the simple back and sleeves – and it is surprisingly fast and easy to make. (See page 230.)

The rib roll neck adds a finish to this warm sweater

The Log Cabin pattern suits a sweater just as well as a quilt

CARDIGAN WITH CREWEL EMBROIDERY

A classic round necked cardigan is transformed into something elegant with the addition of bright crewel-embroidered poppies and leaves. The plain knitting worsted-weight cardigan knits up quickly. (See page 230.)

Popcorn stitch adds texture to a warm striped scarf

Outline-stitch stems and long- and short-satin stitch flowers are worked in Persian yarn on this plain blue cardigan

MULTICOLOR SCARF

Knitted in bulky wool and in bright colors, this knits up quickly and is a good way to use up your scrap yarn. Use two strands of knitting worsted scraps to achieve the same tension as bulky yarn. (See page 232.)

Popcorn stitch

Popcorn, one of the most well-known raised patterns, is easy to work and adds more texture than bobbles.

To work a Popcorn:
K into front and back of stitch twice, then slip 2nd, 3rd, and 4th sts over 1st stitch. The size of the Popcorn can be varied by working fewer or more times into a stitch.

EMBROIDERING KNITTING

SIMPLE EMBROIDERY STITCHES enrich any knitted garment by adding extra color and texture. Four of the most popular stitches are shown here – duplicate stitch, cross stitch, long and short, and bullion knot. As its name suggests, duplicate stitch follows the same stitch pattern as the knitting, and can be used instead of color knitting (see page 46) to work motifs, or in combination with color knitting to add areas of color. Cross stitch is a quick and easy pattern stitch; bullion knots provide interesting texture. Long and short stitch is useful for filling solid shapes in free-form embroidery. You can also experiment with other common embroidery stitches – including chain stitch, daisy stitch, and running stitch.

EMBROIDERY BASICS

It is often easier to embroider on knitting before the garment has been assembled, but after it has been blocked (see page 64). The golden rule is to work with the knitted fabric and not against it. Do not pull the embroidery stitches too tight or the knitting will pucker, and always work with a blunt-ended tapestry needle or yarn needle to avoid splitting the knitted stitches. Embroider with a yarn of the same type and thickness as the knitting – if the embroidery yarn is too thin it will sink into the knitted stitches, and if it is too thick it will stretch the knitting and look lumpy. You can also use embroidery floss or tapestry wool instead of knitting yarn. These products are sold in small, economical amounts and come in a wide range of beautiful colors. Bear in mind that you may need to work with several strands to match the thickness of the knitting yarn.

Duplicate stitch worked on a knitted pocket can form a striking initial or monogram

Duplicate stitch in vertical rows on stockinette

1 Bring needle out on right side of knitting under strand at the bottom of a knit stitch (base of V-shape). Insert needle from right to left behind knit stitch directly above and pull the yarn snug.

2 Insert needle under same strand where thread emerged for first half-stitch. Bring needle out under the connecting strand of the knit stitch directly above it.

Duplicate stitch in horizontal rows on stockinette

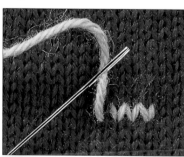

1 Bring the needle up on the right side under the connecting thread at the bottom of a knit stitch. Insert needle from right to left behind the knit stitch above, and pull the yarn snug.

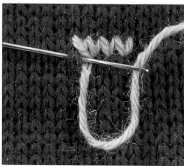

2 Insert needle under the same strand where thread emerged for the first half stitch. Bring needle up again under the connecting strand of the stitch to the left of it.

Cross stitch

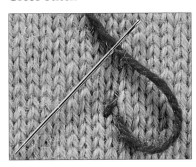

1 Bring yarn out to the front of the work at the bottom of a knit stitch, and take a diagonal stitch up to right. Bring the needle out directly below, and pull the yarn snug.

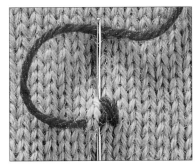

2 To complete the cross, insert the needle directly above where it first emerged. If making a second cross stitch, bring it out at bottom to left and continue as in step 1.

Stem stitch

Work from left to right, taking regular, slanted backstitches. The thread should always emerge on the left of the previous stitch.

Long and short stitch

1 Baste the outline shape with contrasting thread (this is removed afterward). Count down the knitted rows vertically, and bring needle out to front of work about 2 knit stitches inside outline.

2 Insert needle at outline, and bring it out to left of previous stitch and one knit stitch down. Repeat using long and short stitches alternately, closely following the outline. Work stitches in following rows to fill shape.

Bullion knot

1 Similar to a French knot (see page 135), this stitch may be worked singly or in clusters. Bring yarn out on front of work at the position for the knot. Make a backstitch the size of the knot(s) required, bringing needle out to front next to first stitch. Twist yarn around needle point as many times as required to equal the backstitch length.

2 Hold your left thumb on the coiled yarn and pull needle through the coils. Then turn needle back to where it was first inserted, and pull yarn through to the back of the work so that the bullion knot lies flat.

A combination of different embroidery stitches can be used very effectively

Knots form the centers of the flowers, which are worked in long and short stitch

KNITTING IN THE ROUND

KNITTING IN THE round is a more ancient art than flat knitting, and many of the beautiful tribal and traditional peasant designs you will see in museums have been knitted in this way. Since the knitting is worked as a continuous spiral there are no seams to sew up, and a stronger garment is produced. Another advantage is that the right side of the knitting is always facing you, so if you are working a color pattern you can see it clearly at all times. Knitting stockinette stitch is simplified because you knit every row or round. Purling every row produces reverse stockinette stitch.

There are two main ways of working: With a flexible circular needle or with four or more double-pointed straight needles. A circular needle can hold three times as many stitches as a straight needle so it is the best way of knitting large items such as skirts. Small items, such as socks and mittens are usually produced with four or more straight needles rather than a circular needle.

FAIR ISLE HAT AND MITTENS

Traditional Fair Isle patterns are popular decorations for warm hats and mittens. When knitting in the round the pattern will always be facing you.
(See page 232.)

Knitting worsted-weight mittens are decorated on the back and front

A Fair Isle ski hat is decorated with a pompon

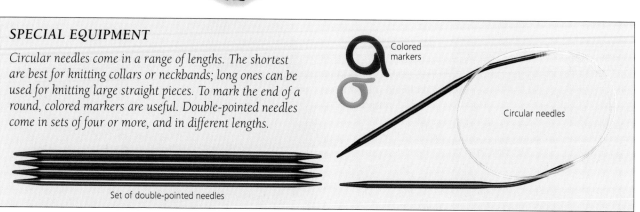

SPECIAL EQUIPMENT

Circular needles come in a range of lengths. The shortest are best for knitting collars or neckbands; long ones can be used for knitting large straight pieces. To mark the end of a round, colored markers are useful. Double-pointed needles come in sets of four or more, and in different lengths.

Colored markers

Circular needles

Set of double-pointed needles

KNITTING WITH A CIRCULAR NEEDLE

Choose a circular needle about two inches smaller than the circumference of the knitting to avoid stretching the stitches. If you haven't used this type of needle before, just work as if each pointed end is a separate needle.

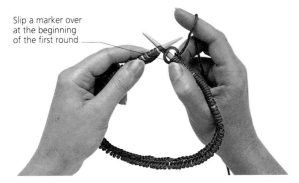

Slip a marker over at the beginning of the first round

1 Cast on the number of stitches needed, then slip a marker between the first and last stitches so that you can see where the first round starts. Hold the needle tip with the last cast-on stitch in your right hand, and the tip with the first cast-on stitch in your left hand. At this point it is crucial to check for any twisted stitches by making sure the cast-on edge is facing in toward the center of the needle. When knitting the first stitch of the round, pull the yarn firmly to avoid a gap.

2 Knit until you reach the marker, then slip the marker over. You are now ready to start the second round. Check again to see if any stitches are twisted. If so, ravel the first row – twisted stitches cannot be corrected in any other way.

To knit flat work on a circular needle

The last cast-on stitch is on left-hand point

A circular needle is ideal for knitting large flat pieces. Hold the needle tip with the last cast-on stitch in your left hand and the needle tip with the first cast-on stitch in your right hand. Knit as with ordinary needles across the row, ending with the last stitch, then turn your work around so that the wrong side is facing you. Purl across the row. Continue to work back and forth, knitting and purling.

KNITTING WITH DOUBLE-POINTED NEEDLES

Double-pointed needles usually come in sets of four, but sometimes as many as six needles can be used. The working method is always the same: One needle is used to knit off the stitches that are equally divided between the other needles.

1 To knit with 4 needles, cast on one third of the stitches onto each of 3 needles. When you complete the stitches on one needle, hold the next one parallel and above it with the point a little bit further forward than the lower one. (Alternatively, cast on all the stitches on one needle and then divide them between the other needles.)

2 Place the 3 needles in a triangle and make sure the bottom edges of all the stitches are facing the center. Place a marker after the last stitch.

3 Use the 4th needle to knit into the first cast-on stitch. Pull the yarn extra firmly on this stitch to avoid a gap in the work. When you have knitted all the stitches off the first needle, use it as the working needle to knit the stitches off the 2nd needle, then use this needle to work the stitches off the 3rd needle.

The marker will show you where each new round starts

4 Continue knitting in this way, holding the 2 working needles as you would normally, and dropping the needles not in use to the back of the work. When you reach the marker, slip it and start the next round.

BUTTONHOLES

THERE ARE FOUR basic types of buttonholes – horizontal, vertical, round, and loop. The horizontal is hardwearing and is the most commonly used. It is suitable for light- and medium-weight garments. The vertical type is better when the knitting will have a vertical pull, such as on pocket flaps. Round buttonholes are worked for small buttons on baby clothes (see eyelets page 43). Loops are suitable for thick jackets, and are sewn to the edge of the knitting.

It is essential that the size and position of the buttonhole match the button to be used. In general, a horizontal buttonhole extends one stitch beyond the button, a vertical hole extends one row above it, and a round hole or loop aligns exactly with the button.

Horizontal buttonhole

Knit up to buttonhole position. On a right-side row, bind off number of stitches required for size of button and then knit to end of row. On next row, work up to stitch before buttonhole and knit into front and back of this stitch. Cast on one stitch less than number bound off. Knit to end of row.

Vertical buttonhole

Turn work at base of buttonhole, holding unused stitches on spare needle. Work on first set of stitches to the depth needed, ending on a right-side row. Join new yarn, and work one less than this number of rows on 2nd set of stitches. Slip these back onto original needle and knit across.

Loop

Mark 2 fixing points on wrong side. With a blunt-ended needle, secure yarn firmly to one point, then loop it over to the 2nd fixing point and take a small stitch. Continue looping and securing yarn until the required thickness has been achieved. Then buttonhole stitch over the loops.

Buttonhole stitch

This stitch is used to cover loops (*above*) and to neaten other buttonholes. Work from right, using a blunt-ended needle. Bring yarn out on right side just below edge. Take a straight downward stitch with thread under needle, pull up stitch to form a loop knot at buttonhole edge and repeat. Work stitches close together.

Buttonband

With some patterns you may need to knit a buttonband – an extra area of fabric onto which buttons are sewn. To knit a buttonband, simply cast on the extra number of stitches required at the end of a row, then work across these and the rest of the stitches until you reach the required depth. Bind off the extra stitches.

Knitted buttons

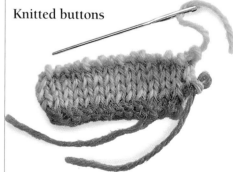

With scrap yarn, cast on 14 stitches. With yarn for button, knit 5 rows; leaving about 8 inches, cut yarn. With this yarn, sew through stitches in last row. Unpick scrap yarn; with another length of yarn, sew through loops. Draw both ends tight and fasten. Stuff button with yarn, and sew up. Use threads to sew on.

TRIMMINGS

THE RIGHT TRIMMING can add that special finishing touch to your knitted garment. Pompons are fun on children's hats, a fringe is the perfect edging for a scarf, and tassels make a jacket look smart or home furnishings more professionally finished. All can be made in the same or contrasting yarn.

Pompons

1 Cut 2 card-board circles to desired size. In centers, cut a hole about one third of total diameter. Place circles together and wrap yarn as shown.

2 Continue wrapping yarn until the center holes are completely filled. If you run out of yarn, wrap a new length in and leave the ends dangling at the outer edge.

Tie a lenght of yarn between cardboard circles

3 Cut through yarn around edges. Ease circles slightly apart and wrap a length of yarn tightly around strands a few times, and secure with a firm knot. Pull off cardboard. Fluff out pompon, and trim with sharp scissors.

Trimmed and finished pompon

Fringe

1 Wrap yarn around a cardboard rectangle slightly deeper than desired length of fringe. Cut along one edge to make the strands. Take several strands and fold.

2 With a crochet hook, draw loop of strands through edge stitch, then pull cut ends through loop to form a loose knot. Adjust and trim.

Tassels

1 Wrap yarn around cardboard cut to desired length. Thread length of yarn under top loops, and tie tightly; leave one end long. Cut through yarn at lower edge.

2 Hide knot and short end of yarn under tassel strands. Wind long end tightly around strands to form a neat top. Thread needle with long end of yarn and push under binding and out through top of tassel. Trim ends if necessary.

BLOCKING & PRESSING

BEFORE A KNITTED garment is sewn together it must be blocked. This means that each knitted piece is shaped to the measurements given in the pattern. The process also helps smooth out any stitch irregularities and flattens curling edges. Before blocking, weave in all the loose ends. The beauty of the garment is in its hand knitted appearance – be careful not to overpress and obliterate this look.

BLOCKING

You will need a large, flat, padded surface. A table covered with a folded blanket and topped with a clean white sheet works well. Place each knitted piece wrong side up on the padding, smooth it out, and pin the corners to the padding with straight steel pins. Take care not to stretch or distort the basic shape, and make sure the knit rows run in straight lines. Then take a tape measure and check the length and width of each piece against those given in the pattern. Stretch or shrink the piece as necessary, and continue pinning at fairly close intervals all around the edges. The edges should be quite smooth: If each pin draws out a point of the knitting, you are either stretching it too much or are not using enough pins.

Block the piece to the measure given in the pattern instructions

PRESSING

After pinning cotton and wool, press very lightly under a damp cloth with a warm iron. Alternatively, hold a steaming iron very close to, but not touching, the knitting. Leave until completely dry. For synthetic yarn, check label instructions.

Stockinette and garter stitch

Press or steam each part of the knitting. If pressing, lift up and reapply the iron since moving it over the surface of the cloth will distort the stitches.

Embossed patterns

Hold a steaming iron or steamer just above the knitting. If you press, use a damp cloth and unpin the piece immediately and lightly pat it into shape so that the texture doesn't become flattened.

Ribbing

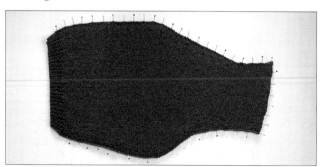

If the garment is all ribbing, use minimum pinning so that the ribbing isn't under any tension. If the ribbing is attached to stockinette, omit the pins on the ribbing section altogether. After pressing or steaming, immediately unpin the piece and gently ease the ribbing into its correct shape.

SEAMS

ONCE YOU'VE FINISHED knitting all the pieces of a garment, you have to sew them together. Don't be tempted to rush this process because clumsy seaming can completely ruin beautiful knitting. Seams should be sewn with a blunt-ended tapestry needle and matching yarn. If the garment yarn is not smooth, use plain yarn in a matching or slightly darker color, making sure the washing instructions are compatible. A ladder-stitch seam is best for straight edges, and can be almost invisible. Backstitch seams make a small ridge inside the garment. If you are joining two pieces of horizontal knitting, use the grafting method.

ORDER OF SEAMING

If given, always follow the assembling instructions included with the pattern. Due to special design features, your pattern instructions may vary slightly from the basic steps listed below:

1 Shoulder seams
2 Set in sleeves (*see below*)
3 Side and sleeve seams: Seam in one continuous line of stitching
4 Collar: Sew right side of collar to wrong side of neckline, matching center back of both pieces
5 Buttonbands
6 Pockets
7 Hems

Backstitch seam

Place the pieces to be joined, right side to right side, carefully matching up the rows of knitting stitch for stitch. Baste together with contrasting yarn. Work backstitch along the seam about ¼ inch in from edges, sewing into the center of each stitch and checking that the stitches correspond on both pieces. To work backstitch: Bring needle one stitch ahead at starting edge, insert it one stitch back and bring it out one stitch ahead of emerging thread. Repeat to end and remove basting thread.

Ladder-stitch seam

Place the 2 pieces in your left hand, edge to edge, and with the 2 right sides facing you. Match the knitting row by row. Pick up the strand between the first and 2nd stitches on one edge, and then the strand between first and 2nd stitches on the other edge. Take care to match the tension of the knitting.

To set in sleeves

The sleeve cap is often slightly larger than the armhole. The following steps will ensure a good fit. Fold the sleeve in half lengthways and mark the center cap. Match it to the shoulder seam on the garment and pin in position. Then pin the 2 pieces together at intervals, easing in the sleeve fullness. Sew the sleeve into the armhole.

Grafting

Slip the stitches off the needles; in order to prevent your work from raveling, press lightly with a steam iron or thread a piece of yarn through the stitches. Place the 2 pieces face up on a padded surface, with the 2 edges to be joined butting. Thread a tapestry needle with matching yarn; you will need about 3 times the length of the seam to be joined.

Insert needle from back to front through first loop on lower piece. *Insert needle from front to back through first loop on upper piece; then from back to front on 2nd upper loop.

Insert needle from front to back in first lower loop, then from back to front in 2nd lower loop. Repeat from *, always going from front to back through a loop you have already gone through from back to front.

MEASURING UP

IF YOU WANT a new pattern to fit perfectly or if you wish to alter an existing pattern, you will need to take accurate measurements. Then, compare these to the measurements of the garment given at the beginning of the pattern. Most patterns give a body measurement, and a finished measurement of the knitted garment which allows for ease of fit. Compare your own measurements with those given on the pattern. After knitting up a stitch gauge sample (page 24), you will have all the information you need to vary the amount of ease, alter measurements, or knit up a pattern in a different stitch.

TAKING MEASUREMENTS

For greatest accuracy, measurements should be taken over underclothes. If you are taking your own measurements, ask somebody else to help you hold the tape measure straight.

Basic body measurements

Armhole: From tip of shoulder bone, down to one inch below armpit.
Shoulder length: From base of neck to tip of one shoulder.

Underarm to waist: Measure from one inch below armpit to waist.
Sleeve: From one inch below armpit to wrist with arm bent. Outer arm, from shoulder tip to wrist.

Overall back length: From base of neck to the required length.

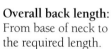

Wrist: Measure around the wristbone.

For a hat

1 Circumference: Measure straight around the head at mid-forehead level.
2 Diameter: Measure across top of head from ear tip to ear tip and then from mid-forehead across top of head to base of skull.

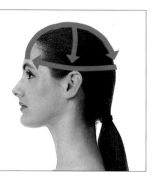

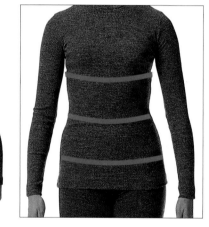

Shoulder width: Measure across the back from shoulder tip to shoulder tip (about 3 inches below the base of the neck for a child, 5 inches on a woman, 6 inches on a man).

Chest or bust: Measure straight across the back, under the arms and across the fullest part at front.
Waist: Measure not too tightly around the narrowest part.
Hips: Measure around the broadest part about 9 inches below the waist.

TO ALTER A PATTERN

Knit a sample square to the required tension and check the gauge. To make the garment larger across the bust, for example, calculate how many extra inches you need. Then, add extra stitches across the width of the front and back to obtain the measurement required. Remember you must allow for complete pattern repeats.

If you want to knit up a favorite garment in a different stitch, you need to check that your gauge matches that originally given. If it doesn't match, you must either change your needle or make adjustments to the width and length as necessary.

CARING FOR YOUR KNITS

KNITTED GARMENTS CAN be pulled out of shape all too easily during washing and drying. Handle garments gently, particularly when they are wet. Some specially treated wool yarns and many acrylic yarns are machine washable, and most yarns will benefit from a short, fast spin before being laid out flat to dry. Check the instructions on the yarn label first, and, if you are in any doubt, use the method given below.

TROUBLE-SHOOTING

Here are some tips for keeping your knitted garments in great condition:

- Snags should never be cut. Ease the yarn back in position with a blunt tapestry needle, and, if necessary, catch with a few small stitches on the wrong side.
- Some yarns are prone to pilling (tiny balls of fluff caused by rubbing). Lay the garment flat and pick off the balls gently by hand. They may also be removed by brushing lengthways with the edge of a stiff, dry synthetic sponge. A small shaver can also be bought from stores for this purpose.
- The texture of mohair can be improved by brushing very gently with a metal 'teazel'.
- Stains require immediate action. Most will respond to cold water. Dab or soak the area – don't rub. Oil-based stains should be treated with an appropriate solvent on the wrong side, following the manufacturer's instructions. Rinse afterward.

MACHINE WASHING

Use only when indicated on the yarn label. Turn the garment inside out and wash on the appropriate cycle. To avoid stretching, place garment in a loosely tied pillowcase before washing. Then, wash it on a short, fast cycle. Remove the garment when damp, lay it on a flat surface away from direct heat or sunlight, and pat it into its original shape. Leave until completely dry.

The pillowcase prevents the garment stretching in the machine's drum

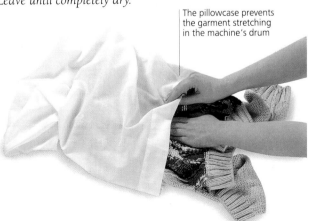

HAND WASHING

Large items should be washed separately in lukewarm water, using a mild detergent made especially for knitwear. If you think strong colors will run, wet a corner of the garment and press it on a white cloth. If it makes a stain, use cold water for a few washes.

1 Work in lather by gently squeezing and pressing the knitting up and down. Never rub or twist. Rinse thoroughly with several changes of lukewarm water.

2 Do not wring; squeeze out excess moisture. Then roll in a clean towel to soak up as much moisture as possible; repeat with a second towel if necessary.

3 Spread the article out on a flat surface, away from direct heat, and ease it into its original shape. Leave until completely dry.

STORAGE

Dust can damage knitted garments. To prevent this, store knitwear flat in a closed closet, drawer, or in a container under the bed, not on an open shelf. Always wash your knits before storage. Never hang up knitted garments as their weight will cause them to stretch out of shape.

CROCHET

*B*ig and bold or light and lacy, crochet is a versatile craft that lends itself to a variety of uses. As tools and materials are minimal – a single hook and a ball of yarn – crochet is extremely portable. Like knitting, it is formed from a continuous length of yarn, but only one stitch at a time is made. By using a large hook and thick yarn, you can create chunky hats and sweaters, for example. If you choose a thin hook and yarn, a combination of stitches will result in patterns that rival lace in their delicacy. These patterns work well on household items, such as bedspreads, or to embellish garments. Easy to work in rows or rings, well-loved patterns include multicolored granny squares, which are ideal for using up scraps of different yarns, and delicate lace medallions, most often created from finer cotton. Crochet is an old craft, and is practiced all around the world. New stitch patterns are regularly created, and each year another generation of designers rediscovers crochet's appeal. With the wealth of attractive patterns and yarns available it is not surprising that crochet has remained such a popular pastime.

HOOKS & YARNS

CROCHET HOOKS COME in different sizes and materials. There are fine steel hooks and larger ones of aluminum, plastic, or wood. Avoid the cheaper plastic versions that may have rough edges. Yarns are sold by weight and/or length. Beginners will find it helpful to choose a smooth yarn in a heavy weight that is not likely to untwist while you work. Generally, the coarser the yarn, the larger the hook needed. Sometimes a hook size is given on the label: Use this as a starting point, but it is essential to obtain the gauge stated in a pattern (see page 83). Fancy yarns can be worked with a larger hook than a smooth yarn of similar weight. If you are mixing more than one yarn in a garment, check that they share the same care instruction.

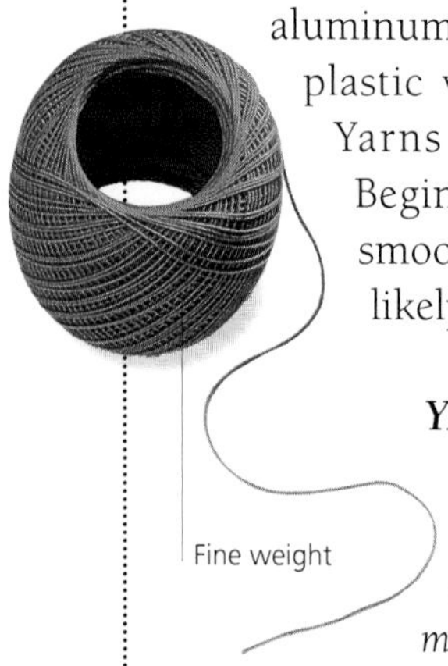

Fine weight

YARNS

There are basic standard terms which describe the most popular weights of yarns and some of their suitable uses. These yarns may be made of different numbers of strands spun together, 2-, 3- and 4-ply are all common. There is often an overlap within these terms so the following is a guide:

Fine weight is usually used for lace work and edgings. It is approximately half the thickness of fingering weight, or finer. Fingering weight, for delicate garments and baby wear, is often a 3-ply yarn. Sport weight is middle of the weight range, for sweaters, cardigans, or afghans, and is the standard on which other yarn weights are based. Knitting worsted suits chunkier jackets and sweaters, and is equivalent to two strands of sport weight. Fisherman (Aran) weight is equivalent to three strands of sport weight, and is used for heavy afghans or jackets. Bulky weight, for warm outdoor garments, is equivalent to four strands of sport weight or two strands of knitting worsted.

Fingering weight

Sport weight

Knitting worsted weight

Fisherman (Aran)

Bulky weight

HOOKS

Steel and aluminum hooks come in a large range of sizes, but wooden hooks are also popular. Afghan crochet needs the very long hook shown on the right.

CROCHET HOOK SIZES

Aluminum hooks

Size	mm
B	2.25
C	2.75
D	3.25
E	3.50
F	3.75
G	4.25
H	5.00
I	5.50
J	6.00
K	6.50
N	9.00
P	10.00

Steel hooks

Size	mm
00	3.50
0	3.25
1	2.75
2	2.25
3	2.10
4	2.00
5	1.90
6	1.80
7	1.65
8	1.50
9	1.40
10	1.30
11	1.10
12	1.00
13	0.85
14	0.75

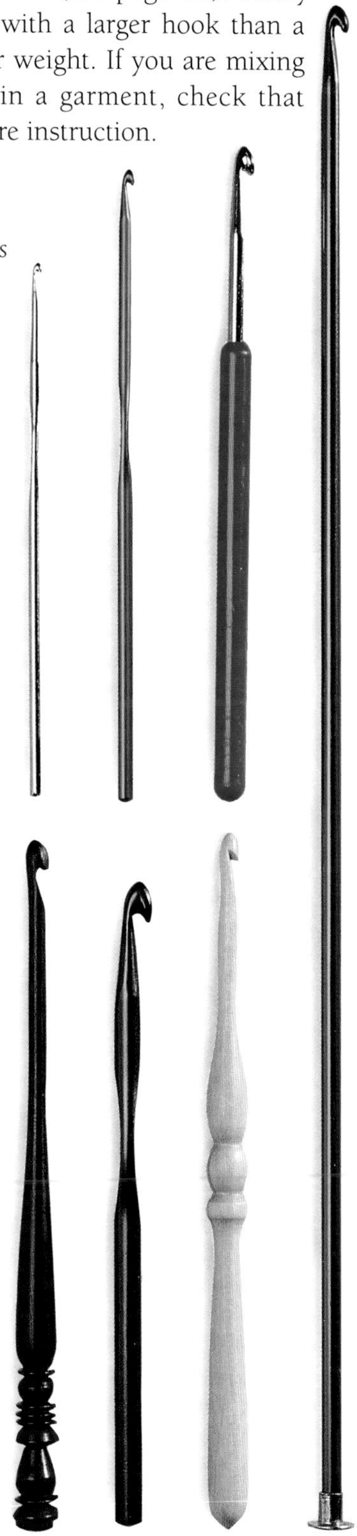

BEGINNING TO CROCHET

CROCHET WORK, like knitting, is created from a continuous length of yarn. However, in crochet a single hook is used to work one stitch at a time. To begin crocheting, you start with a slip knot then continue to make loops (called chains) to form your foundation chain, from which you make your first row. You can hold the hook and yarn as you like, but we show the two most common ways or you can devise a method to suit yourself. The tension of the yarn is controlled with either your middle or forefinger. With practice, you will learn to control the yarn evenly and develop uniform chains.

LEFT-HANDED CROCHETERS

Illustrations show hook and yarn positions of a right-handed person. If you are left-handed, hold the working yarn in your right hand and hold the hook exactly as shown, but in the left hand. If it helps, hold this book in front of a mirror to follow the correct working positions.

HOLDING THE HOOK

Both methods are equally good, so use whichever feels most comfortable.

Pencil position
Grasp the flat part of the hook between thumb and forefinger as if it were a pencil with the stem above your hand.

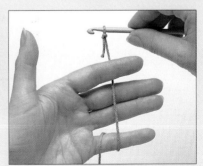

Hold the hook as if it were a pencil

Knife position
With the stem against your palm and your thumb on the flat part, grasp the hook between thumb and fingers.

Hold the hook in the knife position

Making a slip knot

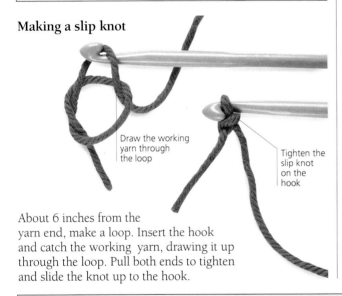

Draw the working yarn through the loop

Tighten the slip knot on the hook

About 6 inches from the yarn end, make a loop. Insert the hook and catch the working yarn, drawing it up through the loop. Pull both ends to tighten and slide the knot up to the hook.

CONTROLLING THE YARN

The way you hold the yarn allows it to flow easily with the right tension. You can wrap the yarn around your little finger, over the next two fingers, and catch it with your forefinger – when your middle finger will control the yarn. Or you can wrap the yarn around your little finger, then under your next two fingers and over your forefinger – when your forefinger will control the yarn. With thick yarn, you can catch it between your fourth and fifth fingers. Use the method that you feel comfortable with.

Forefinger method
Pass working yarn around little finger, under next 2 fingers and over forefinger. With hook through slip loop, and holding slip knot between thumb and middle finger, prepare to make first chain by raising your forefinger.

Middle finger method
Pass working yarn around little finger, and over other fingers. With hook through slip loop, and holding slip knot between thumb and forefinger of your left hand, prepare to make first chain by raising your middle finger.

CHAIN STITCH (CH)

Chain stitch is usually used to form the foundation for the first row in crochet. It is also used as part of a pattern stitch, to make spaces between stitches, for bars in openwork (see page 105), and for the turning chains at the beginnings of rows/rounds (see page 76).

Foundation chain

The foundation chain should be worked loosely and evenly to ensure that the hook can enter each loop easily on the first row. The hook and your tension will determine the size of the chains. Do not try to make them loose by pulling them as you make them, since this tightens up previously made chains. If the chains are too tight, ensure that the yarn is flowing through your fingers easily, or use a larger hook than you will use for the rest of your work. The length of the foundation chain will be specified in the pattern instruction.

Making a chain stitch

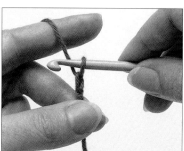

1 Hold hook in your right hand. Keeping working yarn taut, grasp slip knot with thumb and middle finger of your left hand. Push hook forward and take hook under (counter-clockwise), behind and then over yarn, so that yarn passes around hook and is caught in it. This is called a yarn-over – abbreviated as *yo*.

2 Draw hook and yarn back through the slip loop to form the first chain stitch.

3 Repeat steps 1 and 2. After making a few chains in this way, move your left hand up so that you are holding the work directly under the hook for maximum control, and continue.

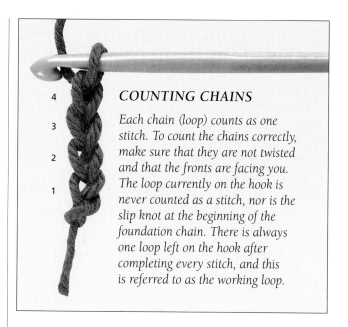

COUNTING CHAINS

Each chain (loop) counts as one stitch. To count the chains correctly, make sure that they are not twisted and that the fronts are facing you. The loop currently on the hook is never counted as a stitch, nor is the slip knot at the beginning of the foundation chain. There is always one loop left on the hook after completing every stitch, and this is referred to as the working loop.

SLIP STITCH (SL ST)

Some of the earliest crochet work found was done in continuous slip stitch. However, this stitch is now only used to join a row into a round (see page 98), to decrease (see page 85), and for joining seams (see page 117).

1 Make a length of evenly worked foundation chain.

2 Insert the hook from front to back under the top of the 2nd chain (*ch*) from the hook. Wrap the yarn around the hook to make a yarn-over (*yo*).

3 Draw yarn through the 2 loops now on the hook, making a slip stitch. To continue working slip stitch, insert the hook into the next and each chain, and repeat step 2 as required.

BASIC CROCHET STITCHES

IT IS EASY to learn crochet stitches because they are all made in the same way. Apart from the chain and the slip stitch, there are five basic crochet stitches, which vary in height (there are others, but these are used infrequently). The difference in the height or length of these stitches is determined by the number of times the yarn is wrapped around the hook. As each stitch has a flatter appearance on the front than on the back, the crocheted piece has more texture when worked in rows and turned because you see both the fronts and the backs of the stitches. The surface has a smoother, flatter look when worked in rows/rounds without turning, as it always shows the front of the stitches.

SINGLE CROCHET

This is a simple compact stitch. It is found in many pattern designs and forms a firm, smooth surface.

HALF DOUBLE CROCHET

Between a single and double crochet in size, this stitch produces a slightly looser surface with an attractive ridge.

Double crochet

Half double crochet

Single crochet

DOUBLE CROCHET

Twice as high as single crochet, this stitch works up quickly. It is the most commonly used stitch.

TRIPLE CROCHET

Three times as high as single crochet, this stitch forms a looser texture.

Triple crochet

Double triple crochet

DOUBLE TRIPLE CROCHET

This extremely long stitch is commonly used in fancy stitch patterns, but is not generally used continuously to make a whole piece, except where it is linked (see page 78).

73

MAKING THE BASIC STITCHES

WHEN YOU ARE working the basic stitches onto the foundation chains, insert the hook from front to back under the top loop of each chain. On subsequent rows, unless instructed otherwise, insert your hook from front to back under the top two loops of each stitch. Turn the work at the end of each row, then make extra chains, called turning chains, to bring the hook level with the height of the stitches in the new row (see page 76). The turning chains may or may not count as stitches at the beginning of a row, according to the pattern. They do count as a stitch in the basic stitch patterns below.

Single crochet (sc)

1 Make a foundation chain. Skip 2 ch and insert hook under top loop of 3rd ch *(right)*. Yo and draw yarn through chain loop only *(far right)*.

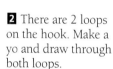

2 There are 2 loops on the hook. Make a yo and draw through both loops.

3 Single crochet made. Continue working sc into the next and all following chains to the end of the row.

4 Turn work and ch 1. This is called the turning chain (t-ch). Skip first st, at base of t-ch, work 1 sc into top 2 loops of 2nd st in previous row. Work 1 sc into next and each st to end, including top of t-ch.

Half double crochet (hdc)

1 Make a length of foundation chain. Skip 2 ch, yo and insert hook under top loop of 3rd ch. Make a yo.

2 Draw yarn through chain loop only; (there are now 3 loops on hook).Yo.

3 Draw yarn through all 3 loops. Half double crochet made. Continue working hdc into next and all following chs to end of row.

4 To make the next and following rows of hdc, turn work and ch 2. This turning chain counts as first hdc in new row. Skip first st, which is at base of t-ch. Work 1 hdc, inserting hook under top 2 loops of 2nd st in previous row. Work 1 hdc into next and each st to end, including into top of t-ch.

Double crochet (dc)

1 Make a length of foundation chain. Skip 3 ch, yo and insert the hook under the top loop of the 4th ch. Yo.

2 Draw yarn through ch loop only (there are now 3 loops on hook). Yo.

3 Draw yarn through 2 loops only (2 loops on hook). Yo.

4 Draw yarn through these 2 loops. Double crochet made. Continue working dc into the next and all following chains to the end of the row.

5 To make next and following rows of dc, turn work and ch 3. This t-ch counts as first dc in new row. Skip first st which is at base of t-ch. Work 1 dc inserting hook under top 2 loops of 2nd st in previous row. Work 1 dc into next and each st to end, including into top of t-ch.

Triple or treble crochet (tr)

1 Make a length of foundation chain. Skip 4 ch, yo twice and insert the hook under the top loop of the 5th ch. Yo.

2 Draw yarn through ch loop only; (there are now 4 loops on hook). Yo.

3 Draw yarn through 2 loops only; (3 loops on the hook). Yo.

4 Draw yarn through 2 loops only, yo again. Draw yarn through remaining 2 loops. Triple crochet made. Continue working tr into the next and all following chains to the end of the row.

5 To make next row of tr, turn work and ch 4. This t-ch counts as first tr in new row. Skip first st which is at base of t-ch. Work 1 tr, inserting hook under top 2 loops of 2nd st in previous row. Work 1 tr into next and each st to end of row, including into t-ch.

Double triple (dtr)

1 Make a length of foundation chain. Skip 5 ch, yo 3 times and insert hook under top of the 6th ch, yo and draw it through the ch loop only; (there are now 5 loops on the hook). *Yo.

2 Draw yarn through 2 loops only.

3 Repeat from * 3 times more.

4 Double triple made. Continue working dtr into next and all following chains to end of row.

5 To make the next and following rows of dtr, turn the work and ch 5. This t-ch counts as the first dtr in the new row. Skip the first st, which is at the base of the t-ch. Work 1 dtr, inserting the hook under the top 2 loops of the 2nd st in the previous row. Work 1 dtr into next and each st to the end of row, including into top of t-ch.

TURNING CHAINS (T-CH)

*To bring the hook up to the height of the stitches, you must add turning chains at the beginning of each row. Each stitch has its own number of chains: The table gives the numbers when the t-ch counts as the first stitch. Sometimes the t-ch may **not** be counted as a stitch (see Straight Edges). Some instructions say ch 2 and turn.*

Stitch	Add to foundation chain	Skip at beginning of foundation row (counts as first st)	For turning chain counts as first st
Single	1	2	1
Half double	1	2	2
Double	2	3	3
Triple	3	4	4
Double triple	4	5	5
Triple triple	5	6	6

STRAIGHT EDGES

To obtain straight edges and keep the number of stitches constant, you need to make the turning chains in one of two ways. The first is most common, but the second is used with very short stitches, or to avoid the gap created by using the turning chain as a stitch. However, the second method creates slightly uneven edges. The instruction to work "even" in a pattern means to work without any increasing or decreasing.

Turning chain counts as first stitch

Skip the first stitch of the previous row at the base of the turning chain. When you reach the end of the row, work a stitch into the top of the turning chain of the previous row.

Turning chain does not count as stitch

Work into the first stitch at the base of the turning chain. When you reach the end of the row, do not work into the top of the previous turning chain.

WORKING IN ROWS

Crochet is normally worked in rows to produce the desired width, and the work is turned between each row: The right side of the work will not always be facing you.

The first row is made by working across the foundation chain from right to left (if you are left-handed, work from left to right).

At the end of the foundation chain or row, turn the work so that the yarn is behind the hook and the new stitches can be worked into the tops of those in the previous row.

BINDING OFF

To prevent the work from raveling when you have finished, it is necessary to fasten the end.

Complete the final stitch, then cut the working yarn and pull it through the last loop on the hook. Pull the yarn tight to close the loop. Thread the working end of the yarn into a tapestry or yarn needle and weave it into the back of the work.

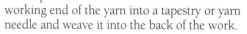

COUNTING STITCHES

To count short stitches, such as single crochet (as shown), it is easier to look at the tops. For longer stitches, count the upright stems – each is counted as a single stitch.

BASIC STITCH VARIATIONS

YOU CAN ACHIEVE interesting textural effects by working the basic stitches, but then inserting the hook into a different part of the work instead of into the top two loops of each stitch. For example, you can work under one top loop at a time, between the stitches, or around the post or stem of the stitch. All crochet stitches can be worked with these variations, but some produce more interesting effects than others. As well as adding surface texture, these stitches can make a garment warmer. To begin any of these variations, first make a length of foundation chain and work one row in your chosen stitch.

WORKING UNDER ONE LOOP

By continually working into only the back loop (abbreviated as bl *as in* blsc*), you can create a pattern with a ridged effect. Working into only the front loop (*fl*) makes a less pronounced ridge with a horizontal line. This technique works well with the shorter stitches, for example single crochet and half double crochet.*

To work into the back loop

From the 2nd row onward work your chosen crochet stitch normally (for example, hdc as shown here), but insert the hook into the back loop of each stitch.

To work into the front loop

From the 2nd row onward work your chosen crochet stitch normally (for example, sc as shown here), but insert the hook into the front loop only of each stitch.

Stitch worked into back loop

Stitch worked into front loop

WORKING BETWEEN TWO STITCHES

This technique of working between the stitches of the previous row is quick and easy, and produces a slightly thicker fabric with a more open look.

To work between two stitches

From the 2nd row onward work your chosen crochet stitch normally (for example, dc as shown here), but insert hook between posts and below all horizontal threads connecting stitches.

WORKING SPIKES

Spikes are arrow-shaped loops of yarn on the surface of the work. They are made by inserting the hook lower down than usual, for example, into one or more rows below the previous one (pattern instructions will always specify where).

To make a simple sc spike

Insert hook into base of next stitch (*inset*), yo and draw it through up to height of a sc in this row, (2 loops on hook) (*right*). Yo and draw it through both loops. Sc spike made.

WORKING AROUND THE POST (RAISED STITCHES)

A raised effect can be achieved by working around the posts of the stitches in the previous row. This can be done either in front (raised front rf), or in back (raised back rb). Whole rows can be worked all in front or all in back, or alternatively one or more stitches around the back then one or more stitches around the front, to produce a large variety of stitch patterns.

To work raised stitches around the front

First work a row of your basic stitch, such as the dc shown here. From 2nd row onward, make each stitch normally, but insert hook in front and from right to left around post of stitch below *(right)*.

A raised stitch worked around the front

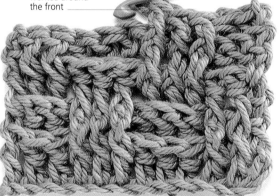

To work raised stitches around the back

Work exactly the same as above, except insert the hook in back and from right to left around post of stitch below *(right)*.

The finished stitch worked around the back

WORKING LINKED STITCHES

Longer stitches can be linked to each other down their sides to eliminate the space between the posts of the stitches. This creates an effect as if several rows of shorter stitches had been worked in the same direction at the same time.

To work a linked triple

1 Insert the hook down through the upper of the 2 horizontal loops around the post of the last stitch made; make a yo.

2 Draw a loop through, insert the hook down through the lower horizontal loop of the same stitch, yo, draw a loop through. (There are 3 loops on the hook.)

3 Insert hook for next stitch, yo, draw it through stitch only, [yo and draw it through 2 loops only] 3 times. Linked triple is made.

To start a row with a linked triple, treat 2nd *(left)* and 4th chains from the hook as the upper and lower horizontal loops of last stitch made.

FOLLOWING PATTERNS

CROCHET PATTERN INSTRUCTIONS indicate, in abbreviated form, how many and what kind of stitches to work and where to insert the hook. They assume you are familiar with the basic stitches and other procedures and that you understand these abbreviations.

Pattern abbreviations

across	to the end of the row
alt	alternate
approx	approximate(ly)
beg	beginning
bet	between
bl	insert hook under back loop only. Ex. blsc – back loop single crochet
ch(s)	chain or chain stitch(es)
ch sp(s)	chain space(s)
cl	cluster
cont	continue
dc	double crochet
dc2tog	work 2 dc together
dec	decrease
dtr	double triple crochet
dtr2tog	work 2 dtr together
fl	insert hook under front loop only. Ex. flsc – front loop single crochet
foll	following
gr	group
hdc	half double crochet
hdc2tog	work 2 hdc together
in	inches
in next	sts to be worked into same stitch
inc	increase
lp(s)	loop(s)
pat	pattern
p or pc	picot
rf	raised front. Ex. rfsc – raised front single crochet
rb	raised back. Ex. rbsc – raised back single crochet
rem	remaining
rep	repeat
rnd	round
sc	single crochet
sc2tog	work 2 sc together
sk	skip
sl st	slip stitch
sp(s)	space(s)
st(s)	stitch(es)
t-ch(s)	turning chain(s)
tog	together
tr	triple or treble crochet
tr2tog	work 2 tr together
ttr	triple triple crochet
ttr2tog	work 2 ttr together
yo	yarn over hook
*	Work instructions immediately following *, then repeat as directed, (see Repeats)
[ ]	Work or repeat all instructions enclosed in brackets as directed immediately after, (see Repeats)

Unless otherwise specified:
• Do not turn the work at the end of a row/round.
• Always count the turning chain as a stitch (see page 76).
• Work into the next available stitch in the previous row.
• Always insert the hook under both top loops of a stitch, unless it is a chain space or loop.
• The instruction, *1 sc*, means work one single crochet into the next sitch, and *5 dc,* work 1 dc into each of next 5 sts.
• For a cluster, the instruction *dc3tog,* or *tr5tog,* means that each stitch is worked into a separate stitch, before joining.
• If all parts of the cluster are to be worked into the next stitch, the instruction would say *dc5tog in next.*

Multiples
In the stitch glossaries the pattern gives the number of stitches required in the row and the number of chains to work for the foundation chain in this way: *Multiple of 5 sts plus 2, plus 2 for foundation ch.* This means make 9, 14, 19, etc, chains in order to work with 7, 12, 17, etc. stitches.

Brackets [ ] or parentheses ( )
These are used in three distinct ways:
• To simplify repetition – see Repeats.
• To indicate at the end of a row/round the total number of stitches that have been worked in that row/round. For example, *(24 dc)* means that the row/round counts as 24 double crochet stitches.
• To give information about different sizes.

Right side/wrong side
Even if a crochet pattern is reversible it is usual to define a right side. When working in the round, the right side is normally facing you. Where the work is turned between rows, instructions specify the first right side row. If you are directed to keep the right side facing you when working rows, bind off at the end of each row and rejoin the yarn.

Repeats
Instructions within brackets are worked the number of times stated, for example *[ch 1, skip 1 ch, 1 dc] 5 times.* A single asterisk marks the beginning of a pattern repeat sequence. For example **ch 1, skip 1 ch, 1 sc; rep from * across.* A double asterisk indicates a smaller repeat in the main repeat sequence. The instruction: *Rep from * to last st* means work complete repeats until only one stitch remains.

Working into the back and front loops alternately makes a broken texture

◄ BACK AND FRONT LOOP HALF DOUBLE CROCHET

Multiple of 2 sts, plus 1 for foundation ch

Row 1: Skip 2 ch, hdc across, turn.
Row 2: Ch 2, *1 blhdc, 1 flhdc; rep from * to last st, 1 hdc, turn.
Row 2 forms the pattern.

BACK LOOP HALF DOUBLE CROCHET ▼

Any number of sts, plus 1 for foundation ch

Row 1: Skip 2 ch, hdc across, turn.
Row 2: Ch 2, blhdc across, turn.
Row 2 forms the pattern.

Working into the back loops only produces a ridged effect

HALF DOUBLE CROCHET BETWEEN STITCHES ▼

Any number of sts, plus 1 for foundation ch

Row 1: Skip 2 ch, hdc across, turn.
Row 2: Ch 2, *1 hdc inserting hook between posts of next 2 sts and below all horizontal connecting threads; rep from * across, turn.
Row 2 forms the pattern.

BACK AND FRONT LOOP SINGLE CROCHET ▲

Multiple of 2 sts, plus 1 for foundation ch

Row 1: Skip 2 ch, sc across, turn.
Row 2: Ch 1, *1 blsc , 1 flsc; rep from * to last st, 1 sc, turn.
Row 2 forms the pattern.

ALTERNATE ROWS BACK AND FRONT LOOP DOUBLE CROCHET ▲

Any number of sts, plus 2 for foundation ch

Row 1: Skip 3 ch, dc across, turn.
Row 2: Ch 3, bldc across, turn.
Row 3: Ch 3, fldc across, turn.
Rows 2 and 3 form the pattern.

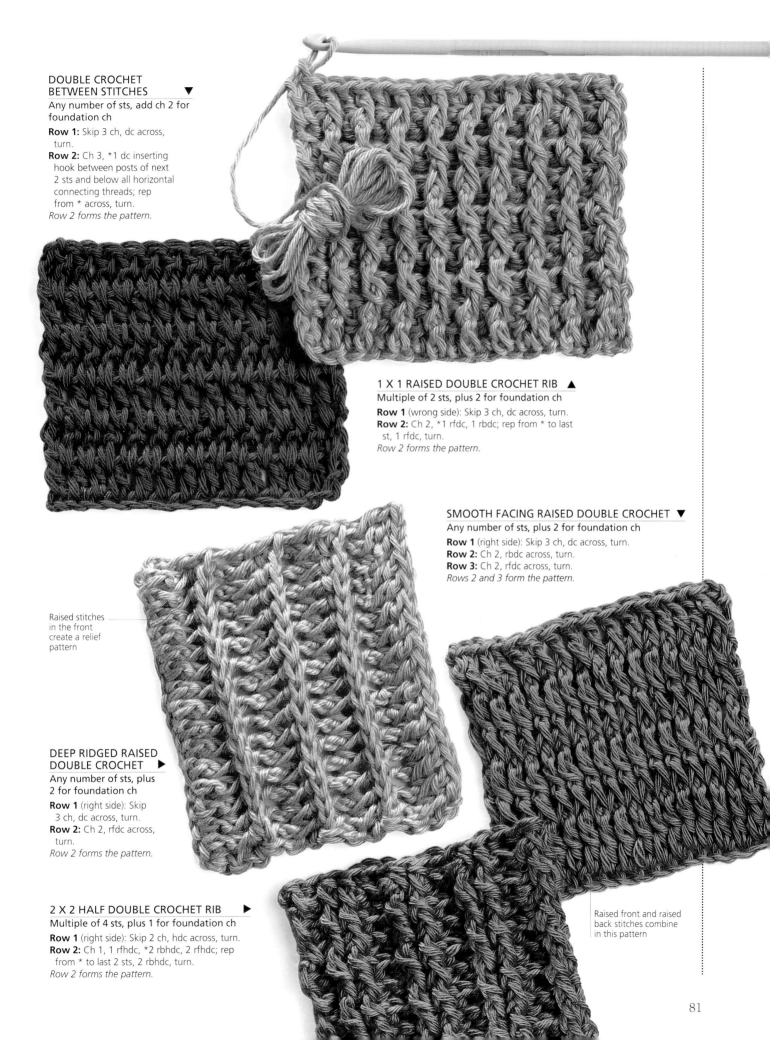

DOUBLE CROCHET BETWEEN STITCHES ▼

Any number of sts, add ch 2 for foundation ch

Row 1: Skip 3 ch, dc across, turn.

Row 2: Ch 3, *1 dc inserting hook between posts of next 2 sts and below all horizontal connecting threads; rep from * across, turn.

Row 2 forms the pattern.

1 X 1 RAISED DOUBLE CROCHET RIB ▲

Multiple of 2 sts, plus 2 for foundation ch

Row 1 (wrong side): Skip 3 ch, dc across, turn.

Row 2: Ch 2, *1 rfdc, 1 rbdc; rep from * to last st, 1 rfdc, turn.

Row 2 forms the pattern.

SMOOTH FACING RAISED DOUBLE CROCHET ▼

Any number of sts, plus 2 for foundation ch

Row 1 (right side): Skip 3 ch, dc across, turn.

Row 2: Ch 2, rbdc across, turn.

Row 3: Ch 2, rfdc across, turn.

Rows 2 and 3 form the pattern.

Raised stitches in the front create a relief pattern

DEEP RIDGED RAISED DOUBLE CROCHET ▶

Any number of sts, plus 2 for foundation ch

Row 1 (right side): Skip 3 ch, dc across, turn.

Row 2: Ch 2, rfdc across, turn.

Row 2 forms the pattern.

Raised front and raised back stitches combine in this pattern

2 X 2 HALF DOUBLE CROCHET RIB ▶

Multiple of 4 sts, plus 1 for foundation ch

Row 1 (right side): Skip 2 ch, hdc across, turn.

Row 2: Ch 1, 1 rfhdc, *2 rbhdc, 2 rfhdc; rep from * to last 2 sts, 2 rbhdc, turn.

Row 2 forms the pattern.

A simple pattern using single crochet spikes

Working linked triples closes the spaces between the stitches

ALTERNATING SPIKED SINGLE CROCHET ▲
Multiple of 2sts plus 1, plus 1 for foundation ch

Special abbreviation
sc spike (single crochet spike): Insert hook into base of st, ie 1 more row down, then complete sc normally.
Row 1 (right side): Skip 2 ch, sc across, turn.

Row 2: Ch 1, 1 sc spike, *1 sc, 1 sc spike; rep from * to last st, 1 sc, turn.
Row 3: Ch 1, 1 sc, *1 sc spike, 1 sc; rep from * to last st 1 sc, turn.
Rows 2 and 3 form the pattern.

▲ LINKED TRIPLES
Any number of sts, plus 3 for foundation ch

Special abbreviation
Linked tr (see page 78).
Row 1 (right side): Skip 4 ch, linked tr across, turn.
Row 2: Ch 4, linked tr across, turn
Row 2 forms the pattern.

Spikes and working into the back loop are both used in this pattern

BASKETWEAVE ▼
Multiple of 8 sts plus 2, plus 2 for foundation ch
Row 1 (wrong side): Skip 3 ch, dc across, turn.
Rows 2, 3, and 4: Ch 2, *4 rfdc, 4 rbdc; rep from * to last st, 1 rfdc, turn.
Rows 5, 6, and 7: Ch 2, *4 rbdc, 4 rfdc; rep from * to last st, 1 rbdc, turn.
Rows 2 to 7 form the pattern.

BACK LOOP SPIKED SINGLE CROCHET ▶
Multiple of 4 sts plus 1, plus 1 for foundation ch

Special abbreviation
sc spike (single crochet spike): Insert hook into base of st, ie 1 more row down, then complete sc normally.
Row 1 (right side): Skip 2 ch, sc across, turn.
Row 2: Ch 1, blsc across, turn.
Row 3: Ch 1, *1 sc spike, 3 blsc; rep from * across, turn.
Row 4: as row 2.
Row 5: Ch 1, *2 blsc, 1 sc spike, 1 blsc ; rep from * across, turn.
Rows 2 to 5 form the pattern.

GAUGE

THE NUMBER OF stitches and rows required to make a piece of crochet of a specific size depends upon four things: The yarn, the hook size, the stitch pattern, and the individual crocheter. A stitch gauge is given at the beginning of every crochet pattern. This indicates the number of stitches and rows in a particular measure, and the entire design is based around this. To achieve the best results, you *must* follow the stitch gauge. But since crochet is a true hand craft, each person's work will be slightly different. Before beginning a project, make a swatch to ensure that your gauge matches that given. If you want to change the yarn or the stitch pattern, you can usually do so as long as you make sure you can still match the gauge.

CHECKING THE GAUGE

Using the weight of yarn, hook size, and stitch pattern given with the instructions, crochet a sample at least 4 inches square. Place the finished sample right side up on a flat surface, taking care not to stretch it out of shape.

Measuring stitches

Lay your ruler across the sample at the bottom of a row of stitches. Insert 2 pins vertically one inch apart. Count the number of stitches between the pins. If a pin falls in the middle of a stitch, measure 2 inches.

Measuring rows
Now turn your ruler vertically and lay it along one side of a column of stitches. Avoiding the edges, place pins horizontally 4 inches apart. Count the rows between the pins. If a pin falls in the middle of a row, measure 2 inches.

MAKING ADJUSTMENTS

If your gauge does not correspond with that given in the instructions, change to a bigger or smaller hook and crochet another sample. Fewer stitches and rows than indicated means your work is too loose and you should try a smaller hook. More stitches and rows than shown means it is too tight and you should try a larger hook. Occasionally you may find it impossible to match the gauge of both stitches and rows at the same time, in which case you should match the stitch gauge and compensate by working more or fewer rows.

THE EFFECT OF YARNS AND PATTERNS

Weight of yarn and stitch pattern affect stitch gauge, so always work a sample before altering written instructions. Fine yarn will work with more stitches to the inch than heavier yarn, as will yarn worked with a smaller hook.

A thick yarn and a finer yarn worked on the same hook size will result in different numbers of stitches per inch

The same yarn and stitch worked on different size hooks will work up to a different stitch gauge

Different stitch patterns worked with the same hook and yarn will also produce different numbers of stitches per inch

INCREASING

MANY CROCHET ITEMS are made of rectangles worked evenly throughout (see page 76). There are times, however, when it is necessary to shape your work. To widen the fabric, you increase or add stitches. This may be done at the beginning and/or the end of a row, or at one or more places within a row.

WORKING SINGLE INCREASES

When it is necessary to increase by a single stitch, the simplest way is to work twice into the same stitch.

At the beginning of a row

When the turning chain counts as a stitch (*see page 76*), use one of these methods. Skip the first st as usual and work 2 sts into the 2nd st, or work 1 st into the first st that you usually skip.

At the end of a row

Work 2 sts into the last st (this will be the turning chain, if it counts as a st).

REPEATED SINGLE INCREASES

When you are making single increases one above another, work each subsequent pair into either the first or second of the previous pair consistently, so as to maintain vertical lines of increase. To slant them to the right on a right side row, work each increase pair into the first of the previous pair; to slant them to the left, work them into the second.

Across a row

Mark the position for each increase. Pattern instructions usually tell you exactly where to place these, but if not, spread them evenly. Work 2 stitches into each marked stitch.

MULTIPLE INCREASES

To increase by more than two stitches at the edge, make additional chain sts. The method is the same for all the basic stitches. Here the turning-chain counts as a st. When several stitches at once are made at an edge, a sharp angle is created.

At the beginning of a row

Add the number of increases needed to the number of turning-chains being used. For example, if you are working double crochet (dc), which needs 2 t-ch, and want to add 5 sts, you will need to work 7 ch. Skip 3 ch (counts as 1 dc) and work 1 dc into each of the remaining 4 new ch sts, making 5 new sts, including turning-chain.

At the end of a row

To make the first additional stitch, insert the hook through the lower part of the last stitch made, picking up the single, vertical thread on its left-hand side. Continue inserting the hook into the base of the stitch just completed to work the required number of additional stitches.

DECREASING

IT MAY BE necessary to shape your crochet work by subtracting stitches; these decreases may be made at the beginning and/or end of a row, or at set places within the row. You can also narrow your work by skipping one or more stitches, but this method may leave holes. Unless you want a decorative effect, it is preferable to decrease by crocheting two or more stitches together.

REPEATED SINGLE DECREASES

When working single decreases one above another in mid row, work consistently either the first or the second part of the decrease cluster into the top of the previous cluster so as to maintain vertical lines of decrease. (See Repeated Single Increases, page 84.)

MULTIPLE DECREASES

To decrease more than two or three stitches, work multiple decreases at the ends of rows. The t-ch counts as a stitch. This method creates a sharp angle. Double crochet (dc) is shown here, but the method is the same for all basic stitches.

At the beginning of a row

Work slip st over each st to be subtracted. Then, make the required number of turning chains to form a new edge st and continue the row in pattern from there.

At the end of a row

Work in pattern until you reach the stitches to be decreased. Leave these sts unworked, turn and make the t-ch for the first st of the next row.

WORKING STITCHES TOGETHER AS ONE (STITCH CLUSTER)

To decrease 1, 2, 3, sts, etc. work 2, 3, 4, sts, etc. together. At the beginning of a row, when the t-ch counts as first st, work the 2nd and 3rd sts together to make a single decrease and the 2nd, 3rd, and 4th together to make a double decrease.

At the end of a row

Work the last 2, 3, or 4 sts together. In mid row work 1, 2, or 3 consecutive sts together in the appropriate positions (*see also Increasing and Repeated Single Decreases*).

At the beginning of a row
Single crochet

Single decrease (sc2tog): Make 1 ch (counts as 1 sc), skip first st, *insert hook into 2nd st, yo and draw through**; rep from *once more into 3rd st (3 loops on hook), ending yo and draw through all loops – single decrease made. Double decrease (sc3tog): Work as for single decrease from *, but rep from * to ** once more into 4th st (4 loops on hook) before ending.

Half double crochet

Single decrease (hdc2tog): Make 2 ch (counts as 1 hdc), skip first st, *yo, insert hook into next (2nd) st, yo and draw through**; rep from * once more into next (3rd) st (5 loops on hook), ending yo and draw through all loops – single decrease made. Double decrease (hdc3tog): Work as for single decrease from *, but rep from * to ** once more into next (4th) st (7 loops on hook) before ending.

Double crochet

Single decrease (dc2tog): Make 3 ch (counts as 1 dc), skip first st, *yo, insert hook into next (2nd) st, yo and draw through, yo and draw through 2 loops only**; rep from * once more into next (3rd) st (3 loops on hook), ending yo and draw through all loops – single decrease made. Double decrease (dc3tog): Work as for single decrease from *, but rep from * to ** once more into next (4th) st (4 loops on hook) before ending.

Triple crochet

The method is the same for longer crochet stitches, such as triple crochet.

Making a single decrease in triple crochet

WORKING WITH COLOR

COLORED YARNS ARE used to create stripes, geometric patterns, and simple pictures in sharp contrasts or subtle gradations. Crochet stitches are generally larger and more varied than knitted ones and are perfect for overlapped and relief effects as well as variegated row structures. These stitches are best used for their own unique character, boldly and with imagination. Single yarns may be used, or strands of more than one giving both variegated color and additional warmth. Yarns may be plain color, two-tone, or patterned in different ways – heather mixtures, mottled or multicolored yarns.

Working stripes is the simplest way of introducing a new color

HORIZONTAL STRIPES

Use single colors for one or more whole rows to create horizontal stripes. Carry the yarns not in use up the side of the work or cut them off and rejoin as required.

VERTICAL STRIPES AND INTARSIA

For blocks of color, join a separate ball for each color area or stripe, which avoids floats entirely. There is no need (as there is in knitting) to twist the yarns around each other at the changeovers to prevent holes appearing.

Work with separate colored balls for intarsia

TEXTURED EFFECTS

Richly textured effects can be achieved using different types of yarn along with changes of color. Multicolored yarns create a new effect when combined with plain colors, or textured yarns. Bouclé and mohair multicolored yarns are shown worked together in this basketweave pattern sample.

Jacquard includes all-over multicolored, geometric, and picture patterns

JACQUARD

When yarn is joined in the middle of a row, the yarn not in use is carried along the back of work. This will form loops, or floats, which may catch in wear and must be worked over every few stitches, or encased during right side rows.

Textured stitches and yarns combined make a rich fabric

YARN ENDS

Provided you can do so without interfering with the visual effect, it is advisable to work over yarn ends whenever possible. Remember that all stray ends must finally be woven into the wrong side.

CHARTS

Most multicolor patterns are presented in the form of graphs, in which each square corresponds to one stitch – normally single crochet, since it is the smallest, squarest stitch. There are two main rules for following color chart grids: Always change to next color required just before you complete the previous stitch and follow odd-numbered rows from right to left and even-numbered from left to right (chart always represents right side of the work).

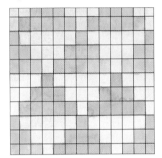 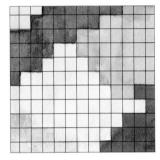

JOINING NEW YARN

When working horizontal stripes, change to the new yarn at the end of the row just before you complete the last stitch. This way, the new color is ready to work the turning chain. If you are working in the round, work the last stitch with the old color and use the new color to make the joining slip stitch.

1 Just before you pick up for the last time to make the last stitch with the old color, drop the old yarn and pick up the new yarn.

2 Draw new yarn through to complete the old stitch – the working loop is now ready in the new color. This sample is in dc, but the same principle applies to all other stitches.

Before working the next stitch, make sure old yarn is kept to the wrong side of the work, or carried along the tops of the next few stitches so that it will become encased.

CHANGING YARN

Change the yarns as for joining, just before you complete the last stitch with the old color. Draw up the float in the new color evenly, making sure the old yarn is appropriately positioned. Single crochet is illustrated here, but the same principle applies to all other basic stitches.

RE-JOINING YARN

Occasionally you will need to join yarn into a piece of crochet that has been fastened off, in order to make a fresh start.

Insert the hook into the appropriate place. Start with a slip knot (or a simple loop, if you prefer) and draw this through. Make the appropriate turning chain for the first new stitch (ch 3 for 1 dc shown here).

FLOATS

To help the tension of floats be more even, catch them into the work every few stitches. When finished, cut in half any unacceptably long float threads and weave them in.

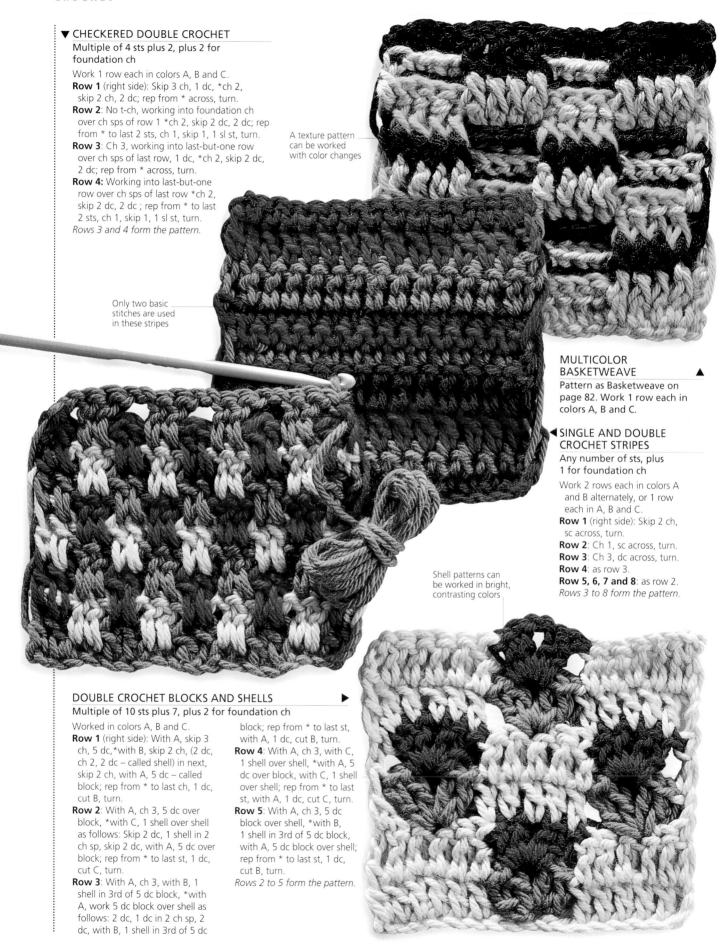

▼ CHECKERED DOUBLE CROCHET

Multiple of 4 sts plus 2, plus 2 for foundation ch

Work 1 row each in colors A, B and C.

Row 1 (right side): Skip 3 ch, 1 dc, *ch 2, skip 2 ch, 2 dc; rep from * across, turn.

Row 2: No t-ch, working into foundation ch over ch sps of row 1 *ch 2, skip 2 dc, 2 dc; rep from * to last 2 sts, ch 1, skip 1, 1 sl st, turn.

Row 3: Ch 3, working into last-but-one row over ch sps of last row 1 dc, *ch 2, skip 2 dc, 2 dc; rep from * across, turn.

Row 4: Working into last-but-one row over ch sps of last row *ch 2, skip 2 dc, 2 dc ; rep from * to last 2 sts, ch 1, skip 1, 1 sl st, turn.
Rows 3 and 4 form the pattern.

A texture pattern can be worked with color changes

Only two basic stitches are used in these stripes

MULTICOLOR BASKETWEAVE ▲

Pattern as Basketweave on page 82. Work 1 row each in colors A, B and C.

◄ SINGLE AND DOUBLE CROCHET STRIPES

Any number of sts, plus 1 for foundation ch

Work 2 rows each in colors A and B alternately, or 1 row each in A, B and C.

Row 1 (right side): Skip 2 ch, sc across, turn.

Row 2: Ch 1, sc across, turn.

Row 3: Ch 3, dc across, turn.

Row 4: as row 3.

Row 5, 6, 7 and 8: as row 2.
Rows 3 to 8 form the pattern.

Shell patterns can be worked in bright, contrasting colors

DOUBLE CROCHET BLOCKS AND SHELLS ►

Multiple of 10 sts plus 7, plus 2 for foundation ch

Worked in colors A, B and C.

Row 1 (right side): With A, skip 3 ch, 5 dc, *with B, skip 2 ch, (2 dc, ch 2, 2 dc – called shell) in next, skip 2 ch, with A, 5 dc – called block; rep from * to last ch, 1 dc, cut B, turn.

Row 2: With A, ch 3, 5 dc over block, *with C, 1 shell over shell as follows: Skip 2 dc, 1 shell in 2 ch sp, skip 2 dc, with A, 5 dc over block; rep from * to last st, 1 dc, cut C, turn.

Row 3: With A, ch 3, with B, 1 shell in 3rd of 5 dc block, *with A, work 5 dc block over shell as follows: 2 dc, 1 dc in 2 ch sp, 2 dc, with B, 1 shell in 3rd of 5 dc

block; rep from * to last st, with A, 1 dc, cut B, turn.

Row 4: With A, ch 3, with C, 1 shell over shell, *with A, 5 dc over block, with C, 1 shell over shell; rep from * to last st, with A, 1 dc, cut C, turn.

Row 5: With A, ch 3, 5 dc block over shell, *with B, 1 shell in 3rd of 5 dc block, with A, 5 dc block over shell; rep from * to last st, 1 dc, cut B, turn.
Rows 2 to 5 form the pattern.

SINGLE CROCHET AND SPIKE CLUSTERS ▼

Multiple of 8 sts plus 5, plus 1 for foundation ch

Special Abbreviation

spcl (spike cluster): Over next st pick up 5 spike loops by inserting hook as follows: 2 sts to right and 1 row down; 1 st to right and 2 rows down; directly over next st and 3 rows down; 1st to left and 2 rows down; 2 sts to left and 1 row down, (6 loops on hook); insert hook into top of next st in current row itself, yo, draw loop through, yo drawn through all 7 loops on hook.

Work 4 rows each in colors A, B and C throughout.

Note: T-ch does not count as a stitch.

Row 1 (right side): Skip 1 ch, sc across, turn.

Row 2: Ch 1, sc across, turn.

Rows 3 and 4: as row 2.

Row 5: Ch 1, 4 sc, *1 spcl, 7 sc; rep from * to last st, 1 sc, turn.

Rows 6 to 8: as row 2.

Rows 5 to 8 form the pattern.

INTERLOCKING DOUBLE CROCHET SHELLS ▼

Multiple of 6 sts plus 1, plus 1 for foundation ch

Work 1 row each in colors A, B and C.

Row 1 (right side): Skip 1 ch, 1 sc, *skip 2 ch, 5 dc in next – called shell, skip 2 ch, 1 sc; rep from * across, turn.

Row 2: Ch 3, 2 dc in first st, *1 sc in 3rd dc of shell, 1 shell in sc; rep from * to last shell, 1 sc in 3rd dc of shell, 3 dc in sc, turn.

Row 3: Ch 1, *1 shell in sc, 1 sc in 3rd dc of shell; rep from * across with last sc in t-ch, turn.

Rows 2 and 3 form the pattern.

Shells in stripes of colors make an attractive pattern

ALTERNATING RELIEF STITCH ▲

Multiple of 2 sts plus 1, plus 2 for foundation ch

Work 1 row each in colors A, B and C.

Row 1 (right side): Skip 3 ch, dc across, turn.

Row 2: Ch 3, *1 rftr, 1 dc; rep from * across, turn.

Row 2 forms the pattern.

The reverse of this pattern also makes an interesting right side

INSET FLOWER BUDS ▶

Multiple of 10 sts plus 3, plus 2 for foundation ch

Worked with color A and with B and C for the flower buds.

Row 1 (right side): With A, skip 3 ch, 2 dc, *ch 3, skip 3 ch, 1 sc, ch 3, skip 3 ch, 3 dc; rep from * across, turn.

Row 2: Ch 2, 2rbdc, *ch 3, skip 3 ch, 1 sc in sc, ch 3, skip 3 ch, 3 rbdc; rep from * across, turn.

Row 3: Ch 2, 2 rfdc, *ch 1, skip 3 ch, 5 dc in sc, ch 1, skip 3 ch, 3 rfdc; rep from * across. Do not turn but work flower buds in B and C alternately over each group of 5 dc thus: Ch 3, dc4tog, ch 1. Bind off – flowerbud completed. Turn.

Row 4: With A, ch 3, 2 rbtr, *ch 3, 1 sc in ch at top of flowerbud, ch 3, skip 1 ch, 3 rbtr; rep from * across, turn.

Row 5: as row 2.

Rows 2 to 5 form the pattern.

GO FOR COLOR

THERE ARE MYRIAD possibilities when using colored yarn, whether you choose to make traditional granny squares in rainbow colors, or bright, geometric patterns. Leftover pieces of yarn are ideal for making attractive and handy accessories. (See pages 233 to 237.)

MULTICOLORED GRANNY JACKET

This granny-square wrap cardigan has everlasting appeal. Crochet it square-by-square and join together.

The shawl collar is worked separately

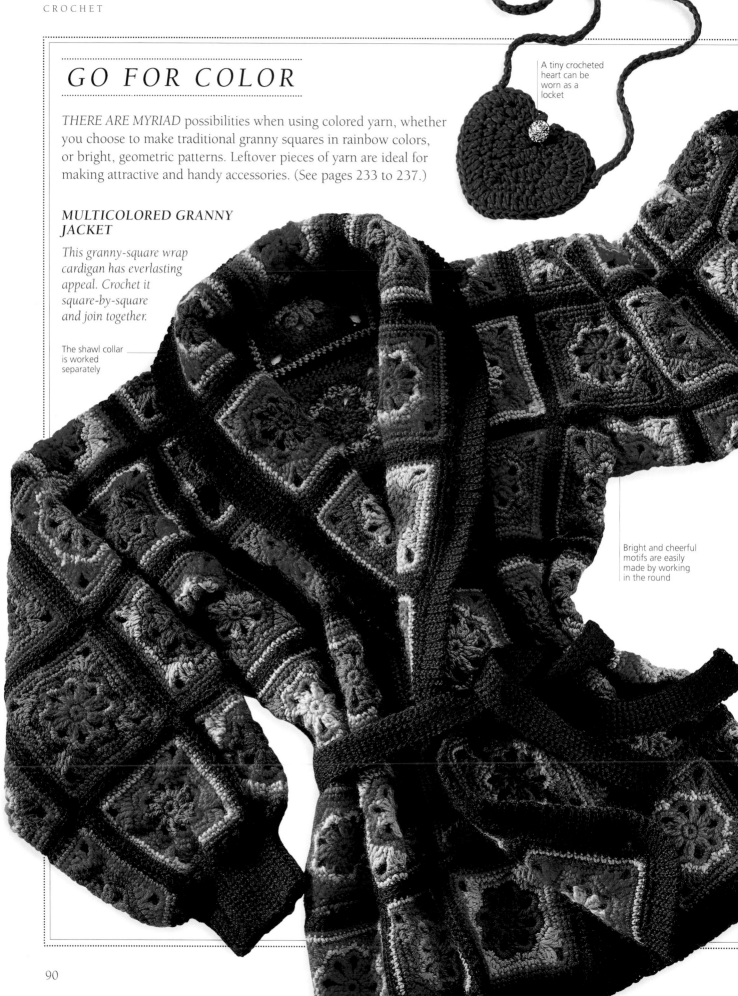

A tiny crocheted heart can be worn as a locket

Bright and cheerful motifs are easily made by working in the round

PURSES

These decorative medallions are easy to make, and are appropriate for people of all ages. They dress up an outfit and also make nice purses.

Picot edging is crocheted directly onto the edges of the purse, joining the two sides together

This starlit spangle purse is made by working only in single crochet

Surprise, surprise, this watermelon wedge is made of crochet. If you thought crochet designs were old-fashioned, think again

This brightly colored small bolster will go with any decor

This pinwheel puff is a fun way of using lots of contrasting colors

PILLOWS

These are a wonderful way of experimenting with a variety of shapes, designs, and colors, and will brighten up any room in the home. The granny-square bolster is ideal for using up scrap yarns in a random array of different colors.

MORE STITCH VARIATIONS

ONE OF THE great strengths of crochet is the versatility of the stitches. Change the height of your stitches from row to row, and you will see many different textures and stripe widths. Within a row, stitches of different heights will produce wave shapes and surface texture. Additional texture can be achieved by crossing stitches to produce a cable effect, or working them into different places. Making long stitches – reaching down below the level of the previous row and picking up around the post – results in raised surface stitches, which are particularly striking when made in contrasting colors.

Simple crossed stitch

1 To make a pair of simple crossed stitches (dc shown here), first skip 1 and work 1 dc into next stitch (*left*). Then work 1 dc, inserting hook into previous skipped stitch (*right*).

2 The crossed dc wraps up and encases previous dc. (See page 93, Crossed Double Crochet.)

Cable crossed stitch (back)

1 To begin cable, first skip 3 sts and then work 3 dtr normally (shown here worked on dc).

2 With hook behind sts, insert it from front. Work 1 dtr into each of 3 skipped sts.

Cable crossed stitch (front)

Work entirely in front of the previous stitches (holding them aside at back if necessary) after inserting hook so as not to encase the stitches, as in Simple Crossed Stitch (*left*).

RAISED SURFACE STITCHES

*There are many variations of raised surface stitches, but they are all made in a similar way. The method shown left involves skipping stitches in the background fabric and working around the post. The surface stitches must be longer than the background stitches. When skipping a stitch would result in a hole, work the raised surface stitch **together with** the background stitch, like a decrease cluster (see page 85). In this typical example the background is made with alternate rows of sc and dc.*

Skip sts in sc row and work raised surface sts in tr around post of chosen stitch. Work at front, alternately a few sts to left and then to right, inserting hook from right to left.

Leaving last loop of each stitch on hook, work raised surface stitch, then background sc (there are now 3 loops on hook). Yo and draw through all loops to complete cluster.

SINGLE AND DOUBLE CROCHET ◄

Any number of sts, plus 1 for
foundation ch

Row 1 (wrong side): Skip 2 ch,
sc across, turn.
Row 2: Ch 3, dc across, turn.
Row 3: Ch 1, sc across, turn.
Rows 2 and 3 form the pattern.

DOUBLE CROCHET V STITCH ►

Multiple of 2 sts, plus 2 for
foundation ch

Row 1 (right side): Skip 3 ch, 2 dc
in next, * skip 1 ch, 2 dc in next;
rep from * to last 2 ch, skip 1 ch,
1 dc, turn.
Row 2: Ch 3, *skip 2 sts, 2 dc in
between 2nd skipped st and next;
rep from * to last 2 sts, skip 1 st,
1dc, turn.
Row 2 forms the pattern

STACKING SINGLE AND DOUBLE CROCHET ▲

Multiple of 2 sts plus 1, plus
1 for foundation ch

Note: T-ch does not count
as a stitch.

Row 1 (right side): Skip 1 ch,
1 sc, *1 dc, 1 sc; rep from
* across, turn.
Row 2: Ch 1, 1 sc, *1 dc, 1 sc;
rep from * across, turn.
Row 2 forms the pattern.

MULTI STITCH WAVE ▲

Multiple of 14 sts plus 1, plus
1 for foundation ch

Special Abbreviation

wave (worked over 14 sts): 1 sc, 2
hdc, 2 dc, 3 tr, 2 dc, 2 hdc, 2 sc.
reverse wave (worked over 14 sts):
1 tr, 2 dc, 2 hdc, 3 sc, 2 hdc,
2 dc, 2 tr.
Work 2 rows each in colors A
and B alternately throughout.
Row 1 (right side): Skip 2 ch,
*wave; rep from * across, turn.
Row 2: Ch 1, sc across, turn.
Row 3: Ch 4, *reverse wave;
rep from * across, turn.
Row 4: as row 2.
Row 5: Ch 1, *wave; rep
from * across, turn.
Row 6: as row 2.
*Rows 3 to 6 form
the pattern.*

This stitch can also
be worked in brightly
colored stripes

DOUBLE CROCHET DIAGONAL BLOCKS ▼

Multiple of 7 sts plus 4, plus
3 for foundation ch

Row 1 (right side): Skip 2 ch, 2 dc
in next, *skip 3 ch, 1 sc, ch 3,
3 dc; rep from * to last 4 ch, skip
3 ch, 1 sc, turn.
Row 2: Ch 3, 2 dc in first sc, *skip
3 dc, (1 sc, ch 3, 2 dc) in 3 ch
loop, 1 dc in sc; rep from *
ending skip 2 dc, 1 sc, turn.
Row 2 forms the pattern.

▲ CROSSED DOUBLE CROCHET

Multiple of 2 sts, plus 2 for
foundation ch

Special Abbreviation

2 cdc (2 crossed double crochet):
Skip next st, 1 dc, 1 dc in skipped
st, working so that the crossed dc
wraps and encases the previous
dc (see Simple crossed stitch,
page 92).

Row 1 (right side): Skip 3 ch,
*2 cdc; rep from * to last st,
1 dc, turn.
Row 2: Ch 1, sc across, turn.
Row 3: Ch 3, *2 cdc; rep
from * to last st, 1 dc, turn.
*Rows 2 and 3 form the
pattern.*

CHEVRONS & MOTIFS

THE BASIC STITCHES can be combined with increasing and decreasing to create zigzags, chevrons, and curves. The same plain stitch, increased and decreased alternately at frequent intervals at the same place in each row, will create a zigzag shape. Using increasing and decreasing in several different ways, you can make a variety of other geometric shapes for motifs to be made up into patchwork items.

SIMPLE CHEVRONS

In these patterns the same row shape is maintained and all rows are parallel throughout. If given the instruction to work even when working chevrons, you must continue increasing and decreasing as established to create the chevrons, but keeping the same number of stitches in each row and the edges of your fabric straight.

1 Increase by working additional stitches into the same place.

2 Decrease by joining stitches together into clusters (*see page 85*).

If the row shapes are to change, for instance so that zigzags alternate with straight rows or angles reverse, then you must use stitches of graduated heights at the same time as increasing and decreasing.

Zigzags and straight rows are combined in this piece

TRIANGLE MOTIFS

There are numerous ways of combining simple triangles to make patchwork throws or bedspreads. These coverlets have long formed a large and popular part of traditional crochet.

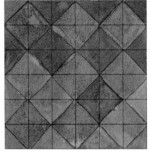

Increase triangle
Start with a single stitch and increase at both edges simultaneously. Make a foundation chain of 3 ch. Skip 2 ch, 2 sc in next, turn (3 sts – right side). Work 11 more rows in sc, making single inc at end of every row and also at beginning of 4th, 7th, and 10th rows (17 sts at end of Row 12).

Decrease triangle
Start with a foundation row the desired length of a triangle side and then decrease at both edges simultaneously to a single stitch. Work a foundation chain of 18 ch. Skip 2 ch, sc across to last 2 ch, sc2tog, turn (16 sts – right side). Work 11 more rows in sc, making single dec at end of every row and also at beginning of 3rd, 6th, and 10th rows (1 st at end of row 12).

Make a diamond by crocheting an increase triangle followed by a decrease triangle

BOBBLES

CROCHET WAS DEVELOPED mainly to meet the nineteenth century demand for lace. But it can also be used to create a lovely array of textured effects. The easily-made bobbles shown here involve the same skills already learned for increasing and decreasing.

A relief effect is created whenever you work a stitch taller than the stitches on either side, for example, a triple crochet in a row of single crochet; the taller stitch cannot lie flat, but sticks out from the surface. Similarly, if you work more than one stitch into the

same place and then join the group into one at the top, the excess will stand out from the surface. The taller and greater the number of stitches in the cluster, the more pronounced the bobble.

Variations can be made using different numbers of stitches and inserting the hook in different positions.

Completed bobbles on single crochet

Popcorn stitch

Work 5 stitches into same place (*left*). Remove hook from working loop. Insert it from front to back under top 2 loops of first stitch in group. Pick up working loop and draw it through. To make popcorn stand out toward back of work, insert hook from back through to front (*right*).

Puff stitch

The puff stitch is about to be completed

Work a cluster of half dc (*above*). Yo, insert hook into st, yo, draw loop through loosely. Without tightening other loops on hook, repeat 4 times. Yo and draw through all loops on hook (*right*). To secure, leave last of 11 loops on hook, yo and draw through remaining 2 loops.

Bobble

Work a decrease cluster of 5 dc (or whatever amount you like) all into same place, in a row made otherwise of sc (*left*). *Yo, insert hook into st, yo, draw a loop through, yo, draw through 2 loops; repeat from * 4 more times always inserting hook into same stitch (6 loops on hook). Yo and draw yarn through all loops to complete (*right*). The bobble is more pronounced when worked during wrong side rows.

Bullion stitch

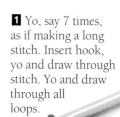

1 Yo, say 7 times, as if making a long stitch. Insert hook, yo and draw through stitch. Yo and draw through all loops.

2 Allow enough yarn to be drawn through loops to give them enough room to stand up as far as you wish. Yo once more and, taking care not to allow post of bullion to tighten, draw through to complete (*right*).

VERTICAL POPCORNS WITH RAISED TRIPLES ▼

Multiple of 11 sts plus 3, plus 2 for foundation ch

Special Abbreviation

pop: Popcorn made with 5 tr (see page 95).

Row 1 (right side): Skip 3 ch, 2 dc, *ch 2, skip 3 ch, 1 pop, ch 1, 1 pop, ch 1, skip 3 ch, 3 dc; rep from * across, turn.

Row 2: Ch 3, 1 rbtr, 1 dc, *ch 3, skip (1 ch, 1 pop), 2 sc in ch sp, ch 3, skip (1 pop, 2 ch), 1 dc, 1 rbtr, 1 dc; rep

from * across, turn.

Row 3: Ch 3, 1 rftr, 1 dc, *ch 2, skip 3 ch, 1 pop, ch 1, 1 pop, ch 1, skip 3 ch, 1 dc, 1 rftr, 1 dc; rep from * across, turn.
Rows 2 and 3 form the pattern.

DIAGONAL SPIKE PUFF ▲

Multiple of 3 sts plus 2, plus 2 for foundation ch

Special Abbreviation

spfcl (spike puff cluster): Yo, insert hook in next st, yo, draw through, yo, draw through 2 loops, (yo, insert hook from front in 3rd previous st, yo, draw through loosely) twice (6 loops on hook), yo, draw through all loops.

Row 1 (right side): Skip 3 ch, *2 dc, 1 spfcl; rep from * to last st, 1 dc, turn.

Row 2: Ch 3, *2 dc, 1 spfcl; rep from * to last st, 1 dc, turn.
Row 2 forms the pattern.

PUFFS AND RAISED CROSSES PANEL ▶

Worked over 11 sts on a background of dc

Special Abbreviation

Puff: Made as hdc5tog in same place (see page 95).

nc (not closed): See Clusters, page 102.

Row 1 (right side): 11 dc.

Row 2 (wrong side): *1 rbtr, 1 puff, 1 rbtr**, 1 dc; rep from * once more and from * to ** again.

Row 3: *1 dcnc in first, skip puff, 1 rftrnc around next (3 loops on hook), yo, draw through all loops, 1 dc in puff, 1 dcnc in next, 1 rftrnc around st before previous puff crossing in front of previous rftr, yo, and draw through 3 loops as before**, 1 dc; rep from * once more and from * to ** again.
Rows 2 and 3 form the pattern.

POPCORNS AND DOUBLE CROCHET ▲

Multiple of 6 sts plus 1, plus 2 for foundation ch

Special Abbreviation

pop: Popcorn made with 5 dc (see page 95).

Work 1 row each in colors A, B and C throughout.

Row 1 (right side): Skip 3 ch, dc across, turn.

Row 2: Ch 1 (does not count as st), *1 sc, ch 1, skip 1; rep from * to last st, 1 sc, turn.

Row 3: Ch 3, *skip (1 ch, 1 sc), (1 pop, ch 1, 1 dc, ch 1, 1 pop) in next ch sp, skip (1 sc, 1 ch), 1 dc; rep from * across, turn.

Row 4: as row 2.

Row 5: Ch 3, dc across, turn.
Rows 2 to 5 form the pattern.

BOBBLE PANEL ◀

Worked over 13 sts on a background of alt dc (right side) and sc rows

Special Abbreviation

bob (bobble): dc5tog in same place (see page 95).

Note: Work each rftr around dc st 2 rows below.

Row 1 (right side): 13 dc.

Row 2 (wrong side): 4 sc, 1 bob, 3 sc, 1 bob, 4 sc.

Row 3: 1 rftr, 1 dc, 1 rftr, 7 dc, 1 rftr, 1 dc, 1 rftr.

Row 4: 6 sc, 1 bob, 6 sc.

Row 5: as row 3.
Rows 2 to 5 form the pattern.

PUFFS AND SINGLE CROCHET ▲

Multiple of 4 sts plus 1, plus 1 for foundation ch

Special Abbreviation

puff: Made as hdc4tog in same place (see page 95).

Row 1 (right side): Skip 2 ch, sc across, turn.

Row 2: Ch 1, 1 sc, *1 puff, 3 sc; rep from * across, omitting 1 sc at end of last rep, turn.

Row 3: Ch 1, sc across, turn.

Row 4: Ch 1, *3 sc, 1 puff; rep from *to last 4 sts, 4 sc, turn.

Row 5: as row 3.

Rows 2 to 5 form the pattern.

BULLION WAVES ▶

Multiple of 10 sts plus 2, plus 1 for foundation ch

Special Abbreviation

bst: Bullion stitch made with (yo) 10 times (see page 95).

Note: t-ch counts as stitch only on right side (bullion stitch) rows.

Row 1 (wrong side): Skip 1 ch, sc across, turn.

Row 2: Ch 3, *5 dc, 5 bsts; rep from * to last st, 1 dc, turn.

Row 3: Ch 1, sc across, turn.

Row 4: Ch 3, *5 bsts, 5 dc; rep from * to last st, 1 dc, turn.

Row 5: as row 3.

Rows 2 to 5 form the pattern.

DOUBLE BULLIONS ▼

Multiple of 6 sts plus 2, plus 1 for foundation ch

Special Abbreviation

bst: Bullion stitch made with (yo) 7 times (see page 95).

Note: t-ch counts as stitch only on right side (bullion stitch) rows.

Row 1 (wrong side): Skip 1 ch, 1 sc, ch 1, skip 1 ch, 1 sc, * ch 2, skip 2 ch, 1 sc; rep from * to last 2 ch, ch 1, skip 1 ch, 1 sc, turn.

Row 2: Ch 3, 1 dc in ch sp, *1 dc, 2 bsts in 2 ch sp, 1 dc, 2 dc in 2 ch sp; rep from * across, working last dc in last sc, turn.

Row 3: Ch 1, 1 sc, ch 1, skip 1, 1 sc, *ch 2, skip 2, 1 sc; rep from * to last 2 sts, ch 1, skip 1, 1 sc, turn.

Row 4: Ch 3, 1 bst in next ch sp, *1 dc, 2 dc in next ch sp, 1 dc **, 2 bsts in 2 ch sp; rep from * to last 6 sts and from * to ** again, 1 bst in next ch sp, 1 dc, turn.

Row 5: as row 3.

Rows 2 to 5 form the pattern.

▼ CROSSED DOUBLE TRIPLE CABLE PANEL

Worked over 19 sts on a background of dc

Note: See page 92 for crossed stitches.

Row 1 (wrong side): 19 dc.

Row 2 (right side): 1 rftr, 1 dc, skip 3, 3 dtr, going in back of last 3 dtr work 3 dtr in 3 skipped sts, 1 dc, 1 rftr, 1 dc, skip 3, 3 dtr, going in front of last 3 dtr but not encasing them, work 3 dtr in 3 skipped sts, 1 dc, 1 rftr.

Row 3 (wrong side): as row 1, except work rbtr instead of rftr over 1st, 10th and 19th sts to keep raised ridges on right side of fabric.

Rows 2 and 3 form the pattern.

DOUBLE CROCHET BOBBLES ▼

Multiple of 4 sts plus 1, plus 2 for foundation ch

Row 1 (right side): Skip 3 ch, dc across, turn.

Row 2: Ch 1, 1 sc, *dc5tog in next, 3 sc; rep from * to last 3 sts, dc5tog in next, 2 sc, turn.

Row 3: Ch 3, dc across, turn.

Row 4: Ch 1, *3 sc, dc5tog in next; rep from * to last 4 sts, 4 sc, turn.

Row 5: as row 3.

Rows 2 to 5 form the pattern.

WORKING IN THE ROUND

THIS TECHNIQUE IS used to make motifs, and larger pieces such as tablecloths. Unlike regular crochet, you work around a central ring and increase regularly every round to keep the work flat. If you increase too much or too little the piece will curl.

Crochet made in the round may be any shape depending on the position of the increases.

An enormous number of patchwork-style designs can be made from motifs. Lace stitches can be incorporated as in the pretty lace doilies shown here (see page 233 for instructions for the beaded doily).

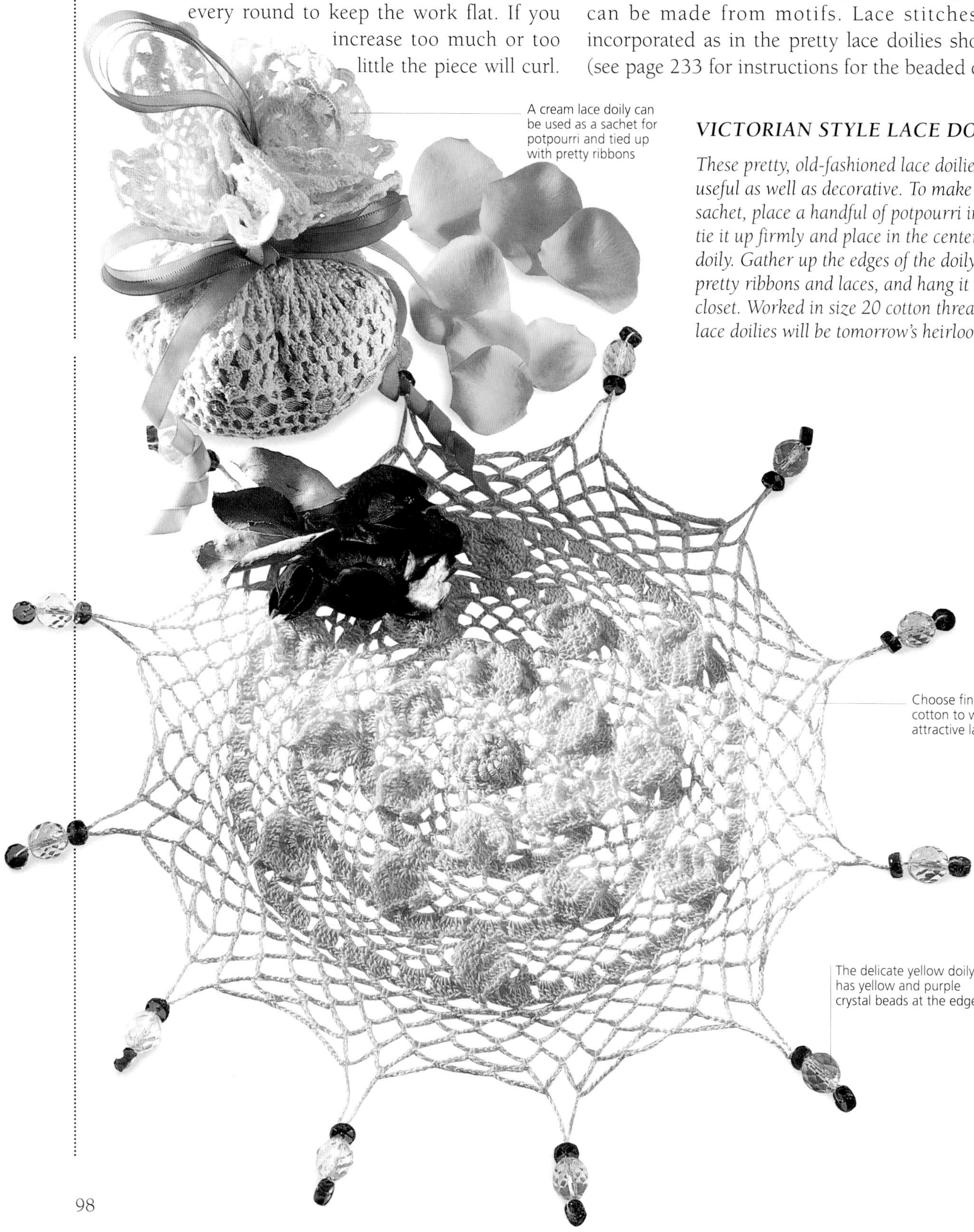

A cream lace doily can be used as a sachet for potpourri and tied up with pretty ribbons

VICTORIAN STYLE LACE DOILIES

These pretty, old-fashioned lace doilies are useful as well as decorative. To make this herb sachet, place a handful of potpourri in muslin, tie it up firmly and place in the center of a lace doily. Gather up the edges of the doily with pretty ribbons and laces, and hang it in your closet. Worked in size 20 cotton thread, these lace doilies will be tomorrow's heirlooms.

Choose fine 20s cotton to work this attractive lacy pattern

The delicate yellow doily has yellow and purple crystal beads at the edge

FOUNDATION RING

Working in the round starts with a foundation ring; the one most often used is closed by working a slip stitch into the first chain (first method below). When it is important to be able to close any central hole in the fabric, use the second method.

Chain foundation ring

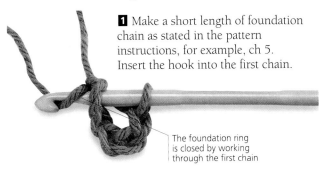

1 Make a short length of foundation chain as stated in the pattern instructions, for example, ch 5. Insert the hook into the first chain.

The foundation ring is closed by working through the first chain

2 Close the ring with a slip stitch, (yo and draw through).

Yarn loop foundation ring

1 Make a loop in yarn. Hold bottom of loop with fingers which normally hold work. Insert hook through loop, yo and draw through. Make correct turning chain (chain 1 for single crochet) and work first round into loop ring, making sure you encase short end of yarn.

2 Close the round with a slip stitch. Close up the center of the ring by drawing the short end of the yarn tight. Secure it by weaving it into the wrong side of the work.

MOTIFS

On the stitch glossary overleaf, unless otherwise specified:
1 Close the foundation chain ring by working a slip stitch into the first chain.
2 At the beginning of each round work a turning chain to stand as the first stitch of the first pattern repeat (see table page 76).
3 At the end of each round close with a slip stitch into the top of this first stitch.
4 Do not turn between rounds – right side is always facing.

WORKING IN THE ROUND

There are two main methods of working in the round: Making one continuous spiral or a series of joined rounds. In the latter case, each round is completed and joined with a slip stitch, but before starting the next round, make a turning chain to match the height of the following stitches (even if the work is not actually turned between rounds). For turning chain table see page 76.

1 Make the correct number of chains for the turning chain, for example, ch 4 for tr.

Work turning chains after the foundation ring

Working into the center of the foundation ring

2 Insert hook into center of foundation ring; work stitches as required for first round.

3 To close the round, work a slip stitch into the top of the turning chain.

All the stitches are worked into the foundation ring

4 Before working another round, make the required turning chain.

A turning chain is worked at the beginning of each round

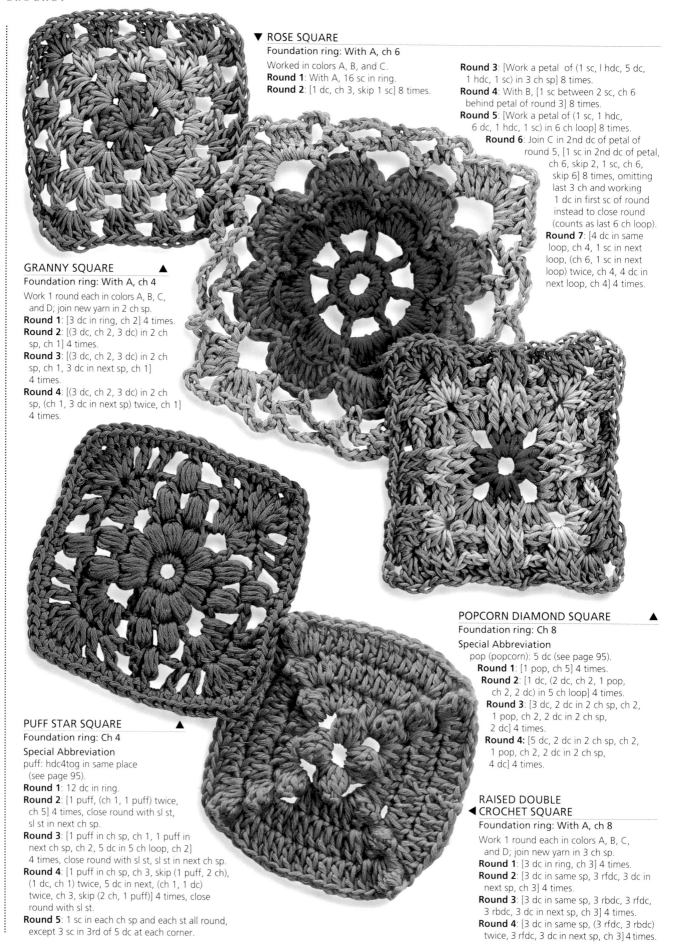

▼ ROSE SQUARE

Foundation ring: With A, ch 6

Worked in colors A, B, and C.

Round 1: With A, 16 sc in ring.

Round 2: [1 dc, ch 3, skip 1 sc] 8 times.

Round 3: [Work a petal of (1 sc, l hdc, 5 dc, 1 hdc, 1 sc) in 3 ch sp] 8 times.

Round 4: With B, [1 sc between 2 sc, ch 6 behind petal of round 3] 8 times.

Round 5: [Work a petal of (1 sc, 1 hdc, 6 dc, 1 hdc, 1 sc) in 6 ch loop] 8 times.

Round 6: Join C in 2nd dc of petal of round 5, [1 sc in 2nd dc of petal, ch 6, skip 2, 1 sc, ch 6, skip 6] 8 times, omitting last 3 ch and working 1 dc in first sc of round instead to close round (counts as last 6 ch loop).

Round 7: [4 dc in same loop, ch 4, 1 sc in next loop, (ch 6, 1 sc in next loop) twice, ch 4, 4 dc in next loop, ch 4] 4 times.

GRANNY SQUARE ▲

Foundation ring: With A, ch 4

Work 1 round each in colors A, B, C, and D; join new yarn in 2 ch sp.

Round 1: [3 dc in ring, ch 2] 4 times.

Round 2: [(3 dc, ch 2, 3 dc) in 2 ch sp, ch 1] 4 times.

Round 3: [(3 dc, ch 2, 3 dc) in 2 ch sp, ch 1, 3 dc in next sp, ch 1] 4 times.

Round 4: [(3 dc, ch 2, 3 dc) in 2 ch sp, (ch 1, 3 dc in next sp) twice, ch 1] 4 times.

PUFF STAR SQUARE ▲

Foundation ring: Ch 4

Special Abbreviation

puff: hdc4tog in same place (see page 95).

Round 1: 12 dc in ring.

Round 2: [1 puff, (ch 1, 1 puff) twice, ch 5] 4 times, close round with sl st, sl st in next ch sp.

Round 3: [1 puff in ch sp, ch 1, 1 puff in next ch sp, ch 2, 5 dc in 5 ch loop, ch 2] 4 times, close round with sl st, sl st in next ch sp.

Round 4: [1 puff in ch sp, ch 3, skip (1 puff, 2 ch), (1 dc, ch 1) twice, 5 dc in next, (ch 1, 1 dc) twice, ch 3, skip (2 ch, 1 puff)] 4 times, close round with sl st.

Round 5: 1 sc in each ch sp and each st all round, except 3 sc in 3rd of 5 dc at each corner.

POPCORN DIAMOND SQUARE ▲

Foundation ring: Ch 8

Special Abbreviation

pop (popcorn): 5 dc (see page 95).

Round 1: [1 pop, ch 5] 4 times.

Round 2: [1 dc, (2 dc, ch 2, 1 pop, ch 2, 2 dc) in 5 ch loop] 4 times.

Round 3: [3 dc, 2 dc in 2 ch sp, ch 2, 1 pop, ch 2, 2 dc in 2 ch sp, 2 dc] 4 times.

Round 4: [5 dc, 2 dc in 2 ch sp, ch 2, 1 pop, ch 2, 2 dc in 2 ch sp, 4 dc] 4 times.

RAISED DOUBLE ◄ CROCHET SQUARE

Foundation ring: With A, ch 8

Work 1 round each in colors A, B, C, and D; join new yarn in 3 ch sp.

Round 1: [3 dc in ring, ch 3] 4 times.

Round 2: [3 dc in same sp, 3 rfdc, 3 dc in next sp, ch 3] 4 times.

Round 3: [3 dc in same sp, 3 rbdc, 3 rfdc, 3 rbdc, 3 dc in next sp, ch 3] 4 times.

Round 4: [3 dc in same sp, (3 rfdc, 3 rbdc) twice, 3 rfdc, 3 dc in next sp, ch 3] 4 times.

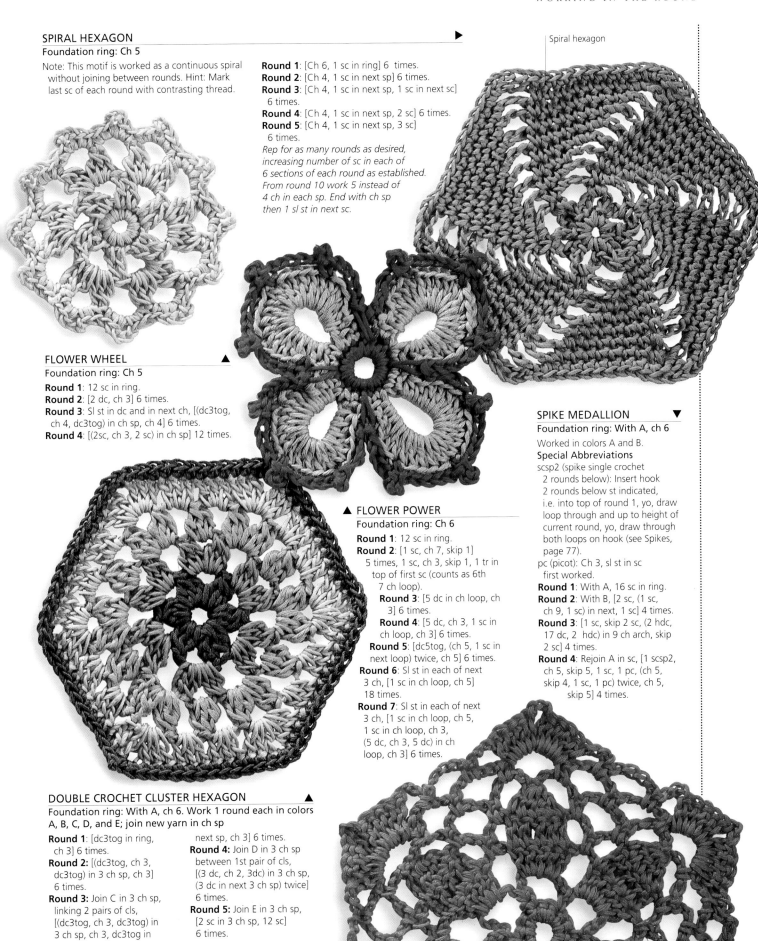

SPIRAL HEXAGON
Foundation ring: Ch 5

Note: This motif is worked as a continuous spiral without joining between rounds. Hint: Mark last sc of each round with contrasting thread.

Round 1: [Ch 6, 1 sc in ring] 6 times.
Round 2: [Ch 4, 1 sc in next sp] 6 times.
Round 3: [Ch 4, 1 sc in next sp, 1 sc in next sc] 6 times.
Round 4: [Ch 4, 1 sc in next sp, 2 sc] 6 times.
Round 5: [Ch 4, 1 sc in next sp, 3 sc] 6 times.
Rep for as many rounds as desired, increasing number of sc in each of 6 sections of each round as established. From round 10 work 5 instead of 4 ch in each sp. End with ch sp then 1 sl st in next sc.

Spiral hexagon

FLOWER WHEEL ▲
Foundation ring: Ch 5

Round 1: 12 sc in ring.
Round 2: [2 dc, ch 3] 6 times.
Round 3: Sl st in dc and in next ch, [(dc3tog, ch 4, dc3tog) in ch sp, ch 4] 6 times.
Round 4: [(2sc, ch 3, 2 sc) in ch sp] 12 times.

▲ FLOWER POWER
Foundation ring: Ch 6

Round 1: 12 sc in ring.
Round 2: [1 sc, ch 7, skip 1] 5 times, 1 sc, ch 3, skip 1, 1 tr in top of first sc (counts as 6th 7 ch loop).
Round 3: [5 dc in ch loop, ch 3] 6 times.
Round 4: [5 dc, ch 3, 1 sc in ch loop, ch 3] 6 times.
Round 5: [dc5tog, (ch 5, 1 sc in next loop) twice, ch 5] 6 times.
Round 6: Sl st in each of next 3 ch, [1 sc in ch loop, ch 5] 18 times.
Round 7: Sl st in each of next 3 ch, [1 sc in ch loop, ch 5, 1 sc in next loop, ch 3, (5 dc, ch 3, 5 dc) in ch loop, ch 3] 6 times.

SPIKE MEDALLION ▼
Foundation ring: With A, ch 6

Worked in colors A and B.
Special Abbreviations
scsp2 (spike single crochet 2 rounds below): Insert hook 2 rounds below st indicated, i.e. into top of round 1, yo, draw loop through and up to height of current round, yo, draw through both loops on hook (see Spikes, page 77).
pc (picot): Ch 3, sl st in sc first worked.

Round 1: With A, 16 sc in ring.
Round 2: With B, [2 sc, (1 sc, ch 9, 1 sc) in next, 1 sc] 4 times.
Round 3: [1 sc, skip 2 sc, (2 hdc, 17 dc, 2 hdc) in 9 ch arch, skip 2 sc] 4 times.
Round 4: Rejoin A in sc, [1 scsp2, ch 5, skip 5, 1 sc, 1 pc, (ch 5, skip 4, 1 sc, 1 pc) twice, ch 5, skip 5] 4 times.

DOUBLE CROCHET CLUSTER HEXAGON ▲
Foundation ring: With A, ch 6. Work 1 round each in colors A, B, C, D, and E; join new yarn in ch sp

Round 1: [dc3tog in ring, ch 3] 6 times.
Round 2: [(dc3tog, ch 3, dc3tog) in 3 ch sp, ch 3] 6 times.
Round 3: Join C in 3 ch sp, linking 2 pairs of cls, [(dc3tog, ch 3, dc3tog) in 3 ch sp, ch 3, dc3tog in next sp, ch 3] 6 times.
Round 4: Join D in 3 ch sp between 1st pair of cls, [(3 dc, ch 2, 3dc) in 3 ch sp, (3 dc in next 3 ch sp) twice] 6 times.
Round 5: Join E in 3 ch sp, [2 sc in 3 ch sp, 12 sc] 6 times.

SHELLS, CLUSTERS & LACE

ATTRACTIVE PATTERNS can be made by grouping stitches together in shells or clusters. Shells are formed by working a group of stitches into the same place, whereas a cluster is made of several adjacent stitches joined together at the top. Work these closely together, or for a delicate look, increase spacing.

SHELLS

These may be all of the same stitch, or of varying stitch heights to create an asymmetric shape. Shells may also contain chains to create spaces. If no stitches are skipped, working more than one stitch into the same place will make an increase (see page 84). If groups of stitches are worked at intervals with other shells between them, no increase is created. See Interlocking Double Crochet Shells, page 89.

CLUSTERS

A cluster is a group of stitches worked into one stitch or space then drawn together at the top with a loop. A shell and a cluster in combination can make a starburst.

1 Work the required number of stitches, leaving last loop of each on hook (see right). These are some- times called not closed (nc).

2 Yo; draw the yarn through all loops as in Double Crochet Whorls.

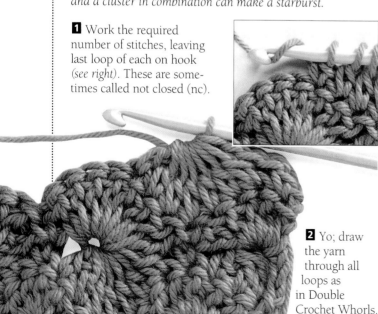

LACE

Lacework consists of shells and clusters as well as meshes (see page 104), single chains, and arches or loops, including picots. There are two ways of working over chains. Working into a space underneath a chain is quicker and easier, so use the second method unless otherwise instructed.

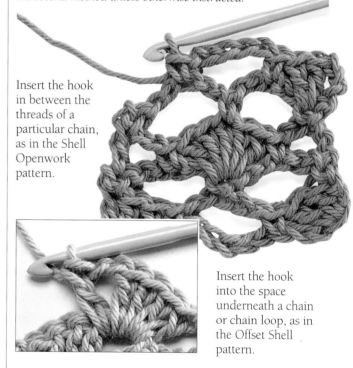

Insert the hook in between the threads of a particular chain, as in the Shell Openwork pattern.

Insert the hook into the space underneath a chain or chain loop, as in the Offset Shell pattern.

PICOTS

These single or multiple chain loops are anchored together for decoration. They are often featured in Irish crochet lace networks (see page 104), and are frequently used as edgings (see page 114).

To make this simple picot the instructions would state, *1 sc in ch sp, (ch 3, sl st in 3rd ch from hook – called picot)*, as in the Shells with Picot pattern.

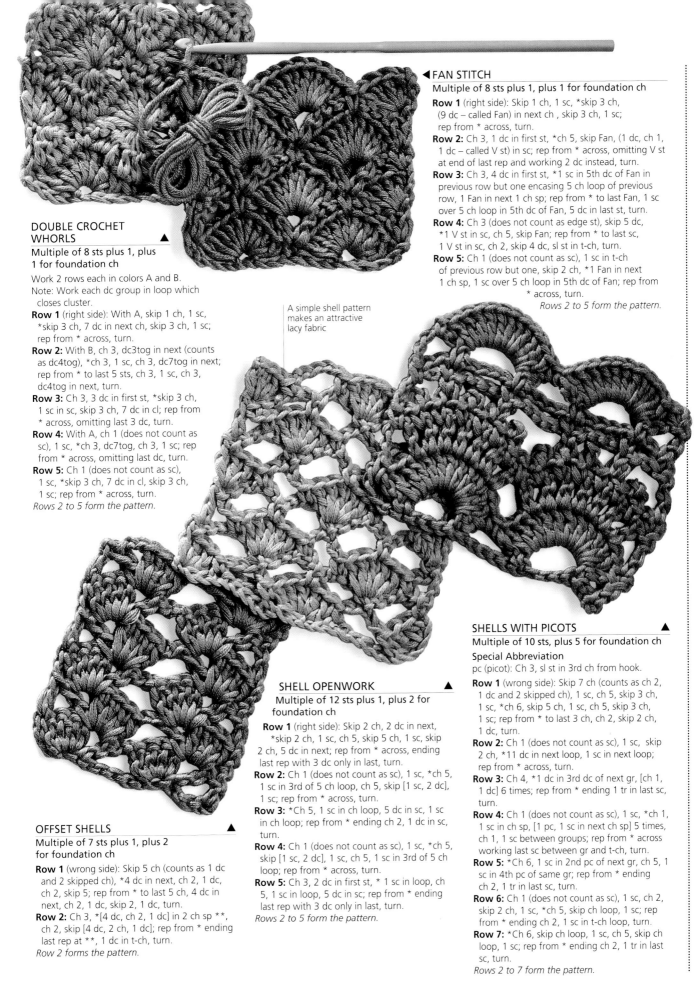

DOUBLE CROCHET WHORLS ▲

Multiple of 8 sts plus 1, plus 1 for foundation ch

Work 2 rows each in colors A and B.
Note: Work each dc group in loop which closes cluster.

Row 1 (right side): With A, skip 1 ch, 1 sc, *skip 3 ch, 7 dc in next ch, skip 3 ch, 1 sc; rep from * across, turn.

Row 2: With B, ch 3, dc3tog in next (counts as dc4tog), *ch 3, 1 sc, ch 3, dc7tog in next; rep from * to last 5 sts, ch 3, 1 sc, ch 3, dc4tog in next, turn.

Row 3: Ch 3, 3 dc in first st, *skip 3 ch, 1 sc in sc, skip 3 ch, 7 dc in cl; rep from * across, omitting last 3 dc, turn.

Row 4: With A, ch 1 (does not count as sc), 1 sc, *ch 3, dc7tog, ch 3, 1 sc; rep from * across, omitting last dc, turn.

Row 5: Ch 1 (does not count as sc), 1 sc, *skip 3 ch, 7 dc in cl, skip 3 ch, 1 sc; rep from * across, turn.

Rows 2 to 5 form the pattern.

A simple shell pattern makes an attractive lacy fabric

FAN STITCH ◀

Multiple of 8 sts plus 1, plus 1 for foundation ch

Row 1 (right side): Skip 1 ch, 1 sc, *skip 3 ch, (9 dc – called Fan) in next ch , skip 3 ch, 1 sc; rep from * across, turn.

Row 2: Ch 3, 1 dc in first st, *ch 5, skip Fan, (1 dc, ch 1, 1 dc – called V st) in sc; rep from * across, omitting V st at end of last rep and working 2 dc instead, turn.

Row 3: Ch 3, 4 dc in first st, *1 sc in 5th dc of Fan in previous row but one encasing 5 ch loop of previous row, 1 Fan in next 1 ch sp; rep from * to last Fan, 1 sc over 5 ch loop in 5th dc of Fan, 5 dc in last st, turn.

Row 4: Ch 3 (does not count as edge st), skip 5 dc, *1 V st in sc, ch 5, skip Fan; rep from * to last sc, 1 V st in sc, ch 2, skip 4 dc, sl st in t-ch, turn.

Row 5: Ch 1 (does not count as sc), 1 sc in t-ch of previous row but one, skip 2 ch, *1 Fan in next 1 ch sp, 1 sc over 5 ch loop in 5th dc of Fan; rep from * across, turn.

Rows 2 to 5 form the pattern.

SHELL OPENWORK ▲

Multiple of 12 sts plus 1, plus 2 for foundation ch

Row 1 (right side): Skip 2 ch, 2 dc in next, *skip 2 ch, 1 sc, ch 5, skip 5 ch, 1 sc, skip 2 ch, 5 dc in next; rep from * across, ending last rep with 3 dc only in last, turn.

Row 2: Ch 1 (does not count as sc), 1 sc, *ch 5, 1 sc in 3rd of 5 ch loop, ch 5, skip [1 sc, 2 dc], 1 sc; rep from * across, turn.

Row 3: *Ch 5, 1 sc in ch loop, 5 dc in sc, 1 sc in ch loop; rep from * ending ch 2, 1 dc in sc, turn.

Row 4: Ch 1 (does not count as sc), 1 sc, *ch 5, skip [1 sc, 2 dc], 1 sc, ch 5, 1 sc in 3rd of 5 ch loop; rep from * across, turn.

Row 5: Ch 3, 2 dc in first st, * 1 sc in loop, ch 5, 1 sc in loop, 5 dc in sc; rep from * ending last rep with 3 dc only in last, turn.

Rows 2 to 5 form the pattern.

OFFSET SHELLS ▲

Multiple of 7 sts plus 1, plus 2 for foundation ch

Row 1 (wrong side): Skip 5 ch (counts as 1 dc and 2 skipped ch), *4 dc in next, ch 2, 1 dc, ch 2, skip 5; rep from * to last 5 ch, 4 dc in next, ch 2, 1 dc, skip 2, 1 dc, turn.

Row 2: Ch 3, *[4 dc, ch 2, 1 dc] in 2 ch sp **, ch 2, skip [4 dc, 2 dc]; rep from * ending last rep at **, 1 dc in t-ch, turn.

Row 2 forms the pattern.

SHELLS WITH PICOTS ▲

Multiple of 10 sts, plus 5 for foundation ch

Special Abbreviation

pc (picot): Ch 3, sl st in 3rd ch from hook.

Row 1 (wrong side): Skip 7 ch (counts as ch 2, 1 dc and 2 skipped ch), 1 sc, ch 5, skip 3 ch, 1 sc, *ch 6, skip 5 ch, 1 sc, ch 5, skip 3 ch, 1 sc; rep from * to last 3 ch, ch 2, skip 2 ch, 1 dc, turn.

Row 2: Ch 1 (does not count as sc), 1 sc, skip 2 ch, *11 dc in next loop, 1 sc in next loop; rep from * across, turn.

Row 3: Ch 4, *1 dc in 3rd dc of next gr, [ch 1, 1 dc] 6 times; rep from * ending 1 tr in last sc, turn.

Row 4: Ch 1 (does not count as sc), 1 sc, *ch 1, 1 sc in ch sp, [1 pc, 1 sc in next ch sp] 5 times, ch 1, 1 sc between groups; rep from * across working last sc between gr and t-ch, turn.

Row 5: *Ch 6, 1 sc in 2nd pc of next gr, ch 5, 1 sc in 4th pc of same gr; rep from * ending ch 2, 1 tr in last sc, turn.

Row 6: Ch 1 (does not count as sc), 1 sc, ch 2, skip 2 ch, 1 sc, *ch 5, skip ch loop, 1 sc; rep from * ending ch 2, 1 sc in t-ch loop, turn.

Row 7: *Ch 6, skip ch loop, 1 sc, ch 5, skip ch loop, 1 sc; rep from * ending ch 2, 1 tr in last sc, turn.

Rows 2 to 7 form the pattern.

MESHES & FILETS

GRIDS OF SQUARES or diamonds characterize most crochet patterns. These can be in the form of close or openwork fabric. Crochet meshes are often embellished, not only with shells (see page 102) and picots (see page 114), but with Clones knots and with the filled spaces of filet lace.

CLONES KNOTS

These are named for an Irish town that was an early center for lace making.

1 To make the knot: Ch 3, *yo, take hook under ch loop just made, yo, bring hook back again over ch loop; repeat from * 4 more times (there are now 9 loops on the hook).

2 Yo and draw through all loops, sl st in 1st of 3 ch.

FILET CROCHET

This is a smooth background of regular squares. Patterns are created by leaving some squares open (spaces) and filling others (blocks). Characteristic images range from simple geometrics to detailed representations of birds and flowers. Filet work is used for edgings as well as for tablecloths, curtains, and clothes.

Filet mesh can be filled with blocks or bars and lacets

CHARTS

Pattern instructions usually come on graph paper. Remember, unless otherwise stated, to read odd rows of a chart from right to left, even rows from left to right. You can usually adapt and use any squared chart as a pattern for filet work.

On filet charts, the spaces are represented by blank squares and the blocks by filled-in squares. The filet ground's vertical stitches are usually double crochet and the horizontal bars ch 2 spaces. Occasional special features called bars and lacets are drawn as they look.

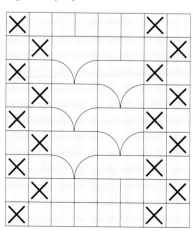

MAKING FILET MESH

For the foundation chain, make a multiple of 3 ch for each square required (which in turn will be a multiple of the number of squares in the pattern repeat), plus 1. Add 4 if the first square is a space, but only 2 if it is a block.

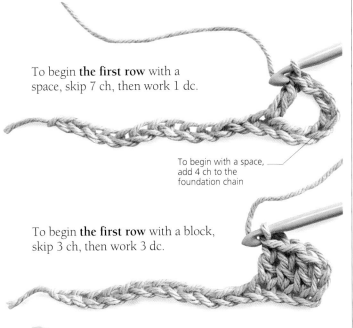

To begin **the first row** with a space, skip 7 ch, then work 1 dc.

To begin with a space, add 4 ch to the foundation chain

To begin **the first row** with a block, skip 3 ch, then work 3 dc.

The last block in the row is worked

Thereafter, work each space as: Ch 2, skip 2, 1 dc. Work each block as: 3 dc.

Alternating blocks and spaces form a simple filet mesh

From row 2, at the beginning of each row, ch 3 to count as the edge stitch (dc), skip the first dc, and then, for each space, ch 2, skip 2 ch (or next 2 dc of a block), 1 dc in next dc; and for each block, work 2 dc in 2 ch sp (or in next 2 dc of a block), 1 dc in next dc.

BARS AND LACETS

Each structure occupies 2 squares and is usually worked alternately.

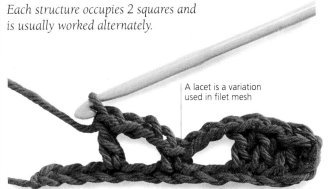

A lacet is a variation used in filet mesh

lacet – ch 3, skip 2, 1 sc, ch 3, skip 2, 1 dc.

A bar is normally worked over the top of each lacet in the mesh

bar – ch 5, skip lacet (or 2 squares), 1 dc.

Filet Variation 1
Sometimes filet charts are interpreted with 1 ch for the spaces. Each square is then narrower.

Filet Variation 2
A mesh with 1-ch spaces and offset squares, that is, with the vertical stitches (dc) worked into the chain spaces of the previous row, produces a nice effect.

Variation 1

Variation 2

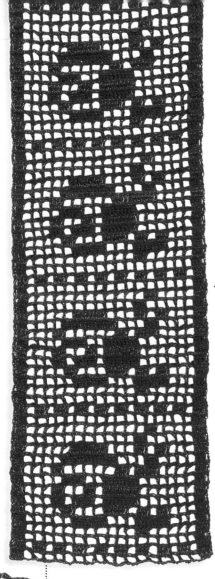

PUFF TRELLIS ▶

Multiple of 3 sts plus 1, plus
1 for foundation ch

Special Abbreviation
Puff V st: [hdc3tog, ch 3, hdc3tog]
in same place (see page 85).

Row 1 (right side): Skip 1 ch,
1 sc, *ch 3, skip 2 ch, 1 sc; rep
from * across, turn.

Row 2: Ch 4, 1 sc in ch loop,
*ch 3, 1 sc ch loop; rep from
* across, ending ch 1, 1 dc in
last st, turn.

Row 3: Ch 3,*1 puff V st in sc;
rep from * across, ending 1 dc
in t-ch loop, turn.

Rows 2 and 3 form the pattern.

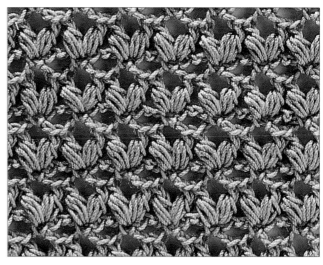

◀ FILET ROSE INSERTION

Foundation: Ch 60

Row 1 (right side): Skip 3 ch, 3 dc,
[ch 2, skip 2, 1 dc] 17 times, 3 dc,
turn (19 squares).

*Follow chart from row 2 for
pattern, repeating rows 3 to 16
as required.*

(chart showing filet rose pattern, rows numbered 1, 3, 5, 7, 9, 11, 13, 15)

BASIC TRELLIS ▶

Multiple of 4 sts plus 2, plus
4 for foundation ch

Row 1 (right side): Skip 5 ch, 1 sc,
*ch 5, skip 3 ch, 1 sc; rep from
* across, turn.

Row 2: *Ch 5, 1 sc in 5 ch loop;
rep from * across, turn.

Row 2 forms the pattern.

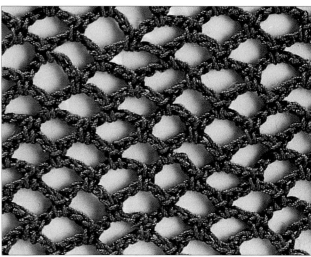

FILET BUTTERFLIES ▼

Multiple of 54 sts (18 squares) plus 7 (2 squares plus 1 st),
plus 4 for foundation ch

Row 1 (right side): Skip 7 ch, 1 dc,
*ch 2, skip 2, 1 dc; rep from *
across, turn.

*Follow chart from row 2 for
pattern, repeating rows 2 to 33 as
required.*

Delicate filet mesh
butterflies are worked in
simple blocks and spaces

(chart showing filet butterfly pattern, rows numbered 1, 3, 5, 7, 9, 11, 13, 15, 17, 19, 21, 23, 25, 27, 29, 31, 33, 35)

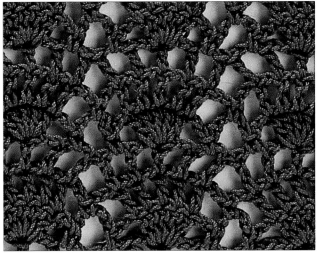

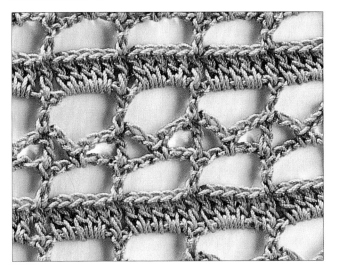

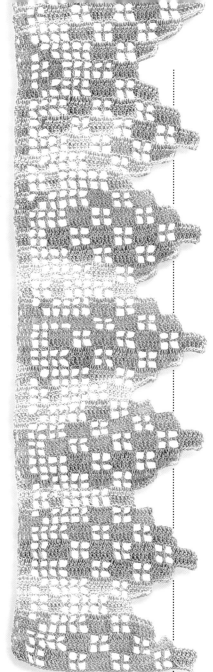

FOUNTAIN NETWORK

Multiple of 12 sts plus 5, plus 1 for foundation ch

Row 1 (right side): Skip 1 ch, 1 sc, *ch 5, skip 3 ch, 1 sc, ch 2, skip 3 dc in next, ch 2, skip 3 ch, 1 sc; rep from * to last 4 ch, ch 5, skip 3 ch, 1 sc, turn.

Row 2: Ch 5 (counts as 1 dc and ch 2), *1 sc in 5 ch loop, ch 2, skip 2 ch, 1 dc in dc, [ch 1, 1 dc] 4 times, ch 2, skip 2 ch; rep from * to last 5 ch loop, 1 sc in 5 ch loop, ch 2, 1 dc in sc, turn.

Row 3: Ch 4 (counts as 1 dc and ch 1), 1 dc in first st, *skip [2 ch, 1 sc, 2 ch], 1 dc in dc, [ch 2, skip 1 ch, 1 dc] 4 times; rep from * ending skip [2 ch, 1 sc, 2 ch], [1 dc, ch 1, 1 dc] in t-ch loop, turn.

Row 4: Ch 1 (does not count as sc), 1 sc, skip [1 ch, 2 dc], *ch 5, 1 sc in 2 ch sp, ch 2, skip [1 dc, 2 ch], 5 dc in dc, ch 2, skip [2 ch, 1 dc], 1 sc in 2 ch sp; rep from * ending ch 5, 1 sc in t-ch loop, turn.

Rows 2, 3 and 4 form the pattern.

FILET DIAMOND BORDER ▶

Foundation: Ch 36

Note: For multiple increases and decreases see pages 84 to 85.

Row 1 (right side): Skip 3 ch, 3 dc, [ch 2, skip 2, 1 dc] twice, 3 dc, [ch 2, skip 2, 1 dc] 5 times, [3 dc] twice, turn.

Follow chart from row 2 for pattern, repeating rows 2 to 12 as required.

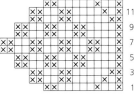

BLOCK, BAR AND LACET ▲

Multiple of 6 sts plus 1, plus 2 for foundation ch

Row 1 (right side): Skip 3 ch, dc across, turn.

Row 2: Ch 3, skip first dc, *ch 5, skip 5, 1 dc; rep from * across, turn.

Row 3: Ch 3, skip first dc, *ch 3, 1 sc in ch loop, ch 3, – called lacet, 1 dc in dc; rep from * across, turn.

Row 4: Ch 3, skip first dc, *ch 5, skip lacet, 1 dc; rep from * across, turn.

Row 5: Ch 3, *5 dc in ch loop, 1 dc in dc; rep from * across, turn.

Rows 2 to 5 form the pattern.

SINGLE CROCHET NETWORK ▶

Multiple of 8 sts plus 1, plus 1 for foundation ch

Note: t-ch does not count as st, except on row 4, 10, etc.

Row 1 (right side): Skip 1 ch, 3 sc, *ch 5, skip 3 ch, 5 sc; rep from * across, omitting 2 of 5 sc at end of last rep, turn.

Row 2: Ch 1, 1 sc, *ch 3, 1 sc in 5 ch loop, ch 3, skip 1 sc, 2 sc; rep from * across, turn.

Row 3: Ch 1, 1 sc, *ch 3, 1 sc in 3 ch sp, 1 sc, 1 sc in 3 ch sp, ch 3, skip 1 sc, 1 sc; rep from * across, turn.

Row 4: Ch 5 (counts as 1 dc and 2 ch), * 1 sc in 3 ch sp, 3 sc, 1 sc in 3 ch sp **, ch 5; rep from * to 2nd last 3 ch sp and from * to ** again, ch 2, 1 dc in last sc, turn.

Row 5: Ch 1, 1 sc, *ch 3, skip 1 sc, 3 sc, ch 3, skip 1 sc, 1 sc in 5 ch loop; rep from * across, turn.

Row 6: Ch 1, 1 sc, *1 sc in 3 ch sp, ch 3, skip 1 sc, 1 sc, ch 3, skip 1 sc, 1 sc in 3 ch sp, 1 sc; rep from * across, turn.

Row 7: Ch 1, 1 sc, *1 sc, 1 sc in 3 ch sp, ch 5, 1 sc in 3 ch sp, 2 sc; rep from * across, turn.

Rows 2 to 7 form the pattern.

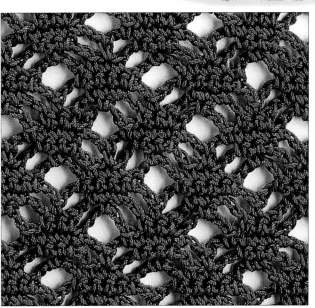

SUMMER SENSATIONS

LACY OPENWORK MAKES cardigans and tops look fresh and summery, with a soft, romantic touch. In addition, this technique can completely transform plain pillows into works of art.

Lacy edging around opening and hem sets off the mesh pattern

The same lace edging is used around the openwork panels to make an attractive feature on the body and sleeves of the jacket

LACY JACKET

This lovely lacy cardigan is ideal for slipping over summer dresses, and for adding a feminine look to T-shirts (see page 237).

Varying stitch heights makes this pretty shell stitch

The front motif is made of three squares sewn together

CROCHET SHELL

This cotton top can be dressed up or down – it looks great with a pretty skirt and just as good with jeans (see page 236).

Add a final feminine flounce with lacy edging

Mesh panel makes openwork corners

PILLOWS

Delicate, lacy decorations for pillow covers are made in the same way as medallions. The doilies are then sewn onto pillows of any color (see page 238).

A flower-bud pattern makes an attractive motif

AFGHAN STITCH

AFGHAN STITCH (SOMETIMES referred to as Tunisian crochet) is traditionally worked with a special hook, which is longer than usual, has a uniform diameter, and a knob (or sometimes another hook) at the other end. The technique is a cross between knitting and crochet. The finished work resembles knitting, but the stitches are thicker and firmer. You should expect to use a hook at least two sizes larger than you would ordinarily use with the same yarn in regular crochet.

The odd-numbered rows are worked from right to left, as loops are picked up and retained on the hook. In the even-numbered rows, the loops are worked off again from left to right.

FOUNDATION ROW

An enormous range of plain, textured, multicolored, and openwork stitch patterns are all possible in afghan stitches. Most patterns are worked with the same two rows given below. Unless a double-ended hook is involved, the work is never turned and so the right side is always facing.

Make a length of foundation chain with the same number of chains as the number of stitches required in the finished row, plus 1 chain for turning.

Row one (forward)

Skip 1 ch, *insert the hook in the next ch, yo, draw the loop through the ch only and keep on the hook; rep from * across. Do not turn the work.

Row two (return)

Yo, draw through 1 loop only, *yo, draw through 2 loops; rep from * across until 1 loop remains on hook. Do not turn the work.

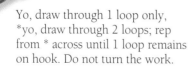

The finished foundation row forms the basis of most afghan stitch patterns.

SIMPLE AFGHAN STITCH

Work basic forward and return foundation row as at left.

Forward (row 3 and all odd rows): Count loop on hook as first st and start in 2nd st. *Insert hook at front and from right to left around single front vertical thread, yo, draw loop through and keep on hook; rep from * across. Do not turn.
Return (even rows): Same as row two.

AFGHAN STOCKINETTE STITCH

Work basic forward and return foundation row as at left.

Forward: Count loop on hook as first st and start in 2nd st. *Insert hook from front through fabric and below chs formed by previous return row to right of front vertical thread and left of back thread of same loop, yo, draw loop through and keep on hook; rep from * across. Do not turn.
Return: Same as row two.

The borders of popcorn pattern also form the joining bands between panels of afghan stitch

A ground of afghan stitch is embroidered in contrasting colors using cross stitch, outline stitch, straight stitch, and French knots

Reverse colorway

DESIGNING A COLORWAY

Reversing the colorway from a light to a dark background gives an entirely different look to the pattern. The bright contrast between the white flowers and the ground emphasizes the freshness of the blue and white color scheme. Experiment with various color schemes to see the different effects that can be created with the same selection of colors used in different parts of the pattern.

AFGHANS

THESE THREE AFGHANS are all made
using simple crochet stitches, and will work up
surprisingly quickly. Use to decorate your favorite
room, or for a little additional warmth when
you are sitting out on the porch.

TRADITIONAL AND MODERN AFGHANS

*This Fan afghan pattern is crocheted in delicate shades
of soft mohair, and has a nostalgic appeal, reminiscent
of ladies' fans of the nineteenth century. Use it as a throw
in cooler late summer evenings. (See page 239.)*

*Crochet the Antique Rose pattern or the Kaleidoscope
pattern in knitting worsted-weight yarn. The blue
background and large rose pattern have a romantic,
feminine look, while the bright, colorful circles with a
border of triangles make a more contemporary looking
afghan. Wrap yourself up in the one of your choice on
chilly evenings, and feel proud of your handiwork.
(To make, see pages 239 and 240.)*

The fan shaped
pattern is completed
with a shell pattern
to make a square

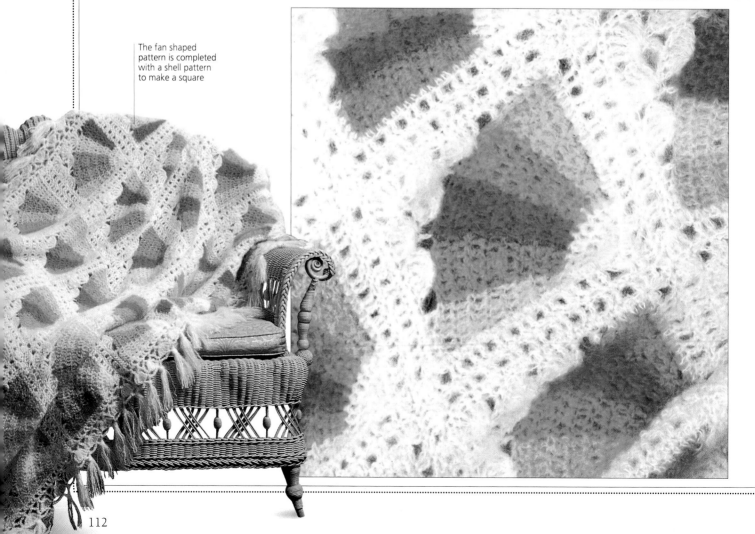

Squares of
plain color are
interspersed with
the Antique Rose
pattern motifs

A red background
sets off circles
which are worked
in nine contrasting
colors to produce
a kaleidoscope
effect

EDGINGS

CROCHET WORK WILL usually lie flatter and have a better finish if an edging is added. Crochet edges and borders can also be used to trim a finished article. If edges or borders are a foundation for your main piece, make them first. If you are to attach them afterward, make them separately. When working edgings, use a smaller size hook than you used for the main piece. This will give the edging a firmer finish.

SINGLE CROCHET EDGING

This basic edging, worked with the right side facing, neatens and strengthens the fabric, and can cover any float threads or stray short ends. (The two rows shown here were worked in a contrasting color for clarity.) It is also a good foundation for a more decorative edging.

BUTTONHOLE LOOPS

Loops for buttons may be made in an edging row/round by skipping the required number of stitches and working chains instead. If you need extra edging rows, work sc into the loops.

CORDED EDGE

This is a very effective edging, usually worked after one round of sc and with the right side facing. Work it in sc, but from left to right.

PICOT EDGING

Picots of varying size and complexity are a regular feature of crochet edgings. To make this triple picot work [ch 3, sl st in 3rd ch from hook] 3 times, then sl st into the top of the last sc made (see Triple Picot below).

WORKING CORNERS AND EDGES

Normally you work one stitch into each stitch across the top of a row and into the underside of a foundation chain. Work 3 stitches into a corner and along the side of the fabric at the rate of 1 stitch per sc row. As a guide, you will need to use 1 and 2 stitches alternately per hdc row, 2 stitches per dc row, 3 stitches per tr row, etc.

Making the corded edge

*Working from left to right, insert the hook into the next stitch to the right, yo. Draw the loop through the work, below the loop which remains on the hook, and up to the left, into the normal working position (*left*). Yo and draw the loop through to complete 1 corded sc (*right*). Repeat from *.

PUFF STITCH
Multiple of 2 sts

Note: All rows worked right side facing.
Row 1: With yarn matching main fabric, sc.
Row 2: With contrasting color, working from left to right and inserting hook from front to back, work * ch1, skip 1, hdc 3tog; rep from * ending with a sl st.
Main fabric represented here by a row of dc.

TRIPLE PICOT ▲
Multiple of 5 sts

Note: All rows worked right side facing.
Row 1: With yarn matching main fabric, sc.
Row 2: With contrasting color, *5 sc, [ch 3, sl st in 3rd ch from hook] 3 times, sl st in top of last sc made; rep from *.
Main fabric represented here by a row of dc.

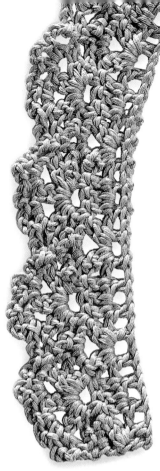

◀ PICOT SCALLOPS

Multiple of 8 sts plus 1, plus 2 for foundation ch

Row 1 (right side): Skip 3 ch, 1 dc, *ch 1, skip 1, 1 dc; rep from * to last ch, 1 dc, turn.

Row 2: Ch 5 (counts as 1 dc, ch 2), dc2tog in first, *skip [1 dc, 1 ch], 3 dc, skip [1 ch, 1 dc], [dc2tog, ch 4, dc2tog – called 2cl] in ch sp; rep from * across, omitting last 2 ch and dc2tog from last 2cl and working 1 dc in same loop, turn.

Row 3: Ch 3 (counts as 1 hdc, ch 1), 1 sc in 2 ch sp, *skip cl, [ch 3, 1 sc – called picot], skip 1, 1 pc, 2 pc in 4 ch loop; rep from * across, omiting 2nd pc at end of last rep and working ch 1, 1 hdc in same loop, turn.

Row 4: Ch 1 (does not count as sc), 1 sc, *ch 1, skip 1 pc, [dc2tog, (ch 3, dc2tog) twice] in next pc, ch 1, skip 1 pc, 1 sc in next pc; rep from * across, turn.

Row 5: Ch 1 (does not count as sc), 1 sc, skip 1 ch, *[2 pc in next 3 ch loop] twice, skip 1 ch, 1 pc in sc; rep from * across.

SHAMROCK STRIPES ▲

Foundation: With A, ch 19

Work 2 rows each in colors A, B, C and D, throughout.

Row 1 (wrong side): With A, skip 5 ch, 1 dc, ch 1, skip 1, 2 dc, ch 8, skip 9, [1 dc, (ch 3, 1 dc) 3 times] in last ch, turn.

Row 2: [In 3 ch sp work (1 sc, 1 hdc, 3 dc, 1 hdc, 1 sc – called petal)] 3 times, ch 6, skip 6 ch, 1 dc in each of last 2 ch of loop, (2 dc – called blk), [ch 1, skip 1, 1 dc] twice, turn.

Row 3: With B, ch 4 (counts as 1 dc, ch 1), skip 1 ch, 1 dc, ch 1, skip 1, (4 dc – called blk), 1 dc in each of next 2 ch, ch 8, in center dc of 2nd petal work [1 dc, (ch 3, 1 dc) 3 times], turn.

Row 4: as row 2, except work blk of 6 dc.

Row 5: With C, as row 3, except work blk of 8 dc.

Row 6: as row 2, except work blk of 10 dc.

Row 7: With D, ch 4 (counts as 1 dc, ch 1), skip 1 ch, 1 dc, ch 1, skip 1, 2 dc, ch 8, skip 9, (1 dc, [ch 3, 1 dc] 3 times) in last dc, turn.

Rows 2 to 7 form the pattern.

DEEP SEA SHELLS ▼

Foundation: Ch 11

Row 1 (right side): Skip 3 ch, 2 dc, ch 2, skip 2, 1 dc, ch 2, skip 2, [1 dc, ch 3, 1 dc] in last ch, turn.

Row 2: Ch 5, [3 dc, ch 1, 3 dc] in 3 ch sp, ch 2, skip 2 ch, 1 dc, ch 2, skip 2 ch, 3 dc, turn.

Row 3: Ch 3, 2 dc, ch 2, skip 2 ch, 1 dc, ch 2, skip 2 ch, [1 dc, ch 3, 1 dc] in 1 ch sp *, ch 2, (1 dc, [ch 1, 1 dc] 7 times) in 5 ch loop **, 1 tr in 1st ch made of foundation, turn.

Row 4: Ch 2, skip 2, 1 sc in ch sp, [ch 3, 1 sc in ch sp] 6 times, ch 2, skip 2 ch, [3 dc, ch 1, 3 dc] in 3 ch sp, ch 2, skip 2 ch, 1 dc, ch 2, skip 2 ch, 3 dc, turn.

Row 5: as row 3 to *, turn.

Row 6: as row 2.

Row 7: as row 3 to **, 1 sc in 2 ch sp of last-but-two row.

Row 8: as row 4.

Rows 5 to 8 form the pattern.

BULLION SPIRALS ▶

Foundation: Ch 12

Special Abbreviation

B st (Bullion stitch): See page 95, made with yo 10 times.

Row 1 (right side): Skip 3 ch, 1 dc, skip 3 ch, (1 dc, [1 B st, 1 dc] 3 times – called shell) in next, skip 3 ch, (3 dc, ch 2, 3 dc – called V st) in next, turn.

Row 2: Ch 7, skip 3 ch, [3 dc in next] 4 times, V st in 2 ch sp, ch 3, 1 sc in centre B st of shell, ch 3, 1 dc in each of last 2 sts, turn.

Row 3: Ch 3, 1 dc, skip 3 ch, shell in sc, skip 3 ch, V st in 2 ch sp, turn.

Rows 2 and 3 form the pattern.

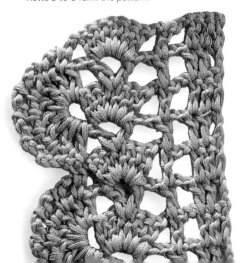

PICOT ARCHWAY ▲

Multiple of 8 sts plus 1, plus 1 for foundation ch

Row 1 (right side): Skip 2 ch, sc across, turn.

Row 2: Ch 1, sc across, turn.

Row 3: Ch 1 (does not count as sc), 1 sc, *ch 3, 2 dc in next, skip 2, 1 sc; rep from * across, turn.

Row 4: Ch 4 (counts as 1 dc, ch 1), 1 dc in first, * 1 sc in 3 ch loop, ch 6, 1 sc in 3 ch loop, (1 dc, ch 3, 1 dc – called V st) in sc; rep from * omitting 2 of 3 ch in last V st, turn.

Row 5: Ch 1, 1 sc in 1 ch sp, *[5 dc, ch 5, sl st in 5th ch from hook, 5 dc] in 6 ch loop, 1 sc in next ch loop; rep from * across.

BUTTONS, CORDS & FINISHES

YOU CAN ADD finishing touches to garments by using matching or contrasting crochet trims. Buttons and cords will liven up children's garments, or women's accessories such as purses. The addition of slip stitches to the surface of a finished crochet piece creates an effect somewhat like weaving.

BUTTONS

Easy to make, chunky crochet buttons offer a colorful, lively way of enhancing handmade garments and accessories. For a crochet loop buttonhole, see page 114.

Bobble Button
Foundation: Ch 2. Note: Close each round with sl st in first sc.
Round 1 (right side): 6 sc in 2nd ch from hook.
Round 2: Ch 1, 2 sc in each dc (12 sts).
Round 3: Ch 1, 1 sc in each sc *(top right)*.
Round 4: Ch 1, (1 sc, skip 1) 6 times (6 sts). Pack button with small amount of yarn *(bottom right)*.
Round 5: Ch 1, (1 sc, skip 1) 3 times. Cut length of yarn to close opening and sew button in place.

CORDS

Ties and drawstrings can be worked quickly and easily in contrasting colors to add bright and decorative touches to crochet or knitted children's clothes and accessories.

Round Cord
Foundation ring: Ch 5 (or as required for thickness of cord). Work in spiral around ring as follows: 1 sl st in top loop of each ch and then of each sl st, until cord reaches required length. For a faster-growing cord, work in sc or dc.

Flat Cord
Ch 2, 1 sc in 2nd ch from hook, turn and work 1 sc in ch at back of sc just made, *turn and work 1 sc, inserting hook down through 2 loops at back of sc just made; rep from * until cord is required length.

SURFACE CHAINS

Plaids require careful planning, but any crocheted design, particularly one with a network of chain spaces, may be decorated in this way with vertical or horizontal lines.

Making surface chains

1 Make a slip knot in new yarn. With right or wrong side of work facing as required, insert hook down through chosen chain space. Yo underneath work, draw through work and loop on hook.

2 *Insert hook down through next chain space or selected position, yo underneath fabric, draw through fabric and loop on hook; rep from * as required.

Make one chain beyond edge of work and bind off. It is important to work loosely so as not to distort the background stitches. It may help to use a larger hook than you used for the main work. Short ends of yarn should be worked over and encased during any subsequent edging rounds or darned into the wrong side of the piece.

Right side

Wrong side

FINISHING & JOINING

FOR A POLISHED, professional look, take special care when finishing and joining your work – its whole appearance and durability depend on it. Make sure all stray ends of yarn are woven neatly and securely into the wrong side. Seams can be sewn, or joined with a crochet hook as below.

JOINING WITH A HOOK

Crochet seams are strong, and quick to work. Slip stitch is the most invisible, and single crochet makes a ridge that can be a feature on the right side. The number of stitches to work per row end is the same as for edgings (see page 114).

Slip-stitch seam

Place the pieces right sides together. *Insert hook through both edge stitches, yo and draw through to complete 1 sl st; rep from *, working fairly loosely.

Single-crochet seam

Place the pieces right sides together (or wrong sides together for a visible seam) and work as for slip-stitch seam, using single crochet instead of slip stitch.

Single-crochet and chain seam

A useful variation of the single crochet seam, this is used when less bulk and/or greater flexibility is called for. Work 1 sc and 1 ch alternately.

Flat slip-stitch seam

Place the pieces edge to edge and wrong sides up. Work 1 sl st into each edge alternately. (See also alternative right.)

JOINING MOTIFS

Straight edges may be joined in the normal way. However, when there are many pieces, particularly squares and triangles, it is worthwhile connecting pairs of motifs in a continuous seam to avoid repeated binding off.

Alternative flat slip-stitch seam

A neat, flat seam may be made using the tops of stitches, as for example, with motifs made in the round. Lay the pieces edge to edge and right sides up. Insert the hook down through the top loop only of each corresponding pair of stitches and join with slip stitch.

Filler motifs join as well as decorate

Many motifs have a final round of picots or loops, and these may be used to join motifs to each other as that round is being worked. Typically the center chain of a loop is replaced by a sl st or sc worked into a loop of the adjacent motif.

After joining, small motifs, which add decoration and strength, can be worked in the spaces between. The main motifs shown here are Flower Wheel (see page 101). For the filler motifs work: Foundation ring: Ch 5. Round 1: [1 sc in ring, ch 2, sl st in motif, ch 2, 1 sc in ring] 4 times.

BLOCKING AND PRESSING

Cotton lace work usually needs careful pinning and pressing. Other crochet, particularly a textured piece, hardly ever requires this treatment. Pinning the article, misting with a fine spray, and leaving it to dry naturally may be just as effective. Be sure to use rust-proof pins.

EMBROIDERY

*U*sing stitches to decorate a fabric is an ancient craft. The variety of individual stitches is legion, and the myriad ways stitches can be combined and applied – to plain or patterned fabric – means that work of great originality is within everyone's reach.

Today, many Good Housekeeping readers enjoy working cross-stitch projects, but there is always the possibility of decorating garments with more ambitious stitchery. Collars, cuffs, and pockets offer conveniently small opportunities of personalizing garments, as do household items such as bed and table linens.

Museums around the world are filled with examples of embroidery. A good collection will contain traditionally-embroidered garments such as waistcoats and christening gowns, as well as pictures, covered boxes, and altar pieces. Not content with using silk, wool, or cotton threads, skilled embroiderers are using metal threads and adding beads and sequins. Special effects were, and continue to be, prized and sought after on both garments and household furnishings.

TOOLS & MATERIALS

THERE IS AN enormous range of background fabrics and threads for any embroidery project. The ones you choose will affect the results of your work. When making your selections, keep in mind that the fabric should be suitable for the finished item – for example, longwearing and washable for a pillow cover. Also be certain that the needle and thread will pass through the fabric easily without splitting the woven threads. Your only other essential piece of equipment is a small, sharp pair of scissors.

FABRICS

Plain or patterned fabric are suitable for embroidery. Woven or geometric patterns are especially useful for stitches that need guidelines to keep them a regular size. A wide range of even-weave fabrics for counted-thread techniques (such as cross stitch) is available. An even-weave fabric has the same number of warp and weft threads per square inch. For example 18-count means that there are 18 threads to the inch. One of the most popular fabrics for embroidered pictures is 14-count Aida cloth. This is also available with a woven colored grid to make stitch counting from charts easier. The colored threads are removed when the stitching is finished.

EMBROIDERY THREADS

These come in a wide range of colors. Some popular thread types are shown below, but don't be afraid to experiment with other yarns supplied for knitting, crochet, and canvas work.

Embroidery floss
A loosely twisted 6-strand thread that is easily divided into single threads.

Pearl cotton
A strong, twisted non-divisible thread with a high sheen.

Flower thread
A fine non-divisible thread with a matte finish.

Matte embroidery cotton
A thick, soft, tightly twisted thread.

Crewel yarn
Fine 2-ply wool or acrylic yarn. Also used in tapestry work.

Persian yarn
Loosely twisted 3-strand wool or acrylic yarn; this is easily divisible.

NEEDLES

Needles come in a range of sizes; the higher the number, the finer the needle.

Crewel or embroidery needle
This is the most commonly used embroidery needle. It has a sharp point and a large eye.

Chenille needle
Similar to a crewel needle, but this has a thicker stem. It is suitable for working with heavier threads on a coarse background fabric.

Tapestry or yarn needle
A thick-stemmed, large-eyed needle with a round-pointed end. Used for lacing embroidery stitches and for pulled threadwork.

Beading needle
A fine, long needle for sewing on tiny beads.

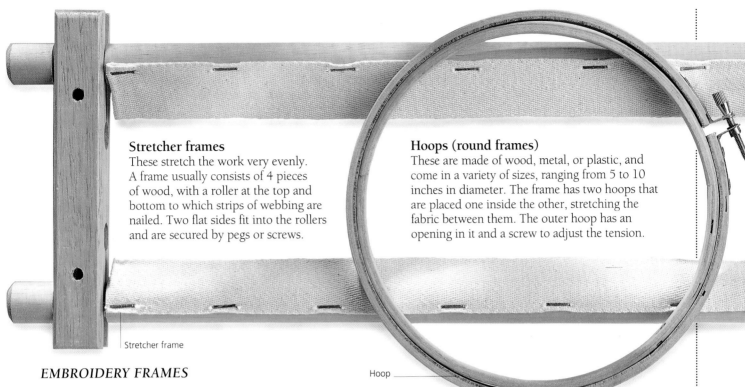

Stretcher frames
These stretch the work very evenly.
A frame usually consists of 4 pieces
of wood, with a roller at the top and
bottom to which strips of webbing are
nailed. Two flat sides fit into the rollers
and are secured by pegs or screws.

Hoops (round frames)
These are made of wood, metal, or plastic, and
come in a variety of sizes, ranging from 5 to 10
inches in diameter. The frame has two hoops that
are placed one inside the other, stretching the
fabric between them. The outer hoop has an
opening in it and a screw to adjust the tension.

Stretcher frame

Hoop

EMBROIDERY FRAMES

*These hold the fabric taut while you work. A frame isn't
essential for small pieces of embroidery, but it does make the
work easier to handle and quicker to stitch. Since the fabric is
held at an even tension, the stitches themselves will be more
even. Also, holding the frame instead of the fabric keeps the
work cleaner than working without one.*

   *There are two basic types of frames, the round frame
(called a hoop) and the straight-sided frame. The hoop is the
most commonly used because it is lightweight and portable,*

*and it only takes a few seconds to mount the fabric in it
correctly. Straight-sided frames, known as stretcher frames,
have a roller at the top and bottom and are generally used
for large pieces of embroidery such as wall hangings; it takes
longer to mount the work, but the fabric is quickly moved into
a new position. Both types of frames are available on floor or
lap stands, which allow you to keep both hands free.*

OTHER USEFUL EQUIPMENT

*Pairs of large and small sharp
scissors for cutting your fabric and
thread are absolutely essential.
You'll also want dressmaker's
carbon paper and special pencils
for transferring your embroidery
designs to fabric. Other useful
items include a thimble, needle
threader, and masking tape to
prevent fabric edges from fraying.*

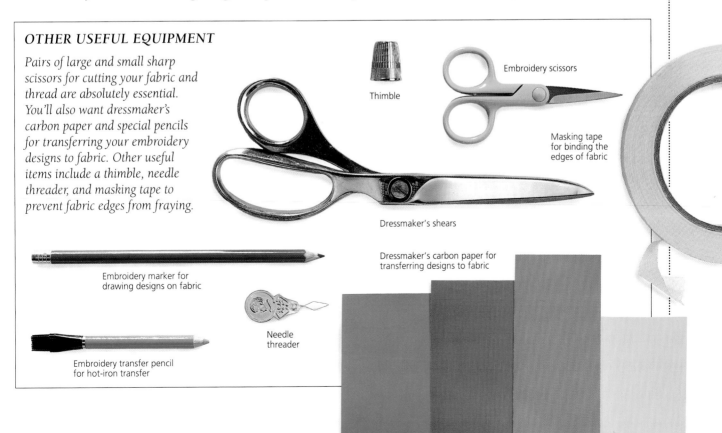

Thimble

Embroidery scissors

Masking tape
for binding the
edges of fabric

Dressmaker's shears

Dressmaker's carbon paper for
transferring designs to fabric

Embroidery marker for
drawing designs on fabric

Needle
threader

Embroidery transfer pencil
for hot-iron transfer

PREPARING A FRAME

LIGHTWEIGHT ROUND FRAMES, called hoops, are ideal for small pieces of fabric, while straight-sided frames, or stretcher frames, are better for larger pieces.

These latter take longer to set up as the fabric has to be stitched to the roller webbing at the top and bottom, and then laced to the sides of the frame.

HOOPS

Before placing the fabric, loosen the tension screw on the outer hoop. The hoop can be repositioned on the fabric as you complete each small area of stitching.

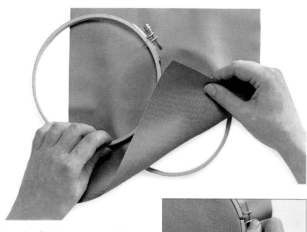

Lay the fabric on top of the inner hoop, with the section to be embroidered facing you *(above)*. Make sure that the fabric is smooth. Push the outer hoop down on top of the fabric on the inner hoop. Gently pull the fabric taut. Tighten the upper hoop by turning the screw, so that the fabric is stretched like a drum and held firmly in position *(right)*.

Irregular shapes

1 Baste the irregular shape onto a larger piece of fabric, with the woven threads of each aligned.

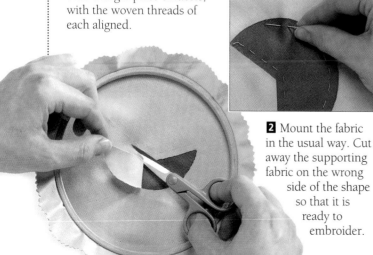

2 Mount the fabric in the usual way. Cut away the supporting fabric on the wrong side of the shape so that it is ready to embroider.

PROTECTING YOUR WORK

You can bind your hoop to prevent fine fabrics from sagging and losing their shape while you work. For a large piece of embroidery, change hoop position every time a section is completed. When you reposition your work be sure to protect finished stitches with a layer of tissue paper.

Wrap woven tape around the inner hoop as shown, and secure the end with a few stitches *(left)*. Place the fabric on the lower hoop and lay white tissue paper on top. Mount the fabric and paper, then tear away the paper *(right)*.

STRAIGHT-SIDED FRAMES

Before you mount the fabric, hem all the edges, or bind them with ³/₄ inch-wide cotton tape. Mark the center point of the fabric on the top and bottom edges.

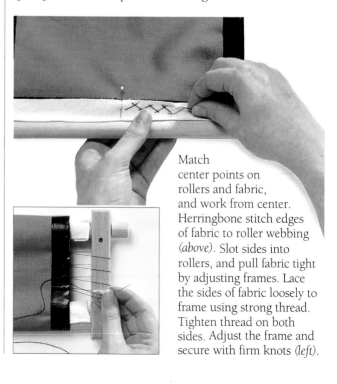

Match center points on rollers and fabric, and work from center. Herringbone stitch edges of fabric to roller webbing *(above)*. Slot sides into rollers, and pull fabric tight by adjusting frames. Lace the sides of fabric loosely to frame using strong thread. Tighten thread on both sides. Adjust the frame and secure with firm knots *(left)*.

EMBROIDERY TECHNIQUES

ONCE YOU HAVE transferred your design to the fabric, you are ready to start the embroidery. If the fabric weave is very open and loose, you will need to bind the edges so that they don't fray – use one of the simple methods given below. When working, try to keep the back of the work as neat as possible by weaving the thread ends behind existing stitches and avoiding large gaps between stitches.

CUTTING AND BINDING FABRIC

The fabric should be cut two inches larger all around than the overall design. But if you want to mount or frame the completed embroidery, add twice this amount (four inches). Take care to cut the fabric straight, following the warp and weft threads of the weave of the fabric.

Binding fabric prevents edges from fraying while you work and is essential on loosely woven fabric. Either tape the edges with masking tape or neaten raw edges with machine zigzag stitch. Alternatively, turn the edges under and sew in place.

PREPARING THE THREADS

The working thread should be 18 inches or less. Longer threads will get tangled, lose their sheen, and fray.

When stitching a large area in one color, cut skeins into 18-inch lengths before you start. Fold bundles in half width-wise, and tie a thread around loop end. Use as needed.

Embroidery floss, matte embroidery cotton and Persian yarn are all loosely twisted threads that can be separated into finer strands. It is best to separate them when you need them.

STARTING AND FINISHING WORK

Don't make a knot when you are starting or finishing a length of thread. Knots show through the work, creating an uneven appearance. Instead, use a small backstitch (page 129), or weave the end into existing stitches on the back of the work.

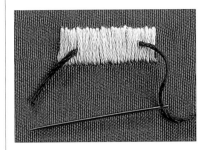

Start a new thread by sliding needle under wrong side of some stitches, keeping thread end about 1½ inches long. Bring needle up on right side of fabric and continue.

To secure the thread at the end of stitching, slide the needle under 1½ inches of the worked stitches on the wrong side of the work, and then cut the thread.

EMBROIDERING THE DESIGN

Always work in a good light and in a comfortable position. Follow the guidelines carefully, inserting the needle on the outside of each line, so that none of the lines will show when the work is finished.

Choose the right needle for the fabric and thread, and try to keep the stitch tension even. Where possible, use a stabbing motion with the needle, and always pull the thread through carefully. Stitching will make the thread twist, particularly if you are working knotted stitches. If this starts happening, just let the needle drop and hang freely for a few seconds until the thread untwists.

Don't make the stitches too long, especially if you are working an article that will receive a lot of wear or be handled frequently. When your embroidery is finished you may find that the long stitches tend to snag and break if they get caught on other objects. For the same reason, on the back of the work, if there is a gap of more than ¾ inch between stitches, secure the first stitch and start the next one with a new piece of thread.

ENLARGING & REDUCING

INSPIRATION FOR EMBROIDERY designs can be found almost anywhere. Start by looking at old embroidery, art postcards, photographs, book illustrations, or wallpaper. Since the original design is unlikely to be the right size, you will need to enlarge or reduce it. The easiest way to do this is with a photocopier, or you may use the grid method shown below. This involves transposing the outline shapes of the basic design from one grid to another of a different size. You will need some good quality tracing paper, a ruler, and a triangle.

INSPIRATION FOR DESIGN

You can find ideas for designs from all kinds of things such as plates, tiles, leaves, shells, or flowers. Old objects, such as this trinket box or book, often have attractive decorations that could easily be copied for embroidery designs. If the design has a lot of detail, try to simplify the outlines to suit the scale of your work.

To enlarge a design

1 Trace shapes on tracing paper, and go over all lines with a black felt-tip pen. Enclose the design in a rectangle. Draw a diagonal line from bottom left-hand corner to top right-hand corner.

2 Place traced rectangle on a sheet of paper large enough for the final design. Align left-hand and bottom edges. Tape down tracing; extend the diagonal line on the tracing across paper.

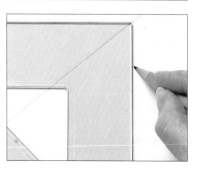

3 Remove paper and complete the diagonal line. At height of new design, using a triangle, draw a horizontal line to cross diagonal. From this point draw a vertical line down to bottom edge.

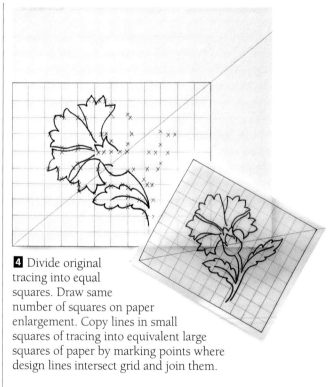

4 Divide original tracing into equal squares. Draw same number of squares on paper enlargement. Copy lines in small squares of tracing into equivalent large squares of paper by marking points where design lines intersect grid and join them.

To reduce a design

Start with step 1 of enlargement instructions; then tape a small piece of paper in the bottom left-hand corner of the tracing. Draw a diagonal line on the paper to correspond to the diagonal line on the tracing. Draw the required width and height of the embroidery on the paper as in step 3. Divide the tracing into squares, and then divide the paper into the same number of squares. Transfer the design as in step 4.

TRANSFERRING A DESIGN

THERE ARE FIVE methods of transferring an original design to fabric. The method you choose as the most suitable will depend on the type of design and texture of the fabric. First iron the fabric, then cut it to size (see page 123). Carefully position the design on the fabric before you transfer it by your chosen method.

Drawing freehand

Designs can be drawn directly onto the right side of fabric with a pencil or embroidery marker – a fine-tipped water-soluble pen. Any lines that show afterward can be removed by dampening the fabric. In the case of sheer fabrics such as organdy, muslin, or voile, draw the design on paper and go over the lines with a medium black felt-tip pen. When the ink is dry, place the fabric over the paper, and trace the design onto the fabric.

Hot-iron transfer

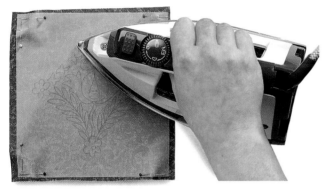

Copy your design onto tracing paper. Turn the paper over and trace the lines with an embroidery-transfer pencil. Position the paper, transfer side down, on the fabric, and pin together. With an iron on low heat, press down for a few seconds; do not move the iron because this may cause smudges. Before unpinning, pull back a corner of the tracing paper to check that the transfer is visible on the fabric.

Basting through tissue paper

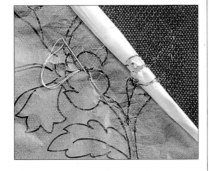

This method is suitable for coarse fabric. Trace the design onto white tissue paper and pin in position on the fabric. Baste over the traced lines, through the paper and fabric, using small uniform stitches. Gently tear off tissue paper. If it doesn't come away easily, gently score the basting lines with a needle. When you have completed the embroidery, remove the basting stitches with tweezers.

Tracing with dressmaker's carbon paper

Dressmaker's carbon paper is made especially for use on fabrics, and is nothing like stationery carbon paper. It works best on smooth fabrics. Use a light color on a dark fabric, and a dark color on a light fabric. Draw the design on thin paper. Place the carbon paper, ink side down, between the fabric and the design. Pin together at the corners, or hold down firmly with one hand. Trace over all the lines of the design with a tracing wheel, or a hard-pointed object, pressing down firmly. Check that you haven't missed any lines before you remove the design and the carbon paper.

Tracing-paper templates

This is a way of transferring simple shapes. It works well on any type of fabric, and is particularly useful for repeating motifs. Draw the design onto thick tracing paper and cut out each separate piece. Pin all the shapes in position on the fabric. Draw around them if the fabric is smooth or baste around them if the fabric is coarse. Use the templates again for a repeating motif. Use clear acetate for a more durable, reuseable template.

125

HEIRLOOM STITCHES

THROUGHOUT THE AGES, and in every culture, people have
made use of needle and thread to create a wide range of
decorative textiles – to be worn, used, or displayed. These
varied examples from North America, the Far East, and Europe
– demonstrating the effects of different stitches – can be used
as inspiration for your own imaginative efforts.

Victorian beaded
purses were
a popular
accessory

These late 19th century
North American Indian cuffs
have two strips of beads
twisted together and
couched to the edge

The flowers on this
Chinese boy's hat
are embroidered
in satin stitches

Insects have seeding
and single straight
stitch details worked
over the satin stitch

Motifs of couched
beadwork with small
clusters of beads
stitched in
individually

The scalloped
edge is worked in
buttonhole stitch

The flowers on this English
1820s hem are worked
in padded satin stitch

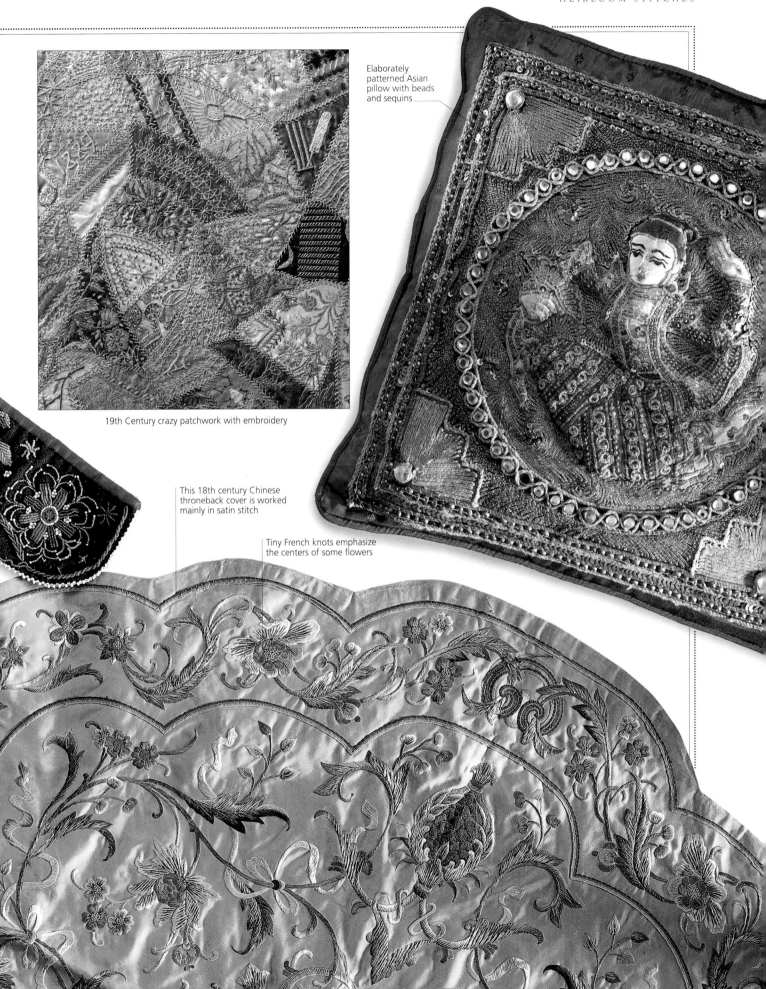

19th Century crazy patchwork with embroidery

Elaborately patterned Asian pillow with beads and sequins

This 18th century Chinese throneback cover is worked mainly in satin stitch

Tiny French knots emphasize the centers of some flowers

FLAT STITCHES

IT MAY SEEM there is an infinite variety of embroidery stitches. In fact, they are all variations on a few basic stitches, categorized into four groups: Flat stitches, crossed stitches, looped stitches, and knot stitches.

The flat stitches are perhaps the simplest and easiest to learn; those shown here are based on two of the oldest known stitches: Running stitch and backstitch. They are all formed with flat, straight stitches. The stitches can be worked in a number of different sizes, grouped with other stitches in varying combinations, or worked in different directions to form borders, outlines, and blocks of color in your designs.

Star worked in split stitch

Bands of encroaching satin stitch are set off by two rows of running stitch

Double running stitch frames the laced running stitch circle

Whipped running stitch borders trim a pocket edge decorated with half sun shapes worked in straight stitches

EMBROIDERED SHIRT POCKETS

Shirt pockets provide an ideal area to decorate with simple or elaborate embroidery motifs. Initials and monograms are the classic embellishment for pockets, but why not let your imagination have free rein: Use a variety of stitches worked together to add pattern and color to shirt pockets for all the family and create a unique effect.

Running stitch

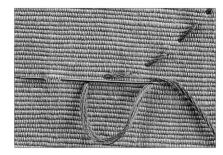

Take several small, even stitches at one time. The stitches on the wrong side of the fabric are usually half the size or less of the stitches on the right side.

Laced running stitch

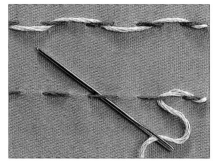

Lace the running stitches with a round-pointed needle by sliding it between the stitches and the fabric. Take the needle alternately through the bottom of one stitch and then the top of the next stitch. Do not pick up any fabric.

Whipped running stitch

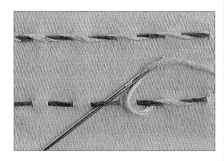

Work a row of running stitches. With a round-pointed needle, weave contrasting thread through each stitch from top to bottom, sliding the needle between the stitches and the fabric. Do not pick up any fabric.

Double running stitch

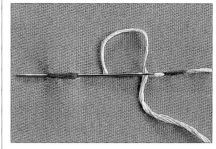

Work a row of running stitches. In same direction, work a second row, in same or a contrasting color, to fill spaces between stitches in first row.

Backstitch

Take a small backward stitch, and bring the needle through to the right side again in front of the stitch you just made. Take another backward stitch, inserting the needle at the point where the first stitch stops. Keep the length of the stitches even.

Stem stitch

Work from left to right, taking regular, slanted backstitches. The thread should always emerge slightly above the previous stitch.

Encroaching satin stitch

Work the first row as for satin stitch. Work subsequent rows so that the head of the new stitch is between the bases of the stitches above.

Split stitch

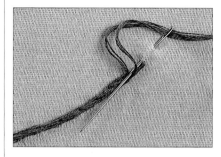

Work in the same way as stem stitch, but the thread of the new stitch should split the thread of the previous stitch.

Straight stitch

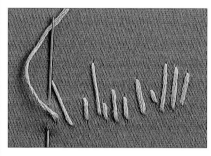

These single, spaced stitches may vary in size. Do not make them too long or too loose.

Satin stitch

Work the straight stitches against each other to completely fill area. Make sure stitches are fairly short and uniform.

Seed stitch

Work very small uniform stitches to cover area to be filled, changing stitch direction as desired. For a stronger effect, work two stitches close together instead.

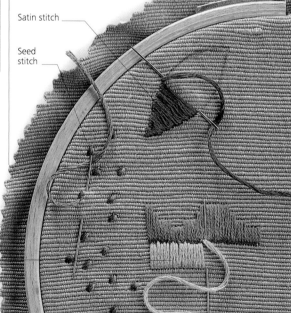

Satin stitch

Seed stitch

Encroaching satin stitch

CROSSED STITCHES

BASIC CROSS STITCH is probably the most popular of all the embroidery stitches; it is quick and easy to master, and can be worked singly or in rows. One stitch fills a small square. This means that designs can be worked out in grid form; it is simple to work out your own design on graph paper, shading the squares with colored pencils.

There is a wide variety of crossed stitches, and all are formed by stitches crossing each other at differing angles. To work a neat row of crossed stitches, the head and base of each stitch should be the same number of rows apart. If the threads in the fabric are too fine to count, work the stitches between two lines of basting stitches and remove them afterward.

EMBROIDERED HANDKERCHIEFS

A few simple cross stitch patterns can enliven a plain or printed handkerchief and make an attractive, personalized gift.

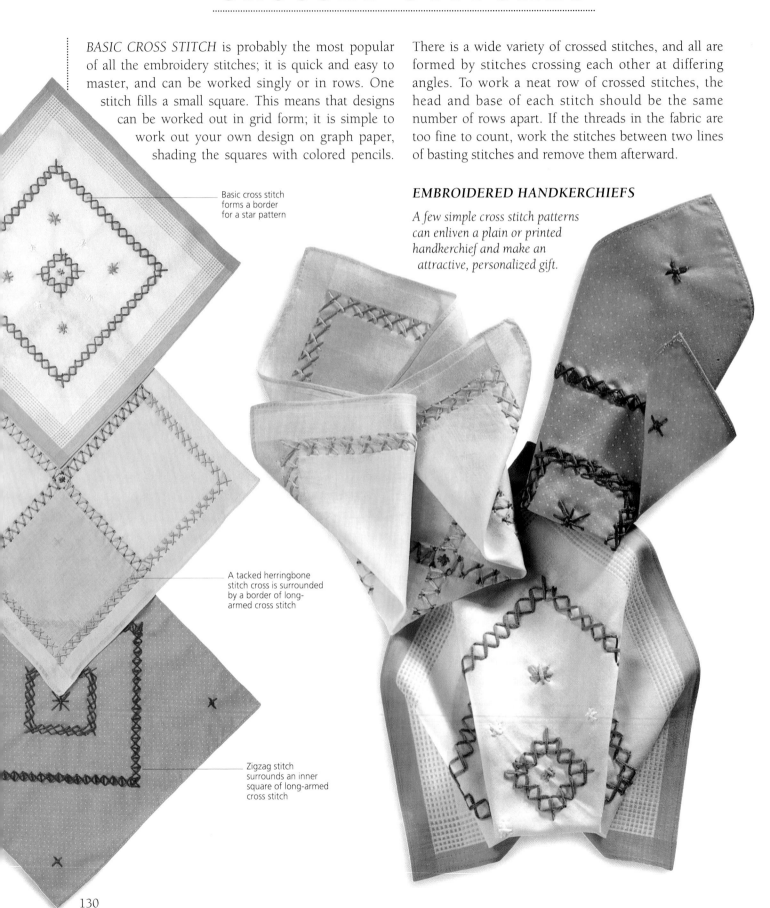

Basic cross stitch forms a border for a star pattern

A tacked herringbone stitch cross is surrounded by a border of long-armed cross stitch

Zigzag stitch surrounds an inner square of long-armed cross stitch

130

Basic cross stitch

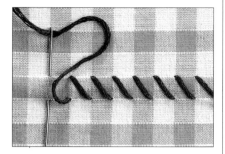

1 Work one or more evenly spaced diagonal stitches in one direction.

2 Cover with one or more diagonal stitches worked in opposite direction.

Long-armed cross stitch

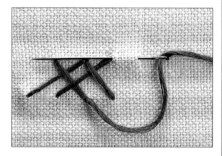

1 Bring the needle through at the stitch base line and take a long diagonal stitch to the right, at desired height of stitches. Measure the diagonal stitch, and bring out needle half this distance to the left, on the top line.

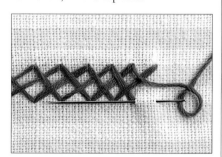

2 Take a diagonal stitch to base line, insert needle directly below the point where needle was inserted on top line. Bring needle out directly below the point where it emerged on the top line.

A wide variety of star shapes can be created using crossed stitches

Herringbone stitch

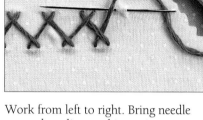

Work from left to right. Bring needle out on base line, and insert it on top line, a little to the right. Take a small stitch to the left along top line. Then, insert the needle on base line directly below the point where needle first entered. Thread should be above the needle. Keep the spacing even.

Tacked herringbone stitch

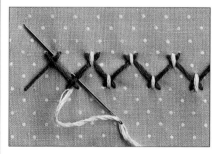

Work a row of herringbone stitch. In a contrasting colored thread, working from right to left, sew each cross together with a small vertical stitch.

Closed herringbone stitch

Work in the same way as herringbone stitch but with no spaces left between the stitches. The diagonals should touch at the top and bottom.

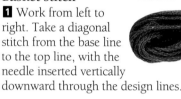

Basket stitch (step1)

Basket stitch (step 2)

Basket stitch

1 Work from left to right. Take a diagonal stitch from the base line to the top line, with the needle inserted vertically downward through the design lines.

2 Take a vertical downward stitch to the left and into the same holes as the two previous crossed stitches.

Zigzag stitch

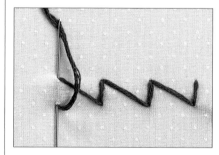

1 Work from right to left. Take alternate upright and long diagonal stitches to the end of the row.

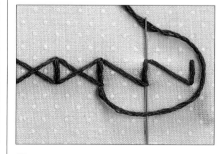

2 Work from left to right. Take upright stitches into the same holes as the previous upright stitches, and reverse the direction of the diagonal stitches so they cross each other.

LOOPED STITCHES

CHAIN STITCH IS the most important of the looped stitches. It is an extremely versatile stitch, which can be worked in thick yarns or fine silk threads.

All the stitches in this group are formed from loops that are held in place with small stitches. They can be used both for outlining and for filling shapes. When used as filling stitches, they are generally worked in rows, and stitched in the same direction, to create an all-over texture.

EMBROIDERED SHIRT COLLARS

Shirt collars provide endless opportunity for imaginative stitch decoration. Here, open Cretan stitch is worked in rows to produce a lattice trimmed with closed Cretan stitch and detached chain stitch (above). Blanket stitch trims the edge and forms shapes decorated with feather stitch and open chain stitch (below).

Lazy daisy flowers and feather stitch stems decorate this shirt collar and front

The buttons each have a lazy daisy to match the collar

Chain stitch

Bring the needle out at the position for the first stitch. Loop thread and hold it down with your left thumb. Insert the needle where it first emerged, and bring the tip out a short distance below this point. Keep the thread under the tip of the needle, and pull the needle through. To make the next stitch, insert the needle into the hole from which it has just emerged.

Lazy Daisy stitch (detached chain)

Work a single chain stitch, as described above. To secure the stitch, insert the needle just below the base of the loop and bring it out at the position for the next chain stitch.

Blanket stitch

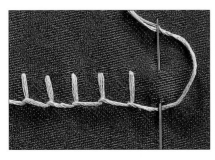

Work from left to right. Bring the thread out at the position for the looped edging. Insert the needle above and a little to the left of this point as shown, and take a straight downward stitch, with the thread under the tip of the needle. Pull up the stitch to form the loop, and repeat.

Checkered chain stitch

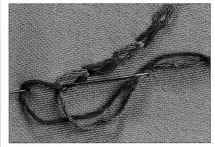

Thread the needle with two contrasting colored threads. Work as for chain stitch, keeping the thread not in use above the point of the needle.

Open chain stitch (ladder stitch)

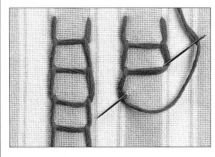

Bring needle out at left guideline. Hold thread down with left thumb, and insert needle at right guideline, opposite point where thread emerged. Bring needle out again at left guideline, with thread under needle. Continue anchoring right side as for left.

Feather stitch

Work vertically from top to bottom. Bring needle out at top center. Hold thread down with your left thumb, and insert needle to right and slightly below. Take a small slanting stitch toward the center, with thread under needle. Insert needle again on left side, and take a slanting stitch down toward the center, with thread under needle. Work looped stitches to left and right alternately.

Double feather stitch (fancy)

This is worked in the same way as feather stitch, but two stitches are taken instead of one.

Closed Cretan stitch

1 Bring the needle through centrally at left side of shape. Take a small stitch on the lower guideline, with the needle pointing inward and the thread under the tip of the needle.

2 Take a small stitch on upper guideline, with needle pointing inward and thread under needle. Repeat steps 1 and 2 until shape is filled.

Open Cretan stitch

Work by making short vertical stitches downward and upward alternately, with the thread always held down to the right under the tip of the needle.

KNOTTED STITCHES

KNOTTED STITCHES PRODUCE various exciting surface textures and look particularly attractive when worked with thick thread. They are formed by looping the thread around the needle, and then pulling the needle through the loops to form a knot or twist on the surface of the fabric.

If you haven't tried a particular knotted stitch before, work several samples on a piece of scrap fabric first because it takes a little practice to get the tension of the knots even. To avoid your thread getting into tangles, always hold the loops of thread down with your left thumb when you pull the needle through.

Scroll stitch and French knots are edged with a row of zigzag coral stitch

EMBROIDERED SHIRT CUFFS

Decorating shirt cuffs can be as subtle or as extrovert as you like. Cream and white embroidery on a white shirt can add just a hint of luxury or contrasting colors can be used according to your mood. Either way you can create an entirely individual look.

Zigzag coral stitch rows are decorated with arrows of bullion knots

Knotted chain stitch rows border small bullion knots and four-legged knot stitches

French knot

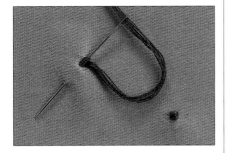

Bring out the needle at the position for the knot. Twist the needle 2 or 3 times around the thread. Turn the needle and insert it just above where the thread first emerged. Holding the working thread taut with the left hand, pull the thread through to the back of the work. For a larger knot, use 2 or more strands of thread.

Bullion knot

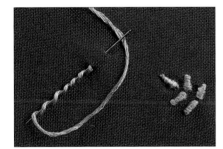

Make a backstitch, the size of the knot required, bringing the needle half way out at the point where it first emerged. Twist the thread around needle as many times as required to equal the size of backstitch. Holding your left thumb on the coiled thread, pull the needle through. Then turn the needle back to where it was inserted, and pull the thread through to the back of the work, so that the bullion knot lies flat.

Scroll stitch

Bring the needle out on the guideline. Loop thread to right. Insert needle in loop, and over working thread as shown. Pull through to form a knot.

Coral stitch

Work from right to left. Bring the thread out, and hold it with your left thumb along the line to be worked. Take a small stitch under and over the looped working thread. Pull thread through to form knot. The spacing of the knots can be varied as required. (*See top right.*)

Zigzag coral stitch

Bring the needle out at top left. Lay thread across fabric to right margin to form first diagonal. Loop the thread; insert the needle and take a small diagonal stitch, bringing the needle tip out at the center of the loop. Pull the needle through the loop to form the knot. Lay the thread across the fabric to left margin for second diagonal, and repeat knot stitch. Continue knotting at right and left margins alternately for form zigzag.

Four-legged knot stitch

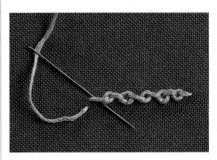

1 Take a vertical stitch and bring the needle out at center right, ready to form horizontal leg of cross.

2 Slide the needle between the vertical stitch and the fabric, without picking up any fabric. Loop the thread around the needle, and pull the needle through to form the knot. Take a small horizontal stitch to left, to form last leg of cross (*see right*).

Zigzag coral stitch

Knotted chain stitch (link stitch)

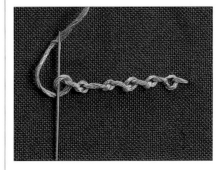

1 Take an upward diagonal stitch, and bring out the needle directly below the point where it has just been inserted. Slide the needle between the stitch and the fabric, keeping the looped thread on the left.

2 Loop the working thread under the tip of the needle and pull through to form the knot.

135

COUCHING & LAIDWORK

COUCHING IS A quick and easy method of laying one strand of thread on the fabric, and catching it down at intervals with a separate strand of thread. More than one strand can be laid down at a time to create bold outlines. Textured and metallic threads, which won't pass through the fabric easily, can be laid down with finer thread. It is also useful for filling large shapes rapidly to produce solid areas of color.

Laidwork is really a continuation of couching. Long threads (grid threads) are laid on the fabric in a grid pattern, and then secured at the intersections with a separate thread. The method produces quite complicated-looking lattice filling stitches.

For the best results, use an embroidery frame in order to keep the fabric taut, and make sure that the grid threads are evenly spaced.

Basic method

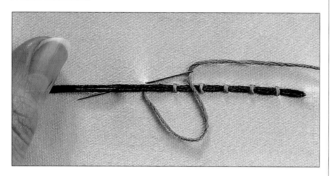

Work from right to left. Bring out the strand to be laid and use your left thumb to hold it in place. Bring out the working (couching) thread just below the laid strand. Take a vertical stitch over the laid strand, bringing the needle out to the left, below the laid strand, ready for the next stitch. At the end of the line, take both the couching thread and laid thread through to back of work, and secure.

To fill an area

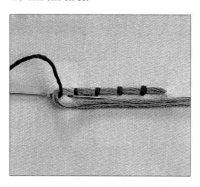

1 Work a line of basic couching. At the end of the line, turn the loose laid thread to the right and take a horizontal stitch across the turning point.

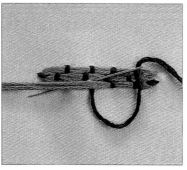

2 Turn the work upside-down and couch second row of threads next to first, placing stitches between those on the previous row. Continue until the area is filled.

To couch a circle

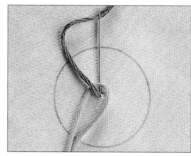

1 Bring out the needle with the laid thread at the center of the circle, and pass the needle through the looped couching thread.

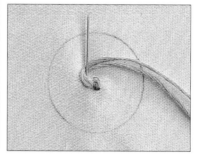

2 Insert the needle at the center to secure the laid thread. With your left thumb, guide the laid thread into a spiral, and couch over it.

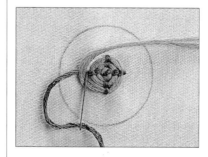

3 Make sure all the couching stitches line up as shown, as if on the spokes of a wheel. Bring threads to the back and secure.

Variations

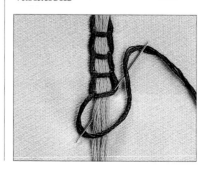

Couching can be worked with two contrasting colored threads or with open chain stitch as shown here (see page 133).

Squared laidwork (open lattice)

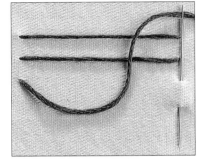

1 To lay horizontal threads, bring needle out at top left-hand guideline, lay thread across to opposite point on right guideline. Insert needle, and bring it out below this stitch, ready to form next horizontal thread. Continue back and forth until all horizontal threads are laid, keeping tension fairly loose so that stitches do not pucker. At end of last stitch, take thread to back of work and secure.

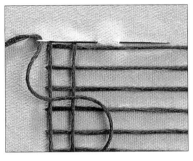

2 To create the lattice effect, lay the vertical stitches across the horizontal threads in the same manner.

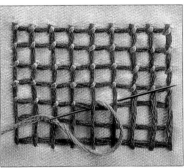

3 Bring out the couching thread at the top left corner of the grid. Secure each intersection of the vertical and horizontal threads with a small, slanting stitch.

Variations

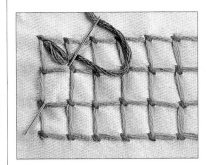

1 Make the squared laidwork, and make a series of 4 detached chain stitches (*see page 133*) within 4 lattice squares. Make the anchoring stitch at the center of the 4 squares.

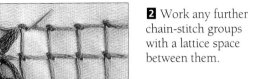

2 Work any further chain-stitch groups with a lattice space between them.

EMBROIDERED PARTY SHOES

Plain black velvet children's shoes can be dressed up with embroidery and circles couched in metallic thread – and transformed into sophisticated party slippers for that first grown-up evening out. The same techniques in cotton thread could be applied to tennis shoes for casual wear.

Spirals of metallic gold thread make little coin-like motifs

Lazy Daisy stitch decorates an open lattice of laidwork

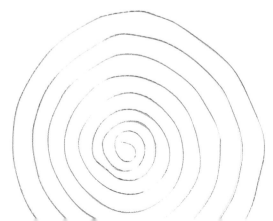

ALPHABETS & MONOGRAMS

EMBROIDERED INITIALS, MONOGRAMS, and messages are used to personalize clothes and gifts. Cross stitch is the traditional way to work the name and date on samplers, and is still the most popular lettering stitch for embroidered pictures.

The smooth, even look of satin stitch is perfect for scrolled initials on table linen, pillowcases, towels, and handkerchiefs. You can use techniques such as padded satin stitch, braidwork, and openwork to add variety to your lettering designs.

Any design incorporating lettering should be easy to read. You can trace examples of alphabets from books and magazines. Transfer the outlines of the letters on to your background fabric. If possible, work on a frame or hoop so that you can keep the stitches even and prevent the fabric from puckering.

The letters and words in a full name or message must be spaced out carefully. Trace all the words onto paper. Then hold the paper away from you and study the effect. If necessary, adjust the spacing before transferring the lettering to the fabric.

SATIN STITCHES

Two variations on satin stitch (see page 129) are ideal for working initials. Before you embark on a monogram, practice working the shapes to obtain a smooth outline.

Satin stitch initials personalize a blue handkerchief

Padded satin stitch

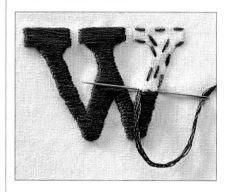

Raising the satin stitch above the surface of the fabric gives it more definition. Fill in outlined area with satin stitch. Then, working in a different direction, add a second layer of satin stitch.

Negative satin stitch

This is an effective technique for monograms and crests. Choose a simple, well defined letter shape. Work the background in satin stitch, leaving the letters in unstitched fabric. Outline the design in stem stitch (*see page 129*) or chain stitch (*see page 133*).

BRAID AND RIBBON LETTERING

For joined lettering, try to plan out the design so that only one piece of ribbon or braid is required for the complete design. If you must add a separate piece, place it underneath the ribbon or braid previously laid down. Raised braids can be couched in a matching or contrasting color.

Fine ribbon and braid can be used for lettering. Hem the short ends by pressing the narrow raw edges to the wrong side. Stitch in place down the center with small running stitches or backstitches.

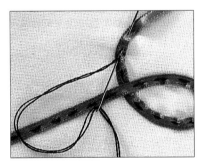

When you reach an intersection, leave a gap in the running stitches. On the return, thread the ribbon or braid through this gap, and continue stitching.

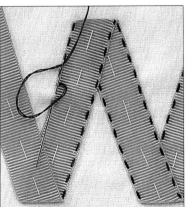

A wide braid or double-sided ribbon may be twisted over to form angles and corners for straight-sided lettering. Baste in position and press. Then stitch along both edges so that they lie flat and even.

A background of openwork stitches emphazises the satin stitch letter

OPENWORK

Satin stitch lettering looks very attractive against a fine openwork background. Work the lettering first, then the background, and outline the letters in stem stitch. Two useful openwork filling stitches are shown below.

Cloud filling stitch

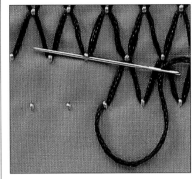

Work rows of small, vertical, evenly spaced stitches across the background area. Use a tapestry needle to lace a second thread through these stitches to form a trellis pattern.

Wave stitch

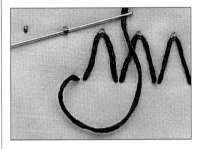

1 Work a row of small, evenly spaced vertical stitches. Bring out needle below and to the right of last stitch, and work a row of arched loops by passing the needle under the vertical stitches.

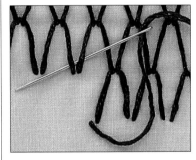

2 On following rows, continue to make arched loops by passing the needle under the pairs of stitch bases in the row directly above.

SAMPLERS

The word sampler comes from the Latin "exemplum", meaning an example to be followed. In the 16th and 17th century, samplers were worked by the high born ladies of the European courts as a method of recording stitches and designs. In the 18th to 19th century they became the province of the school room, to teach the alphabet, a skill necessary for marking bed linen. The designs became more stylized, with decorative borders, religious scripts, and pictures of the home or school. The name of the young embroiderer and the date were usually incorporated.

Detail from a modern cross-stitch sampler

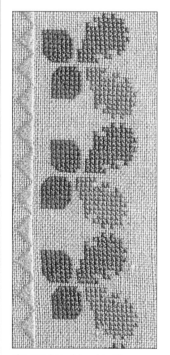

The strawberry (above) is still a favorite motif. It was first used as a Christian symbol denoting perfect righteousness. Flowers and fruit (right) are worked in cross stitch, stem stitch, and satin stitch

A house motif from a modern cross-stitch sampler with straight-stitch detail

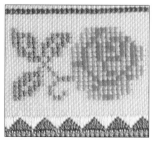

Alphabet detail from a modern sampler, based on an 1822 design

Alphabets in cross stitch and Algerian-eye stitch are divided by narrow bands of pulled threadwork

Crowns and coronets were originally embroidered on the household linens of the aristocracy. By the 18th century, they had become a traditional motif for filling awkward spaces in a design

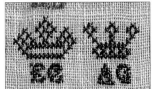

A typical cross-stitch house motif

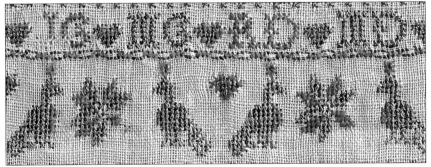

The peacock was a symbol of eternal life in ancient Christian art, and became a popular sampler motif

SCHOOLROOM SAMPLER

All the details shown on this page are from a splendid sampler made by Catherine Gairns in 1831. Two thirds of it is packed with lettering, and the rest is filled with traditional motifs. It was necessary for a young girl to learn how to embroider lettering so that she could mark household linens.

19th century schoolroom samplers were worked almost exclusively in cross stitch, called sampler stitch

141

PULLED THREADWORK

THIS TECHNIQUE HAS been used for centuries to decorate clothing and household items. Stitches are looped around the fabric threads and pulled tightly, to make holes. This combination of stitches and holes creates lacy patterns. Threadwork was traditionally done on cream or white linen with matching thread. Today, we have a wider choice of fabrics, and many of the patterns look lovely when worked in colors.

TOOLS AND MATERIALS

Work on an even-weave fabric, using a thread that is similar in weight to a single thread of the fabric you are using. The working thread must be fairly strong. Pearl cotton, soft embroidery cotton, and crochet cotton are all suitable. Use a round-pointed needle to exaggerate the holes, but make sure it will still slip between the threads easily. Working in a frame isn't essential, but it helps to have both hands free to count the threads and pull the stitches tight.

BASIC WORKING METHOD

If necessary, finish raw edges to prevent fraying (see page 123). Run a line of basting stitches in a contrasting color across the length and width of the fabric to help you count the stitches, and remove them when the work is finished.

Work the stitch patterns in rows, starting at the center and moving outward. Count the fabric threads carefully, and always pull the embroidery thread tight.

Secure the first thread with a few backstitches on the wrong side of the work. Then, when you have finished a row of the pattern, unpick the backstitches, and weave the loose thread under some of the embroidery stitches. Secure all other threads by weaving the ends under worked stitches.

The size of stitches can be varied by stitching over more or fewer threads than the numbers stated in the instructions.

Pin stitch hem

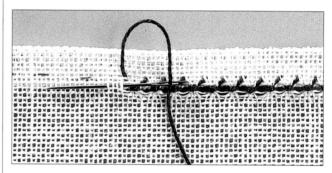

1 Bring needle out on right side, 2 threads above folded hem. Insert needle 2 threads down (through single thickness) just under hem, and bring it out 4 threads to left. Backstitch over same 4 threads and pull tight.

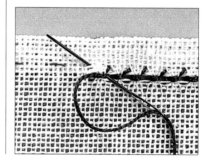

2 Take a 2nd backstitch over the 4 threads, and bring out needle 2 stitches above hemline to start next stitch sequence.

TO MITER THE CORNERS ON A HEM

If you want to make place mats or napkins with pulled-threadwork borders, you must miter the corners of the hems so that they lie flat.

1 Press raw edges to wrong side of fabric. Turn under folded edge again by the same amount to form a double hem, and press. Open fabric.

2 Crease marks will form 4 squares at each corner. Taking one corner at a time, cut off corner by cutting inner square in half diagonally. Fold in sides so that edges just meet at inner corner of inner square. Turn under raw edges.

3 Refold and baste hems. Slip stitch mitered corner edges. Machine or hand stitch hem.

Coil filling stitch

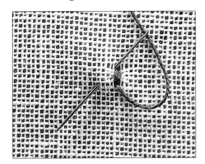

1 Bring out needle on right side. Take 2 vertical satin stitches across 4 threads, into same holes. Take a 3rd satin stitch into top hole, bringing out needle 4 threads to left, on base line of stitches just worked.

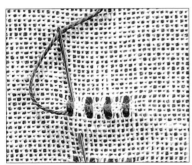

2 To begin next row, bring needle out 4 threads below and 2 threads to right of stitches just worked. Continue working rows from right to left, and left to right, alternately.

Faggot stitch

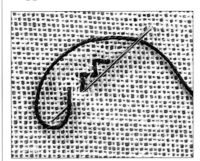

1 Bring out needle on right side of fabric. Work diagonally, and take horizontal and then vertical stitches over an equal number of threads alternately.

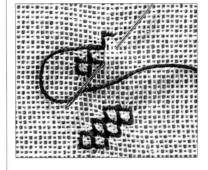

2 On the next row, make squares by working into the holes of the previous row.

Coil filling stitch is made from groups of satin stitches worked in horizontal rows

Honeycomb stitch

 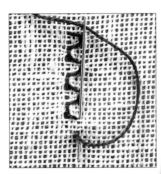

1 Bring the needle out on right side of work. Insert needle 3 threads to right, and bring it out 3 threads down. Take a backstitch into base of stitch just made, and bring it out 3 threads down. Insert needle 3 threads to the left, and bring it out 3 threads down. Take a backstitch into the base of stitch just made, and bring it out 3 threads down. Repeat sequence to end of row.

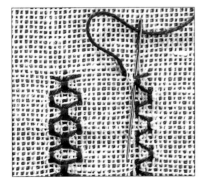

2 Turn the work at end of row, and embroider the next row in the same way.

Honeycomb stitch forms a regular lattice filling, and is worked from top to bottom

Faggot stitch is a useful basic stitch for patterning and background filling

Chessboard filling stitch

1 Work 3 rows of satin stitch from left to right, and right to left, alternately. Each satin stitch is worked over 3 threads, and each block is made up of 3 rows of 8 stitches.

2 At end of 3rd row, turn the work as shown, and bring out needle 3 vertical threads down and one horizontal thread to the left, ready to start next block.

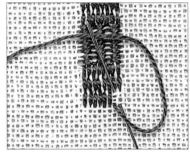

3 Repeat step 1. Work all other blocks in the same way, turning the work after each to change the stitch direction.

Diagonal raised band

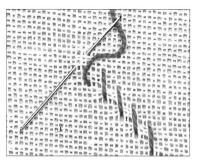

1 Bring needle out on right side at bottom right-hand corner. Insert it 6 threads up to form first vertical stitch, and bring it out 3 threads down and 3 to left. Pull thread very tight to make a ridged effect. Repeat.

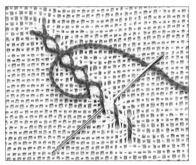

2 Insert needle 6 threads to right to form first horizontal stitch, and bring it out 3 threads down and 3 to left, ready to start next stitch. Pull tight. Repeat.

Wave stitch

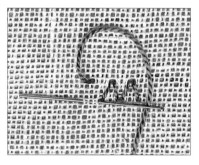

1 Working from right to left, bring needle out on right side of work, and insert it 4 threads down and 2 to the right, to form the first diagonal stitch. Bring it out 4 threads to the left and insert it at the point where the thread emerged.

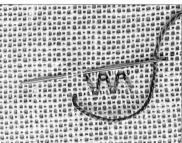

2 Bring out the needle, 4 threads to the left in line with top of V-shape formed, to start the next diagonal stitch. Repeat to end of row.

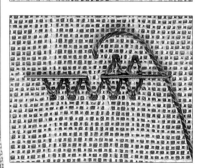

3 To start second row, insert needle 8 threads down from top of V-shape formed. Turn the work upside-down and work second row of zigzags as in step 1.

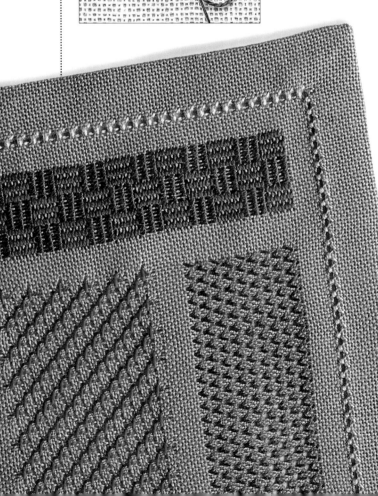

Chessboard filling stitch is shown in blue, diagonal raised band in red, and wave stitch in green

DRAWN THREADWORK BORDERS

IN DRAWN THREADWORK, some of the warp and weft threads of the fabric are removed, and the remaining threads in the drawn area can then be pulled together in clusters with the embroidery thread to form open patterns. The technique is used mainly for border decorations on table cloths and place mats.

TOOLS AND MATERIALS

If you are a beginner, you will find it easier to remove the threads from a coarse open-weave fabric rather than a closely woven one. To hemstitch the border, use stranded cotton or pearl cotton similar in thickness to a single thread of the ground fabric you have chosen, and work with a round-pointed tapestry needle.

How to remove the fabric threads

1 Cut your chosen fabric to size, allowing for a mitered hem around all four sides (*see page 142*). Mark out the hem allowance with a row of basting stitches or an embroidery marker. Decide on the number of threads that will make up the depth of the border and mark the inner border line, then mark the center point on each side.

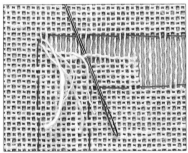

2 Using a pair of sharp embroidery scissors, carefully cut horizontal fabric threads at the center mark on each side of border. Gently ease out threads with a tapestry needle until you reach corners.

3 Trim loose thread ends. Then fold them back, and backstitch over ends. Remove basting stitches. Turn up hem allowance, and baste in position, ready for hem stitching.

Hemstitch

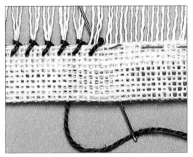

1 Work from left to right on the wrong side of the fabric. Bring needle out 2 threads below hem, and opposite first loose thread in border. Take a diagonal stitch to right, and insert needle under first 3 or more loose threads in border; pull together.

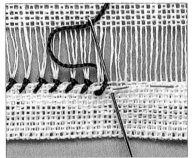

2 Take vertical stitch, bringing needle out on wrong side, to right of bundle and 2 threads below hem. Repeat.

Ladder stitch variation

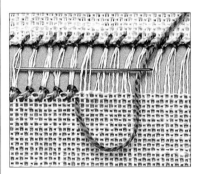

Complete a row of hemstitch. Turn the work upside-down and work hemstitch along opposite edge of border, catching the same loose threads into bundles, forming a ladder-like pattern.

To finish corners

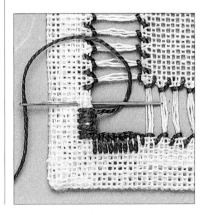

If the open squares at the corners are small, they can be left as they are, or they can be reinforced with blanket stitch (*see page 133*).

SMOCKING

AN ATTRACTIVE WAY of reducing the fullness in fabric is to gather material into tiny pleats, and work over them with embroidery stitches. The patterns can be worked in one stitch only or several stitches can be combined into elaborate patterns, according to the effect desired. When the embroidery is finished, the gathering stitches are removed and the fabric relaxes slightly. Extensively used in England in the eighteenth and nineteenth centuries to create comfortable garments for rural workers, it remains a popular and interesting way to shape and decorate clothes for children and adults. It also can be used for accessories, and all sorts of items for the home such as pillows, lampshades, and curtains.

MATERIALS AND TOOLS

Any type of fabric can be smocked if it is supple enough to be gathered. Regular repeating patterns, such as checks and dots, are popular because the pattern can be used as a guideline for the gathering stitches. Work with a crewel needle and strong cotton thread for the gathering stitches. The embroidery can be worked in either embroidery floss, pearl cotton, or matte embroidery cotton.

CUTTING THE FABRIC

Smocking is always worked before a garment is made up. The amount of fabric needed is usually three times the finished width of the smocked area. Less fabric is required when working on a thick material.

GATHERING THE FABRIC

Work the rows of gathering stitches from right to left, on the wrong side of the fabric, using a strongly contrasting thread. The contrast color will help you remove the gathering thread easily when the smocking is finished.

To gather fabric

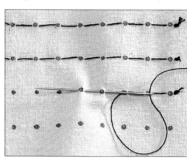

1 Cut a length of thread, longer than row of dots to be gathered, and tie a knot. Make running stitches along each row, picking up a piece of the fabric at each dot. Leave thread ends loose.

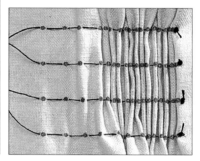

2 Pull up each gathering thread to the required width and tie together in pairs at the end of the rows. Make sure all pleats are even and that gathers are not pulled too tightly.

MARKING THE FABRIC FOR GATHERING

In England, the rows for the gathering stitches are marked on the wrong side, in America, on the right. In either case, the easiest way to do this is with a smocking-dot transfer. This is an iron-on transfer with rows of equally spaced dots printed across it. The space between dots is usually 1/4 to 3/8 inch, and 3/8 to 1/2 inch between rows. In general, the finer the fabric, the closer the dots and rows. Make sure the dots are in line with the threads of the fabric, then iron in position, following the hot-iron transfer method on page 125.

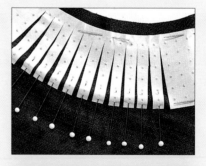

To mark a curved area, such as a yoke, slash the transfer and pin in place before ironing.

You can make your own guide from thin cardboard and mark out dots in pencil. Position the points on a row of dots, and mark the next row at the base of each V.

SMOCKING STITCHES

These stitches are worked on the right side of the gathered fabric. All the stitches shown here are worked from left to right, beginning at the top left-hand corner. Make sure the embroidery thread is attached and fastened off very securely. Hold the needle parallel to the gathering threads, and take the stitches through about one-third of the depth of each pleat, to keep them elastic, and to ensure that the embroidery thread doesn't become entangled with the gathering thread. Leave the first row of gathers free of embroidery so that the smocked panel can be joined to another piece. Smocking stitches vary considerably in tension, so work a sampler first to see how tight or loose a stitch will be. Intricate patterns can be made with a combination of smocking stitches, although equally impressive results can be achieved by working only one or two. Other embroidery stitches such as Lazy Daisy (see page 133), cross stitch (see page 131) and chain stitch (see page 133) may be worked over two or more pleats between the rows of smocking for extra decoration. The gaps between rows should not be too wide or the pleats will puff out.

Stem stitch

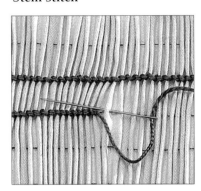

Working it like a basic stem stitch, use this stitch for the top row of smocking. Bring needle out to left of first fold. Take a stitch through top of each fold, keeping thread below needle.

Cable stitch

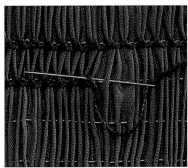

1 Bring needle out to left of first fold. With the thread below the needle, take a stitch over the 2nd fold, and bring the needle out between the first and 2nd folds.

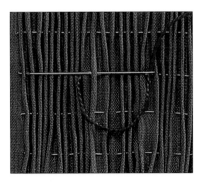

2 With thread above needle, take a stitch over 3rd fold, and bring needle out between 2nd and 3rd folds. Continue to the end of the row, keeping the thread alternately above, then below, needle.

Wheat stitch

This variation of stem stitch produces a tight stitch. Work a row of stem stitch, then work a second row just below, keeping the thread above the needle to alter stitch direction.

Double cable stitch

Work one row of cable stitch, starting with the thread below the needle. Work a 2nd row underneath it, starting with the thread above the needle.

Honeycomb stitch

1 This stitch is worked across 2 lines of gathering stitches. Bring needle out at left of first fold on top of line of gathering stitches, and take a backstitch over first 2 folds to draw them together. Take a 2nd stitch over 2 folds, bringing needle out at lower line of gathering stitches, between first and 2nd fold.

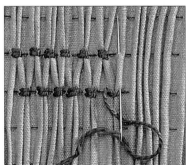

2 Take a backstitch over 2nd and 3rd folds to draw them together. Take a 2nd stitch over these folds, bringing needle out at top line of gathering stitches, between 2nd and 3rd fold.

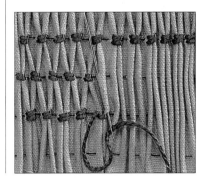

3 Continue working stitches on top and bottom lines of gathering stitches alternately.

Wave stitch

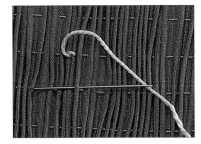

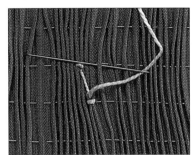

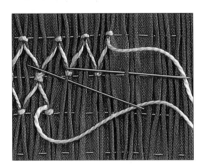

1 Work across 2 lines of gathering. Bring needle out left of 1st fold on top line. With thread above needle, take a stitch over 2nd fold. Bring it out between 1st and 2nd folds. With thread at lower line, and above needle, take stitch over 3rd fold. Bring needle out between 2nd and 3rd folds.

2 With thread below needle, take stitch over 4th fold. Bring it out between 3rd and 4th folds. With thread at top line and below needle, take a stitch over 5th fold. Bring it out between 4th and 5th folds.

3 Next row, work between 3rd line of gathering and bases of stitches above.

Trellis diamond

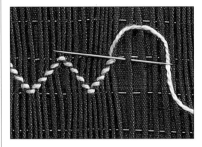

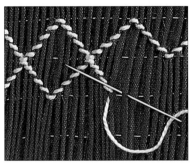

1 Work one row of stem stitch in a chevron pattern between 2 lines of gathering stitches, keeping thread below needle when working up, and above needle on the way down.

2 Start at 2nd line of gathering stitches, and work another row of stem stitch chevron pattern between lines 2 and 3, inverting chevrons to form a diamond trellis.

Surface honeycomb stitch

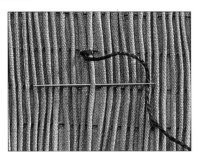

1 Work across 2 lines of gathering. Bring the needle out to the left of 1st fold, on the top line. With the thread above the needle, take a stitch over and to the left of the 2nd fold. With the thread at the lower line and above the needle, insert the needle between the 2nd and 3rd folds; bring it out to the left of the 2nd fold.

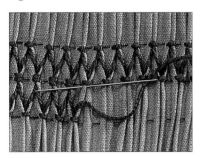

2 With the thread below the needle, take a stitch over 2nd and 3rd folds: Bring it out to left of 3rd. With the thread at the top line and below the needle, insert the needle between 3rd and 4th folds. Work next row between the 2nd and 3rd rows of gathering stitches.

This drawstring bag is worked in trellis diamond and surface honeycomb stitches

TO FINISH

When a smocked piece is finished, steam press on the wrong side, or lay a damp cloth on top and lightly pass a hot iron over the work, taking care not to flatten it. Then remove the gathering threads.

If you find that the smocking is too tight, take out the gathering stitches, lay the work wrong side on the ironing board, and pin it out to size. Steam press as above.

BEADS & SEQUINS

THROUGHOUT THE AGES, in every culture, and in every part of the world beads and sequins have been used to add extra sparkle and richness to textiles and to denote the wearer's wealth and standing. Fashions change, and today we see beading on everything from glittering evening clothes to T-shirts. However, beads and sequins can also be used creatively to highlight areas on embroidered pictures and hangings – for example, a single pearl bead looks wonderful in the center of a flower, or two flashing green sequins can suggest a cat's eyes.

BEADING

Use an ordinary sewing needle for beads with large holes. If, however, the beads have very small holes, you will need a fine beading needle, see page 120.

Sewing on beads individually

Bring out the needle and thread the bead. If the bead is round, insert needle back through same hole. With a long shaped bead, hold down with the thumb and insert needle close to edge of bead. Repeat.

Couching rows of beads

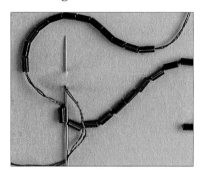

Use two needles. Bring out 1st needle, and thread beads. Bring out 2nd needle close to left of first bead and take a small stitch over thread. Slide next bead up, and repeat.

Strand fringe

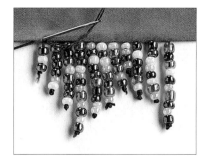

Tie first bead onto thread, and knot securely. (If beads are large, start with a small bead.) Thread beads for one fringe strand; secure to hem with a small backstitch. Repeat for each strand.

APPLYING SEQUINS

With matching sewing thread, sequins may be stitched on almost invisibly. An embroidery thread in a contrasting color can add to the decorative effect.

Two-stitch method

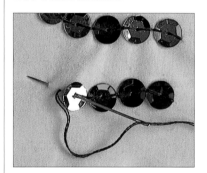

Use to secure one or more sequins. Bring out needle and thread sequin. Take a backstitch over right edge of sequin and bring out needle at left edge. Stitch through sequin again and repeat.

Invisible stitching

Bring out needle and thread on sequin. Take a stitch over its left edge; place a 2nd sequin so that right edge covers eye of 1st. Bring out needle at left edge of 2nd sequin and insert needle in its eye.

Securing sequins with beads

Bring out needle; thread on a sequin and a bead. Insert needle through sequin eye and pull thread so that bead holds sequin in its place. Bring out needle at position for next sequin.

SPECIAL EFFECTS

ONCE YOU HAVE mastered the basic embroidery stitches, you might like to experiment with some of the traditional forms of embroidery that depend upon a combination of stitches to achieve a particular effect. Four of the the most popular are shown here – blackwork, whitework, stumpwork, and crewel work.

CREWEL WORK

This type of embroidery gets its name from the very fine wool yarn with which it is worked. Since it is difficult to create small, intricate stitches in wool, the designs are generally bold and free-flowing. Crewel work has always been popular for home furnishings, and also looks very decorative on clothing and accessories. Traditional themes include exotic animals, birds, flowers and trees. The basic shapes are usually worked in a simple outline stitch and then filled in with a variety of broader stitches. Choose a firm, medium-weight fabric on which to stitch your designs.

Crewel-work design

This landscape shows how outline shapes can be enhanced with textured filling stitches. Branches are worked in stem stitch, berries are French knots, and the foreground is satin stitch. Useful stitches include split and herringbone.

STUMPWORK

This is an interesting way of making embroidery more three-dimensional. It is done by combining padded appliqué and embroidery stitches. Stumpwork was very popular in the last century for decorating boxes and screens. It is also very effective on pictures and wall hangings. Choose lightweight fabrics for the best results.

Appliqué shapes are stitched to a background fabric and one end is left open for stuffing. Once the appliqué is stitched closed, you can embroider the surrounding area and the padded shapes. Raised stitches with a clearly defined surface texture – such as padded satin stitch, couching – and any of the knotted stitches combine well with padded appliqué. Instructions for the padded appliqué sachet and turkey-stitch sunflower are on page 241.

Padded appliqué

1 Cut out your appliqué shape, slightly larger than finished size, and hand stitch to right side of fabric (*see appliqué, page 200*). Leave a small section open to insert the stuffing. Push in some batting and distribute it evenly.

2 Sew up the opening neatly by hand. The padded appliqué motif may then be left as it is or decorated with embroidery stitches or even beadwork.

French knots decorate this appliquéd heart

The petals are embroidered with seeding and couching

WHITEWORK

The general name given to any type of
white embroidery on white fabric, whitework
is a beautiful way of decorating fine bed linen,
tablecloths, and blouses.

When only one color is used for both the background
fabric and the embroidery, subtle contrasts, such as the
look of the thread against the fabric and the texture of
the stitch, become important. Most surface stitches will
be enhanced by working them in a thread with a high
sheen on a matte background fabric. Bands of pulled and
drawn threadwork (see pages 142 to 145) will add texture
to the design. For an even stronger contrast, hem sections of
fabric with a close buttonhole stitch to prevent fraying, then
cut away sections within the buttonhole. This technique is
called cutwork, and the basic method is given below.

The pillow shown right is worked with high-sheen pearl
cotton thread on crisp linen. It has a cutwork border, and
strongly defined surface embroidery done with whip stitch
and French knot. The narrow satin ribbon is threaded
through a band of open chain stitch.

Cutwork border
is edged with
buttonhole stitch

Cutwork

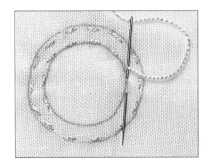

1 This is easier
to work in a frame.
Outline the section
of the background
fabric that is to be
cut away with a
small running
stitch in embroidery
floss or cotton
pearl thread.

2 Work a close
buttonhole stitch
in matching thread
around this outline.
The ridged edge of
the buttonhole stitch
should just cover the
running stitch, as
shown above.

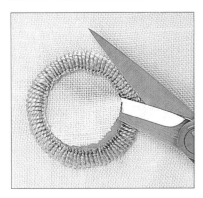

3 From the
wrong side of fabric,
carefully cut out the
fabric shape close
to the base of the
buttonhole stitching.

BLACKWORK

A form of counted-thread embroidery, blackwork depends on
simple stitches worked in one color over a precise number of
fabric threads; it forms repetitive geometric patterns, and the
spacing of the stitches creates dark, medium, and light areas
within the design. Traditionally, the embroidery is worked in
black thread on linen. It was very popular in Tudor England,
and was used to decorate clothing and bed linen.

Work the design using backstitch, running stitch, double
running stitch, and cross stitches for stars. Outline different
patterned shapes in chain stitch, stem stitch, or couching.
Work small parts of the design in satin stitch to create solid
black areas to contrast with lighter, open-stitch patterns.
A combination of straight and crossed stitches can be used
to form elaborate borders and large motifs, as shown below.

BLOCKING & MOUNTING

ONCE FINISHED, MOST pieces of embroidery only require a light pressing on the wrong side of the background fabric. However, if the work has become badly distorted, it will need to be soaked and blocked to remove any creases and to ease it back into shape. There are as many ways to display finished work as there are different types of embroidery. If you plan on framing your work, it must first be mounted.

PRESSING

Never put an iron on the right side of a piece of embroidery as it will flatten the stitches, and may scorch the piece.

Place embroidery, right side down, on a padded surface. Cover it with a damp or dry cloth (depending on type of fabric). With iron at correct setting for fabric, press very gently all over.

BLOCKING

Check that the background fabric and floss on yarn will not run when wet (see page 153), otherwise the piece will have to be blocked dry. With modern fabrics this isn't usually a problem, but care should be taken with old or ethnic fabrics.

1 Soak the embroidery in cold water, and roll it in a clean towel to remove the excess moisture.

2 Cover a soft board with plastic or cotton, and pin it in position. Lay the embroidery on top of the covered board, right side up. Using steel pins, pin the embroidery at each corner, keeping the pins outside the area of work. Stretch the piece, and pin at one-inch intervals, starting at the center. Leave pinned until completely dry.

MOUNTING

To frame embroidery, the piece first must be mounted on stiff cardboard. The board should be cut to the same size as the work, or slightly larger to accommodate a mat or a frame with an edge that might hide some of the stitching.

1 Press the finished embroidery, and lay it right side down on a table. Center the cardboard on top, and turn the edges of the fabric to the back of the board.

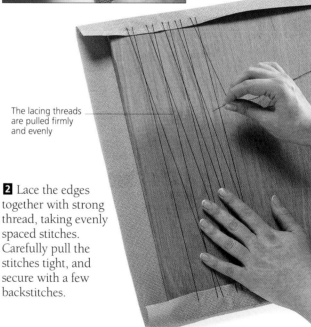

The lacing threads are pulled firmly and evenly

2 Lace the edges together with strong thread, taking evenly spaced stitches. Carefully pull the stitches tight, and secure with a few backstitches.

3 Fold and lace the side edges, in the same way, pulling evenly so that the work is stretched smoothly across the board.

CLEANING

DUST, DIRT AND moths are the three main enemies of embroidered textiles. Regular inspection, a gentle wash when necessary, and careful storage will guard against all three. If the embroidery is delicate, it is better to play it safe; take it to a specialist rather than attempting to clean it yourself.

HAND WASHING

Most modern embroidery threads are colorfast, but you should still make a test before washing. You can either test scraps of the threads in hot water, or press a wet cotton ball against the wrong side of the work, and check for staining. Dark colors and shades of red are the most likely to run; if this happens, take the piece to a reliable dry cleaner.

If the embroidery is lined, the lining should be removed and washed separately. It is a good idea to measure your upholstery covers before washing so that they can be blocked to the correct size afterward.

1 Press a wet ball of cotton onto the threads to see if any dye runs into it. If it does, do not wash.

2 Wash all embroideries very gently by hand in lukewarm water, using pure soap flakes or a mild detergent recommended for delicate fabrics. Do not rub the piece; rinse several times in lukewarm water until the water runs clear. The final rinse should be in cold water.

3 Roll up the embroidery in a thick towel to blot the excess water. Repeat if necessary.

4 Pull gently to shape, or block if necessary, and dry flat at room temperature.

STORAGE

If a piece is not in use, wrap it in plenty of acid free paper and store flat, or roll it up with tissue paper. If it has to be folded, rearrange the piece from time to time so that the creases don't set. Check the embroidery for moths and mildew, and clean it when necessary.

DUST

The best way to keep dust at bay is with a vacuum cleaner. Use an upholstery attachment and keep the nozzle just above the surface of the work. Dust between raised stitches can be gently removed with a sable paint brush.

Brush gently over the stitches to avoid raising the pile

NEDLEPOINT

Stitches worked on canvas are used to create household articles that are both beautiful and long-lasting. Simple to work, easily portable, and requiring little equipment, needlepoint is suitable for many different types of designs, making it one of the most popular crafts. Historically, needlepointers usually followed charted designs, but today there is a wide variety of ready-to-work canvases, some of which are partially completed for the stitcher. Needlepoint stitches are used to interpret both historical and contemporary designs. Very simple stitches can be used to produce quite complex motifs, while elaborate stitches can make a simple design more visually and texturally interesting. Inspiration for needlepoint ranges from the mainly geometric patterns of the Orient to the floral and figurative designs of Colonial America and Europe. The bold triangular shapes of Bargello or Florentine suit all types of interiors.

As with most traditional crafts, a wide range of patterns and techniques has been developed over the years, but just one stitch is often enough to work most needlepoint projects.

TOOLS & MATERIALS

THE ESSENTIALS ARE square-mesh canvas, a tapestry needle, and yarn. Needlepoint canvas comes in a wide range of mesh sizes to suit different purposes. It is important to choose a yarn that is sufficiently thick to cover the threads of the mesh, and a needle that will pass through the holes easily.

CANVAS

Most canvases are made from cotton or linen. They are purchased by the yard, and are white, brown, or creamy-beige in color. If you are going to work with dark colors, choose brown canvas because even a small gap in your stitching can show up as a white dot and spoil the effect.

The mesh size or gauge of canvas is determined by the number of threads to the inch – the larger the number, the finer the canvas. *A fine gauge such as 22 threads per inch is used for detailed work and a coarse gauge of 3 threads per inch for chunky rugs. Many needlepoint projects call for a 10 gauge canvas. Some common types are shown below; others include interlock, rug, and plastic. The first two are suitable for wall hangings and rugs, the latter is often sold pre-cut for making place mats and decorations.*

Interlock canvas
This is made of single horizontal threads, and fine twisted vertical threads in pairs, which make the canvas less liable to distort or fray.

Mono canvas
Sold in the largest range of gauges, the mesh consists of single threads. It is not suitable for working half cross stitch or cross stitch (*see pages 161 and 164*).

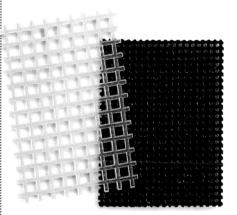

Double or Penelope canvas
This mesh is made of pairs of threads. You can work over each pair, or split them if you want to take smaller stitches.

Perforated paper and plastic canvas
Perforated paper (*above right*), available in a variety of colors, is suitable for making decorations and cards. Plastic canvas is molded into a medium-gauge mesh and sold in pieces.

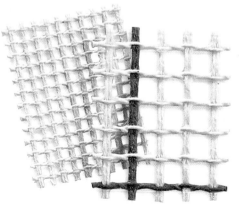

Rug canvas
Interlocking construction gives rug canvas (*left*) its shape. It has a wide range of mesh sizes and uses – needlepoint and latch-hook are two of the most popular.

YARNS

Crewel, tapestry and Persian are needlepoint yarns. They are durable, color-fast, and come in a wide variety of lovely shades. Other yarns include rug wool, a thick, long-lasting single-strand yarn, crochet and embroidery cottons, silk floss, and metallic thread.

Tapestry
A single-strand yarn is slightly finer than three strands of Persian yarn. One strand will cover 10-mesh canvas.

Crewel
This is the finest tapestry yarn – slightly finer than one strand of Persian yarn. It can be worked singly or in 2, 3, or 4 strands together.

Persian
This is made up of 3 easily divisible strands. Use the number of strands to suit the gauge of the canvas.

NEEDLES

Tapestry needles are specially made for needlepoint work. They have large eyes for easy threading and blunt, round-pointed ends which slip through the mesh without piercing it. Choose a size that will fit comfortably through the mesh holes without distorting the canvas. A size 18 needle is suitable for 10- and 12-mesh canvas.

Your needle and yarn should pass easily through the canvas

NEEDLEPOINT FRAMES

Stretching your work on a frame will keep the canvas from being distorted and has the advantage of leaving both hands free. A flat frame (see page 122), is best. Some people prefer to roll up their work and carry it with them.

OTHER USEFUL EQUIPMENT

Only a few additional accessories are necessary: Sharp scissors and masking tape. If you make your own designs you will need waterproof pens and paints to outline and color the canvas.

A waterproof felt-tip pen for transferring designs onto canvas

Acrylic paints to tint canvas or for painting on designs

Masking tape for binding the edges of canvas to stop it from fraying

Paint brush to color the canvas

Embroidery scissors with small, sharp blades for snipping off thread ends

Dressmaker's shears for cutting canvas to size

GENERAL TECHNIQUES

NO SPECIAL SKILLS are needed for working needlepoint. Aside from learning the basic stitches, all you need to know is how to start and finish off the thread ends neatly, and a few basic rules about handling the canvas and yarn so that your work is not damaged or distorted before the project is completed.

HANDLING CANVAS

It is unusual for modern canvas to fray. However, if you are working on a large piece, it is a good idea to bind the edges with masking tape. A comfortable and convenient way of working a large piece of canvas is to keep it rolled up, with the design on the inside. Use clothespins on the edges to hold the canvas in place while you are stitching a particular area. Always make a paper pattern of the finished shape before you start. You will need this to block the canvas when the work is finished.

NUMBERS OF THREADS

The most important thing to remember is that the yarn must cover the canvas, otherwise the mesh will show through. If you are not using a kit, always work a small sample first. If the stitching looks too thin, add extra strands of yarn.

FORMING THE STITCHES

There are two ways of working the stitches – the sewing method and the stabbing method. When using a frame, you will find it easier to use the stabbing method; for hand-held needlepoint, try both and see which method suits you best.

Sewing method

Each stitch is formed in one movement. Insert the needle into the canvas from the right side and bring it out at the position for the next stitch. Pull the thread through.

Stabbing method

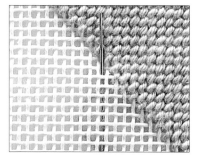

Each stitch is formed in two movements. Insert needle into canvas from right side and pull thread through to back. Re-insert needle at position for next stitch, and pull through to front.

BASIC WORKING METHOD

The working thread should be no longer than 18 inches, otherwise it will start to fray as it is pulled through the canvas mesh holes. If the thread starts to twist and tangle, let the needle drop down from the work until the thread has straightened out. Avoid starting and ending new threads in the same place in any area, because the extra thickness of the thread ends will form a ridge on the right side of the work.

Starting a thread

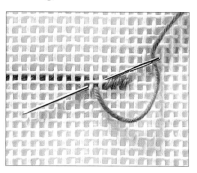

Leave an end at the back, about one inch long. Work the first few stitches over this to secure it, and cut off any surplus. Never start with a knot; it may make the work look lumpy and come undone.

Ending a thread

Take the needle and thread through to back of canvas. Weave the thread through the backs of the last few stitches; cut off any surplus.

NEEDLEPOINT KITS

These are ideal because they already contain canvas, needle, and yarns in the amounts required. Moreover, the design is either printed in color on the canvas or provided in chart form. The chart will resemble graph paper, with each square representing one mesh of the canvas. Unless otherwise stated, start stitching at the center and work toward the outer edges.

Sometimes a design that will receive hard wear, such as a footstool cover, is marked out with lines of horizontal stitches called tramé. These stitches add extra thickness and strength to the piece, and the needlepoint is worked over them in matching yarn.

CREATING YOUR OWN DESIGNS

DESIGNING YOUR OWN needlepoint is fascinating because there are so many directions your design can take. You start by drawing out a design to full size and paint or trace it onto the canvas. Beginners may find it easiest to start with a tent-stitch design. Add more decorative stitches as you become more inventive.

DESIGN INSPIRATION

Flowers, paintings, plates, and fabrics are all sources of inspiration. Start by making sketches. Be sure that the scale is suitable for your project – a small pattern may look exquisite on a pin cushion but can look weak on a large item. Positioning is also important; if your pattern has small details around the edges of the design they may get lost when the work is sewn up.

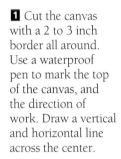

After making initial sketches, draw the design to full-size. Use colored pencils to shade in as much detail you like. Draw a clear outline around the outer edges of the design, and a vertical and horizontal line across the center.

CHARTING YOUR OWN DESIGNS

If you want to work out the design accurately, chart it on graph paper. Remember, the scale of the graph paper may not be the same as your canvas.

In a chart for a tent-stitch design *(see tent stitches, page 161)* each square is usually colored to represent one stitch taken over one intersection of the canvas. For decorative stitches *(see pages 162 to 168)*, think of the lines of the graph paper as the canvas mesh, and mark the color, length, and direction of each stitch on your chart.

TRANSFERRING THE DESIGN

The design may be marked on the canvas with acrylic paints or felt-tip pens. Make sure these are waterproof, otherwise they may stain the work when it is blocked (see page 178).

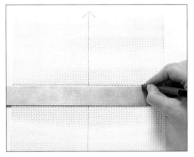

1 Cut the canvas with a 2 to 3 inch border all around. Use a waterproof pen to mark the top of the canvas, and the direction of work. Draw a vertical and horizontal line across the center.

2 Place the canvas over the drawing, match up the center lines, and tape or pin them together. Draw the outer edges of the design onto the canvas with a waterproof pen.

3 Now either paint the design on the canvas or draw out the main details with a pen. Use your initial design as a guide to color and detail. Make sure the ink or paint is dry before stitching.

NEEDLEPOINT STITCHES

NEEDLEPOINT STITCHES ARE worked vertically, diagonally, or horizontally over the threads of the canvas, and normally cover it. Textures and patterns are created by the direction and size of the different stitches. The best way to master the stitches is to work them: Stitch a sampler of the ones you like best to serve as a reference for the future. The sampler will also help you discover the variety of ways the various stitches can be combined to produce different designs.

The instructions on the following pages state the number of threads in each direction over which the stitches should be formed. Once you familiarize yourself with the stitches, you can vary their length depending on the effect you want to achieve. But don't work stitches over more than ten canvas threads as the loops will be so long they may snag. Unless otherwise stated, all the stitch patterns given may be worked on either single or double canvas.

NEEDLEPOINT MAGIC

The wall hanging shown above demonstrates the rich variety of patterns and textures that can be achieved by combining different needlepoint stitches. Place bands of smooth texture stitches, such as Tent stitch (see page 161) or Upright Gobelin stitch (see page 166) next to stitches with strongly defined raised patterns such as Scotch stitch (see page 163) and Algerian Eye stitch (see page 168).

TENT STITCHES

EACH SMALL DIAGONAL stitch in tent stitch is worked in the same direction over one intersection of canvas. It is versatile enough to translate any detail or subtle shading, so many people use only this stitch.

There are three variations – half cross stitch, Continental stitch, and basketweave stitch. They all look the same from the front. Half cross stitch is the easiest of the three and uses the least yarn. However, it cannot be used on single canvas because the stitches slide. Half cross stitch and Continental stitch tend to distort the canvas, so use a frame if you are working a large area. Basketweave is the best to use over a large area because it doesn't distort the canvas. However, it does use more yarn than the other two stitches.

Half cross stitch

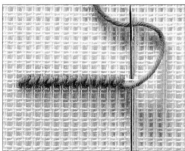

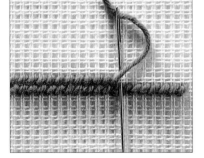

1 Work in horizontal rows from left to right. Bring the needle out and take it up to the right over one canvas intersection. Insert needle under one horizontal thread, and bring it out ready to form the next stitch.

2 At end of row turn canvas upside down and start next row.

Continental stitch

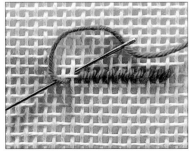

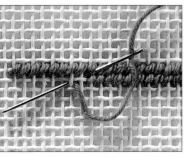

1 Work in rows from right to left. Bring needle out and take it up right over one intersection. Take the needle diagonally under one intersection to left.

2 At end of row turn canvas upside down for return row.

Basketweave stitch

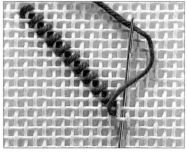

1 Work down and up the canvas diagonally. Take a stitch up to right over one intersection. Insert needle downward under two horizontal threads.

All tent stitches look the same on the front; half cross stitch is shown here

2 To return, take a diagonal stitch up to right over one intersection. Stitch under 2 vertical threads to left.

The back of the work will show the difference between the tent stitches – half cross stitch (left), Continental stitch (center), basketweave stitch (right)

DIAGONAL STITCHES

ALL THE STITCHES in this section are worked so they slant diagonally over the canvas threads. Each stitch sequence produces a distinctive overall pattern, and many of them can be worked in different colors to form striped, zigzag, and checkerboard designs. Diagonal stitches distort the canvas more than any other type of stitches, so don't work them too tightly and use an embroidery frame if possible.

Slanted Gobelin stitch

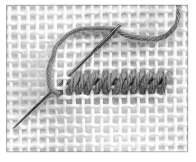

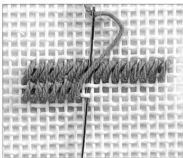

1 Work on single canvas only, from right to left, then left to right alternately. Bring needle out, and insert it 2 horizontal threads up, and one vertical thread to right. Bring needle out 2 horizontal threads down, and one vertical thread to left of stitch just made.

2 In next row, work new stitches one stitch length below stitches in previous row; slant them in same direction.

Encroaching Gobelin stitch

Work as above, but take each stitch over 4 or 5 canvas threads. Slant over one vertical thread. On new row, overlap tops of stitches by one thread.

Condensed Scotch stitch

1 Work the graduating stitches in diagonal rows, starting at top right. The basic unit of the pattern is a group of 4 diagonal stitches worked over 2, 3, 4 and 3 canvas intersections. Repeat this 4-stitch sequence to end of row.

2 On next and subsequent rows, repeat the same stitch sequence, placing the shortest stitch next to the longest stitch of the previous row.

Striped patterns can be made by working the rows in diagonal stitch in two or more colors

Slanted Gobelin stitch is an elongated version of tent stitch and forms neat, ridged rows

Use encroaching Gobelin stitch for shading and blending colors

Scotch stitch

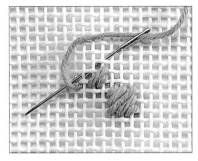

1 This stitch is made of squares of 5 graduated diagonal stitches worked over one, 2, 3, 2, and one canvas intersections. Worked diagonally, each square covers 3 vertical and horizontal threads. Repeat this stitch sequence to the end of the row.

2 Reverse working direction and fit squares of new row in between squares of previous row.

Scotch stitch variation

Work horizontal and vertical lines of tent stitch spaced 3 intersections apart to form a grid. Fill in each square of the grid with Scotch stitch (*see above*).

Work Scotch stitch in one color for texture or several colors for striped and checked patterns

Scotch stitch variation is made by working a tent-stitch grid and filling in each square

Checker stitch

1 Work diagonally over 4 horizontal and 4 vertical canvas threads. Start at top left. On first row, fill each square with 7 diagonal stitches, worked over one, 2, 3, 4, 3, 2, and one intersections.

2 On second row, work 16 small tent stitches into each new square, fitting them into squares of previous row.

In Checker stitch, squares of graduated diagonal stitch alternate with tent stitch

Byzantine stitch

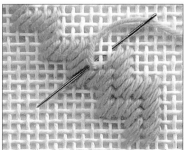

1 The zigzag rows of stitches are worked diagonally from top to bottom, then bottom to top of canvas alternately. Each stitch is worked over 2 canvas intersections. Form steps or zigzags by making 3 diagonal stitches across canvas, and then 3 diagonal stitches up or down canvas alternately.

2 Fit the steps of a new row into steps of preceding row.

Byzantine stitch covers the canvas quickly and is useful for filling large areas of background

CROSSED STITCHES

BASIC CROSS STITCH is the most important stitch in this category and it is always worked on double canvas. All the other patterns in this section are formed by either diagonal or straight stitches crossing over each other; a backstitch can secure the crossed stitches and be worked in a contrasting color.

CROSS STITCH

Cross stitch can be worked horizontally or diagonally on double canvas over one or more intersections according to the canvas gauge. The top stitches of the crosses should always lie in the same direction to ensure an even finish.

Horizontal method

1 Work from right to left, then left to right alternately. Bring out needle and take it up to left, over 2 canvas intersections. Insert needle, bringing it out under 2 horizontal threads.

2 Cross this stitch with a diagonal backstitch over same intersection, but slanted in opposite direction. The needle comes out where it just emerged, ready to make the next cross stitch.

Diagonal method

Work from bottom left. Make first stitch as for horizontal method. Cross it with a stitch slanting in opposite direction, bringing out needle under 2 vertical threads in position for next cross stitch.

Oblong cross stitch

1 Work in 2 steps, from right to left, then left to right. Bring out needle, and take stitch up to left over 4 horizontal and 2 vertical threads. Take stitch under 4 horizontal threads. Repeat to end of row, then cross them with stitches worked in opposite direction.

2 At end of row, bring out needle 4 threads down ready to start first stitch of new row.

Oblong cross-stitch variation

Work oblong cross stitch as above. Then, in a contrasting color, take a backstitch across center of each cross. Each backstitch covers 2 vertical threads.

Cross stitch

Oblong cross stitch

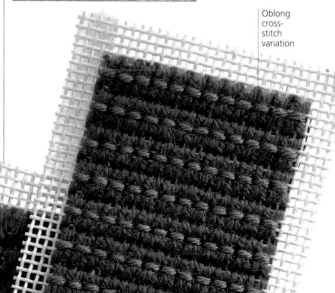

Oblong cross-stitch variation

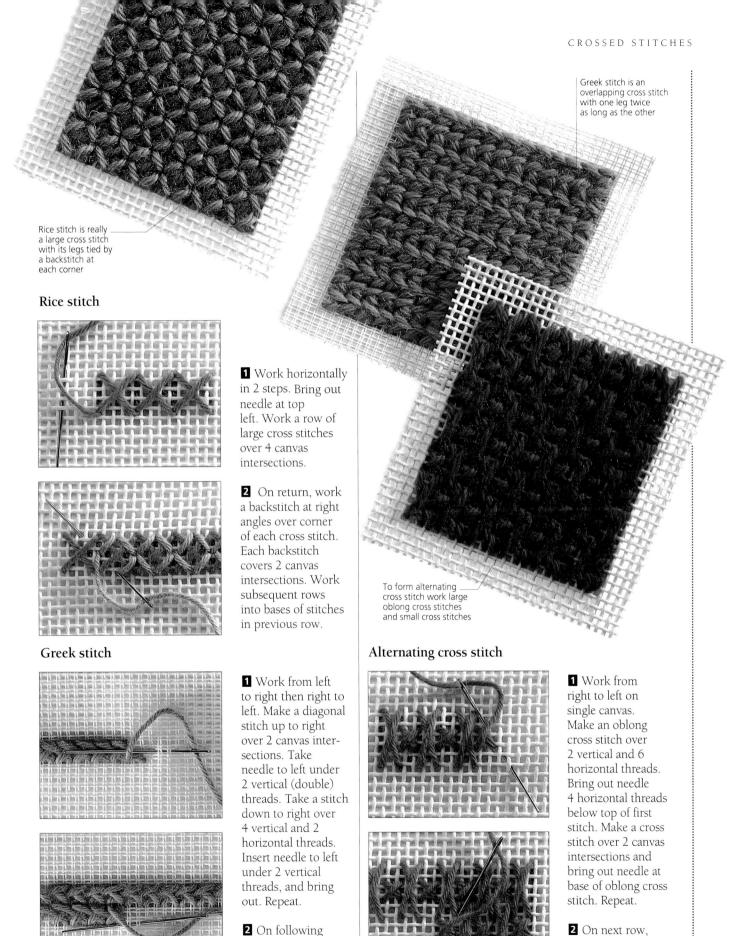

Rice stitch is really a large cross stitch with its legs tied by a backstitch at each corner

Greek stitch is an overlapping cross stitch with one leg twice as long as the other

To form alternating cross stitch work large oblong cross stitches and small cross stitches

Rice stitch

1 Work horizontally in 2 steps. Bring out needle at top left. Work a row of large cross stitches over 4 canvas intersections.

2 On return, work a backstitch at right angles over corner of each cross stitch. Each backstitch covers 2 canvas intersections. Work subsequent rows into bases of stitches in previous row.

Greek stitch

1 Work from left to right then right to left. Make a diagonal stitch up to right over 2 canvas inter-sections. Take needle to left under 2 vertical (double) threads. Take a stitch down to right over 4 vertical and 2 horizontal threads. Insert needle to left under 2 vertical threads, and bring out. Repeat.

2 On following rows, work stitches in bases of those in previous row.

Alternating cross stitch

1 Work from right to left on single canvas. Make an oblong cross stitch over 2 vertical and 6 horizontal threads. Bring out needle 4 horizontal threads below top of first stitch. Make a cross stitch over 2 canvas intersections and bring out needle at base of oblong cross stitch. Repeat.

2 On next row, place cross stitches beneath oblong cross stitches.

STRAIGHT STITCHES

QUICK AND SIMPLE to work, straight stitches are most interesting when stitches of different lengths are combined. As a rule, straight stitches cover single canvas best, although there is no reason why you shouldn't try them on double canvas. All the stitches are worked in horizontal rows unless otherwise stated.

Upright Gobelin stitch

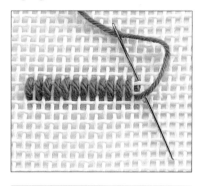

1 Work rows from left to right, then right to left. Bring needle out, and take it up over 2 horizontal threads. Insert needle down to right under one vertical and 2 horizontal threads, and bring it out ready to start next stitch.

2 In subsequent rows, work the tops of the stitches into the bases of the stitches above.

Gobelin filling stitch

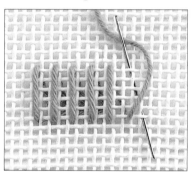

1 Work a row of stitches as for upright Gobelin stitch, taking each stitch over 6 horizontal threads and spacing them 2 vertical threads apart.

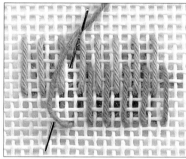

2 When working subsequent rows place the stitches between stitches of the row above. The bases of the new stitches should be 3 horizontal threads below the bases of previous stitches.

Random long stitch

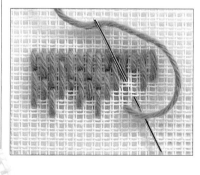

Work as for upright Gobelin stitch, but vary the length of the stitches by taking them over either one, 2, 3 or 4 horizontal threads at random.

Upright Gobelin stitch is a hardwearing stitch producing a close, ridged surface

In Gobelin filling stitch the rows overlap to produce a basketweave effect

Random long stitch is very quick for working large areas of double canvas

Long and short stitch

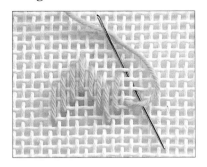

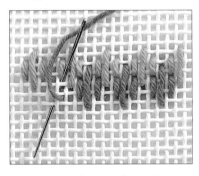

1 Moving up one thread for each of first 4 stitches, work row of long stitches over 4 horizontal threads. Then work 3 stitches, moving down one thread for each. Repeat.

2 Work next 2 rows in same sequence, taking smaller stitches worked over 2 threads. Continue working one row of long stitch and 2 rows of shorter stitch alternately.

Hungarian stitch

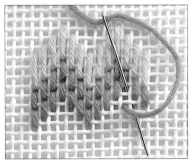

Work groups of 3 stitches over 2, 4 and 2 horizontal threads, with a space of 2 vertical threads between each group. On subsequent rows, work groups into previous spaces .

Hungarian stitch (bottom left),
Long and short stitch (top left),
Hungarian stitch grounding
(top right), and Hungarian
diamond stitch (bottom right)

Hungarian diamond stitch

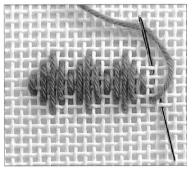

1 Work stitches one vertical thread apart. Make groups of 4 graduated stitches in a repeated sequence over 2, 4, 6, and 4 horizontal canvas threads.

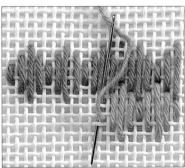

2 On all subsequent rows, work the longest stitches into the bases of the shortest stitches in the previous row.

Hungarian stitch grounding

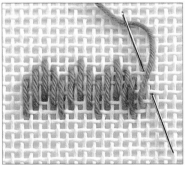

1 The first row is worked in same way as zigzag long stitch, but stitch sequence is shorter. Take 3 vertical stitches over 4 horizontal threads moving up, and 2 stitches moving down.

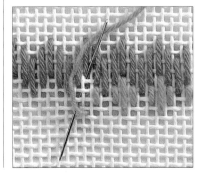

2 On 2nd row, work Hungarian stitch between spaces left in previous row. Work these 2 rows alternately.

STAR STITCHES

THESE ARE COMPOSITE stitches formed from diagonal, crossed, and straight stitches. Star stitches tend to be large stitches, which may be framed in other stitches, and produce clear shapes rather than overall textures. Work them fairly loosely on single canvas with a thick thread that will cover the mesh.

Smyrna cross stitch

1 From top left, work a cross stitch over 4 intersections. Bring needle out through center hole between bases. Take a vertical stitch up over 4 threads. Bring needle out, 2 threads to left and 2 threads down. Take one horizontal stitch to right.

2 Bring needle out 4 threads to right on baseline. On subsequent rows, work tops of stitches into previous bases.

Large Algerian eye stitch

1 To form star, work 16 stitches clockwise into same central hole over 4 canvas threads or over 4 canvas intersections at corners of square. To space out stitches, leave 2 canvas threads unworked between each converging stitch.

2 When stars are completed, frame each one with backstitches worked over 2 canvas threads.

Algerian eye stitch

Work rows from right to left, then left to right. Start at top right corner. Work 8 stitches clockwise over 2 canvas threads or 2 canvas intersections into same central hole. Leave 2 canvas threads between each. Work next star into sides of last one. On next row, work counterclockwise.

Ray stitch

Work left to right, then right to left. Work 7 stitches counterclockwise over 3 threads or 3 intersections into same hole. Space out stitches one thread apart.

Algerian eye stitch

Smyrna cross stitch

In this version of Algerian eye stitch, each star is framed with backstitches

Ray stitch is one quarter of a very large Algerian star

LOOPED STITCHES

THESE STITCHES FORM a series of knotted loops. The loops can be cut to produce a soft, fluffy pile that looks like the surface of a carpet. The stitches can be worked on their own on rug canvas or combined with areas of smoother, flatter stitching on finer canvas to create interesting changes in texture on the work.

Turkey stitch

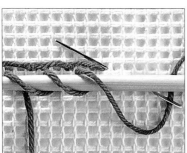

1 Start at bottom left, and work horizontally. From front of canvas, insert needle and take it up to left under one horizontal and 2 vertical threads. Bring out needle, leaving a short thread end on surface of work. Insert needle to right over 3 vertical threads, bringing it out one vertical thread to left of yarn end.

2 Work the following stitches in the same way, forming even loops around a knitting needle, as shown above.

3 Work subsequent rows, one horizontal thread above the preceding row. Cut all loops when work is finished.

Work Turkey stitch on single canvas and completly cover the canvas

Velvet stitch is worked as loops and these are then cut to form a soft pile

Velvet stitch

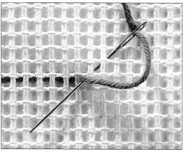

1 Work this loop stitch on single or rug canvas from left to right. Bring out needle and take a diagonal backstitch up to right over 2 canvas intersections.

2 Take needle up to right again and insert in the same place as before, but this time hold the thread down with your finger to form a loop. (Working the loops over a thick knitting needle will ensure that they are all the same size.) Bring needle out 2 horizontal threads down.

3 Hold loop down with finger and take a diagonal backstitch up to left over 2 canvas intersections. Repeat sequence to end of row. On each row, position new stitches above those just done.

4 When work is finished, cut the loops to form the pile, and trim if necessary.

NEEDLEPOINT PROJECTS

NEEDLEPOINT CAN BE worked on furnishings and accessories, and on large or small items. The only constraint on your imagination is the fact that needlepoint is always worked on canvas. You may want to try bold geometric patterns, or decorative florals in the style of classic country house chintzes of the 19th century. Whatever style you choose, you can work these doorstops, pillows, jewelry boxes, and purses to complement your own taste. (See pages 242 to 244.)

GIFT BOXES

Small jewelry boxes in different shapes make attractive gifts.

This strawberry heart box will keep your treasures safe

Make a gift of this golden yellow beehive box

A singing bird decorates this pretty chickadee box

DOORSTOP

Show off your needlepoint skills by working the covering for this doorstop – the inside is a brick. As well as this attractive bow, a lot of simple patterns could be adapted to this size.

This surprise parcel is a doorstop that is both useful and decorative

These pillows have the inspirational names of Santa Fe and Albuquerque – and an Old West feeling

OLD WEST PILLOWS

All sizes and shapes of pillows can be done in needlepoint. Big, bold, colorful designs based on kilims or Navajo rugs look good against solid colors. Make several in complementary colors.

PURSE

Small flower motifs decorate a needlepoint purse. After the design is worked on canvas it is sewn up and lined with fabric.

This floral purse is pretty enough to use in the evenings

FOLK-ART FLORAL

Patterns familiar from the folk art originating in Northern Europe provide lots of inspiration. The bold outlines make this type of design suitable for a beginner.

171

BARGELLO WORK

SOMETIMES KNOWN AS Florentine work or flame stitch, Bargello is formed of straight, upright stitches repeated in zigzag rows. By altering the size and spacing of stitches, the zigzags can be made into undulating waves or into sharp peaks. Bargello has always been popular, and with good reason – the basic stitch covers single canvas quickly, and the patterns can be worked in colorful bands or subtly shaded.

This Bargello bag is worked in an attractive diagonal pattern, which is reflected in the border

CANVAS AND THREADS

Bargello stitches never cover double canvas adequately. For the best results, always work on single canvas and make sure the yarn is thick enough to cover the mesh. The working thread can be about 22 inches long – slightly longer than for other types of needlepoint because these stitches create very little friction when the thread is pulled through the canvas.

Since you will be changing color frequently, it saves time to keep several needles threaded with the different colors so that you don't have to keep re-threading the same needle.

ROW DESIGNS

These patterns are worked horizontally across the canvas. The first line of stitching is worked from the center point of the canvas out to the left- and right-hand edges. This line sets the structure of the pattern. All the other rows are worked from right to left or left to right, above and below it, to fill the canvas completely.

BASIC ZIGZAG

The easiest way to learn Bargello is to start with a basic 4-2 zigzag pattern. Each stitch is taken over four horizontal threads, and then up or down two horizontal threads.

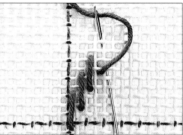

1 Bring out needle at center point of canvas. Insert it 4 horizontal threads up. Bring it out 2 horizontal threads below top of stitch and one vertical thread to the right.

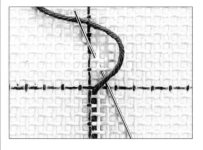

2 Take 3 more stitches in the same way to travel up the canvas. On the 3rd stitch, bring the needle out 6 horizontal threads below top of last stitch.

3 Work next 3 stitches down canvas to form first inverted V of zigzag. Continue working 3 stitches up and down canvas in this way to form zigzag pattern.

4 Work row of stitches of new color into bases of first row.

THE EFFECTS OF COLOR

All Bargello designs are worked in bands of different colors. A three-color repeat is effective, but of course you can use as many colors as you like.

Different color combinations can change the look of the design completely. If you choose three tones of the same color, for example, you will achieve a soft, harmonious effect. Alternatively, you can make distinct stripes by selecting strongly contrasting colors. Experiment with different colors to see the effects that you can achieve.

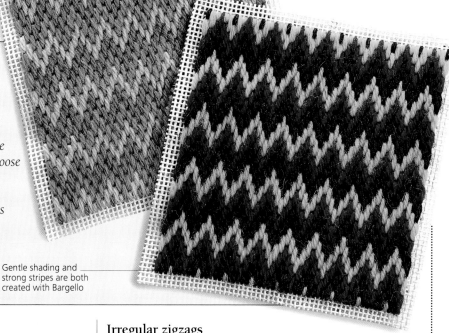

Gentle shading and strong stripes are both created with Bargello

ROW PATTERN VARIATIONS

The Bargello stitch zigzags can either be softened into gentle curves, or be made more spiky, by altering the size of the stitches and the steps between them.

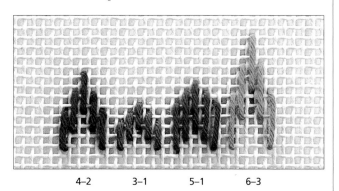

| 4–2 | 3–1 | 5–1 | 6–3 |

The sampler shown above demonstrates what happens when the stitch length and step is changed from 4-2. The first number gives the stitch length, and the 2nd number gives the step up or down between stitches. Keep to your chosen stitch length throughout so that each subsequent row can be fitted above or below it.

Step zigzags

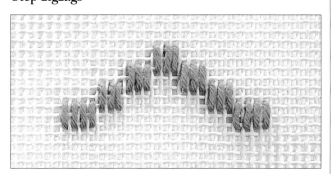

To create a squared-off outline, rather than a sharp outline, work 2 or more stitches along the same line of horizontal threads, before taking a step up or down the canvas.

Irregular zigzags

Peaks and valleys at different levels can be created by varying the number of stitches on any horizontal line and by changing the height of the step between them.

Curves

Curves are produced by working 2 or more stitches along the same line of horizontal threads at the top and base of each peak.

These curves are worked in contrasting tones of the same family of colors

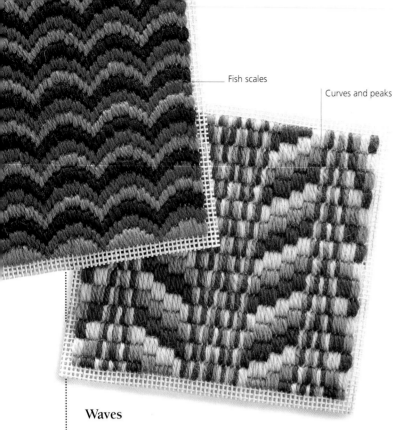

Fish scales

Curves and peaks

Fish scales

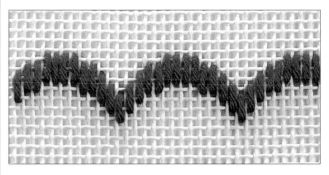

Curving the tops of the peaks, and keeping the bases pointed, this technique creates a pattern of half-circles which resembles the scales of a fish.

Curves and peaks

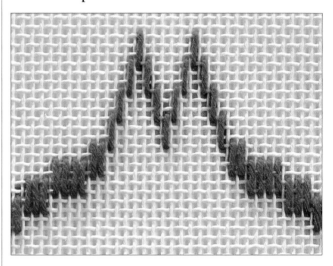

To achieve attractive, contrasting shapes, combine curves and steep peaks in the same pattern row. This pattern is especially effective in shaded colors as it gives the effect of a row varying in thickness as well as shape.

Waves

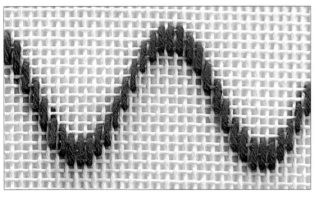

Curves can be made more gradual by altering the step formation, adding extra stitches at each peak.

CHARTING YOUR OWN DESIGNS

It is easy to work out your own Bargello designs on graph paper. Each square of the grid represents one square of the canvas, and the colored lines denote the stitches.

When charting a design, start at the center and work out toward the edges so that it looks well balanced

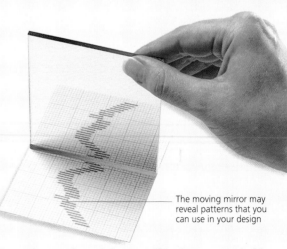

The moving mirror may reveal patterns that you can use in your design

To see how a charted design will look in repeat, hold a mirror at right angles to the graph paper. Slide the mirror along the chart to see other interesting patterns.

TWO-WAY BARGELLO

The first row sets the pattern and is worked as usual. The pattern is then reversed to form a mirror-image, and the spaces between the two rows are filled with upright stitches.

Two-way 4-2 zigzag

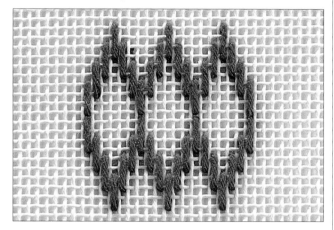

1 Work the first row as shown on page 172. Work a 2nd row beneath it, reversing direction of zigzags, to form diamonds.

2 Fill in the diamond shapes with bands of stitching, and fit subsequent diamonds above and below this pattern row.

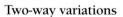

Two-way variations

Any row can be turned into a two-way pattern by reversing the first row. With some patterns, you may need to fill in the motifs with stitches of varying lengths. The spaces between the rows may become an important element in the design.

FOUR-WAY BARGELLO

Square designs like pillows or bags can be worked in four directions. Each starts from the center and goes out toward the edges of the canvas to build up one large motif.

Basic method

1 Cut the canvas into a square. Draw 2 diagonal lines from corner to corner. Work 4 stitches into the center hole of canvas, placing them at right angles to each other to form a cross.

2 Develop the pattern by working out to the edges of the canvas, filling each quarter section of the canvas in an identical way.

Four-way variations

As with any type of Bargello, the four-way pattern can be quite simple, or you can vary the sizes of the stitches and the steps between them to create more intricate and complex designs.

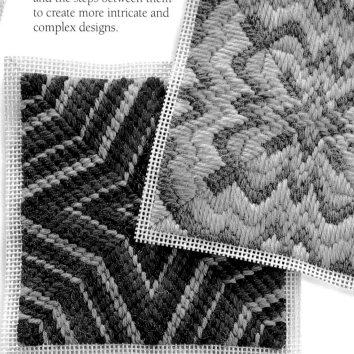

CHRISTMAS TREASURES

LITTLE THINGS MEAN a lot at Christmas, so delight your friends and family with these beautiful miniature needlepoint designs for gift tags, cards, decorations, and a stocking. For instructions, see page 245.

Christmas pudding gift tag

Christmas tree gift tag

GIFT TAGS

To make a present extra special, add a pretty little petit point gift tag mounted on colored cardboard. It will be a lasting memento of a very happy Christmas.

Crackers gift tag

Christmas tree card

Gift box card

GREETING CARDS

These petit point Christmas cards are only 2 1/4 inches wide by 3 1/4 inches high, so they won't take long to stitch. Make your own cards to display them, or buy the cards from a craft shop.

Snowflake
decoration

Crackers
decoration

DECORATIONS

Needlepoint decorations
won't break like glass baubles,
or fall apart like paper chains.
Mount your work in light-
weight gold-colored plastic
frames, and hang it on the wall
or on the Christmas tree.

Bells
decoration

A tent stitch Christmas stocking
is quick to work and will last
for many festive seasons

Fill the brightly colored
stocking with sugar candies
and a child will love it

CHRISTMAS STOCKING

The perfect stocking for the perfect
gift – decorated with holly, bells, and
a bright, happy robin.

177

BLOCKING & JOINING

AFTER COMPLETING YOUR needlepoint, examine it carefully to make sure that you haven't missed any stitches. If you have, you can easily fill these in with matching yarn. The next step is to 'block' or remold the needlepoint back into its original shape using your paper pattern as a guide. Don't worry if your work appears to be quite distorted – this often happens, especially if you have been using diagonal or crossed stitches that pull against the weave of the canvas. If you are making an item such as a bag or pillow, the final step involves joining the needlepoint and the backing together with a visible or invisible seam.

BLOCKING

If your work shows very little distortion, steam the wrong side lightly with a steamer or iron, and leave it to dry thoroughly. If it's badly distorted, use the method below.

Wet and tack method

1 Pin your paper pattern to a piece of board and tape a piece of plastic over the top. Place the needlepoint right side down on top of the pattern and spray with water, or moisten with a sponge or cloth.

2 Starting at the center top, hammer a tack through the unworked canvas. Stretch the needlepoint gently into shape, using more water if necessary. Tack at center bottom and sides.

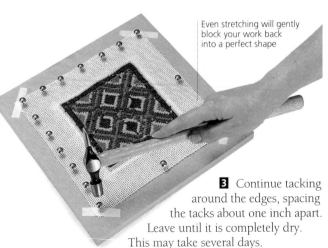

Even stretching will gently block your work back into a perfect shape

3 Continue tacking around the edges, spacing the tacks about one inch apart. Leave until it is completely dry. This may take several days.

JOINING

All sections of a needlepoint design should be blocked separately before they are stitched together. Seams can be a decorative feature or relatively invisible.

Half cross-stitch seam

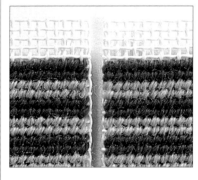

1 Trim the canvas edges to about half an inch. Turn these back onto wrong side, checking that folds run along a thread of canvas. With right sides up, lay the pieces edge to edge, matching pattern row for row.

2 Using matching or contrasting yarn, bring out needle through first hole of left-hand piece. Insert it through 2nd hole of adjacent piece, and bring it out through 2nd hole of left-hand piece. Repeat.

TO SEW A FABRIC BACKING TO A PILLOW COVER

Fine and medium gauge canvas can usually be stitched to a fabric backing with a sewing machine. Check the stitch tension on a scrap of canvas and backing fabric before you start. If you are using a coarse gauge canvas, sew the pieces together with backstitch (see page 129).

Join your backing to your needlepoint work with an even backstitch

CARE & REPAIR

NEEDLEPOINT WORKED WITH wool yarn stays clean with little care. A light, routine cleaning with a vacuum cleaner to remove the dust should be all that is necessary. If you used silk threads, send it to a specialist for cleaning and repairs. If your threads are colorfast, you may be able to wash the piece in warm soapy water. Small tears in the canvas or frayed stitches should be mended quickly.

MINOR REPAIRS

Broken threads can be repaired with a patch of the same canvas type and gauge. A large tear in the canvas calls for expert attention so the patch will not show.

Frayed stitches

Carefully remove frayed stitches and a few good stitches either side, so loose ends can be secured under new stitching. Work new stitches in matching colors.

Broken canvas threads

1 Cut a canvas patch a few meshes larger all around than the damaged area. From the wrong side, use a sharp pair of embroidery scissors and a tapestry needle to remove the stitches around the broken mesh, in an area slightly larger than the patch.

2 Baste patch in position on wrong side, aligning canvas mesh exactly. Trim off any broken mesh threads so that the patch lies flat.

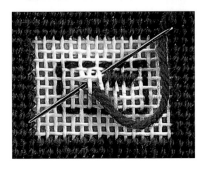

3 Restitch area through both layers of canvas with matching yarn, removing basting stitches as you work.

HAND WASHING

Check that the yarn is colorfast by pressing a damp cotton ball onto the back to see if color comes off. Make a paper pattern of the needlepoint shape to block the washed canvas.

1 Use a container large enough for the piece to lie flat. Fill with warm water, add a mild soap suitable for your fiber, and froth up to make suds; immerse the needlepoint.

2 Let the needlepoint soak, and gently press up and down on the back with a sponge without rubbing. Drain off the water. Then rinse in the same way, until the water runs clear.

3 Place the needlepoint on a flat surface, right side up, and blot off the excess water with a clean dry sponge. Re-block the piece, following the instructions on the opposite page.

STORING NEEDLEPOINT

Ideally, needlepoint should be placed between sheets of acid-free tissue paper and stored flat away from dust and sunlight. Or cover a cardboard cylinder with acid-free paper and wrap the needlepoint around it, right side out. Then wrap this in acid-free tissue paper.

PATCHWORK
& QUILTING

Perennially popular with needlecrafters, patchwork and quilting are used to reproduce treasured designs, as well as to create the heirlooms of tomorrow. These crafts have, for generations, been the hub of social gatherings, where quilters contribute their talents toward the completion of a single quilt. While both techniques can be used alone, they are most often combined into intricate patterns. Using patchwork and appliqué, myriad effects are possible. And whether you create a design or use one of the hundreds of established pattern blocks, your choice of fabrics and their placement will make your project unique; the beauty of quilting is subtle.

The motifs used in patchwork and quilting are inspired by everyday objects, political opinions, dreams, and remembrances – you are limited only by your imagination. The techniques are easy to master, and machine stitching and new cutting techniques make them even more accessible.

EQUIPMENT

PATCHWORK AND QUILTING require little in the way of specialty equipment. The correct needle and thread are important and, depending on the complexity of your design, you may need a template, a rotary cutter and board (see page 186), and a quilting hoop. One other vital piece of equipment is a steam iron, which is used in every step of creating patchwork. Steam helps set seams and removes wrinkles from the fabric.

PATCHWORK AND QUILTING TOOLS

The correct needle will make your patchwork or quilting much easier. Most fabric shops sell packs of needles specifically for quilting. Apart from the equipment described below, most of the other tools needed are likely to be found in your sewing box.

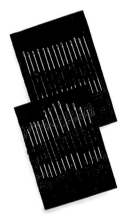

Thimble
Absolutely necessary for quilting – if you have never used a thimble before, you should learn to use one now.

Thread
Use No. 50 cotton thread for hand sewing and a No. 40 cotton thread or a polyester/cotton thread for machine sewing. Always use a 100% cotton thread for quilting.

Needles
Sharps are used for hand sewing; betweens for quilting. A size 8 between needle is recommended for beginners.

Pins
Smooth, fine dressmaker's pins with glass or plastic heads are recommended.

Beeswax
Run your thread over a cake of beeswax to strengthen the thread and prevent it from kinking when hand sewing or quilting.

Seam ripper
To remove machine-sewn stitches.

Embroidery scissors
Use these to clip into seam allowances or to cut thread.

Dressmaker's shears
Use these for cutting fabric only. They should be extremely sharp.

Templates
Used for cutting pattern pieces, these are plastic or metal, or can be made from cardboard or clear acetate (see page 184).

Quilting hoop
Wooden hoops, around 14 inches diameter, help to keep an even tension on your work as you are quilting.

FABRICS & PATTERNS

MOST TRADITIONAL-STYLE patchwork quilts are constructed of printed fabrics. However, this should not keep you from experimenting with a variety of textures, colors, and designs and exploring the different effects created. Let your imagination and taste guide you. Beginners should use only 100% cotton fabrics, which are easy to work with, keep a crease, and wear well. Choose those with a medium weave, since loosely woven fabrics have little strength and tightly woven fabrics will be difficult to quilt. Wash fabrics in hot water to test for shrinkage and colorfastness, and iron carefully before using.

COLOR VALUE

In art, value is the relative lightness or darkness of a color. In patchwork, this quality can be more important than the color itself. A design can differ substantially depending upon the placement of fabrics of different values. For the best results, combine a mix of light, medium, and dark values.

In addition, color values are affected by surrounding fabrics. This can be a useful point to exploit if you are working with a limited number of colors and wish to make the best possible use of their difference in value.

PRINT SCALE

Medium-scale prints, which can be compact or widely-spaced are generally the best for patchwork. Small-scale prints can add a subtle texture to a design, while large-scale prints can give the impression of more than one fabric. Stripes and plaids can also be used.

Small-scale prints

Medium-scale prints

Large-scale prints

Stripes and plaids

BATTING

A soft, fibrous material, this is used as a filling between a quilt top and back. Batting can be bought in a roll of different widths, fibers, and weights. Different weights will suit various quilting purposes.

TEMPLATES

TEMPLATES ARE DURABLE patterns used for cutting out the pieces of a patchwork design. They can be purchased from specialty shops, and are available in metal and plastic in a variety of shapes. Plastic and window templates can be positioned on the fabric to create special effects. Window templates provide for the seam allowance other types do not.

It is also easy to make your own templates. Accuracy is extremely important, so be sure to measure carefully and use sharpened dressmaker pencils when making the templates and marking the lines on fabric. Always mark patchwork pieces on the wrong side of the fabric. Sharp cutting tools are also necessary for making templates from cardboard or plastic.

TEMPLATE-MAKING SUPPLIES

If you are making a quilt with many pieces, make several templates for each piece and discard when they are worn out.

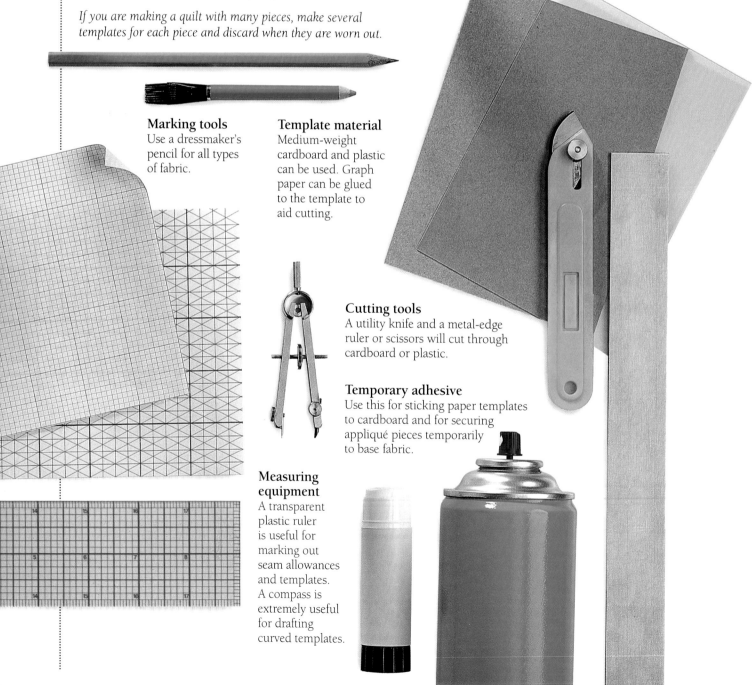

Marking tools
Use a dressmaker's pencil for all types of fabric.

Template material
Medium-weight cardboard and plastic can be used. Graph paper can be glued to the template to aid cutting.

Cutting tools
A utility knife and a metal-edge ruler or scissors will cut through cardboard or plastic.

Temporary adhesive
Use this for sticking paper templates to cardboard and for securing appliqué pieces temporarily to base fabric.

Measuring equipment
A transparent plastic ruler is useful for marking out seam allowances and templates. A compass is extremely useful for drafting curved templates.

MAKING TEMPLATES

Trace pattern pieces from a book, magazine or other source. Alternatively, draw your own design on graph paper. For machine sewing templates or window templates you will need to add a ¹/₄ inch seam allowance all around each pattern piece. Label the pieces with letters and the pattern name, then draw a grainline (see below).

1 Cut out your paper pieces and spray the wrong side with temporary adhesive. Leaving ¹/₂ inch between pieces, press onto sheet of medium-weight cardboard or clear acetate.

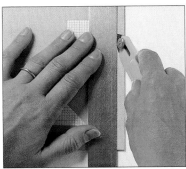

2 Place the cardboard or acetate on a cutting mat or stack of newspaper and use a utility knife and a metal-edge ruler to cut out the templates – either along the edge of the paper or along the marked seamline.

3 For complicated or curved designs, mark notches in the edges of templates to aid in matching the pieces when you sew them together. Cut out notches using a utility knife.

CUTTING OUT FABRIC PIECES

Mark the seamline and cutting lines on the wrong side of the fabric if you are hand sewing. Mark just the outer cutting line if you are machine sewing. As a general rule, mark the longest edge of a patchwork piece along the fabric grain.

For hand sewing

1 Position the pieces at least ¹/₂ inch apart when marking them on fabric.

2 Either mark the cutting lines, or judge by eye, and cut the pieces apart.

For machine sewing

When marking the shapes on fabric, position pieces with edges touching.

GRAIN OF FABRIC

Selvages are the finished edges of fabric. The lengthwise grain or warp runs parallel to the selvages and has little give. The crosswise grain or weft runs perpendicular to selvages and has a slight give. A fabric has its maximum give when it is cut on the bias, which runs at a 45° angle to the selvages. This information is essential when it comes to positioning and cutting out patchwork pieces. For example, the borders of a quilt should be strong, therefore cut them with the longest edges on the length-wise grain of the fabric. Curved patchwork should be cut with the curves on the bias of the fabric so that the pieces are easier to manipulate.

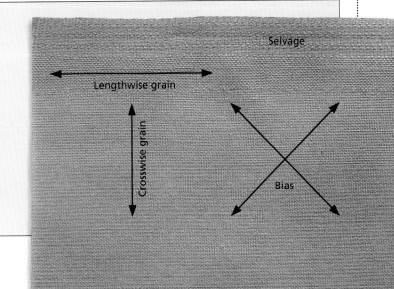

Selvage

Lengthwise grain

Crosswise grain

Bias

ROTARY CUTTING

ROTARY CUTTING is a fast and accurate method of cutting patchwork pieces without using templates. It is particularly effective when cutting long strips for sashing, borders, bindings, and for Seminole patchwork (see page 194).

ROTARY CUTTING EQUIPMENT

A few simple tools will enable you to cut your pieces without templates.

Roll the blade of the cutter against the ruler. The lines aid in measuring fabric

Cutting mat
This self-healing surface will grip the fabric to prevent slipping, and will keep the rotary cutter's blade sharp.

Rotary ruler
Made in clear plastic and marked with straight and angled lines. Roll the blade against the ruler's edge.

Rotary cutter
This accurately cuts through several fabric layers. Buy one with a large blade, and change the blade often.

Cutting material

1 Align the selvages evenly, and iron fabric. If the grain of the fabric is not straight, align it before cutting pattern pieces.

2 Place fabric on cutting board with raw edges at right and selvages at top. Place a triangle along straight fold of fabric. Place rotary ruler against left edge of triangle. Remove the triangle.

3 Press down firmly on the rotary ruler to prevent shifting. Run the blade of rotary cutter along edge of the ruler, keeping the blade upright. Move your hand carefully up the ruler as you cut. Always push the blade away from you.

4 Fold fabric in half again, aligning fold with selvages and matching cut edges. Using rotary ruler, measure desired width of strip. With line of ruler along cut edge, cut a strip as you did in Step 3.

5 To make squares, cut a strip 1/2 inch wider than the finished size of the square. Cut off selvages, then place the ruler over the strip and cut a piece to the same width as the strip to create 4 squares.

6 To cut half-square triangles, cut strip 7/8 inch wider than finished square. Follow steps 1 to 5. Cut squares in half.

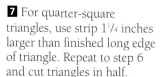

7 For quarter-square triangles, use strip 1 1/4 inches larger than finished long edge of triangle. Repeat to step 6 and cut triangles in half.

PATTERNS

A QUICK WAY to determine the difficulty of a patchwork design is to count the number of pieces in the design – the more pieces there are, the more difficult the design will be, and the more time it will take you to complete it. It is also helpful to study a design to see how many seams need matching, whether several seams must match at one point, and whether there are set-in patches or curved seams. Beginning quilters should select designs with few pieces and seams that are easy to match, such as the Shoo Fly design. The designs shown on here are graded in order of difficulty. Work your way up gradually to the more challenging designs and have the satisfaction of seeing your skills improve.

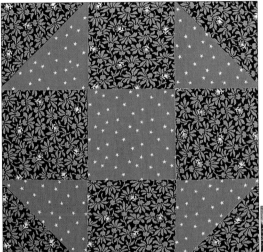

Shoo Fly

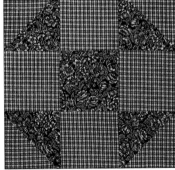

Shoo Fly variation

Grape Basket variation

EASY

Shoo Fly is one of the easiest patchwork patterns to construct. It is composed of nine squares, four of which are pieced from right-angle triangles. Both blocks are made using fabrics in the same color family. The same design can look very different depending upon the scale of the overall pattern; experiment to see the various effects.

MEDIUM

Grape Basket is a block of medium difficulty. There are many more seams than in Shoo Fly. The illustrations show a variety of fabrics, creating an old-fashioned block, and the graphic look achieved by using solid colors.

DIFFICULT

Diamond Star is a challenging block because there is an eight-seam join in the middle and the pieces at the edges must be inset (see page 193). The large illustration shows plaids and stripes, which have to be carefully matched. The variation shows how contrasting values create a feeling of depth.

Diamond Star

Grape Basket

Diamond Star variation

187

PIECING

ACCURACY IS CRUCIAL when joining many little patchwork seams together. Always sew pieces with the right sides of the fabric together and the raw edges exactly even with each other.

Seam allowances in patchwork are a quarter of a inch wide whether you are sewing by hand or machine, and must be marked on the patches when sewing by hand. Hand sewing takes more time but produces a unique look. Stitches made by hand must be evenly spaced, and not too crowded. Today, quilters often machine-piece the quilt top, to save time, and do the quilting by hand.

If machine sewing, use a standard straight stitch at a length of 10 to 12 stitches per inch. The edge of the presser foot or a marked line on the throat plate of the sewing machine should be used as a stitching guide.

HAND PIECING

Work with 18 inch lengths of matching thread knotted at the end. It helps to run the thread over a cake of beeswax to strengthen it and prevent it tangling as you work. Sewing lines are marked on the wrong side of the fabric; seams are sewn from corner to corner along the marked lines.

Holding the needle correctly is essential for good sewing

1 With a thimble on the middle finger of your sewing hand, hold the needle between your thumb and forefinger with the eye of the needle resting against the thimble.

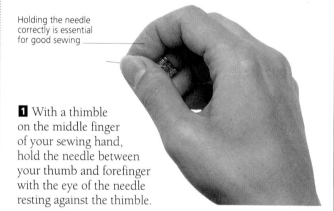

2 Hold the fabric so that you can see the sewing lines on each side. Make two backstitches at the beginning of the seam and work evenly spaced running stitches along the marked seam lines.

3 Check your stitching to ensure that they are exactly on the marked lines, front and back. Make two backstitches at the opposite corner.

Basting

Use a temporary stitch to secure the pieces before sewing them together. For easy removal, use light colored thread that will contrast with the surrounding fabric. Make spaced running stitches about 1/4 inch long.

Joining rows

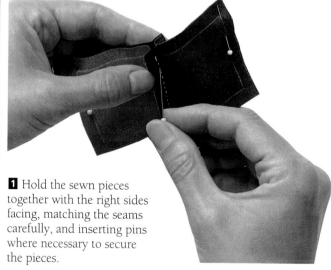

1 Hold the sewn pieces together with the right sides facing, matching the seams carefully, and inserting pins where necessary to secure the pieces.

2 At each seam, knot or backstitch the thread, then insert needle through seam allowance to other side so that you are leaving seam allowances free. Knot or backstitch again before sewing the rest of the seam.

Hand sewing over papers

1 Using outer edge of a window template, cut out fabric pieces. Use inner edge to cut out papers. Center a paper on wrong side of a fabric piece, then pin. Fold one seam allowance over paper without creasing it; baste one stitch through fabric and paper, leaving tail of thread free and unknotted.

2 Fold adjacent seam allowance over paper, forming a sharp corner. Baste over corner to secure, bringing needle up in middle of next seam allowance. Repeat for remaining edges. Cut thread, leaving end free. Remove pin. Press gently and repeat for other patches.

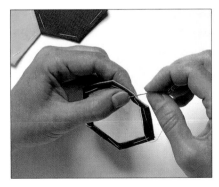

3 To join, place pieces with right sides facing, matching corners. Whip stitch edges together from corner to corner, backstitching at each end. Do not sew in papers. Remove basting stitches and papers. Gently press finished work.

MACHINE SEWING

Before joining the patchwork pieces, test the sewing machine's tension by stitching on a fabric scrap.

1 Hold the patches together; pin if necessary. Place the edge of the patches beneath the presser foot. Lower it and needle into the edge of the fabric. Stitch forward slowly, guiding the fabric with your hand. At end of the seam, pull out a length of thread and break it.

2 Backstitch to secure stitches, using reverse lever on sewing machine, or make stitches tiny. It isn't necessary to backstitch at each edge of each patch – only where you know that a seam or edge will be under stress, or when insetting (*see page 193*).

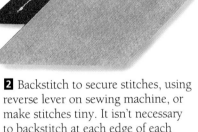

3 Patches can be sewed together in a chain to save time and thread. Feed each new set of patches beneath presser foot. Feed dogs will draw them beneath needle. Cut chain apart with scissors after sewing, and press seam allowances.

CORRECTING MISTAKES

If stitches cause the fabric to pucker, remove them carefully.

Use a seam ripper to remove unwanted stitches. Cut through every 3rd or 4th stitch on one side. On the opposite side, pull the thread – it should lift away easily.

Joining rows

Make sure that the matching seam allowances are pressed in opposite directions to reduce bulk and to make matching the seam easier. Pin the pieces together directly through the stitching, and to the right and left of the seam to prevent the pieces from shifting as you sew.

To save time, several sections of patches can be sewn up at one sitting and then snipped apart

BASIC PATCHWORK

FOR YOUR FIRST patchwork pattern, choose one of the simpler ones – we show some patterns here in order of increasing difficulty. The assembly diagrams will help you construct the patchwork blocks. Draw these patterns on graph paper to the desired size, and make templates (see page 184) to mark and cut out the patches you need. When pieces are asymmetrical, such as in the Box design, you will need to reverse some of the pieces when cutting out. Simply flip the template over and mark the outline on the fabric as usual. Blocks are assembled in sections, starting with the smallest pieces and building up from these.

Turnstyle

This four-patch design is relatively simple, and a good starting point for beginners. It is made up of identical quarters which are rotated through a circle in order to make the pattern. It is also known as Oh Susannah. Cut 4 dark and 4 light of A, and 4 medium of B. (Total of 12 pieces.)

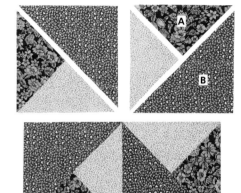

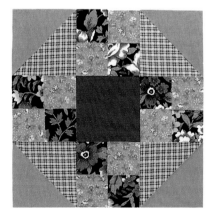

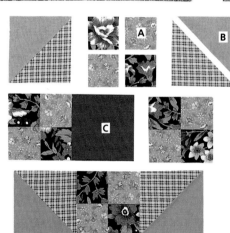

Prairie Queen

This is a nine-patch block where all the patches are pieced except the center one. The corner patches are half-square triangles, and the others simple quarters. Cut 8 medium and 8 dark of shape A, 4 light and 4 bright of B; and 1 bright of C, making 25 pieces in all.

Old Tippecanoe

Irregular sized patches make up this block. If shape A is the basic square, shape B is its quarter-square triangle, and shape C is its half-square triangle. You will need 1 dark of shape A; 8 light, 4 medium, and 8 bright of shape B; and 4 dark of shape C. There are 25 pieces in all.

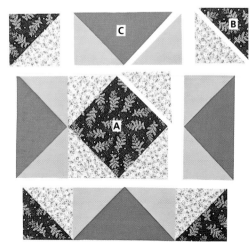

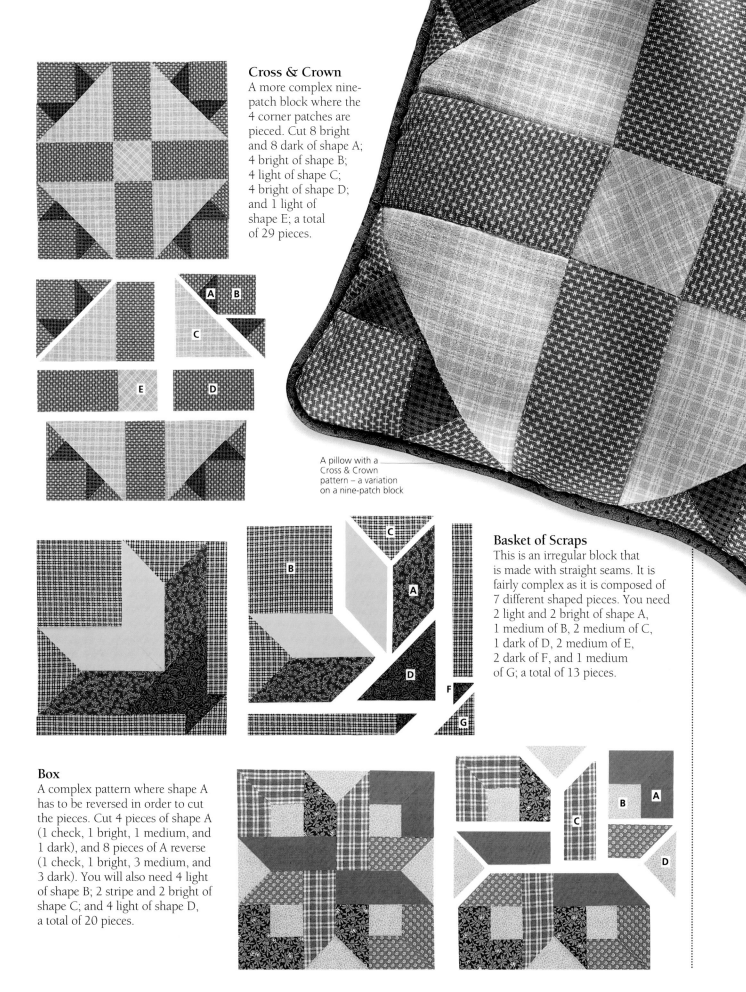

Cross & Crown

A more complex nine-patch block where the 4 corner patches are pieced. Cut 8 bright and 8 dark of shape A; 4 bright of shape B; 4 light of shape C; 4 bright of shape D; and 1 light of shape E; a total of 29 pieces.

A pillow with a Cross & Crown pattern – a variation on a nine-patch block

Basket of Scraps

This is an irregular block that is made with straight seams. It is fairly complex as it is composed of 7 different shaped pieces. You need 2 light and 2 bright of shape A, 1 medium of B, 2 medium of C, 1 dark of D, 2 medium of E, 2 dark of F, and 1 medium of G; a total of 13 pieces.

Box

A complex pattern where shape A has to be reversed in order to cut the pieces. Cut 4 pieces of shape A (1 check, 1 bright, 1 medium, and 1 dark), and 8 pieces of A reverse (1 check, 1 bright, 3 medium, and 3 dark). You will also need 4 light of shape B; 2 stripe and 2 bright of shape C; and 4 light of shape D, a total of 20 pieces.

SPECIAL TECHNIQUES

PATCHWORK CHALLENGES a sewer's ingenuity. There are times when you will need to execute some intricate maneuvers to create certain types of designs involving complex seams and joins. These techniques may seem daunting to the beginning patchworker, but are easily mastered with a bit of experience. Practice some of these techniques with scrap fabrics so that you'll be confident when you begin a project.

CURVED SEAMS

Curved seams have to be eased to fit so the pieces join smoothly and the seam does not pull or pucker.

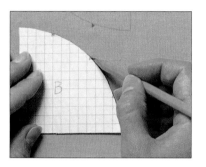

1 Cut out pieces with curves on bias of fabric. When joining curved edges, curves bend in opposite directions. Mark evenly spaced notches on seamline for matching.

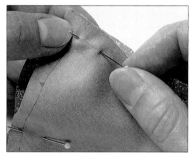

2 Match central notches on both pieces and pin together, then align side edges and pin. Match and pin any other notches, then continue pinning, easing and smoothing pieces to fit.

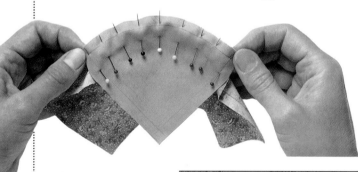

3 Sew pieces together by hand or machine, securing beginning and end of seam with backstitches. Carefully press seam allowance toward darker fabrics, clipping where necessary so seam allowance lies flat and the front of the work lies flat.

EIGHT-SEAM JOIN

Sew the diamonds together, beginning and ending the seam with backstitches ¹/₄ inch from the edges. Sew two pairs of diamonds together to form each half of the design.

1 To hand sew halves together, insert a pin exactly through point of center diamond on wrong side of one piece, exactly ¹/₄ inch away from edge to be joined. The same pin should be inserted through right side of other piece at the same point.

2 Pin the remainder of the seam, then stitch carefully. Press from the wrong side, opening up the seam allowance around the center point to reduce the bulk.

The points of the pieces should all meet accurately at one center point in the finished point.

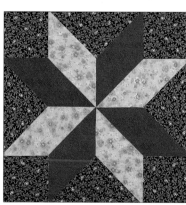

The stitching passes directly over the point of the uppermost diamond

A machine-sewn eight-seam join should look like this on the back.

SETTING IN

*This is done when
you have to sew
a piece into an
angle formed by
other joined pieces.
When sewing the initial*

*pieces, end your stitching ¹/₄ inch from the edge. Backstitch or
knot the end. Mark a dot on the corner of the piece to be inset
to show the exact position of the corner.*

Hand sewing

1 If sewing by hand, pin the patch
to be inset into the angle with right
sides together,
matching the dots
exactly. Stitch seam
fromthe outer edge
toward the center.
Make a backstitch
at the central dot.

2 Swing the
adjacent edge of the
patch to align it with
the other edge of the
angled piece, then
continue stitching
the adjacent seam
backstitching at
the end.

Machine sewing

1 To sew by
machine, pin the
patch to be inset
into the angle with
right sides together,
matching the dots
exactly. Stitch the
seam from the
center toward the
outer edge. Break
the thread.

2 Swing the
adjacent angled piece
to the other edge of
the patch and pin.
Stitch from center
to outer edge. There
should be no puckers
on the right side of
the work. Clip off
any threads.
Press carefully.

The seams are
carefully matched
at the corners

PRESSING

*Always press seam allowances to one side to make the
seams stronger, not open as in dressmaking. If possible,
press seam allowances toward the darker fabric. If this is
not possible, trim the seam allowance so that the dark
fabric does not show through to the right side. If you are
pressing small patchwork pieces, it may be easier to press
from the right side: Place the light piece of the patchwork
wrong side down on the ironing board, then with the tip
of the iron, smooth the dark fabric upward and open.*

Finger pressing

To save time or when
sewing over batting,
use this method to
crease fabrics in
position without an
iron. Run your index
finger or a thumb-
nail several times
over the area until
the crease holds.

Hand sewing

Because the
seam allowances
are left free, you
must open them
up before pressing,
in order to reduce
the bulk at the join.

Machine sewing

Press every piece
before it is crossed
by another. Always
press intersecting
seam allowances in
opposite directions.
After joining, press
the new seam
allowance toward
darker fabric.

SEMINOLE PATCHWORK

CREATED BY THE Seminole Indians of Florida around the turn of the century, this form of patchwork is a variation on strip piecing. Seminole patchwork has become increasingly popular and is often used for long borders and insertions. You will need a rotary cutter, and it is essential that you are accurate when matching and sewing seams. Although the finished result looks intricate, the method is not difficult.

Cutting and sewing the strips

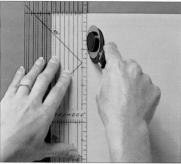

1 Choose a pattern from below and, using a rotary cutter, cut the required number of strips. Coat the strips lightly with spray starch to make them easier to handle and press. Sew the strips together in the combinations given with the design. Press the seam allowances toward the darker fabrics.

2 Cut the strips into pieces of the required width, and arrange on your cutting mat to follow the design shown.

3 Sew the pieces together in a chain (*see page 189*) either alternating the pieces or offsetting them as directed. Press the strip carefully.

4 Use a rotary cutter to trim the top and bottom edges evenly if necessary. Remember to leave a ¼ inch seam allowance all around.

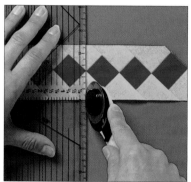

5 You can straighten the angled ends of Seminole patchwork by making a straight cut through the patchwork. If you have seams that do not quite match, make your cut through this area.

6 Re-arrange the pieces, aligning the diagonal edges. Sew these edges together, matching the seams carefully.

NOTE:
The instructions on these pages assume you are working with 45-inch wide fabrics. Cut all the strips across the full width of the fabric, then trim off ½ inch from the selvage ends, to leave you with a 44-inch long strip.

The colorful strips of Seminole patchwork are easy to master

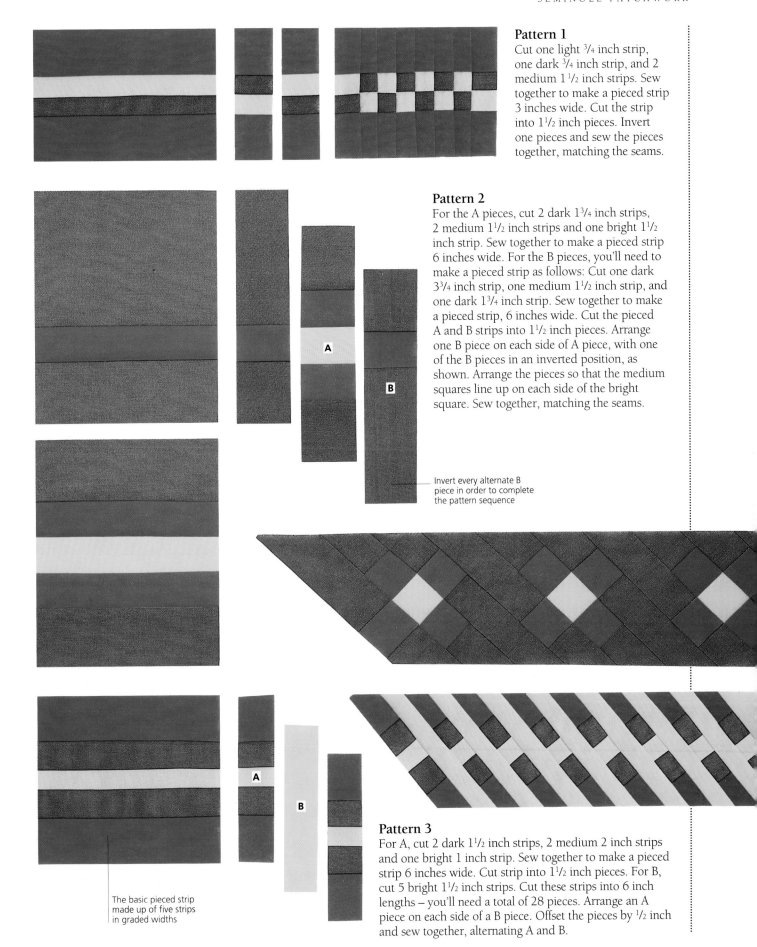

Pattern 1

Cut one light ³/₄ inch strip, one dark ³/₄ inch strip, and 2 medium 1 ¹/₂ inch strips. Sew together to make a pieced strip 3 inches wide. Cut the strip into 1¹/₂ inch pieces. Invert one pieces and sew the pieces together, matching the seams.

Pattern 2

For the A pieces, cut 2 dark 1³/₄ inch strips, 2 medium 1¹/₂ inch strips and one bright 1¹/₂ inch strip. Sew together to make a pieced strip 6 inches wide. For the B pieces, you'll need to make a pieced strip as follows: Cut one dark 3³/₄ inch strip, one medium 1¹/₂ inch strip, and one dark 1³/₄ inch strip. Sew together to make a pieced strip, 6 inches wide. Cut the pieced A and B strips into 1¹/₂ inch pieces. Arrange one B piece on each side of A piece, with one of the B pieces in an inverted position, as shown. Arrange the pieces so that the medium squares line up on each side of the bright square. Sew together, matching the seams.

Invert every alternate B piece in order to complete the pattern sequence

The basic pieced strip made up of five strips in graded widths

Pattern 3

For A, cut 2 dark 1¹/₂ inch strips, 2 medium 2 inch strips and one bright 1 inch strip. Sew together to make a pieced strip 6 inches wide. Cut strip into 1¹/₂ inch pieces. For B, cut 5 bright 1¹/₂ inch strips. Cut these strips into 6 inch lengths – you'll need a total of 28 pieces. Arrange an A piece on each side of a B piece. Offset the pieces by ¹/₂ inch and sew together, alternating A and B.

FOLDED STAR

THIS TYPE OF patchwork is composed of folded rectangles or circles, arranged in overlapping layers to form a star design on a base of lightweight foundation fabric. Folded star pattern is ideal for wallhangings and pillows or could be framed as a sampler. Use highly contrasting fabrics to make the most of this technique and arrange one color of fabric in each round. To achieve a perfect star, ensure that the points of each round are the same distance away from the center. The instructions for making a folded star are given in the pattern instructions (page 247). This pattern is not suitable for a quilt that will receive heavy use as the folds conceal unfinished edges that could fray from wear and frequent washing. The technique of folding also means that the amount of fabric used makes the finished work thick and heavy.

CRAZY PATCHWORK

PROBABLY THE EARLIEST type of patchwork, this technique was born out of the necessity to mend tattered clothing or blankets. During the Victorian era crazy patchwork evolved into an art form in its own right when women used it as a medium for displaying their fine needleworking skills.

Crazy patchwork can be as simple or as elaborate as you wish to make it. It is an enjoyable technique that can make use of all the bits of fabric that you hate to part with, but that you can't use in a larger project. To make a Victorian-style crazy quilt, collect all the rich silks, brocades, and velvet fabrics you can find. Sew them in a random fashion to a base fabric, then embroider over the seams with silk embroidery floss in a variety of fanciful patterns. You can also stitch small motifs in the middle of some of the patches.

This flower has a chain stitch stem. Metallic thread is used for the couched surface decoration

Padded appliqué emphasizes the cat's shape. The face is worked in small, straight stitches

Here, the details are worked in straight stitch, buttonhole, and double feather stitch. Sequins add an exotic touch

LOG CABIN PATCHWORK

THIS PATCHWORK TECHNIQUE involves sewing strips of fabric around a central shape to produce a variety of effects. It is essential that you work with strongly contrasting fabrics so that one half of the block is light and the other half is dark. Identical Log Cabin blocks can be arranged to make numerous different pattern combinations.

There are two main ways to sew a Log Cabin block. One is to sew all the pieces onto a muslin base. This is a good method for combining fabrics of different weights and textures as the base provides a firm foundation. However, the finished product will be difficult to quilt since there is an extra layer of fabric that must be sewn through. You can get around this by using batting for the base, or placing the batting on the base and sewing and quilting at the same time.

The second method, shown here, does not require any templates, unless you are using an unusual shape for the center of the block. Rotary cutting will simplify the cutting process and save time.

TRADITIONAL LOG CABIN BLOCK

The red square in the middle represents the hearth of the log cabin, while the strips symbolize the logs of the cabin walls. The dark and light portions of the block show the effect of sunshine and shadow on the cabin in day and night. To construct the block, begin in the middle and work around in a counter-clockwise direction.

Working without templates

1 Make sure the light and dark fabric you choose contrast sharply. Then cut strips to desired width plus half inch seam allowance – making sure to cut across entire width of fabric.

2 The center can be any shape, although it is usually a square. If you choose another shape, you must make a template and cut the shape with a rotary cutter. Red is traditionally used for the center.

3 With right sides facing, place the center square against a light strip, matching the edges. Stitch, then cut the strip even with the square. Press the seam allowance toward the center.

4 Alternatively, if you wish to use the same fabric for all the first strips in your quilt, sew the center pieces to the first strip one after another, leaving only a small space between each. Cut the pieces apart, trimming them to the same size as the center square.

5 Choose a different light fabric for the second strip and sew to the pieced center, trimming away the excess fabric so it is even with the center. Press lightly.

6 Again, to make all the blocks exactly the same, sew these pieces to the 2nd strip leaving only a small space between each. Cut the pieces apart, trimming them to the same size as the pieced center. Continue adding around center if you want every block to have the same fabric arrangement.

7 Pick a dark fabric for the 3rd strip. Continuing counter-clockwise, sew the pieced center to the 3rd strip, trimming away the excess strip so it is even with the center. Press lightly.

8 Select a different dark fabric for the 4th strip. Sew to the pieced center, trimming away the excess fabric as before. Press lightly.

9 Continue working counter-clockwise, adding 2 light strips, then 2 dark strips in turn around the center. Avoid placing the same fabrics next to each other. Trim the strips and press lightly after each addition.

10 Once you have made the required number of blocks for your quilt or wall hanging, arrange the blocks in a variety of positions to see the different effects you can achieve by transposing the dark and light portions of the blocks. Examples are shown here.

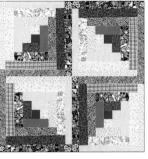

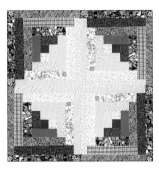

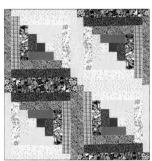

An arrangement of Log Cabin blocks makes a strong pattern

APPLIQUÉ

If you have ever patched a pair of jeans or sewn a merit badge onto a child's scout uniform then you have appliquéd. The word means applied, and the technique is simply to stitch one fabric on top of another. Functional or purely decorative, appliqués can be hand or machine made, and the stitches used to secure the appliqués to the background fabric can be invisible, such as a slip stitch, or visible and part of the decorative effect, such as satin stitch.

APPLIQUÉ QUILT

Huge stylized flower motifs are appliquéd around the border of this quilt, and the shape of the motif is echoed in the quilting on the plain white background.

In appliqué work, you can use many different fabrics in one project, provided that the finished item will not be subjected to heavy wear and frequent washing. The combination of diverse fabrics, such as tweeds, corduroys, silks, and satins, and the use of buttons, beads, and sequins, can create marvelous effects. Beginners may wish to appliqué using felt because it is easy to work with and doesn't fray. Or, choose tightly woven 100% cotton fabrics that are not likely to fray.

APPLIQUÉ DESIGNS

If you are a beginner, select an appliqué design with straight lines or gradual curves and a relatively small number of large or medium-sized pieces. As you become adept at turning the edges under smoothly and sewing them invisibly to a fabric background, you can graduate to more complex shapes and designs. Templates for hand and machine appliqué have no seam allowances so that you can mark the exact outline of the piece on the fabric. Basting lines on your base fabric will help you place the appliqué pieces.

Cutting appliqués

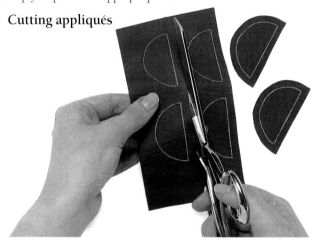

Make templates (to finished size) as on page 184. Mark outline on right side of fabric, leaving ½ inch in between each. Cut out pieces, adding a ¼ inch seam allowance.

Preparing the base fabric

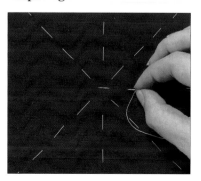

Cut fabric for base 1 inch larger than desired size. Fold base in half horizontally, vertically, and then diagonally, and press folds. Open fabric and baste along each fold with contrasting thread. Press flat.

HAND APPLIQUÉ

Floral, geometric, or pictorial themes all work well in appliqué. If necessary, enlarge or reduce your design and transfer it to paper.

1 Draw the design and label each piece by letter. Trace the design and make a template for each appliqué. Label each template with the correct letter. Mark outline of appliqués on right side of fabric and cut, adding a ¼ inch seam allowance.

2 Use tip of a sharp pair of scissors to clip into curved edges perpendicular to marked outline of piece; do not clip beyond the outline. Make extra clips along deep curves for ease in turning.

3 Using a design tracing, pencil outlines of pieces on right side of base about ¼ inch within outline, to avoid marks showing around edges.

4 Following placement lines, arrange appliqués on the base. Position the background pieces first, with foreground pieces overlapping if necessary. Pin or baste pieces to base.

5 Turn the raw edges of the appliqués ¼ inch to the wrong side, using the tip of your needle as a tool for turning.

6 Using matching thread and making tiny invisible slip stitches, sew the appliqués to the base fabric, starting with the background pieces and finishing with the appliqués that are topmost.

7 Turn completed design to wrong side and very carefully cut away base fabric within all the larger appliqué pieces, leaving a ¼ inch seam allowance. This eliminates any puckers, and makes quilting easier.

8 Remove the pins or basting threads after the appliqué work is finished. Press the appliqués lightly on a thick towel so that the seam allowances do not show through to the right side.

SPECIAL APPLIQUÉ TECHNIQUES

Complex shapes will require you to use special techniques in order to achieve a smooth edge to your appliqué pieces, and prevent the seam allowance from distorting the shape.

Points

Trimming your seam allowance will help you make neat points

1 First clip into seam allowance ¼ inch away from tip on each side and trim seam to ⅛ inch. Trim off point ⅛ inch away from marked turning line. Fold the point to the wrong side along the turning line.

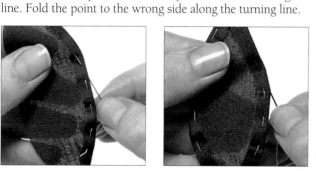

2 Fold one edge of appliqué ¼ inch to wrong side. Steam-press, then baste in place. Fold second edge to wrong side, overlapping first edge at top and bottom. Steam and baste.

Valleys

A sharp dip in an appliqué is called a valley. Clip into the seam allowance to the marked outline. Fold the edges to the wrong side. The seam allowances will separate, leaving virtually no fabric at the valley. Appliqué as normal; when you reach the dip, work a few extra stitches.

Circles

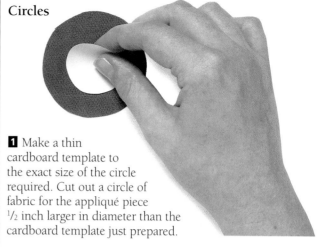

1 Make a thin cardboard template to the exact size of the circle required. Cut out a circle of fabric for the appliqué piece ½ inch larger in diameter than the cardboard template just prepared.

2 Work a row of basting stitches close to the edge of the fabric circle.

3 Place the cardboard template in the middle of the wrong side of the fabric circle. Gently pull the basting stitches to gather the edge of the fabric circle around the cardboard template. Make a few backstitches to secure the end of the thread.

4 Press the circle gently so that there are no puckers on right side. Then, remove the cardboard from the circle without distorting shape.

MACHINE APPLIQUÉ

Before starting, change to a new needle and a zigzag foot; use 100% cotton thread to match the appliqué. Because the seam allowances are not turned under, technically you do not need to add an allowance when cutting out your pieces. However, it is not easy to keep the pieces from puckering when stitching very close to the edges. Therefore, the steps shown here show a seam allowance, which is trimmed away after stitching. Test your stitch on a scrap of fabric. Use a standard width of 1/8 inch for medium-weight fabrics. Fine fabrics will require a narrow stitch width, and heavy fabrics need a wider one. The tension should be even and should not pucker the fabric. If the bobbin thread shows through to the right side, loosen the top tension of the sewing machine.

1 Cut out the appliqués and prepare the base as directed on page 200. Follow steps 1, 2, and 4 for Hand Appliqué. Arrange the pieces in their correct position on the base fabric and attach, using a fabric glue stick and basting stitches.

2 Machine-stitch along the marked outline of each appliqué, using matching thread to make short straight stitches.

3 Using sharp embroidery scissors, carefully trim away the excess seam allowance beyond the stitching line, cutting as close to your machine stitches as possible.

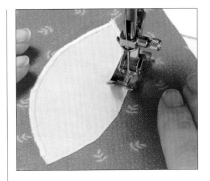

4 Zigzag-stitch over line of stitches, covering raw edges of fabric. Gently guide fabric around curves so that machine sews smoothly. Work slowly so that you have complete control over your stitching.

STITCH EFFECTS

Use zigzag satin stitch to add details that are too small to make in fabric, such as veining on leaves, or to delineate flower petals. You can also use machine-embroidery stitches to create a variety of other embellishments. A highly contrasting thread will also create special effects in machine appliqué, with black or dark gray creating a stained glass appearance.

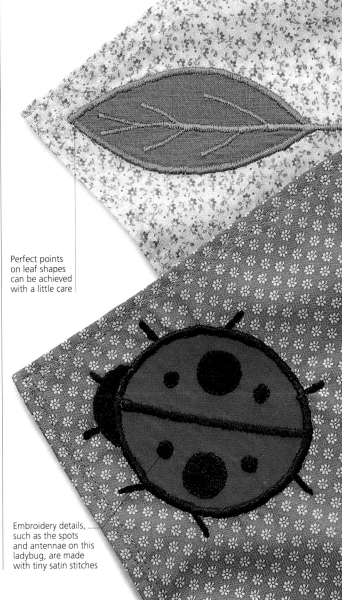

Perfect points on leaf shapes can be achieved with a little care

Embroidery details, such as the spots and antennae on this ladybug, are made with tiny satin stitches

CONSTRUCTING A QUILT

THERE ARE MANY ways to join patchwork blocks together to make a quilt. Each method produces very different results, even when the same patchwork blocks are used. Shown here are some of the traditional ways of joining patchwork blocks. Sashing refers to fabric strips that surround each block of a quilt. In edge-to-edge, the blocks are sewn directly together. Connector squares, or posts, join the short sashing strips that frame individual blocks. Appliqué is used to hide seams and decorate the blocks.

SCRAP QUILT

This Evening Star scrap quilt features blocks set together with gray sashing strips and navy posts (connector squares).

SASHING

The medallion-style blocks of this Lone Star quilt are framed with green sashing.

EDGE-TO-EDGE SETTING

This variation on the Card Trick design has a pieced ribbon border. The blocks form a secondary pattern.

BALTIMORE QUILT

The seams between the blocks of this Baltimore Album-style quilt are decorated with red appliqué made to resemble lace.

ASSEMBLING A QUILT

A QUILT IS a sandwich composed of three layers – the quilt top, the batting, and the quilt back. The layers are held together with quilting stitches or by tying (see pages 206 to 210). Baste the layers carefully before you quilt to prevent creases and puckers forming on the back of the finished quilt.

Putting quilt layers together

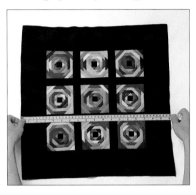

1 Measure your quilt top to find the size of quilt back. Add a 2 inch margin all around. This will be trimmed off later. You may have to join pieces for quilt back, but usually only one central seam is required. If the quilt is large, you may need to join 3 pieces together.

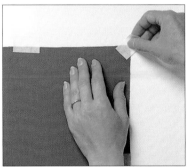

2 Press the quilt back carefully and lay it on a large flat surface, wrong side up. If you can, tape edges of quilt back in place to prevent fabric from shifting as you work.

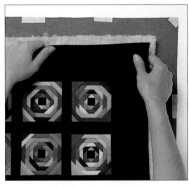

3 Cut a piece of batting the same size as the quilt top. Place in the center of the quilt back. Carefully iron the quilt top and remove any loose threads or bits of fabric. Then, place it right side up on the batting.

4 Pin the layers together with long straight pins so that they don't shift while basting.

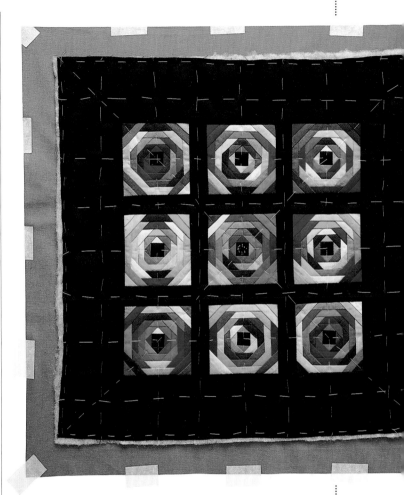

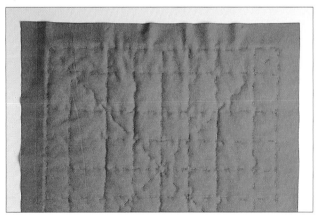

5 Baste the quilt together from the center out to the edges, first horizontally and vertically, then diagonally in each direction. Secure any open areas of quilt with additional basting, working out from the center.

HAND QUILTING

THE MAIN PURPOSE of quilting is to hold the top, batting, and backing layers together to prevent them from shifting when the quilt is being used or washed. Quilting stitches are simply running stitches that pass through all three layers, anchoring the layers together firmly. The stitches can be worked on plain fabric or pieced work, according to the design. Quilting stitches also help bring your quilt to life by providing another design that adds dimension to your work, and serves to highlight or offset the piecing.

1 Cut an 18 inch length of quilting thread and knot the end. Pass thread through top of quilt, pulling it so that knot becomes buried in batting. The knot will make a popping sound as it passes through quilt top.

2 You may want to use a thimble. With one hand below the quilt to guide the needle upward, begin working a series of running stitches through all 3 layers of quilt. The stitches should be the same length on the front and back.

3 Try to make 3 or 4 stitches at a time, rocking needle from surface to quilt back and up to surface again, then pull stitches through. If quilt is in a frame, you can pull quite firmly, which will give your stitches greater definition.

4 If you have trouble pulling the needle through, use a balloon to grip the needle.

5 When you reach the end of your length of thread, make a knot close to the surface of the quilt. Then make a backstitch through the quilt top and batting, pulling the knot beneath the surface and burying it in the batting.

USING A HOOP

Quilting frames can be quite bulky, and few of us have the room for one. Luckily, any size project can be quilted using a large (20 inch) hoop specifically designed for this purpose. (You will still need to baste the quilt.) The tautness, or surface tension, of the quilt in the hoop can vary from very firm to slightly pliant – experiment to find the tension you prefer.

1 Unscrew wing nut on your hoop and separate inner and outer rings. Place inner ring on a flat surface, then position center of your project over it. Place outer ring over inner, and tighten screw after adjusting tension.

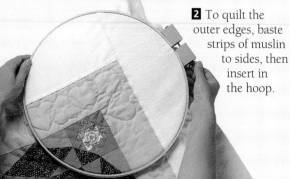

2 To quilt the outer edges, baste strips of muslin to sides, then insert in the hoop.

MACHINE QUILTING

QUICKER THAN HAND quilting, machine quilting is sometimes an effective way of finishing those quilts that are too thick to stitch by hand. Use a medium color printed fabric for the quilt back. The secret to successful machine quilting is to maintain an even tension between the top thread and the bobbin, so test your tension on a scrap quilt "sandwich", and adjust before sewing the quilt itself.

SETTING UP THE MACHINE

Use a size 80/12 needle, and use a 50 three-ply mercerized cotton thread. Wind the bobbin with thread to match the quilt back so that any uneven stitches will not show. If the quilt is well basted and not too thick, you can use a regular presser foot. Work at a table large enough to support the entire quilt – if it hangs off, it will hinder the operation. If the top is being pushed ahead of the batting, use a walking foot (see below).

Quilting by machine

1 To secure the thread ends at the beginning or end of a line of stitching, stitch forward and reverse several times, then cut off the surplus threads close to the surface of the quilt.

2 You can use a spacer guide, which attaches to the walking foot, to sew parallel lines without marking them.

3 Place your hands on each side of the needle and smooth the quilt as you sew. Pulling or pushing the fabric may cause skipped stitches or puckers on the back. Check the back often to catch problems as they occur.

4 First stabilize the quilt by basting as straight a line as possible down the horizontal and vertical centers of piece. Then quilt each quadrant in turn, from center outward to edges.

5 Beginners should try a small project first. The simplest technique is to stitch-in-the-ditch, which means to stitch as close to the seam as possible, opposite the pressed seam allowances.

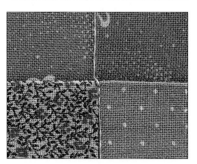

6 If you are sewing along a seam where the position of the seam allowances alternate, just make a small stitch across the intersection and alternate your quilting line too.

7 Roll large quilts in a scroll-like fashion and only uncover the area you wish to quilt. Secure the roll with bicycle clips.

WALKING FOOT

You can use a walking foot (or even feed foot) with most sewing machines. This contains a set of feed dogs similar to those in the throat plate. With both sets working in unison, the fabric layers move evenly beneath the needle.

QUILTING PATTERNS

THE EARLIEST QUILTS were often stitched in straight and diagonal lines, creating simple squares and diamond shapes. The elaborate use of interwoven curves and circles creates a more decorative effect. These medallions set on a plain colored fabric are called wholecloth motifs.

If you want to create your own filling designs for a simple outline shape, bear in mind that the filling lines are there to secure the batting. Always try to create an evenly spaced design. See page 248 for the pattern designs to trace for yourself.

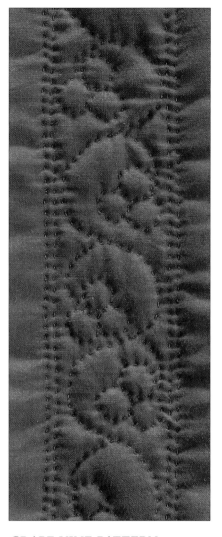

GRAPE VINE PATTERN

This variation on a grape vine pattern makes a suitable border to work continuously around a quilt.

LEAF PATTERN

In this early American quilt, the outline of the leaf is filled with an elaborate pattern of veins. The outer rows of stitches become progressively wider apart.

JAPANESE PATTERN

Sashiko is the name for the folk quilting of Japan, and is often worked in strongly contrasting colors or in white on black. This repeating pattern is called Asanoha or hemp leaf.

PETAL BORDER

An interlacing of simple curves makes a petal design border, with a motif based on the same pattern at each corner.

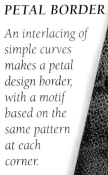

WHOLECLOTH MOTIFS

This medallion design (above left) shows a feathered circle with lattice center. The center can be varied according to taste. The clam shell is another traditional motif (below).

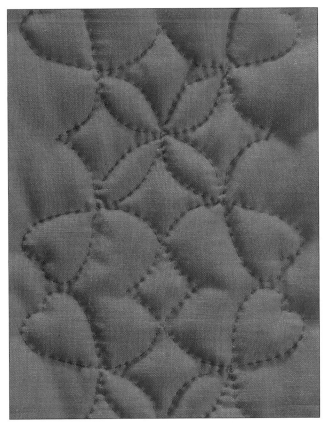

CONNECTED HEARTS

A border of linked hearts and curves is based on a traditional pattern. It can form a filling pattern or a border.

TIED QUILTING

TIED QUILTING IS a quick and simple alternative to hand or machine quilting. It is effective when making quilts for children or projects that have a thick layer of batting. It is worked by making a series of double knots through all three layers to secure them. If the quilt is tied from the back, the ties will be virtually invisible on the front, leaving only small indentations that can form an attractive pattern of their own.

Alternatively, if you wish to make the ties a decorative feature, tie the quilt from the front so that the ends are visible, or use a contrasting color thread to make the ties stand out from the background.

TYING THE QUILT

Ties must be spaced every 2¹/₂ inches if you are using polyester batting, and closer if using cotton batting. You can use silk or cotton thread, embroidery floss, or yarn for the ties. Work with a crewel needle and an 18 to 24 inch length of your chosen thread.

Separate ties

1 Assemble the quilt layers as directed on page 205. Decide on where you wish the ends of the ties to show, and work from that side of the quilt. Leaving a short end of thread, make a backstitch through all three layers.

Knotted ties on the front of a quilt can be used as decoration

2 Make another backstitch in the same spot and cut the thread, leaving a short end.

3 Tie the ends together in a double knot. Trim the ends evenly. Continue tying knots across the quilt, spacing them evenly.

Joined ties

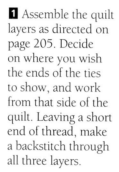

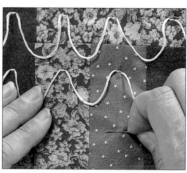

1 If the ties are going to be spaced close together, work the 2 backstitches, then go on to the next area without cutting the thread. Continue with the same length of thread until you run out.

2 Cut the thread in between the ties, then tie the ends into a double knot.

BINDING A QUILT

ADDING THE BINDING is the last step in making a quilt, and it is the finishing touch that determines the overall appearance. The edges should lie smoothly without puckers or ripples. Therefore, you should bind the quilt carefully, using binding that matches the rest of the quilt in weight and quality.

JOINING THE BINDING

Cut 1 1/2 inch-wide strips across the width of the fabric on straight grain. Cut enough strips to fit around the raw edges of the quilt plus 4 inches. Sew the strips together, then press the seams to one side. Press the binding in half lengthwise with wrong sides facing one another; then press one long edge to the center crease, again with wrong sides facing. You will need room to spread out, so choose a suitable work space.

Adding the binding

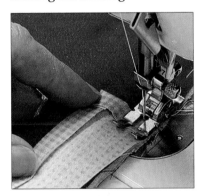

1 Place the middle of one side edge of the quilt on your sewing machine, right side up. Fold one end of binding 1/2 inch to wrong side and place on quilt top with right sides together and raw edges even. Stitch the binding to the quilt making a 1/4 inch seam.

2 As you approach first corner, shorten your stitch length and align binding to next edge of quilt, leaving a fold of binding that lines up with quilt edge. Stitch up to edge of fold. Stop stitching.

  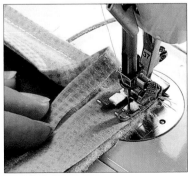

3 Lift the needle and the presser foot and refold the binding so that the fold is on the edge of the quilt that you have just sewn. Lower the needle exactly into the fold so that it does not catch your previous fold; lower the presser foot and continue stitching. Adjust the stitch length to normal after about 1/2 inch. Continue machine stitching to the next corner.

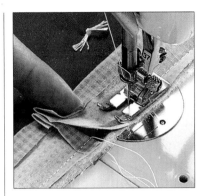

4 Sew each corner in the same way. When you reach the starting point, allow the binding to overlap the beginning fold by 1/2 inch. Trim away any excess binding.

5 Wrap the folded pressed edge of the binding over to the back, overlapping the stitching line. Pin in place. Slip stitch the binding to the quilt back using matching thread.

6 When you reach the end of the binding strip, fold the end of the binding 1/2 inch to the wrong side to make a neat join at the point the ends overlap.

7 Use a pin to adjust the tucks at each corner into a perfect miter. Carefully stitch the mitered corners in place.

RUGMAKING

*R*ugs, like other handcrafted items, can be beautiful and decorative as well as functional. Rugmaking developed from a need to create useful items from readily available materials. We cover two of the most popular and easy-to-master techniques – braiding and hooking. Braiding involves interlacing fabric strips into ovals, rectangles, and circles. No special equipment is required, and the technique is very adaptable. Durable and colorful, soft rugs, runners, mats, and chair pads can be created from fabric remnants of wool or cotton. When working hooked rugs, the yarn or fabric is forced through the backing fabric to create rugs, pillow covers, and wall hangings. Rugs can also be worked on canvas using a latch-hook; the yarn is cut before use so that a thick pile is created. Hooked or knotted rugs can be worked in many different types of designs which are charted out or drawn directly on the backing. Today, when so many items are factory produced, Good Housekeeping readers are rediscovering handcrafted rugs that are a joy to create, use, and display.

TOOLS & EQUIPMENT

THREE BASIC METHODS of rugmaking are described in this section – hooking, knotting, and braiding. They can all be used as colorful wallhangings and pillows as well as on the floor. Hooked rugs are worked by pulling loops of fabric or yarn through a woven backing fabric with a hand hook or a punch hook. The pile on knotted rugs is formed by tying yarn to open-mesh canvas with a latch hook. No special tools or backing fabrics are required for braided rugs. Instead, braided strips of fabric are laced together with strong thread to form a solid mat. If your rug is to be used on the floor, particularly in a heavily trafficked area, you should choose materials that are very hardwearing.

Hand-hook method

Punch-hook method

Latch-hook method

Braided method

TOOLS AND BACKING FABRICS

The hand hook, the traditional tool for making fabric rugs, is like a crochet hook with a wooden handle. The punch hook is also used for hooked rugs. It has a hollow shaft through which yarn is threaded. The latch hook has a hinged bar for knotting loops of yarn onto canvas. The fabric folder, which pre-folds fabric strips, is useful for braided rugs.

For hand-hook and punch-hook rugs use burlap, a closely woven fabric made from jute, as a backing; choose the strongest available. Another popular backing for these rugs is evenweave cotton/linen-mix fabric. It is more expensive than burlap, but more durable. Latch-hook rugs require a canvas (rug canvas), which has 3 to 5 mesh holes per inch.

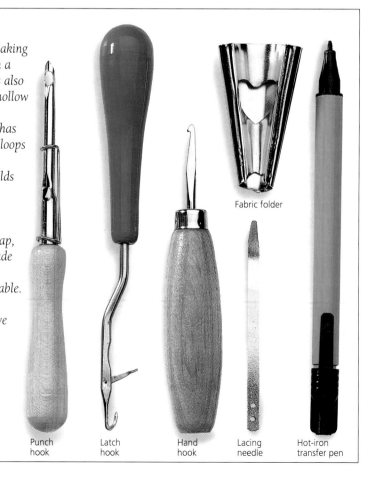

Burlap

Evenweave cotton linen-mix fabric

Rug canvas

Punch hook

Latch hook

Hand hook

Lacing needle

Fabric folder

Hot-iron transfer pen

YARNS AND FABRICS

Rug yarn is a smooth, heavy, 4- to 6- ply yarn suitable for hand-hook, punch-hook, and latch-hook rugs. It is available in balls and hanks. You can use Rya yarn for both punch-hook and latch-hook rugs; several strands of the twisted 2-ply yarn are generally used together. Both these yarns can be bought in ready-cut lengths for latch-hook rugs, which is more convenient but more expensive than cutting the yarn into lengths yourself. Any scraps of closely woven fabric can be used for hand-hooked and braided rugs. The fabric should be washed first to pre-shrink it. Wool is the most hard wearing fabric to use and repels dirt best.

Rug yarn

Rya yarn

Pre-cut yarn

Fabric strips

PREPARATION OF BACKING

The edges of the backing must be strengthened to prevent fraying while the rug is being worked.

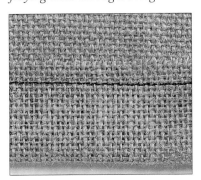

For a hand-hook or punch-hook rug, cut the woven backing to size, allowing an extra 4 inches around the edges so that it can be secured to a frame. Turn a ½ -inch hem around each edge, and machine stitch.

For a latch-hook rug, cut the canvas to size, leaving a 1- to 2-inch hem allowance around the edges. Turn the hems to the back of the canvas and work the first knots through both layers of canvas.

TRANSFERRING DESIGNS TO THE BACKING

Once you have made initial sketches for your design, you can draw it out free-hand on the backing fabric with a waterproof marking pen. Or make a full-size drawing and transfer it using one of the methods given below.

Hand-hook and punch-hook rugs

Draw your design onto tracing paper with a hot-iron transfer pen (left), then turn the tracing face down on to the backing and press carefully (right).
Note: If you are making a punch-hook rug, remember that you will be working the design on the wrong side of the backing. This means that the design should be transferred to the underside of the backing as a mirror image to the way you want it to look on the pile of the rug.

Latch-hook rugs

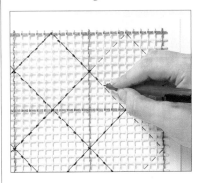

Center the design (right-side up) underneath the canvas, and tape or pin them together. The design outlines are quite visible through the canvas. Trace the design onto it with a waterproof felt-tip pen.

TO FINISH RUGS

To sew a large rug together, and for lacing braided rugs, use carpet thread. The edges of hooked rugs can be finished with a woven cloth tape called rug binding.

 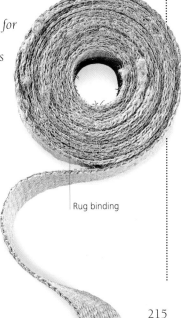

Carpet thread

Rug binding

HAND-HOOKED RUGS

HAND-HOOKED RUGS are worked by pulling loops of a continuous strip of fabric or yarn through a woven backing fabric. The loops stay in place because they are tightly packed together. In order to keep the loops at an even height, the backing must be stretched taut on a straight-sided frame before you start hooking (see page 121). The hand hook is the traditional tool that was used by early American settlers to make superb, finely detailed rag rugs from strips cut from worn-out clothing. Thin strips of fabric work best, as hand hooks tend to split the strands of wool when they are pulled through the backing.

The beribboned toy sheep is framed with a rustic fence border

SHEEP RUG

The folk-art simplicity of early American rugs is captured in this charming design, with the curly texture of the sheep formed by the wool strips. To make, see page 249.

PATCHWORK RUG

A traditional patchwork design is combined with the art of rugmaking to produce a beautiful and useful object. For instructions, see page 249.

Amish quilt patterns in glowing colors are the inspiration for this hand-hooked rug

PREPARATION OF FABRIC

Wash the fabric to remove any finishings, especially if it is new. Use a sharp pair of scissors to cut the fabric into long, thin strips. The width of the strips will depend on the type of fabric used and the effect you want to achieve, so experiment on a piece of backing fabric first. For a homespun look, ¹/₄ inch strips usually work well. Fabrics can be cut as wide as ¹/₂ inch or as thin as ¹/₈ depending on the look you wish to achieve. Cut woven fabrics along the grain, and knitted fabrics along their length. Never cut the strips on the bias.

Basic method

1 Work from right to left. Hold the fabric strip on the wrong side of the backing with your left hand, letting it run loosely between your thumb and forefinger.

2 Hold the hook like a pencil in your right hand, with the hook facing upward. From right side, push hook between 2 threads of backing. Hook around fabric strip, and pull up one end to right side of the backing.

3 To form first loop, push hook through backing fabric again, two threads to left of fabric end that you have just pulled up to right side. Keep holding strip loosely on underside of work with your left hand. If you hold it too tightly, you may pull out the end as you hook up loop.

4 Hook around the fabric and pull up a loop the required size to the right side of work. As a rule, the height of the loop is the same size as the width of the strip.

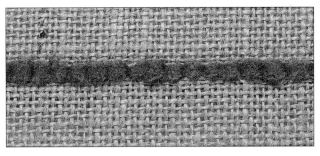

5 Continue pulling up loops of the fabric strip, leaving one or 2 threads of backing fabric between them. On the wrong side of the work, the hooking should look like a smooth row of running stitches. If any of these stitches are forming loops on the wrong side, you are not pulling up the loops on the right side far enough.

6 Leave one or 2 threads of backing between each row of loops. Always start and finish each row by pulling up ends of strip to right side of work. Trim these ends to same height as loops if necessary, when the rug is completed.

WORKING A DESIGN

Create the details of the design first, and then fill in the background. First, outline the detail with a row of loops. Then, fill in the outlined area with rows of loops. Never carry the yarn or fabric strips from one area to another, because the trailing loops on the wrong side may break as you continue hooking. If the rug starts to buckle, you may be spacing the loops and rows too close together. If so, increase the space by one thread of the backing fabric. If too much of the backing fabric is showing through, decrease the spacing by one thread of the backing.

PUNCH-HOOKED RUGS

PUNCH-HOOKED RUGS are worked on a woven backing fabric stretched in a straight-sided frame. The finished effect is similar to a hand-hooked rug because the technique produces a raised pile formed by tightly packed loops of yarn or fabric. The main difference is that a punch-hooked rug is worked with the wrong side of the rug facing toward you, so you must remember to transfer a mirror-image of your design onto this side. Once you have got the knack, a punch hook is quicker to manipulate than a hand hook because it automatically feeds the yarn through the backing, and regulates the height of the loops. Yarns are easier to use than strips of fabric because they slide more freely up and down the shaft of the hook.

TOOLS

Punch hooks come in several sizes for a range of different weights of yarns. Be sure to choose a size that allows the yarn to pass easily through the eye of the hook's needle. The punch hook can be adjusted to form loops of different height, from about 1/4 inch to 3/4 inch, by turning and locking the handle.

The yarn should move freely through the eye of the needle

1 Thread hook with yarn, following hook manufacturer's instructions. When eye is threaded, pull yarn slightly to check it is moving freely.

2 Hold the hook like a pencil, with the grooved side facing in the direction you are working. If the grooved side is not facing the correct way, the yarn will not feed through the needle properly.

3 Push needle portion down through backing fabric up to the wooden handle.

4 Withdraw the needle until it just touches the surface of backing. Do not lift it off. Slide the needle along the surface of backing for a few threads, and push it in again.

5 Continue in this way, changing direction when necessary. Leave a few threads of the backing fabric between each row of loops.

6 Check to make sure loops are even. If not, slip a knitting needle through them and pull them up to same level as the rest.

To end a piece of yarn

When you come to the end of a length of yarn, push hook through backing (*left*). Pull yarn slightly, and cut it off behind eye. Remove hook. Trim yarn ends even with pile (*right*).

LATCH-HOOKED RUGS

LATCH-HOOKED RUGS are worked on canvas, and no frame is needed. The yarn is pre-cut to a given length, and each piece is knotted separately onto the backing. It is easiest to work with rug yarn, but different types and textures of yarn, as well as strips of ribbon and braid can also be knotted with the hook. Since this type of rug has a dense pile, fine details get lost. You will find that strong patterns work best.

HOOKING

Cut the yarn into lengths and hem the canvas, as shown right. Work the rows of knots horizontally, starting at the bottom. Check that all knots lie in the same direction.

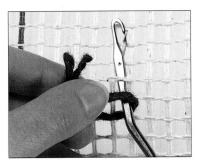

1 Fold length of yarn in half around shank of hook. Hold yarn ends together; insert tip of hook under one horizontal canvas thread and push it through to right side until latch of hook opens.

2 Take the 2 yarn ends through the latch, and place them underneath the hook.

3 Pull hook toward you so that the latch closes around the yarn. Keep pulling until the 2 ends of the yarn have been drawn through the loop to form a knot.

4 Check that the knot is tight by giving the 2 ends of the yarn a tug. Work one knot between each pair of vertical canvas threads along the same horizontal row.

YARN AND FINISHING TECHNIQUES

Pre-cut yarn is available, or you can cut your own. Each strand should be twice the required pile length plus about $^1/_2$ inch to allow for the knot. The minimum convenient length is about $2^1/_2$ inches, giving a pile of about 1 inch. Try out a few sample knots on the canvas first. Finish your rug with a concealed hem that can be left plain or trimmed with a fringe.

Preparing the yarn

Cut through the loops along the long, open edge of the strip to make your own yarn lengths

Cut a long strip of cardboard twice as wide as the required pile length plus $^1/_2$ inch for the knot. Fold cardboard in half lengthways. Wrap the yarn around the strip without overlapping.

How to make a hem

Fold outer 1 to 2 inches to back of the canvas. Check that warp and weft threads on both layers of canvas are aligned, and work first few rows of knots through this double thickness.

How to add a fringe

Turn up a hem, as shown. Leave the first row of canvas mesh holes along the folded hem edge unworked. When the rug is finished, knot longer lengths of yarn onto the hem to form a fringe.

BRAIDED RUGS

THIS TYPE OF rug is made from braided strips of fabric. The braids are then coiled and laced together, until the rug is the desired size. You will need a large quantity of fabric because the strips will be reduced to about a third of their length when braided. Wool is the best fabric for a hardwearing rug, while medium weight cottons are also attractive and colorful. Use the same type and weight of fabric throughout so that the texture of the rug is even. There are two basic ways of using color. Stripes or bands can be made by braiding in one color, and then changing to another. Alternatively, multicolor effects can be created by braiding the strips in three different colors, or by introducing strips of patterned fabric.

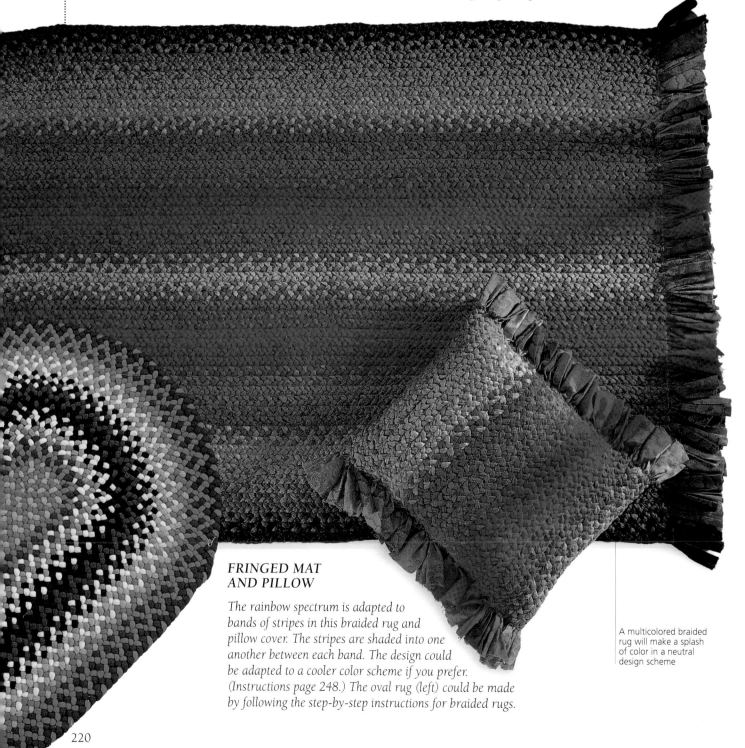

FRINGED MAT AND PILLOW

The rainbow spectrum is adapted to bands of stripes in this braided rug and pillow cover. The stripes are shaded into one another between each band. The design could be adapted to a cooler color scheme if you prefer. (Instructions page 248.) The oval rug (left) could be made by following the step-by-step instructions for braided rugs.

A multicolored braided rug will make a splash of color in a neutral design scheme

PREPARING THE FABRIC

Wash the fabric first, especially if it is new. Cut it into strips of equal width along the lengthwise grain of the fabric. These are usually 1 to 1½ inches wide, depending on the weight of the fabric, and how thick you want the finished braids to be. Before you cut up all the fabric, experiment by making a few short braids with different strip widths.

Joining the strips

1 Cut diagonally across one short end of each strip.

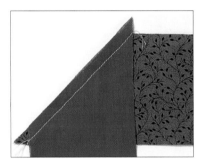

2 Place the 2 strips with right sides together, and with diagonal ends matching, as shown above. Machine stitch or backstitch together across the diagonal.

3 Open out the joined strips. Press seam open, and trim off the protruding corners.

Folding the strips

1 Lay each strip out flat, right side down. Fold the side edges into the center.

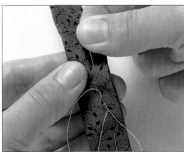

2 Fold in half again down the center line. Baste along the open edges to hold the folded strip in position, or press flat with an iron. Pressing will produce a flatter finished braid.

BRAIDING THE STRIPS

It helps to have both hands free when braiding. Once you have joined the three strips together, you can use a table clamp to anchor the braid while you work, or pin a safety pin to the top of the braid and slip it onto a cup hook screwed into the wall. When you want to stop braiding, clip a clothespin to the braid end to keep it from raveling. Using a fabric folder on each strip will help keep the folds even.

1 Join 2 strips together, as shown at right. Insert a 3rd strip inside the fold, with the open edge facing right. Stitch across the top 3 strips to hold them in position.

2 Fold the right strip over the center strip, keeping the open edge to the right.

3 Fold the left strip over the new center strip, keeping open edge to the right.

4 Continue braiding by alternately taking the right strip, and then the left strip, over the center strip. Always keep the open edges to the right of each strip so they will be hidden as you braid.

Make sure your strips are firmly held and make the braiding as even as possible

JOINING STRIPS TO THE BRAID

Every so often, you will need to stitch new fabric strips to the ends of the braiding strips to increase the overall length of the braid. Trim the braided strips to different lengths so that the joins don't fall in the same place. Stitch a new strip to a braided strip when it is about to come over to the center, so that the seam will be hidden by the next strip that is crossed over it.

1 Clip a clothespin onto the ends of the braid to keep it from raveling. Cut diagonally across the end of the strip.

2 Cut across the end of the new strip and stitch the two strips together across the diagonal. Refold them and continue braiding.

ROUND RUGS

A braided round rug must be worked in a spiral. In order to make the curved braid lie flat, extra loops have to be added to the outer edge. These extra loops are called "round turns". A round turn may need to be repeated as many as twelve times when forming the tight curves at the center of a rug. As the rug gets larger, fewer round turns are necessary, and you can continue braiding in the normal way.

1 Join the 3 fabric strips together and braid in the usual way.

2 To start making a round turn, bring the left strip over to the center.

3 Bring what is now the left strip over the center strip again.

4 Bring the right strip over to the center tightly, so that the braid curves to the right. Continue braiding normally until you want to make another round turn.

OVAL RUGS

To make an oval rug, start with a length of straight braid in the center and then coil the remaining braid around it in a spiral. To curve the braid, you will need to make three round turns at each end of your length of straight braid (see steps 1 to 4 for making round rugs).

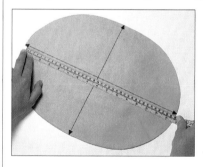

1 The length of straight braid that starts off the spiral depends on the size of the finished rug. The length of braid equals the difference between the length and width of the finished rug.

2 Lay out the straight length of braid, then work 3 round turns to coil the braiding back on itself. Braid straight to the next turn, and make 3 round turns so the braid wraps around the starting end. Continue straight braiding, making round turns as necessary.

LACING THE BRAIDS

This method of joining is quicker and stronger than sewing through the fabric. You will need a darning needle to secure the lacing thread to the fabric and a blunt-ended tapestry needle or a lacing needle (specially designed for braided work) for the lacing. Lace heavy weight braids together with carpet thread, and lighter fabrics with strong quilting thread. Always work on a flat surface. Here, a contrasting thread was used to show detail, but thread usually matches.

Straight lacing

Lay braids side by side. Slide needle through first loop of right-hand braid, then corresponding left-hand loop. Pull the thread tight. Continue lacing, pulling thread tight so that the join is nearly invisible.

Curved lacing

On a circular mat, the outer braid will be longer than the inner. Working as for straight lacing, skip an occasional loop on the outer braid so that the rug stays flat.

Oval lacing

1 For an oval mat, you need to use a combination of straight and curved lacing. Begin lacing about halfway down the center braid, and work toward the first curve.

2 When you reach the curve, change direction, and work to the 2nd curve.

INTERBRAIDING

Another joining method requires the use of a large crochet hook. The braids do not lie as flat as when laced, and the method is easier to work with straight braids. On curves, you must bring two successive strips through the same loop.

Make one braid, and work the second next to it. As each strip comes to the inside *(left)*, pull it through the corresponding loop of the finished braid with the crochet hook *(right)*.

FINISHING OFF

When the rug is completed, the end of the braid must be turned back and secured. Neatly stitch the ends into the rug.

To finish a straight braid

Thread the ends of the strips back into the loops of the braid on the wrong side. Secure with small stitches in matching thread. Trim off excess fabric at ends.

To finish a curved braid

1 Before completing the braid, taper the end of each strip into a long, thin point.

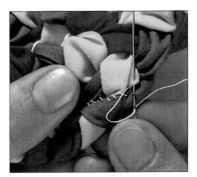

2 As you continue braiding, the braid will get thinner and thinner. Tuck the ends into the loops of the adjoining row, and secure with small stitches in matching thread.

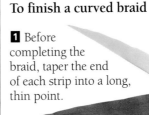

FINISHING TECHNIQUES

THE RAW EDGES of a hooked rug are usually finished with rug binding. A knotted rug will also be more hardwearing if you sew a strip of rug binding over the back of the hem on all sides. Lining is worth considering, but it isn't absolutely necessary to line your rug. In fact some people say it is better for dirt and grit to drop through the backing fabric rather than for it to get trapped between the backing and the lining. However, if you wish to do so, choose a heavy hessian or other strong, closely woven fabric.

BINDING

In order to protect the raw edges of a rug from wear and tear, it is necessary to bind them. Rug binding is a strong woven tape designed for this purpose. Buy enough to go around the edge of the rug, plus an extra two inches to overlap the ends. To attach the binding you will need heavy linen or cotton thread, a strong needle, and a thimble.

Binding a rectangular rug

1 Trim backing, leaving ³/₄ inch around worked area. Lay binding on right side of rug, so that inner edge of binding is in line with outer edge of worked area. Ease tape around corners, and stitch in position close to inner edge of tape.

2 Fold binding and backing over to wrong side of rug. Miter corners by folding excess binding inside to form a neat diagonal pleat. Sew tape to rug, and sew mitered corners together.

Binding a round or oval rug

Trim backing fabric, leaving ³/₄ inch allowance. Cut out notches around curves so that backing will lie flat when folded over to wrong side. Bind as for a rectangular rug, folding excess tape into narrow darts on wrong side of rug.

LINING

If you want to line your rug, use a strong, closely woven fabric like heavy hessian. The turn-through method is a quick way of lining small mats that can be turned inside-out easily. For large rugs, use the back-to-back method. When stitching the lining to the rug, check that the grain on both pieces is running in the same direction.

Turn-through method

Trim rug to size, leaving ¹/₂ inch of backing. Cut lining to same size. Place rug and lining right sides together. Sew together at edge of work, leaving an opening. Turn to right side and slip stitch opening.

Back-to-back method

Cut backing and lining 1 inch larger than worked area. Miter corners of both, and fold hem of each to wrong side. Pin wrong side of lining and rug together. Stitch edges together with herringbone stitch (*see page 131*).

AFTERCARE

Keep some of your spare yarn or fabric for future repairs. To repair a hooked rug, carefully cut and pull out the stitches in the damaged area from the wrong side. Hook or knot the area with the spare yarn.

Shake out your rug, and vacuum it regularly. Clean off stains quickly with a damp cloth, and then use a reliable stain remover. To store a rug, roll it up (do not fold) with the pile inside, and wrap it in a clean sheet.

PATTERN INSTRUCTIONS

KNITTING

SQUARE KNITTED PILLOW
Page 26

Materials: Use scrap yarn, and knit on appropriate needles. Purchased 14" square pillow form.

Front: Knit 4 pieces 4½" by 9" in the following patterns: A Marriage Lines (see page 29), B Ladder stitch (see page 27), C Basketweave (see page 29), D Three by Three Rib (see page 27) and one piece 4½" square in E Garter Stitch Ridges (see page 29).

Back: Knit piece 13½" square in st st. Arrange the pieces according to the chart, or as you desire. Join pieces. Sew the front and back together along three sides. Insert the pillow form and ladder stitch along the fourth side.

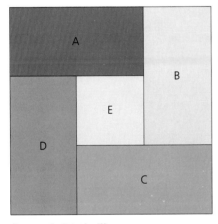

Square knitted pillow

RECTANGULAR KNITTED PILLOW
Page 26

Materials: Use scrap yarn, and knit on appropriate needles. Purchased 18" by 14" pillow form.

Front: Knit 6 pieces 7" by 6", in the following patterns: A Seeded Texture (see page 28), B Mock Fisherman's Rib (see page 27), C Square Lattice (see page 29), D Chevron Rib (see page 28), E Double Moss Stitch (see page 28), F Diamond Brocade (see page 28).

Back: Knit piece 18" by 14" in st st. Arrange the patterns according to the chart, or as you desire. Join 3 pieces together in a strip along their long sides; repeat with the other 3 pieces. Join the 2 strips horizontally. Sew the front and back together along three sides. Insert the pillow form and ladder-stitch along the fourth side.

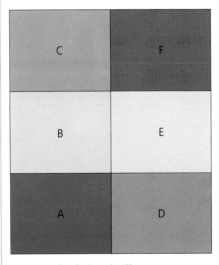

Rectangular knitted pillow

HERRINGBONE-STRIPED TOP
Page 37

Materials: Bulky weight yarn, 16 (20 – 20) oz; knitting needles No. 10 or size to give gauge.

Sizes: Directions are for Small size. Medium and Large sizes are in (). If only one number appears it applies to all sizes.

Gauge: 4 sts = 1"; 6 rows = 1".

Finished measurements: Bust: 35½" (37¾" – 40½"); Front width at underarm: 18¼" (19¼" – 20¾"); Back width at underarm: 17¼" (18¼" – 19¾"); Length to underarm: 17½"; Sleeve width at underarm: 13¼" (13¾" – 14¼").

Front: Cast on 73 (77 – 83) sts. Work in k1, p1 ribbing for 1½", inc'g 0 (1 – 0) st on last row – 73 (78 – 83) sts.

Next row (wrong side):

Herringbone pattern:

Row 1 (right side): K3, [p2, k3] across.

Row 2: P2, [k2, p3] to last st, k1.

Row 3: P2, [k3, p2] to last st, k1.

Row 4: K2, [p3, k2] to last st, p1.

Row 5: K2, [p2, k3] to last st, p1.

Row 6: P3, [k2, p3] across.

Row 7: P1, [k3, p2] to last 2 sts, k2.

Row 8: P1, [k2, p3] to last 2 sts, k2.

Row 9: K1, [p2, k3] to last 2 sts, p2.

Row 10: K1, [p3, k2] to last 2 sts, p2.

Rows 11 to 20: Rep rows 1 to 10.

Row 21: Rep row 1.

Rows 22 to 27: Rep rows 6, 5, 4, 3, 2, 1, thus reversing pat.

Rows 28 to 32: Rep rows 10, 9, 8, 7, 6.

Rows 33 to 42: Rep rows 23–32. Rep rows 1 through 42 once more, then rep rows 1 through 12 once.

Shape armholes: Continuing in pat, bind off 2 sts at beg of next 2 rows – 69 (74 – 79) sts. Work Herringbone pat for 6 more rows, dec'g 0 (1 – 0) sts at end of last row – 69 (73 – 79) sts.

Ribbed yoke: Work in k1, p1 ribbing until armholes measure 7" (7¼" – 7½").

Shape shoulders: Bind off ribbing 17 (18 – 21) sts at beg of next 2 rows, then rem 35 (37 – 37) sts loosely for neck.

Back: Cast on 69 (73 – 79) sts. Work in k1, p1 ribbing for 1½". P one row. Work in st st until same length as front to underarm. Place a marker each end for underarm. Work 8 rows more.

Ribbed yoke and shoulders: Work as for front.

Sleeves: Cast on 41 (43 – 43) sts. Work in k1, p1 ribbing for 4½" for turned cuff. Continue in st st, inc'g 1 st each end on 13th row, then every 16th (16th – 12th) row 5 (5 – 6) times more – 53 (55 – 57) sts. Work even until 21" from beg, or desired length including turned cuff. Bind off.

Finishing: Sew shoulder seam. Mark center top of sleeves. With marker at shoulder seam, sew sleeves in place, sewing upper side edges to bound-off sts at underarm of sweater. Sew side and sleeve seams.

HONEYCOMB, BLACKBERRY & DOUBLE DIAMOND SWEATER
Page 30

Materials: Traditional Aran yarn 30 (32 – 34 – 36 – 38) oz; 1 pr size 6 needles,1 pr size 10 needles.

Sizes: Instructions given for 36". Changes for 38", 40", 42", 44" are in (). If only one number appears it applies to all sizes.

Finished measurements: 38" (40" – 42" – 44" – 46").

Gauge: 16 sts/20 rows = 4" over double moss st using size 10 needles.

Special abbreviations

K2B = knit into back of next 2 knit sts.

T3B = slip next st onto cn, hold at back of work, K2B from left-hand needle, p1 from cn.

T3F = slip next 2 sts onto cn, hold at front of work, purl st from left hand needle, K2B from cn.

C2F = knit into back of 2nd stitch on needle, then knit into 1st stitch, slipping both sts off needle at same time.

C4B = slip next 2 sts onto cn, hold at back of work, knit 2 sts from left-hand needle, k2 from cn.

C4F = slip next 2 sts onto cn, hold at front of work, k2 from left-hand needle, k2 from cn.

C5F = slip next 3 sts onto cn, hold at front of work, k2 from left-hand needle, K2B, p1 from cn.

Double moss (odd no of sts):

Row 1: K1, *p1, k1, rep from * as directed.

Row 2: P1, *k1, p1, rep from * as directed.

Row 3: as row 2.

Row 4: as row 1.

PANEL A – Honeycomb pattern: 8 st, 8 row repeat.

Row 1: K8.

Row 2: P8.

Row 3: C4B, C4F.

Row 4: P8.

Row 5: K8.

Row 6: P8.

Row 7: C4F, C4B.

Row 8: P8.

PANEL B – Blackberry pattern: 8 st, 4 row rep.

Row 1: P8.

Row 2: P3tog, [k1, p1, k1] into next st; rep once more.

Row 3: P8.

Row 4: [K1, p1, k1] into next st, p3tog; rep once more.

PANEL C – Double Diamond pattern: 15 sts, 24 row rep.

Row 1: P5, K2B, p1, K2B, p5.

Row 2: K5, p2, k1, p2, k5.

Row 3: P4, T3B, k1, T3F, p4.

Row 4: K4, p2, k1, p1, k1, p2, k4.

Row 5: P3, T3B, k1, p1, k1, T3F, p3.

Row 6: K3, p2, [k1, p1] twice, k1, p2, k3.

Row 7: P2, T3B, [k1, p1] twice, k1, T3F, p2.

Row 8: K2, p2, [k1, p1] 3 times, k1, p2, k2.

Row 9: P1, T3B [k1, p1] 3 times, k1, T3F, p1.

Row 10: K1, p2, [k1, p1] 4 times, k1, p2, k1.

Row 11: T3B, [k1, p1] 4 times, k1, T3F.

Row 12: P2, [k1, p1] 5 times, k1, p2.

Row 13: T3F, [p1, k1] 4 times, p1, T3B.

Row 14: as row 10.

Row 15: P1, T3F, [p1, k1] 3 times, p1, T3B, p1.

Row 16: as row 8.

Row 17: P2, T3F, [p1, k1] twice, p1, T3B, p2.

Row 18: as row 6.

Row 19: P3, T3F, p1, k1, p1, T3B, p3.

Row 20: as row 4.

Row 21: P4, T3F, p1, T3B, p4.

Row 22: as row 2.

Row 23: P5, C5F, p5.

Row 24: K6, p4, k5.

Row 25: P5, K2B, T3F, p5.

Repeat rows 2–25.

Back: On size 6 needles, cast on 88 (91 – 97 – 100 – 103) sts. Work 20 rows in twist rib as follows:

Row 1: *P1, C2F, rep from * to last st, p1.

Row 2: *K1, p2; rep from * to last st, k1.

Inc 1 (2 – 0 – 1 – 2) sts on last row – 89 (93 – 97 – 101 – 105) sts. Change to size 10 needles.

Row 1: Double moss st 5 (7 – 9 – 11 – 13) sts, p1, row 1 panel A twice, p1, C2F, p1, row 1 panel B, p1, C2F, row 1 panel C, C2F, p1, row 1 panel B, p1, C2F, p1, row 1 panel A twice, p1, double moss st 5 (7 – 9 – 11 – 13) sts.

Row 2: Double moss st 5 (7 – 9 – 11 – 13) sts, k1, row 2 panel A twice, k1, p2, k1, row 2 panel B, k1, p2, row 2 panel C, p2, k1, row 2 panel B, k1, p2, k1, row 2 panel A twice, k1, double moss st 5 (7 – 9 – 11 – 13) sts.

Continue with pattern as set working 5 (7 – 9 – 11 – 13) sts double moss st at each end of rows till length from cast on edge 17½" (18" – 18" – 18½" – 18½"), ending with row 2.

Shape raglan: Cast off 6 sts at beg next 2 rows.

Row 1: K1, C2F, p2tog, work in pattern to last 5 sts, p2tog, C2F, k1.

Row 2: K1, p2, k1, work in pattern to last 4 sts, k1, p2, k1.

Repeat these 2 rows 21 times more – 33 (37 – 41 – 45 – 49) sts remain; continue decreasing inside twist rib on every row until 25 sts left. Transfer sts to stitch holder.

Front: As back till 51 sts remain. Divide for neck and transfer center 9 sts to stitch holder. Dec 1 st neck edge on alternate rows 8 times, at same time continue raglan shaping as for back till 2 sts remain. Work other side of neck.

Sleeves:

Note: Sleeves have a central panel of 35 sts consisting of 2 purl sts, 8 sts panel A, 15 sts panel C, 8 sts panel A, 2 purl sts. The rest of the sleeve and the increases consist of double moss st.

With size 6 needles, cast on 43 sts. Work 20 rows in twist rib as back, inc 0 (2 – 2 – 2 – 2) sts on last row – 43 (45 – 45 – 45 – 45) sts. Change to size 10 needles. Work 4 (5 – 5 – 5 – 5) sts in double moss st at each edge of sleeve. Inc 1 st each end every 4th row 15 times – 73 (75 – 75 – 75 – 75) sts. Work until length at center of sleeve measures 17" (18" – 18" – 19" – 19").

Shape raglan as back until 17 (19 – 19 – 19 – 19) sts left. Leave sts on holder.

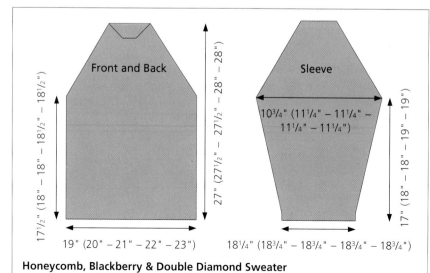

Honeycomb, Blackberry & Double Diamond Sweater

Neckband: Join both raglan seams of left sleeve and front raglan seam of right sleeve. Using size 6 needles, right side facing, pick up 25 sts from back neck, 17 (19 – 19 – 19 – 19) sts from top left sleeve, 14 sts down left front, 9 sts from center front, 14 sts up right front, 17 (19 – 19 – 19 – 19) sts from top right sleeve – 96 (100 – 100 – 100 – 100) sts. Work 22 rows in k1, p1 rib. Cast off loosely in rib. Sew neckband seam, fold to inside and slip stitch in place, loosely enough to pass over head.

Finishing: Join back raglan seam of right sleeve. Join side and sleeve seams.

EMERALD ISLE VEST

Page 36

Materials: Fisherman weight yarn 11 (11 – 14 – 14) oz; size 7 knitting needles or size for gauge; size G crochet hook; double pointed or cable needle; five ³/₄" buttons.

Size: Instructions are for Size 8, Sizes 10, 12, and 14 –16 are in (). If only one number appears, it applies to all sizes.

Gauge: 9 sts = 2"; 6 rows = 1". Cable panel: 18 sts = 3¹/₂".

Finished measurements: Bust: 32¹/₂" (34¹/₂" – 36³/₄" – 39"). Back width at underarm: 16" (17" – 18¹/₄" – 19¹/₄"). Each front width at underarm: 8³/₄" (9¹/₄" – 10" – 10¹/₄").

Special abbreviations

TW2: Sl next st to cn and hold in front of work, k1, k1 from cn.

TW6: Sl next 3 sts to cn and hold in back of work, k3, k3 from cn.

Cable pattern (worked over 18 sts):

Rows 1, 3, 5, 7 (wrong side): K2, p2, k2, p6, k2, p2, k2.

Rows 2, 4, 6: P2, TW2, p2, k6, p2, TW2, p2.

Row 8: P2, TW2, p2, TW6, p2, TW2, p2. Rep these 8 rows for cable panel.

Back: Cast on 66 (71 – 76 – 81) sts. Beg p row, work in st st until 3" from beg, ending p row. Mark each end for waistline. Continuing in st st, inc 1 st each end of next row, then every 2¹/₂" twice more – 72 (77 – 82 – 87) sts. Work even until 11" from beg, or desired length to underarm, ending p row.

Shape armholes: Bind off 5 (6 – 6 – 7) sts at beg of next 2 rows. Dec 1 st each end every row twice, then every k row 3 (3 – 4 – 4) times – 52 (55 – 58 – 61) sts. Work even until armholes measure 7" (7¹/₂" – 7¹/₂" – 8"), ending p row.

Shape shoulders: Bind off 7 (8 – 8 – 9) sts at beg of next 2 rows, 8 (8 – 9 – 9) sts at beg of next 2 rows. Bind off rem 22 (23 – 24 – 25) sts for neck.

Left front: Cast on 2 sts.

Row 1 (wrong side): Inc in each st – 4 sts;

mark beg of row 1 for front edge.

Row 2: Inc in first st, k2, inc in last st.

Row 3: Inc, p4, inc.

Row 4: Inc, p1, k5, inc – 10 sts.

Row 5: Inc, p6, k2, inc.

Row 6: Inc, k1, p2, k6, p1, inc.

Row 7: Inc, k2, p6, k2, p2, inc.

Row 8: Inc, p1, TW2, p2, TW6, p2, k1, inc – 18 sts.

Row 9: Inc, p2, k2, p6, k2, p2, k2, inc.

Row 10: Inc, k1, p2, TW2, p2, k6, p2, TW2, p1, inc.

Row 11: Inc, k2, p2, k2, p6, [k2, p2] twice, inc – 24 sts.

Row 12: Inc, k3, place marker on needle, p2, TW2, p2, k6, p2, TW2, p2, place marker, k1, inc. (Note: Carry markers).

Row 13: Inc, p to marker, k2, p2, k2, p6, k2, p2, k2, p to last st, inc – 28 sts, with 6 st sts at side edge, 18 sts in cable panel, and 4 st sts at front edge.

Working cable pat, beg row 6, over the 18 sts between markers, and st st outside markers, continue to inc 1 st every row at side edge 1 (3 – 3 – 5) times more and at front edge 10 (10 – 13 – 13) times more, working inc's in st st and working side edge even when side inc's are completed – 39 (41 – 44 – 46) sts after all inc's are completed. Keeping cable pat and st st, work even until 3" above last inc at side edge. Mark side edge for waistline. Working front edge even, inc 1 st at side edge on next row, then every 2¹/₂" twice more – 42 (44 – 47 – 49) sts. Work even until side edge measures same as back to underarm, end with wrong-side row.

Shape armhole and V-neck:

Row 1 (right side): Bind off 5 (6 – 6 – 7) sts, work in pat to last 2 sts, k2tog (neck dec).

Keeping pat, at arm edge dec 1 st every row twice, then every 2nd row 3 (3 – 4 – 4) times; at same time, at neck edge, dec 1 st every 2nd row twice more, then every 3rd row 11 (11 – 12 – 12) times – 18 (19 – 20 – 21) sts. Work even until 2 rows more than Back to shoulder, end at arm edge.

Shape shoulder: Keeping pat, at arm edge bind off 9 (9 – 10 – 10) sts once, 9 (10 – 10 – 11) sts once. Mark straight edge of front for 5 buttons evenly spaced, having first just below beg of V-neck and last just above end of lower shaping.

Right front: Work same as left front through row 2, marking end of row 1 for front edge.

Row 3 (wrong side): Inc, p4, inc – 8 sts.

Row 4: Inc, k5, p1, inc.

Row 5: Inc, k2, p6, inc.

Row 6: Inc, p1, k6, p2, k1, inc.

Row 7: Inc, p2, k2, p6, k2, inc.

Row 8: Inc, k1, p2, TW6, p2, TW2, p1, inc.

Row 9: Inc, k2, p2, k2, p6, k2, p2, inc.

Row 10: Inc, p1, TW2, p2, k6, p2, TW2, p2, k1, inc.

Row 11: Inc, [p2, k2] twice, p6, k2, p2, k2, inc – 24 sts.

Row 12: Inc, k1, place marker, p2, TW2, p2, k6, p2, TW2, p2, place marker, k3, inc. Beg row 13, work to correspond to left front, reversing all shaping and making buttonholes opposite markers of left front as follows: From front edge, k2, bind off 2, complete row in pat. On next row cast on 2 sts over bound-off sts.

Finishing: Back ties: Make 2. With crochet hook, ch about 19" (20" – 21" – 22") or desired length; sl st in 2nd ch from hook and each rem ch. Fasten off. Sew shoulder seams, easing fronts to match back shoulder edges. Sew side seams, tacking in end of a tie at waistline.

Crochet edging:

Round 1: From right side, with crochet hook, join at center of lower back edge; with care to keep edge flat, sc around entire outer edge of vest, join with sl st in first sc.

Round 2: Do not turn, working left to right, sc in each sc around for corded edge, join. Fasten off. Work same edging around each armhole edge.

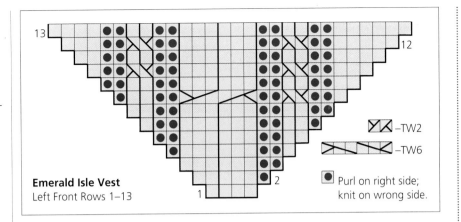

Emerald Isle Vest
Left Front Rows 1–13

—TW2

—TW6

● Purl on right side; knit on wrong side.

13

12

2

1

DIAMOND-KNIT SHAWL
Page 42

Materials: Knitting worsted 14 oz; 29" – 36" circular knitting needle No. 8 or size to give gauge. Crochet hook size E.

Finished measurements: Upper edge: 63½". Length to point: 34½".

Gauge: 12 sts (1 pat) = 2½".

Note: Work back and forth on circular needle; do not join round.

Beg upper edge, cast on 297 sts.

Next Row: K2, p to last 2 sts, k2.

Pattern:

Row 1 (right side): K2, sl 1, k1, psso, k4, k2tog, * yo, k1, yo, sl 1, k1, psso, k7, k2tog; rep from * to last 11 sts, yo, k1, yo, sl 1, k1, psso, k4, k2tog, k2.

Rows 2, 4, 6 and 8: K2, p to last 2 sts, k2.

Row 3: K2, sl 1, k1, psso; k2, k2tog, k1, * [yo, k1] twice, sl 1, k1, psso, k5, k2tog, k1; rep from * to last 10 sts, [yo, k1] twice, sl 1, k1, psso, k2, k2tog, k2.

Row 5: K2, sl 1, k1, psso, k2tog, k2, * yo, k1, yo, k2, sl 1, k1, psso, k3, k2tog, k2; rep from * to last 9 sts, yo, k1, yo, k2, sl 1, k1, psso, k2tog, k2.

Row 7: K2, sl 1, k1, psso, k2tog, k1, * yo, k1, yo, k3, sl 1, k1, psso, k1, k2tog, k3; rep from * to last 8 sts, [yo, k1] twice, sl 1, k1, psso, k2tog, k2.

Row 9: K2, sl 1, k1, psso, k2tog, * yo, k1, yo, k4, sl 1, k2tog, psso, k4; rep from * to last 7 sts, yo, k1, yo, [k2tog] twice, k2.

Row 10: K2, p2tog, p to last 4 sts, p2tog tbl, k2.

Rep rows 1 through 10 for pat until 9 sts rem. Then work as follows:

Row 1: K2, sl 1, k1, psso, k1, k2tog, k2.
Row 2: K2, p3, k2.
Row 3: K2, sl 1, k2tog, psso, k2.
Row 4: K2, p1, k2.
Row 5: K2tog, k1, k2tog.
Row 6: K1, p1, k1.
Row 7: Sl 1, k2tog, psso.
Fasten off.

Edging: Cast on 4 sts.
Row 1 (wrong side): K2, yo, k2.
Rows 2, 4 and 6: K.
Row 3: K3, yo, k2.
Row 5: K2, yo, k2tog, yo, k2.
Row 7: K3, yo, k2tog, yo, k2.
Row 8: Bind off 4 sts, k to end.
Continue working these 8 rows until edging when slightly stretched fits around shawl. Bind off and sew in place.

KALEIDOSCOPE
Page 51

Materials: Yarn, 150g Red A, 50g Yellow B, 200g Blue C, 100g Green D, 200g Blue-mix E. (Note: B and D should be mercerized cotton; A, C and E should be novelty yarns of a comparable weight); pair each size 5 and 8 knitting needles or size for gauge: Two ½" buttons.

Size: One size fits all. This is a very loose-fitting garment.

Gauge: 17 sts = 4"; 24 rows = 4".

Note 1: Garment is worked sideways in vertical rows.

Note 2: For front, k row 1 and all odd-numbered rows for right side of work; p all even-numbered rows. For back, p row 1 and all odd-numbered rows for wrong side of work; k all even-numbered rows.

Houndstooth pattern for front (see above, Note 2 for back):

Row 1 (right side): K1 D, *k1 B, k3 D; rep from * to last 3 sts, end k1B, k2D.
Row 2: *P3 B, p1 D; rep from * to end.
Row 3: *K3 B, k1 D; rep from * to end.
Row 4: P1 D, *p1 B, p3 D; rep from * to last 3 sts, end p1 B, p2 D. Rep rows 1 to 4 for pattern.

Underarm increasing for right front:

K and then p in same st on k rows; p and then k in same st on p rows. When several sts are added at one time, cast on instead of inc'g.

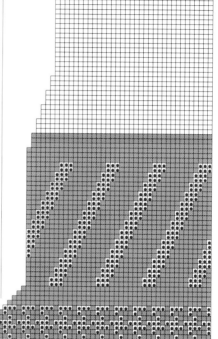

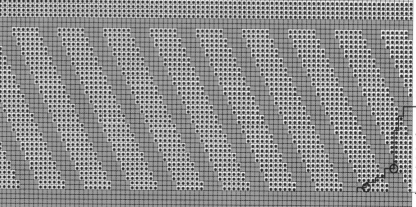

Center back · End right front · Shape neck

Begin left front

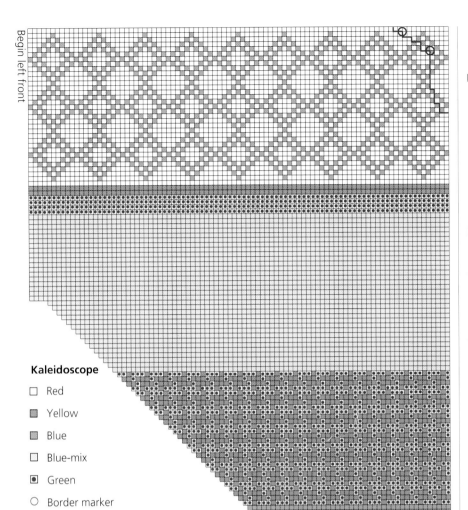

Kaleidoscope

- ☐ Red
- ▦ Yellow
- ▨ Blue
- ☐ Blue-mix
- ☒ Green
- ○ Border marker

Underarm decreasing for left front:

For k rows: k1, sl next st k-wise, k next st, psso. When several sts are decreased at one time, bind off at beg of row instead of dec'g. For p rows: P to last 3 sts, p2tog, p last st.

Neck edge decreasing for right front:

For k rows: k to last 3 sts, k2tog, k last st. When 2 dec's are indicated, k to last 5 sts, [k2tog] twice, k last st. For p rows: *p1, p2tog. When 2 dec's are indicated, p1 [p2tog] twice.

Neck edge increasing for left front:

For k rows: k to last 2 sts, *insert needle under thread between last st knitted and next st and k, k1*, k last st. When 2 incs are indicated, k to last 3 sts, rep between *s twice, k last st. For p rows: P2, * insert needle under thread and p1 between last purled st and next st, p1*, p to end. When 2 incs are indicated, rep between *s once more, then p to end.

Right front:

With larger needles and A, cast on 34 sts for wrist edge. Following chart for colors and shaping, work in st st. For example, with yarn A, work 18 rows even on 34 sts. **Next Row:** Inc 1 st at beg of row, then inc 1 st at beg of every 3 rows 5 times more, being sure to

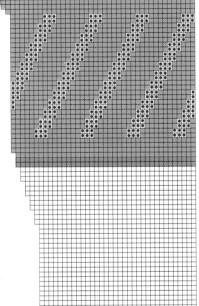

work the two rows of Yellow (B) where indicated on chart, and starting the next pattern on the chart. Begin Houndstooth pattern, given above, on row 67, keeping pat as established while increasing along the underarm.

Left front:

With larger needles and A, cast on 79 sts for center front. Following

chart for patterns, neck shaping and underarm decreases, work in st st out to wrist edge.

Back: Note: Back is an exact duplicate of the front pieces, except that it is worked in one piece from right sleeve wrist edge across to left sleeve wrist edge, with a vertical stripe of 6 rows of color C at the center back. The back neck is worked straight across without any shaping. With larger needles and A, cast on 34 sts for right sleeve wrist edge. Following chart, purl all odd number rows, knit all even number rows.

Finishing: Sew front to back at upper edge of sleeves and shoulders, matching patterns.

Cuffs: With C and smaller needles, with right side of work facing, pick up 1 st in every other row along wrist edge – 33 sts. Work in p1, k1 ribbing for 2½". Bind off in ribbing. Sew side and sleeve seams.

Waistline ribbing: With C and smaller needles, with right side facing, pick up 1 st in every row around entire lower edge. P1 row, dec'g 73 sts evenly spaced – 161 sts. Work in k1, p1 ribbing for 2½". Bind off in ribbing.

Left front border: As indicated on chart, place markers at neck edge for border shaping. With color C and smaller needles, starting at shoulder seam, with right side of work facing, pick up and k 16 sts up to the first marker; pick up and k 7 sts between this and next marker; pick up and k 95 sts along center front, and waistline ribbing, ending at lower edge. Work 1 row in k1, p1 ribbing.

Next Row: Keeping ribbing as established, work 16 sts (k1, p1, k1) in next st, p1, k1, p1, k1, p1, (k1, p1, k1) in next st; continue in ribbing over rem'g 95 sts. Work 4 rows more in ribbing. Bind off in ribbing. Mark for 2 buttons, placing the lower one 1" up from the bottom and the second 1½" above.

Right front border: As indicated on chart, place markers at neck edge for border shaping. With C and smaller needles, starting at lower edge, pick up and k 95 sts to first marker; pick up and k 7 sts between markers; pick up and k 16 sts to shoulder seam, and 46 sts along back of neck. Work 1 row in k1, p1 ribbing. Next Row: Keeping ribbing as established, work 95 sts; (p1, k1, p1) in next st, k1, p1, k1, p1, k1, (p1, k1, p1) in next st; continue in ribbing over rem'g 62 sts.

Buttonhole row: Keeping established ribbing, bind off 2 sts in line with each button marker. **Next Row:** Cast on 2 sts over bound-off sts. Work 2 rows even. Bind off in ribbing. Sew on buttons. Sew neckband seam.

LOG CABIN TURTLENECK
Page 56

Materials: Aran weight tweed yarn, 100g balls: 5 Purple MC, 1 each of Dark Blue, Fuchsia, Red, Teal, Gray, Medium Blue; Sizes 6 and 7 (8 – 9) knitting needles or size for gauge and 16" long sizes 6, 7, and 8 circular needles; 4 stitch holders.

Size: Instructions are for Small (8–10). Changes for Medium (12–14) and Large (16) are in (). If only one number appears, it applies to all sizes.

Note: This sweater is made with the same number of stitches for all sizes. The changes in measurements are made by using different size needles.

Gauge: 17 sts = 4"; 13 rows = 2" on size 7 needles; 16 sts = 4"; 12 rows = 2" on size 8 needles; 15 sts = 4"; 11 rows = 2" on size 9 needles.

Finished measurements: Bust: 39" (41½" – 44¼"). Width of sleeve at underarm: 18½" (20" – 21¾").

Front: With smaller needles and MC, cast on 83 sts. Work in k1, p1 ribbing for 3", inc'g one st at end of last row – 84 sts. Change to larger needles and work in st st, following chart for pattern. Complete chart once, then repeat chart to row 56. Row 57: Following chart, work 36 sts and place on holder; work center 12 sts and place on another holder; work rem 36 sts and place on a third holder.

Shape neck and shoulders: Right side:
Rows 1, 3, 5, and 7: P.
Rows 2, 4, 6 and 8: Bind off 2 sts at beg of each row – 28 sts. Work even until chart is complete. Bind off all sts across row.

Left side: Complete as for right side, reversing shaping.

Back: Work same as for front, eliminating pattern. Work even in st st in MC until back measures same as front.

Shape neck and shoulders: Bind off 28 sts. K center 28 sts and place on holder for back of neck. Bind off rem 28 sts.

Sleeve: With smaller needles and MC, cast on 31 (33 – 35) sts. Work in k1, p1 ribbing for 3". Change to larger needles and p1 row, inc'g 19 sts evenly spaced – 50 (52 – 54) sts. Work even in st st until piece measures 5" from beg. Increase one stitch at each end of next row and every 5 rows 14 times – 78 (80 – 82) sts. When sleeve measures 20" from beg, bind off loosely.

Finishing: Sew front to back at shoulders.
Collar: With smallest circular needle and MC, with right side facing, pick up and k 76 (80 – 84) sts around neck edge including sts from front and back holders. Place marker at beg of round and work in k1, p1 ribbing for 2½" more. Change to largest size circular needle and continue in ribbing for 2" more. Bind off in ribbing. For placement of sleeves, mark front and back at each side edge 9¼" (10" – 10¾") from shoulder seams. Sew sleeves between markers. Sew side and sleeve seams.

CARDIGAN WITH CREWEL-EMBROIDERED POPPIES
Page 57

Materials: Knitting worsted-weight yarn 100g balls – 4 (4 – 5) balls Dark Blue MC, 1 ball Terra Cotta CC. For embroidery: ½ yd lightweight Dark Blue fabric; Persian Yarn, 40-yd skeins – 1 each Green, Red, and Terra Cotta; 8 yd skeins – 2 each Lt. Green, Maroon, Lt. Terra Cotta, Yellow, Lt. Blue, Blue, 1 skein Gold, 3 skeins Pink; sizes 7 and 9 knitting needles or size for gauge; 3 stitch holders; six ⅝" diameter buttons; tapestry needle.

Sizes: Instructions are for Small (6–8). Changes for Medium (10–12) and Large (14–16) are in (). If only one number appears, it applies to all sizes.

Gauge: 15 sts = 4"; 20 rows = 4".

Finished measurements: Bust: 36¼" (39¼" – 42¾"); sleeve width at underarm: 21½".

Back: With smaller needles and MC, cast on 69 (75 – 81) sts. Work twisted ribbing as follows:
Row 1 (right side): K1, p1, *k1 tbl, p1; rep from *, ending k1.
Row 2: P1, *k1 tbl, p1; rep from *. Rep rows 1 and 2 for 3", ending with a wrong-side row. Change to larger needles and work in st st with MC only until piece measures 6½" from beg, ending with a p row. Continue in st st, working in pattern as follows:
Note: When changing colors, to prevent holes, twist colors together on wrong side and carry unused color loosely across back.
Row 1: With MC, k.
Row 2: With MC, p.
Row 3: K1 MC, *k1 CC, k5 MC; rep from *, ending k1 CC, k1 MC.
Rows 4, 6 and 8: With MC, p.
Rows 5, 7, and 9: With MC, k.
Row 10: P4 MC, *p1 CC, p5 MC; rep from *, ending last rep, p4 MC.
Rows 11 and 13: With MC, k.
Rows 12 and 14: With MC, p.
Rep rows 1 to 14 for pat until piece measures 21" from beg, ending with a p row.
Shape shoulders and neck: With MC, bind off 22 (24 – 26) sts; k across center 25 (27 – 29) sts and place them on a holder for neck; bind off rem sts.
Left front: With smaller needles and MC, cast on 31 (35 – 37) sts. Work twisted ribbing for 3", ending with a wrong-side row, inc'g 1 st at end of row on small and large sizes only – 32 (35 – 38) sts. Change to larger needles and work in st st with MC only until piece measures 6½" from beg, ending with a p row – working p row as follows: P 13 (12 – 13),

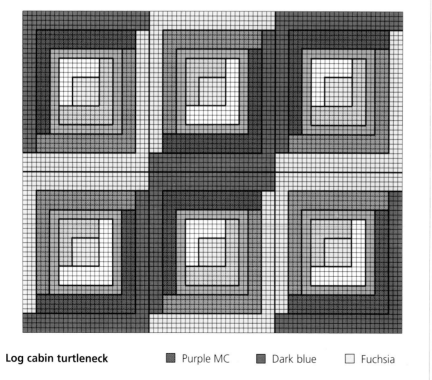

Log cabin turtleneck   ■ Purple MC   ▨ Dark blue   ☐ Fuchsia
   ▨ Red   ▨ Teal   ☐ Gray   ▨ Medium blue

Front

Center

Back

Place on fold

Sleeve

■ Red

□ Maroon

□ Yellow

■ Light blue

■ Blue

□ Gold

■ Pink

Cardigan with crewel-embroidered poppies

1 square =1"

place a marker on needle, p rem sts.

Note: Move marker up on each row and continue to work the 13 (12 – 13) sts to marker with MC only, and remainder of sts in pat as follows:

Row 1: With MC, k.

Row 2: With MC, p.

Row 3: K1 (0 – 1) CC, *k5 MC, k1 CC; rep from *, ending k0 (5 – 0) MC.

Rows 4, 6, and 8: With MC, p.

Rows 5, 7, and 9: With MC, k.

Row 10: P3 (2 – 3) MC, *p1 CC, p5 MC; rep from *, ending p1 CC, 3 (2 – 3) MC.

Rows 11 and 13: With MC, k.

Rows 12 and 14: With MC, p.

Rep rows 1 to 14 for pat. Work as established until piece measures 19"

from beg, ending with a right-side row.

Shape neck: Continuing in pat established, work 4 (4 – 5) sts and place them on a holder. At same edge, bind off 2 sts every other row 3 times; then dec 1 st 0 (1 – 1) time – 22 (24 – 26) sts rem. Work even until front measures same as back to shoulders. For shoulder, at side edge, bind off 22 (24 – 26) sts.

Right Front: Work as for left front, reversing pat and shaping.

Sleeves: With smaller needles and MC, cast on 37 (39 – 41) sts. Work twisted ribbing for 3", ending with a right-side row. Change to larger needles and p one row, inc'g 8 (6 – 4) sts evenly spaced – 45 sts. With MC only, work in st st until

piece measures 4½" from beg. Inc 1 st each end every 4 rows 3 times – 51 sts. Work pat as follows, continuing increases every 4th row until you have 81 sts.

Row 1: With MC, k.

Row 2: With MC, p.

Row 3: K1 MC, *k1 CC, k5 MC; rep from *, ending k1 CC, k1 MC.

Rows 4, 6, and 8: With MC, p.

Rows 5, 7, and 9: With MC, k.

Row 10: P4 MC, *p1 CC, p5 MC; rep from *, ending last rep p4 MC.

Rows 11 and 13: With MC, k.

Rows 12 and 14: With MC, p.

Rep rows 1 to 14 for pat until sleeve measures 20" from beg. Bind off loosely.

Finishing: Lightly block pieces. Enlarge and trace patterns to dark blue fabric, reversing design for left front and sleeve. Cut fabric around outline of patterns and baste to wrong side of sweater pieces 1 – 2 rows from edges and ribbing. From wrong side, baste over patterns to right side of sweater pieces, using basting as a guide for embroidery. Work scroll motifs in rows of Terra Cotta outline stitch with Lt. Terra Cotta outline stitch details. Using outline stitch, work green vines and stems; use outline stitch to fill in lower part of leaves with green and upper part with lt. green. Work flowers with long and short satin stitch and centers with French knots, see chart for colors. Remove basting thread and trim and clip fabric close to embroidery. After embroidery is complete, sew front to back at shoulders.

Neckband: With smaller needles and right side facing, with MC pick up and k all sts from holders and 4½ sts per inch along front neck edges. Work in twisted ribbing for 8 rows. Bind off in ribbing.

Left front band: With smaller needles and right side facing, with MC, pick up and k 4½ sts per inch along center front. Work in twisted ribbing for 8 rows. Bind off in ribbing. Mark for 6 buttons, placing the top one 1" down from the neck edge and the bottom one 1½" up from the lower edge, with the others evenly spaced between.

Right front band: With smaller needles and right-side facing, with MC, work same as left front band in twisted ribbing for 3 rows.

Buttonhole row: Bind off 2 sts to correspond to each marker.

Next Row: Cast on 2 sts over bound-off sts. Work 3 more rows in ribbing. Bind off in ribbing. Sew on buttons. Sew in sleeves; sew side and sleeve seams.

MULTICOLOR SCARF

Page 57

Materials: Approximately 250g of Bulky yarn in ten colors; size 10 knitting needles or size for gauge.

Gauge: 4 sts = 1" in st st.

Cast on 33 sts. With A color, work moss stitch as follows: K1, *p1, k1; repeat from * to end. Repeat this row for 4¹/₂"; ending on wrong side row. Change to color B.

Work popcorn pattern as follows:

Row 1: K.

Row 2: P.

Row 3: K1, *make popcorn as follows: k into front and back of lp twice, then slip 2nd, 3rd, and 4th sts over 1st st, k5; repeat from * to last 7 sts, k5, make popcorn, k1.

Row 4: P.

Row 5: K.

Row 6: P.

Row 7: K4, *make popcorn, k5; repeat from * to last 5 sts, make popcorn, k4.

Rows 1 to 7 form the pattern; repeat for 4¹/₂", ending on right side.

With C, p 1 row, work double moss stitch as follows:

Row 1: *K2, p2; repeat from * to last st, k1.

Row 2: P1, *k2, p2; repeat from * to end.

Row 3: *P2, k2; repeat from * to last st, p1.

Row 4: K1, *p2, k2; repeat from * to end.

Rows 1 to 4 form the pattern; repeat these rows for 4¹/₂", ending on wrong side.

With D, rep popcorn pattern for 4¹/₂", ending on right side.

With E, p 1 row. Rep moss stitch for 4¹/₂", ending on right side.

With F, p 1 row. Rep popcorn pattern for 4¹/₂", ending on right side.

With G, p 1 row. Rep double moss for 4¹/₂", ending on wrong side.

With H, rep popcorn pattern for 4¹/₂", ending on right side.

With I, p 1 row. Rep moss stitch for 4¹/₂", ending on wrong side.

With J, rep popcorn pattern for 4¹/₂". Cast off.

To make fringe: Cut lengths of yarn measuring 10" in A and J. With 6 lengths double, pull through end of scarf with crochet hook and knot to form contrasting fringe on each end.

FAIR ISLE MITTENS AND HAT

Page 60

Materials: Knitting worsted-weight yarn, 50g balls: 3 Cream A, 1 each Blue B, Ochre C, Rust D. Set of size 3 and size 5 double-pointed needles.

Size: One size.

Gauge: 7 sts and 7¹/₂ rows = 1"on size 5 needles, over pat.

Finished measurements: Mittens: 4" width across back. Length 10¹/₂". Hat:

width around 18", depth 11".

Right mitten: With size 3 needles and A cast on 58 sts; divide evenly on 3 needles. Taking care not to twist sts, join and work around in k1, p1 ribbing for 3". Change to size 5 needles. Work in st st (k every round) for 11 rounds. Join D.

Next round 1: *K1 A, k1 D; rep from * around.

Round 2: *K1 D, k1 A, rep from * around Break off D. With A, k two rounds.

Thumb opening: K 32 sts in pattern from chart (round 1) slip next 8 sts on st holder, cast on 8 sts, work in pat to end. Follow chart rounds 2 to 26.

Round 27 to 29: With A, k.

Round 30: Join in D, *k1 A, k1 D; rep from * around.

Round 31: *K1 D, k1 A, rep from * around.

Shape top:

Round 1: *K1, sl 1, k1, psso, k23, k2tog, k1, place marker on needle; rep from * once, carry markers.

Dec round 2: *K1, sl 1, k1, psso, k to within 3 sts of marker, k2tog, k1; rep from * once.

Rep Dec round 2, 8 times more – 18 sts. Break yarn, leaving a 15" end. Graft sts tog (see page 65).

Thumb: With A, k sts from holder, pick up 1 st in sp before cast-on sts, 1 st in each cast-on st, 1 st in next sp – 18 sts. Divide evenly on 3 needles. Work in st st until thumb measures 2¹/₂" or desired length.

Dec round: K2tog around. Rep last round

once – 5 sts. Break A, leaving 8" end. Thread end through sts and sl from needles; draw up tightly, fasten securely.

Left mitten: Work to correspond to right mitten, following chart for left mitten and working thumb opening as follows: k 18 sts in pat, sl next 8 sts to holder, cast on 8 sts, work in pat to end.

Hat: With 3 needles and A, cast on 128 sts; divide on 3 needles. Taking care not to twist sts, join and work around in k1, p1 ribbing for 4". Change to 5 needles. Work in st st for 5 rounds.

Round 6: Join D, *k1 A, k1 D; rep from * around.

Round 7: *K1 D, k1 A; rep from * around.

Break D, k two rounds A. Join B. Follow hat chart, rounds 1 through 25 once, 4 pat reps round hat. Break B. With A k two rounds. Rep rounds 6 and 7 once. Break D.

Shape top:

Dec round: *K2tog, k14; rep from * around – 120 sts.

Having 1 less st between decs on each successive round (k13, k12, k11, etc.), rep Dec round 14 times more – 8 sts. Break yarn, leaving a 12" end. Thread through sts and sl from needles; draw up tightly, fasten securely.

Pompon: Around two 2" cardboard circles together, wind yarn in color B. For finishing pompon, see page 63.

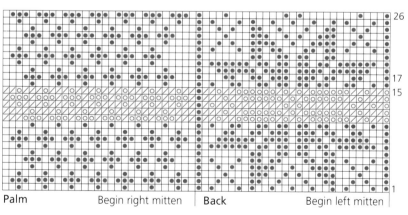

| Palm | Begin right mitten | Back | Begin left mitten |

26 17 15 1

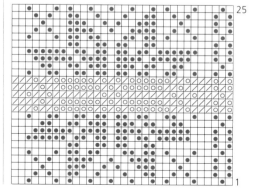

25 1

Fair Isle mittens and hat

- ⊙ Blue B
- ○ Rust D
- ⁄ Ochre C
- ☐ Cream A

CROCHET

BEADED DOILY
Page 98

Materials: 1 oz No 20 Crochet cotton; 24 small glass or ceramic beads approx ¼" diameter and 12 large beads; size 8 steel crochet hook or size for gauge; needle small enough to fit through beads.

Size: 9" diameter.

Gauge: Doily measures 3¼" diameter after round 10.

Special abbreviation

Bst = Bullion stitch (see page 95) made with [yo] 10 times.

Note: Do not turn between rounds – right side is always facing.

To make: Ch 4, join with sl st to form ring.

Round 1: Ch 3 (does not count as st), 12 Bsts in ring, sl st to top of first Bst.

Round 2: Ch 1 (does not count as st), 2 sc in each Bst all round, sl st to first sc.

Round 3: Ch 1 (does not count as st), 1 sc in same place, [ch 3, skip 1, 1 sc] 11 times, ch 1, skip 1, 1 hdc in first sc – 12 lps.

Round 4: [Ch 4, 1 sc in next lp] 11 times, ch 2, 1 dc in hdc.

Round 5: [Ch 5, 1 sc in next lp] 11 times, ch 2, 1 dc in dc.

Round 6: [Ch 4, (3 dc, ch 2, 3 dc) in next lp, ch 4, 1 sc in next lp] 6 times, [sl st in next ch of first 4 ch loop] twice.

Round 7: Ch 1 (does not count as st), *1 sc in ch lp, ch 4, 3 dc, (2 dc, ch 2, 2 dc) in 2 ch sp, 3 dc, ch 4, 1 sc in next lp, ch 4; rep from * 5 more times omitting last ch 4 and ending ch 2, 1 dc in first sc.

Round 8: *Ch 4, 1 sc in next lp, ch 4, 5 dc, (2 dc, ch 2 – called tip of V, 2 dc) in 2 ch sp, 5 dc, [ch 4, 1 sc in next lp] twice; rep from * 5 more times omitting last (ch 4, 1 sc) and ending ch 2, 1 dc in dc.

Round 9: *[Ch 4, 1 sc in next lp] twice, ch 4, skip (7 dc, 2 ch, 7 dc), 1 sc in next lp, ch 4, 1 sc in next lp; rep from * 5 more times omitting last (ch 4, 1 sc) and ending ch 2, 1 dc in dc.

Round 10: Ch 3 (counts as first dc), 2 dc inserting hook under stem of dc which closed previous round, ch 1, *5 dc in next lp, ch 1; rep from * all round, 2 dc in first lp, sl st to top of 3 ch – 24 blocks of 5 dc.

Round 11: Ch 1 (does not count as st), * 1 sc in 3rd of 5 dc, ch 4, (3 dc, ch 2, 3 dc) in 3rd of next 5 dc, ch 4, 1 sc in 3rd of next 5 dc, ch 4, inserting hook through 2 ch sp at tip of V in Round 8 and then in 3rd of next 5 dc work 1 dc, ch 4; rep from * 5 more times omitting last ch 4 and ending ch 2, 1 dc in first sc.

Round 12: *Ch 4, 1 sc in next lp, ch 4, 3 dc, (2 dc, ch 2, 2 dc) in 2 ch sp, 3 dc, [ch 4, 1 sc in next lp] 3 times; rep from * 5 more times omitting last (ch 4, 1 sc) and ending ch 2, 1 dc in dc.

Round 13: *[Ch 4, 1 sc in next lp] twice, ch 4, 5 dc, (2 dc, ch 2, 2 dc) in 2 ch sp, 5 dc, [ch 4, 1 sc in next lp] 3 times; rep from * 5 more times omitting last (ch 4, 1 sc) and ending ch 2, 1 dc in dc.

Round 14: *[Ch 4, 1 sc in next lp] 3 times, ch 4, skip (7 dc, 2 ch, 7 dc), 1 sc in next lp [ch 4, 1 sc in next lp] twice; rep from * 5 more times omitting last (ch 4, 1 sc) and ending ch 2, 1 dc in dc.

Round 15: as round 10 – 36 blocks of 5 dc.

Round 16: Ch 1 (does not count as st), *1 sc in 3rd of 5 dc, ch 4, (3 dc, ch 2, 3 dc) in 3rd of next 5 dc, ch 4, [1 sc in 3rd of next 5 dc, ch 4] twice, inserting hook through 2 ch sp at tip of V in round 13 and then in 3rd of next 5 dc work 1 dc, ch 4, 1 sc in 3rd of next 5 dc, ch 4; rep from * 5 more times omitting last ch 4 and ending ch 2, 1 dc in first sc.

Rounds 17 to 19: Work as for rounds 12 to 14 with additional ch 4 lps as established.

Round 20: as round 10 – 48 blocks of 5 dc.

Round 21: Ch 1 (does not count as st), *1 sc in 3rd of 5 dc, [ch 4, 1 sc in 3rd of next 5 dc] 3 times, ch 4, inserting hook through 2 ch sp at tip of V in round 18 and then in 3rd of next 5 dc work 1 dc, ch 4, [1 sc in 3rd of next 5 dc, ch 4] 3 times; rep from * 5 more times omitting last ch 4 and ending ch 2, 1 dc in first sc.

Round 22: *Ch 5, 1 sc in next lp; rep from * all round, ending ch 2, 1 dc in dc.

Round 23: *Ch 6, 1 sc in next lp; rep from * all round, ending ch 3, 1 dc in dc.

Round 24: *Ch 7, 1 sc in next lp; rep from * all round, ending ch 3, 1 tr in dc.

Round 25: *Ch 8, 1 sc in next lp; rep from * all round, ending ch 4, 1 tr in tr. Fasten off.

Round 26: Thread all beads onto yarn to form drops of 3 beads as follows: * thread through 1 small, 1 large and 1 small bead, then around last small and back through large and first small beads in opposite direction; rep from * 11 more times. (Note: To move drops along yarn, pull gently on last small bead.) Rejoin yarn in center of any ch lp. *Ch 10, locate drop directly under hook and close firmly with ch 1, ch 9, 1 sc in next lp, [ch 8, 1 sc in next lp] 3 times; rep from * 11 more times, sl st where yarn was joined. Fasten off.

WATERMELON WEDGE
Page 91

Materials: Knitting worsted-weight yarn, 1 skein each Red A, White B and ½ oz each Pale Green C, and Dark Green D, few yds. Black E; size H crochet hook or size for gauge; 12" square pillow form; yarn needle.

Size: 12" square.

Gauge: 15 dc = 4"; 2 dc rows = 1".

To make: Front and back alike: Using A, ch 4.

Row 1 (right side): Skip 2 ch, 2 dc in next, turn – 3 sts.

Rows 2 to 22: Always turning at end of row and working ch 3 to stand as first dc of first rep of next row, cont as follows:

Row 2: [2 dc in next] 3 times – 6 sts.

Row 3: [1 dc, 2 dc in next] 3 times – 9 sts.

Row 4: [2 dc, 2 dc in next] 3 times – 12 sts.

Row 5: [3 dc, 2 dc in next] 3 times – 15 sts.

Row 6: [4 dc, 2 dc in next] 3 times – 18 sts.

Cont working 1 additional single dc at beg of each of 3 reps every row as established and change color to work row 20 using C and rows 21 and 22 using D – 66 sts.

Row 23: Using B, ch 1, 1 sc, 1 hdc, 16 dc, 2 dc in next, 26 dc, 2 dc in next, 16 dc, 1 hdc, 2 sc, turn.

Row 24: 5 sl sts, 2 sc, 1 hdc, 25 dc, 2 dc in next, 26 dc, 1 hdc, 2 sc, sl st, turn.

Row 25: Ch 1, skip sl st, 2 sc, 1 hdc, 10 dc [2 dc in next, 11 dc] twice, 2 dc in next, 10 dc, 1 hdc, 2 dc, sl st, turn.

Row 26: Ch 1, skip sl st, 4 sl sts, 2 sc, 1 hdc, 40 dc, 1 hdc, 2 sc, sl st, turn.

Row 27: Ch 1, skip sl st, 5 sl sts, 2 sc, 1 hdc, 9 dc, 2 dc in next, 10 dc, 2 dc in next, 9 dc, 1 hdc, 2 sc, sl st, turn.

Row 28: Ch 1, skip sl st, 4 sl sts, 2 sc, 1 hdc, 24 dc, 1 hdc, 2 sc, sl st, turn.

Row 29: Ch 1, skip sl st, 4 sl sts, 1 sc, 1 hdc, 5 dc, 2 dc in next, 6 dc, 2 dc in next, 5 dc, 1 hdc, 1 sc, sl st, turn.

Row 30: Ch 1, skip sl st, 4 sl sts, 1 sc, 1 hdc, 12 dc, 1 hdc, 1 sc, sl st, turn.

Row 31: Ch 1, skip sl st, 4 sl sts, 1 sc, 1 hdc, 4 dc, 1 hdc, 1 sc, sl st, turn.

Row 32: Ch 1, skip sl st, 3 sl sts, ch 3, hdc3tog, turn.

Edging: Ch 1, sc along edge of piece, matching colors and working 3 sc in each corner; sl st in first sc and fasten off. Thread yarn needle with black and work lazy-daisy stitch seeds (see page 133) at random on portion of piece in A. With wrong sides together and sewing through back loops only, sew front to back on 3 sides. Insert pillow form and sew 4th side.

STARLIT
Page 91

Materials: Knitting worsted-weight yarn, 2 oz. each colors A, B, and C; size E crochet hook or size for gauge; 1/2" ring for button.

Gauge: 4 sc = 1".

Note: At the end of each round close with a slip stitch into the top of the first stitch. From round 2, at the beginning of each round work ch 1 (does not count as first stitch). Do not turn between rounds – right side is always facing.

To make: With A, ch 2.

Round 1: Sk 1, 6 sc in next.

Round 2: 1 sc, [ch 5 to beg point, sk 1 ch, 4 sc, 1 sc in next sc on center] 5 times, ending ch 5 to beg point, sk 1 sc, 4 sc – 6 sc on center and 6 points.

Round 3: Join B in sc nearest tip of any point, [4 sc, sk 1 sc in center, working in underside of ch of next point, 4 sc, ch 2, sk 1 ch] 6 times.

Round 4: [3 sc, 2 sl st, 3 sc, 3 sc in 2 ch sp] 6 times. Fasten off B.

Round 5: Join C in center sc of any point, [3 sc in center sc of point, 4 sc, sk 2 sl sts, 4 sc] 6 times.

Round 6: Sl st in next sc, [3 sc in center sc of point, 4 sc, sc2tog, 4 sc] 6 times.

Round 7: Sl st in next sc, [3 sc in center sc of point, 5 sc, sk 1, 5 sc] 6 times. Fasten off C.

Round 8: Join B in any sc, 1 sc in each sc around. Fasten off. Make 2nd star.

Finishing: Wrong sides tog, whip st through back lps only from center st of one point to center st of 5th point.

Strap: With 2 strands B, make ch 28". Sew ends to center st of first and 5th points.

Button: Sc over plastic ring until it is covered. Sew to sixth point of front. Make ch lp to fit button on 6th point of back.

SWEET HEART
Page 90

Materials: Knitting worsted-weight yarn (4 oz skein) – 1 skein red; size H crochet hook or size for gauge; button.

Gauge: 4 dc = 1".

Note: Work rounds in continuous spiral.

To make: (Make 2): Chain 8.

Round 1 (right side): Sk 2, 2 dc in next, 1 dc, 1 hdc, 1 sc, ch 1; holding rem 2 ch in back and working along other side of ch, 1 sc in same ch, 1 hdc, 1 dc, 2 dc in next, ch 2, sl st in same ch as first dc of round – top center of heart.

Round 2: 1 sc in next ch made at beg of Round 1, (1 sc, 1 hdc) in next ch, (1 hdc, 1 dc) in dc, 2 dc in next, 2 dc, 1 hdc, 1 sc in each of 2 rem ch of ch 8, ch 1; working on other side of ch, 2 sc, sk ch 1

of Round 1, 1 hdc, 2 dc, 2 dc in next, (1 dc, 1 hdc) in next, (1 hdc, 1 sc) in next ch, 1 sc in next ch, sl st in sl st.

Round 3: 2 sl sts, (1 sc, 1 hdc) in next, *(1 hdc, 1 dc) in next, 2 dc in next, (1 dc, 1 hdc) in next, ** 3 hdc, 3 sc, 1 sc in ch, 3 sc, 3 hdc; rep from * to ** once, (1 hdc, 1 sc) in next, 2 sl sts.

Round 4: 3 sl sts, (1 sc, 1 hdc) in hdc, (1hdc, 1 dc) in next, 2 dc in next, 1 dc, 2 dc in each of next 2, 2 dc, 2 dc in next, 4 dc, (1 dc, ch 1, 1 dc) in next, 4 dc, 2 dc in next, 2 dc, 2 dc in each of next 2, 1 dc, 2 dc in next, (1 dc, 1 hdc) in next, (1 hdc, 1 sc) in next, sl st to center. Fasten off.

Strap: Make 45" ch. Turn, sk 1 ch, sl st across. Fasten off, leaving a 20" end.

Finishing: Block pieces. Holding hearts with wrong side tog, working through both pieces, with crochet hook or needle, attach strap securely to one side of heart as in photograph; continue joining pieces tog around bottom to opposite side, attach other end of strap. Sew button to one side. Make ch loop on other side.

GRANNY SQUARE BOLSTER
Page 91

Approximate size: 23⅝" x 6¾" (diameter).

Materials: 4 oz sport weight yarn, main color MC and total of 6 oz sport weight yarn in at least 20 assorted contrast colors C of your choice. Size B crochet hook (or size for gauge). Polyester stuffing for bolster; material for bolster, 1 piece 24½" x 22" and two circular pieces 7¼" diameter.

Gauge: Square motif measures 2⅝"; square and circular motif 6¾" diameter.

Note: At the beginning of each round work a turning chain to stand as the first stitch of the first pattern repeat as follows: Sc – ch 1; dc – ch 3. At the end of each round close with a slip stitch into the top of this first stitch. Do not turn between rounds – the right side is always facing.

To make square motif: (Make 72) using any C, ch 6, join with sl st to form ring.

Round 1: [3 dc in ring, ch 2] 4 times.

Round 2: Sl st in each st to corner in 2 ch sp, [(1 dc, ch 1, 1 dc, ch 2, 1 dc, ch 1, 1 dc) in 2 ch sp, ch 1, skip 3 dc] 4 times. Fasten off.

Round 3: Join next C in any corner 2 ch sp, [(1 dc, ch 1, 1 dc, ch 2, 1 dc, ch 1, 1 dc) in 2 ch sp, ch 1, skip (1 dc, 1 ch, 1 dc), (1 dc, ch 1, 1 dc) in ch sp, ch 1, skip (1 dc, 1 ch, 1 dc)] 4 times.

Round 4: Sl st in each st to corner 2 ch sp, {(1 dc, ch 1, 1 dc, ch 2, 1 dc, ch 1, 1 dc) in 2 ch sp, [ch 1, skip (1 dc, 1 ch, 1 dc),

(1 dc, ch 1, 1 dc) in ch sp] twice, ch 1, skip (1 dc, 1 ch, 1 dc)} 4 times. Fasten off.

Round 5: Join MC in any corner 2 ch sp, {(1 dc, ch 1, 1 dc, ch 2, 1 dc, ch 1, 1 dc) in 2 ch sp, [ch 1, skip (1 dc, 1 ch, 1 dc), (1 dc, ch 1, 1 dc) in ch sp] 3 times, ch 1, skip (1 dc, 1 ch, 1 dc)} 4 times. Fasten off.

To make circular motif: (Make 2).

Note: Avoid joining in new colors in same place as previous round ended. Using any C, ch 4, join with sl st to form ring.

Round 1: [1 dc in ring, ch 1] 12 times.

Round 2: Sl st in ch sp, [2 dc in ch sp, ch 1, skip 1] 12 times.

Round 3: [2 dc, 1 dc in ch sp] 12 times – 36 sts. Fasten off.

Round 4: (and every alt round): With MC, sc all around. Fasten off.

Round 5: With next C, [2 dc, ch 1] 18 times. Fasten off.

Round 7: With next C, [3 dc, ch 1] 18 times. Fasten off.

Round 9: With next C, [4 dc, ch 1] 18 times. Fasten off.

Round 11: With next C, [5 dc, ch 1] 18 times. Fasten off.

Round 13: With next C, [6 dc, ch 1] 18 times. Fasten off.

Round 15: With next C, [7 dc, ch 1] 18 times. Fasten off.

Sew square motifs to make panel of 9 by 8 motifs.

Shell edging: With right side facing and using MC, work along both short sides of panel as follows: Join in corner ch sp, *(1 sc, ch 3, 3 dc – called shell) in corner 2 ch sp, [skip (1 dc, 1 ch, 1 dc), 1 shell in ch sp] 4 times, skip (1 dc, 1 ch, 1 dc), 1 shell in corner 2 ch sp; rep from * 7 more times, omitting final shell and ending with 1 sc in corner 2 ch sp. Fasten off. Leaving shell edging free, sew short sides of panel to circular motifs to complete crochet bolster cover.

Using 1/2" seam allowances, stitch and stuff bolster. Insert bolster into crochet cover and sew up seam.

Tassels (Make 2): For each tassel wind yarn approx 100 times around 4" wide card and cut through one edge to make strands. Fold strands in half and tie firmly. Attach to each end of bolster in center of circular motif.

GOLDEN GIRL
Page 91

Materials: 1 100yd. ball sport weight yarn; size 2 steel crochet hook or size for gauge; 5/8" plastic ring.

Gauge: 5 sc = 1"; 6 rows = 1".

To make: Ch 23.

Row 1: Sk 1, sc across, turn – 22 sc.

Row 2: Ch 1, sc across, turn. Rep row 2 until piece measures 8"; mark edge for beg of flap.

Flap: Work 4 rows even, then dec 1 st each end every row until 2 sts rem. Fasten off.

Joining and edging: Fold up 4" at straight end; pin in place. With folded end up, join yarn at beg of pocket at right-hand side working through both thicknesses, work 1 sc, * ch 3, sl st between vertical threads of same sc (picot made), work 4 sc**; rep from * to **, working 3 sc in corners and working along folded lower edge, side, then along flap to point; ch 10 from button lp, continue as from * to **, ending sl st in first sc. Fasten off.

Strap: Join yarn on right side at beg of flap, ch to desired length, turn, sl st in each ch. Fasten off. Join end to left-hand side.

Button: Sc over plastic ring until it is covered. Fasten off. Join yarn in back of button, ch 1, join at opposite point. Fasten off. Sew button to bag.

MULTICOLORED GRANNY JACKET
Page 90

Materials: 14 oz knitting worsted Black A, 4 oz each Green B, Dark pink C, Pink D, Orange E, Scarlet F, Blue G, Purple H, Emerald I, and 2 oz Mauve pink J; crochet hook size G or size to give gauge.

Size: One size fits all.

Gauge: Each motif = 4 1/2" square.

Finished measurements: Bust (incl ribbing): 45 1/2". Back at underarm: 19".

Motif: Make 93.

Note: Rounds 1 and 2 form center of motif; make 5 centers in J and 11 centers each in B, C, D, E, F, G, H, and I. Make each motif different, selecting a new color for each round as you work, through round 6; on round 7 rep center color. At the beginning of each round work a turning chain to stand as the first stitch of the first pattern repeat, as follows: Sc – ch 1; dc – ch 3; tr – ch 4. At the end of each round, close with a slip stitch into the top of this first stitch. Do not turn between rounds – the right side is always facing.

Round 1: Ch 2, sk 1, 8 sc.

Round 2: [2 dc in sc, ch 3] 8 times. Fasten off.

Round 3: Join new color in any 3 ch lp, [5 sc in 3 ch lp] 8 times. Fasten off.

Round 4: Join new color in center sc of any 5 sc grp, [3 sc in center sc, 1sc, sc2tog, 1 sc] 8 times. Fasten off.

Round 5: Join color in any sc2tog, [(1 tr, ch 3, 1 tr – corner) in sc2tog, dc2tog, 7sc, dc2tog] 4 times. Fasten off.

Round 6: Join color in any corner sp, [5 sc in corner sp, 11 sc] 4 times. Fasten off.

Round 7: Join center color in center sc of any corner, [3 sc in corner sc, 15 sc] 4 times. Fasten off.

Round 8: Join A in center sc of any corner, [3 sc in corner sc, 17 sc] 4 times. Fasten off.

Half motif: Make 1. With any color ch 2, 5 sc in 2nd ch from hook. Fasten off.

Row 2: Join same color in first sc, ch 6, [2 dc in next, ch 3] 3 times, 1 dc. Fasten off.

Row 3: Join new color in 3rd ch at beg of row 2, 1 sc in same ch, 4 sc in next 6 ch lp, [5 sc in next lp] twice, 4 sc in next lp, 1 sc in last dc. Fasten off.

Row 4: Join new color in first sc of row 3, ch 1, sk first, 1 sc (counts as sc2tog), [3 sc in next, 1 sc, sc2tog, 1 sc] 3 times, 3 sc in next, sc2tog. Fasten off.

Row 5: Join new color in first st of row 4, 1 sc in same st, 2 sc, * dc2tog, (1 tr, ch 3, 1 tr) in next, dc2tog, **7sc; rep from * to **, 3 sc. Fasten off.

Row 6: Join new color in first sc, 5 sc, 5 sc in corner sp, 11 sc, 5 sc in corner sp, 5 sc. Fasten off.

Row 7: Join center color in first sc, 7 sc, 3 sc in corner sc, 15 sc, 3 sc in corner sc, 7 sc. Fasten off.

Row 8: Join A in first sc, 3 sc in same sc, 7 sc, 3 sc in corner sc, 17 sc, 3 sc in corner sc, 7 sc, 3 sc in last sc, do not fasten off.

Finishing: With colors evenly distributed, arrange motifs, following charts and having center edge of half motif to outside. From right side, with A, working through lps from center sc of one corner to center sc of next corner, sew tog with overcast st. Sew shoulders. Sew sleeve seams (C to C).

Collar: With A, work 1 row sc along one long edge of facing strip (outer edge); do not work in seams. With wrong sides tog, pin collar and facing strips tog. Having facing strip to underside, sew inner edges of collar and facing strips to front edge of jacket through all thicknesses, sewing A and B motifs of strips to A and B section of jacket neck and center motif of strip to half motif.

Sleeve ribbing: Right side facing, join A in corner sc of any motif on one free edge; ch 16, sl st in 2nd ch from hook

and each rem ch; 15 sl sts. Insert hook, yo and draw up lp in next 3 sc on motif edge, draw last lp on hook through rem 3 lps on hook, turn.

* Row 1: Ch 1, working in back lps only, sl st in each sl st, turn.

Row 2: Ch 1, working through back lps only, sl st in each sl st, insert hook, yo and draw up a lp in next 3 sc on motif, draw last lp through 3 lps on hook. Rep from * around, end at motif edge. Break A, leaving 12" end. Sew rib closed.

Jacket ribbing: Pin collar and facing tog along outer edges. Work ribbing through both thicknesses. Right side facing, join A in any sc on lower edge at side; ch 6, sl st in 2nd ch from hook and each rem ch; 5 sl sts. Sl st in next sc on motif edge.

* Row 1: Ch 1, turn, working in back lps only, sl st in each sl st.

Row 2: Ch 1, turn, working in back lps only, sl st in each sl st; sl st in next sc on motif edge through both lps. Rep last 2 rows twice; at end of last row, insert hook, yo and draw up a lp in each of next 2 sc on motif edge, drawing last lp through 2 lps on hook. Rep from * to within 3 sts of center sc at corner. Work 3 ribs to each of next 5 sc, work up front edge as before, end at seam between 4th and 5th motif. Work 1 rib to 1 st around neck to seam between 4th and 5th motif on left front. Finish ribbing to correspond to first half, working around to beg. Sew ends tog same as for sleeves. Sew in sleeves.

Tie: With A make ch 48" long, sk 1, sl st across, turn.

Row 2: Ch 1, sl st in back lp across. Rep row 2 for 1 1/4". Fasten off.

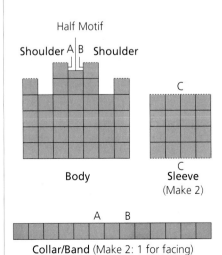

Half Motif

Shoulder A|B Shoulder

Body

C
Sleeve
(Make 2)

A   B
Collar/Band (Make 2: 1 for facing)

Multicolored Granny Jacket

PINWHEEL PUFF

Page 91

Materials: Knitting worsted weight yarn – 3½ oz each Red A, Amethyst B, Blue C, Green D, Yellow E, orange F, size H crochet hook or size for gauge; 12" diameter round pillow form.

Size: 12" diameter.

Gauge: 4 sc = 1"; 4 rows = 1".

Note: Leave each yarn at end of each section of color. On rounds 2–16, bring yarn loosely across back to beginning of section, then work over strand. On rounds 17–22, cut yarn at end of each section.

To make: With A, ch 4, join with sl st in first ch to form ring, ch 1.

Round 1: Working into ring, work 2 sc each A, B, C, D, E and F; do not join.

Round 2: Working around in a spiral, skip first sc, *2 sc in next, 1 sc in first sc of next color, changing to new color; repeat from * around.

Round 3: *1 sc, 2 sc in next, 2 sc in first sc of next color, changing to new color in last stitch; repeat from * around.

Round 4: *2 sc, 2 sc in next, 1 sc, 1 sc in first sc of next color, changing to new color; repeat from * around.

Round 5: *2 sc in next, 1 sc in each sc of section, 1 sc in first sc of next color, changing to new color; repeat from * around.

Rounds 6 to 22: Staggering increases so they do not fall directly over one another, continue in this manner, increasing 1 stitch in each section on each round and moving each section 1 stitch to the left on each round; end last round with sl st in last st; fasten off – 24 sts in each section. Make second piece in same way, but in following color order – A, F, E, D, C and B. Hold pieces together, right side out. Using matching colors, sc around through both layers, inserting pillow form before closing completely.

CROCHET SHELL

Page 109

Materials: 12 250 yd balls sportweight cotton yarn, size 1 crochet hook or size for gauge.

Size: 6–8. Changes for size 10–12 are in (). If only one number appears, it applies to all sizes.

Gauge: 10 mesh = 3"; 5 rows = 2".

Finished measurements: Bust: 31" (33½"). (Garment will give to fit.) Sleeve width: 10½" (11¾").

Note: Ch 3 at beg of each row counts as 1 dc. To work 1 mesh, following initial ch 3 or dc, work ch 1, sk 1, 1 dc.

Back: Ch 108 (116).

Row 1 (right side): Sk 3 ch, 1 dc, *ch 1, sk 1 ch, 1 dc; rep from * across, turn – 52 (56) mesh.

Row 2: Ch 3, 1 dc in first ch sp, *ch 1, 1 dc in next ch sp; rep from * across, ending in top of t-ch, turn.

Rep row 2, called mesh pattern, until 28 rows have been completed.

Shape armholes:

Row 1: Sl st in each st across to 4th dc, ch 3, 1 dc in next ch sp, cont in mesh pat to last 2 sps – 46 (50) mesh, turn.

Row 2 (Dec): Ch 3, sk first sp, 1dc in next sp (dec), cont in mesh pat, ending sk 1 dc, 1 dc in top of t-ch (dec), turn.

Row 3: as row 2.

Row 4: Ch 3, 1 dc in next sp, cont in mesh pat across, ending ch 1, 1 dc in t-ch, turn – 42 (46) mesh. Work even in pat until armholes measure 6½" (7"). Fasten off. Mark center 22 sps on last row for neck edge.

Front Square Motif (make three 4" sq.):

Special abbreviation

Puff – made as hdc4tog in same place (see page 95).

Note: Beg each round with ch 2 (does not count as st) and end with sl st in top of first st and in next ch; work all rounds with right side facing.

Ch 5, sl st in first ch made to form ring.

Round 1: In ring work [1 Puff, ch 3, 1 Puff, ch 2] 4 times.

Round 2: [(1 Puff, ch 3, 1 Puff) in 3 ch sp, ch 2, 4 dc in 2 ch sp, ch 1] 4 times.

Round 3: [(1 Puff, ch 3, 1 Puff) in 3 ch sp, ch 2, 3 dc in 2 ch sp, sk 1 dc, 3 dc, 3 dc in 1 ch sp, ch 1] 4 times.

Round 4: [(1 Puff, ch 3, 1 Puff) in 3 ch sp, ch 2, 3 dc in 2 ch sp, sk 1 dc, 8 dc, 3 dc in 1 ch sp, ch 1] 4 times.

Round 5: [(1 Puff, ch 3, 1 Puff) in 3 ch sp, ch 2, 3 dc in 2 ch sp, sk 1 dc, 13 dc, 3 dc in 1 ch sp, ch 1] 4 times.

Fasten off. Sew squares tog to form a strip.

Edging: Working across long side of strip, from right side join yarn in right corner, 2 sc in corner sp, *1 sc in each st and sp to seam, 1 sc in seam; rep from * twice, end 2 sc in last corner sp – 79 sc. Fasten off. Rep on opposite side, do not fasten off.

Side mesh:

Row 1: Ch 3, working along short side, 1 dc in corner sp, ch 1, sk Puff, 1 dc in 2 ch sp, [ch 1, sk 1, 1 dc] 4 times, ch 1, sk 1 dc, (1 dc, ch 1, 1 dc) in next , [ch 1, sk 1, 1 dc] 5 times, ch 1, sk Puff, (1 dc, ch 1, 1 dc) in corner sp, turn. Work 5 (7) more rows even in mesh pat; fasten off. With right side facing, join yarn in right corner at opposite end of strip and rep mesh pat to match first side.

Lower front:

Row 1: With right side facing, join in lower left corner (i.e. garment right), ch 3; working in sps along side of row [1 dc in sp, ch 1] 6 (8) times, [1 dc in sc, ch 1, sk 1 sc] 39 times, 1 dc in sc, [ch 1, 1 dc in sp] 6 (8) times, turn – 51 (55) mesh.

Row 2: Work mesh pat, turn.

Puff-St pattern:

Row 1: Ch 3, 1 dc in first sp, work 5 (7) mesh, ch 1, 1 Puff in next sp, *[ch 1, 1 dc in next sp] 10 times, ch 1, 1 Puff in next sp; rep from * twice more, [ch 1, 1 dc in next sp] 11 (13) times, ch 1, 1 dc in top of 3 ch, turn.

Row 2: Ch 3, 1 dc in first sp, work 10 (12) mesh, *[ch 1, 1 Puff in next sp] twice, [ch 1, 1 dc in next sp] 9 times; rep from * twice more, ending [ch 1, 1 Puff in next sp] twice, [ch 1, 1 dc in next sp] 5 (7) times, ch 1, 1 dc in top of 3 ch.

Row 3: Rep Puff-St pat row 1.

Rows 4 to 6: Rep Puff-St pat rows 1–3.

Repeat last 6 rows once. Repeat row 2 of lower front once; fasten off.

Upper front:

Row 1: With right side facing, join in upper right corner (i.e. garment left), work as for row 1 of lower front.

Row 2: Rep row 1 of Puff-St pat.

Shape armholes:

Next 4 rows: Keeping Puff-St pat, dec at armholes as for back – 41 (45) mesh Keeping Puff-St pat, work 2 rows even.

Shape neck:

Mark 14 (16th) ch sp in from each side. Working on first side cont pat as established, ending with last dc in first marked sp, turn.

Dec Row: Ch 3, sk first sp (dec); beg in next sp, work Puff-St pat across.

Keeping pat, rep Dec row every 2nd row twice more. Work even in pat until same length as back to shoulder – 10 (12) mesh. Fasten off. Join in next dc following 2nd marked sp, and work 2nd side to correspond to 1st.

Sleeve (Make 2): Ch 74 (82).

Row 1: Rep row 1 of back – 35 (39) mesh. Work as for back for 2½".

Shape cap: Work as for back armhole shaping through row 3. Rep row 3, 9 (10) times more – 7 (9) mesh. Fasten off.

Finishing: Sew side and sleeve seams; sew in sleeves.

Lower edge:

Round 1: With right side facing, join and work 1 sc in first sp at lower left of back, *ch 2, sk 1 sp, 5 dc in next ch sp, ch 2, sk 1 sp, 1 sc in next sp; rep from * around, ending ch 2, sk 1 sp, sl st in first sc; do not turn.

Round 2: *Ch 2, 1 dc in next dc, [ch 3, 1 rfsc around post of same dc (picot made), 1 dc in sp before next dc] 4 times, work picot, ch 2, 1 sc in next sc; rep from * around. (Note: Thread round elastic through base of first row of edging, fit to waist and fasten, if desired.)

Sleeve edging: Same as for lower edge.

Neck edging: With right side facing, join yarn in right shoulder seam, work approx 41 sc across back neck; keeping shape of neck, continue to sc around, having approx 28 sc across the center 14 mesh at front neck, and the total number of sc a multiple of 8. Join in first sc.

Round 1: 1 sc, *ch 2, sk 3 sc, 5 dc in next sc, ch 2, sk 3 sc, 1 sc; rep from * around, sl st in first st.

Round 2: Rep round 2 of lower edge.

LACY JACKET
Page 108

Sizes: Directions are for size Small. Medium and Large sizes are in (). If only one number is given, it applies to all sizes.

Materials: (175-yd ball); 14 (14 – 16) sportweight cotton; crochet hook size F or size to give gauge.

Gauge: 18 sts and 12 rows = 4".

Finished measurements: Bust: 36" (39" – 41½"). Sleeve width: 14" (14½" – 15½").

Note: Ch 2 at beg of each row counts as 1 hdc. To work 1 mesh, following initial ch 2 or hdc, work ch 1, 1 hdc.

Back Panel: Ch 44 (52 – 56).

Row 1 (right side): Sk 2 ch, 1 hdc as follows: Yo, insert hook, yo, draw lp through and up to about ¼", yo, draw through 3 lps on hook (long hdc made; make hdc in same way throughout); hdc across, turn – 43 (51– 55) hdc.

Row 2: Ch 2, sk first st, *ch 1, sk 1, 1 hdc; rep from * across, turn – 21 (25 – 27) mesh.

Row 3: Ch 2, * 1 hdc in ch sp, 1 hdc in hdc; rep from * across, turn.

Rows 4, 5, 6: Rep rows 2, 3, 2.

Diamond pat:

Row 7: Ch 2, work 9 (11 – 12) mesh, ch 1, sk 1 mesh, 4 hdc (block) in next ch sp, ch 1, sk sp, 1 hdc in hdc, continue mesh across, turn – 1 block at center, 10 (12 – 13) mesh each side.

Row 8: Ch 2, work 8 (10 – 11) mesh, ch 1, sk 1 mesh, 4 hdc in next ch sp, ch 1, sk block, 4 hdc in next ch sp, ch 1, sk sp, 1 hdc in hdc, continue mesh across, turn.

Row 9: Ch 2, work 7 (9 – 10) mesh, ch 1, sk 1 mesh, 4 hdc in sp, ch 1, sk 3 hdc of block, 1 hdc, ch 1, sk sp, 1 hdc in hdc, ch 1, sk 3 hdc of block, 4 hdc in sp, continue mesh across, turn. Continue Diamond pat rows 10–17 from chart, then rep rows 8–17, 3 times more. Work even in mesh until 22" from beg, or ½" less than desired length

to shoulders. Fasten off.

Edging:

Row 1: With right side facing, working along side edge, join in corner, ch 2, work 2 hdc at end of each row across side edge only, turn.

Row 2: Ch 2, hdc across, turn.

Row 3: Ch 1, (1 sc and 3 hdc) in first st – shell made, * sk 2 sts, (1 sc and 3 hdc) in next; rep from * across. Fasten off. Work same edging on opposite side edge.

Left front panel: Ch 28 (32 – 32). Work rows 1–6 of back panel – 27 (31 – 31) hdc; 13 (15 – 15) mesh.

Diamond pat:

Row 7: Ch 2, work 5 (6 – 6) mesh, ch 1, sk 1 mesh, 4 hdc in next ch sp, ch 1, sk sp, continue mesh across – 1 block at center, 6 (7 – 7) mesh each side. Work even in Diamond pat as established, following chart rows 8–17, 4 times. Work even until about 2" less than back to shoulder, ending at side edge.

Shape neck:

Row 1: Ch 2, work 6 (7 – 7) mesh, sk 1 ch, 1 hdc in hdc (mesh dec), turn.

Row 2: Ch 2, sk first sp, 1 hdc in hdc, work 5 (6 – 6) mesh. Work even on 5 (6 – 6) mesh until same length as back to shoulders. Fasten off.

Edging: Along side edge only, work same as back edging.

Right front panel: Work same as left front panel, reversing shaping.

Side panels (Make 2): Ch 20 (20 – 24). Work rows 1–6 of back panel – 19 (19 – 23) hdc. Rep'g row 2 of back, work even in mesh until 7¼" (7½" – 8") less than back to shoulder. Fasten off.

Edging: On each side edge, work edging as for back panel.

Sleeve, upper panel: Ch 28 (32 – 32). Work rows 1–6 of back panel – 27 (31 – 31) hdc.

Diamond pat:

Row 7: Ch 2, work 5 (6 – 6) mesh, ch 1, sk 1 mesh, 4 hdc in next ch sp, ch 1, sk sp, work mesh across – 1 block at center, 6 (7 – 7) mesh each side. Work even in Diamond Pat as established until 3 diamonds are completed. Work 1 row mesh. Fasten off.

Under panel: Ch 24 (24 – 28). Work same as side panel until 3" (3" – 3¼") less than length of upper sleeve panel – 23 (23 – 27) hdc.

Divide for underarm:

First half: Work even on 5 (5 – 6) mesh until panel is same length as upper panel. Fasten off.

Second half: Sk center sp on last full row. Work on rem 5 (5 – 6) mesh to same length as first half. Fasten off.

Edging: On each side edge of upper and under sleeve panels, work edging as for back panel.

Finishing: Block pieces. Sew front shoulders to corresponding sts on upper edge of back panel. Beg lower edge, sew side panels to front and back panels by tacking center sts of shells tog. In same way, sew upper and under sleeve panels tog. Mark center of side panels at underarm. Sew sleeves in place, sewing underarm edges to upper edge of side panel each side of marker.

Outer edging:

Round 1: With right side facing, beg lower edge back seam, work 1 round hdc evenly spaced around entire outer edge, inc at corners and dec around neck edge as required to keep work flat, and end with sl st into first st, do not turn.

Round 2: *(1 sc and 3 hdc) in next hdc – called shell, sk 2 sts; rep from * around, sl st in first st. Fasten off. Work same edging on sleeves.

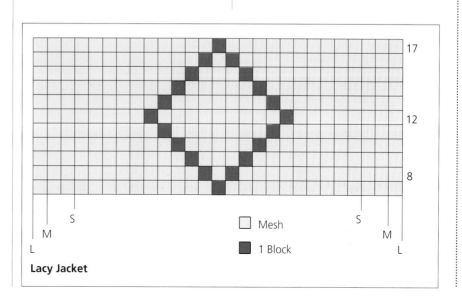

17
12
8

S   S
M   M
L   L

□ Mesh
■ 1 Block

Lacy Jacket

DECORATIVE DOILY
Page 109

Materials: 1 ball 250 yds 10s cotton, size 6 steel crochet hook or size for gauge; 16"-square pillow; ecru sewing thread.

Gauge: First 3 rounds make 3" square.

Finished size: 13" square.

Special abbreviation

Pc (picot) – ch 3, sl st in 3rd ch from hook.

Note: At the beginning of each round, work a turning chain to stand as the first stitch of the first pattern repeat as follows: Sc – ch 1; dc – ch 3; tr – ch 4. At the end of each round, close with a slip stitch into the top of this first stitch. Do not turn between rounds – the right side is always facing.

To make: Ch 5, join with sl st into first ch to form ring.

Round 1: [Tr3tog in ring, ch 5] 5 times.

Round 2: [1 tr, ch 4, sk 1, 1 tr, ch 4, sk2] 6 times.

Round 3: *(Tr3tog, [ch 3, tr3tog] twice) in tr, ch 4, skip 4 ch, [1 hdc in tr, ch 4, skip 4 ch] twice; rep from * 3 more times.

Round 4: Sl st across to 2nd of 3 cls, *(1 tr, ch 9, 1 tr) in 2nd of 3 cls, ch 5, skip 3 ch, 1 tr in next cl, [ch 5, skip 4 ch, 1 tr] 3 times, ch 5, skip 3 ch; rep from * 3 more times.

Round 5: Sl st across to 5th of 9 ch loop, *(1 dc, ch 5, 1 dc) in 5th of 9 ch loop, ch 2, skip 1 ch, 1 dc, [ch 2, skip 2 ch, 1 dc] 12 times, ch 2, skip 1 ch; rep from * 3 more times.

Round 6: Sl st across to 3rd of 5 ch loop, *(1 dc, ch 5, 1 dc) in 3rd of 5 ch loop, [ch 2, skip 2 ch, 1 dc] 15 times, ch 2, skip 2 ch; rep from * 3 more times.

Round 7: Sl st across to 3rd of 5 ch loop, *(2 dc, ch 5, 2 dc) in 3rd of 5 ch loop, [ch 5, skip 2 dc, (1 dc, ch 5, 1 dc) in next dc, ch 5, skip 2 dc, 2 dc in next dc] twice, ch 5, skip 2 dc, (1 dc, ch 5, 1 dc) in next dc, ch 5, skip (2 dc, 2 ch); rep from * 3 more times.

Round 8: *2 dc, ch 5, 1 sc in ch lp, ch 5, [2 dc, ch 5, skip ch lp, 1 dc in dc, 8 dc in ch lp, 1 dc in dc, ch 5, skip ch lp] 3 times; rep from * 3 more times.

Round 9: *2 dc, ch 4, [1 sc in ch lp, ch 4] twice, [2 dc, ch 4, skip ch lp, 10 sc, ch 4, skip ch lp] 3 times; rep from * 3 more times.

Round 10: * 2 dc, ch 4, [1 sc in ch lp, ch 4] 3 times, [2 dc, ch 4, skip ch lp, 10 sc, ch 4, skip ch lp] 3 times; rep from * 3 more times.

Round 11: *2 dc, ch 4, [1 sc in ch lp, ch 4] 4 times, [2 dc, ch 4, skip ch lp, 10 sc, ch 4, skip ch lp] 3 times; rep from * 3 more times.

Round 12: *2 dc in first of 2 dc, ch 4, 2 dc in next dc, ch 4, [1 sc in ch lp, ch 4] 5 times, [2 dc in next dc, ch 4, 2 dc in

next dc, ch 4, skip ch lp, sc2tog, 6 sc, sc2tog, ch 4, skip ch lp] 3 times; rep from * 3 more times.

Round 13: *2 dc, ch 4, 1 sc in ch lp, ch 4, 2 dc, ch 4, [1 sc in ch lp, ch 4] 6 times, [2 dc, ch 4, 1 sc in ch lp, ch 4, 2 dc, ch 5, skip ch lp, sc2tog, 4 sc, sc2tog, ch 5, skip ch lp] 3 times; rep from * 3 more times.

Round 14: *2 dc, ch 4, [1 sc in ch lp, ch 4] twice, 2 dc, ch 4, [1 sc in ch lp, ch 4] 7 times, [2 dc, ch 4, {1 sc in ch lp, ch 4} twice, 2 dc, ch 5, skip ch lp, sc2tog, 2 sc, sc2tog, ch 5, skip ch lp] 3 times; rep from * 3 more times.

Round 15: *2 dc, ch 4, [1 sc in ch lp, ch 4] 3 times, 2 dc, ch 4, [1 sc in ch lp, ch 4] 8 times, [2 dc, ch 4, {1 sc in ch lp, ch 4} 3 times, 2 dc, ch 5, skip ch lp, {sc2tog} twice, ch 5, turn, 1 sc in last dc made, turn, skip ch lp] 3 times; rep from * 3 more times.

Round 16: Sl st across to 2nd of 4 ch loop, *[1 sc in 4 ch lp, ch 4] 4 times, 1 sc in each of 2 dc, ch 4, [1 sc in ch lp, ch 4] 9 times, 1 sc in each of 2 dc, ch 4, [1 sc in ch lp, ch 4] 12 times, skipping (2 dc, 1 sc, 2 dc) over each pineapple motif; rep from * 3 more times.

Round 17: 4 dc in each ch lp and 1 sc in each of 2 sc at corners around – 448 sts.

Round 18: *7 sc, 1 pc; rep from * around

To complete: Center doily on pillow top and tack in place with ecru thread.

DUTCH TILES AFGHAN
Page 111

Materials: Knitting worsted (110-g) ball: 14 balls – White MC; 2 balls each Light blue B, and Royal D; one ball of Medium blue C; afghan hook size J or size for gauge; standard crochet hook size H; tapestry needle.

Gauge: 4 sts, 3 rows = 1" in simple afghan stitch (see page 110).

Size: Approx. 47" by 68" plus fringe.

Special abbreviaton

Pop – popcorn made with 5 dc (see page 95).

Panel: Make 3. With afghan hook and MC, ch 43 loosely. Work in simple afghan stitch for 201 rows. Next Row: Sl st in each vertical bar across; fasten off.

Embroidery: Following chart, embroider each panel, repeating rows 1 through 40; end row 41. Work cross sts over vertical bar.

Panel borders:

Row 1: With right side facing, using standard crochet hook and A, join in right corner of long edge of one panel, ch 1, 1 sc in end of each row across, ending 1 sc in sl st row – 202 sc. Fasten off.

Row 2: With right side facing, join B in first st, ch 1, sc across. Fasten off.

Row 3: With D, rep row 2.

Row 4: With A, rep row 2; do not fasten off, turn.

Row 5: Ch 3, dc across, turn.

Row 6: Ch 3, *1 Pop, ch 2, sk 1, rep from * to last st, 1 dc, turn.

Row 7: Ch 3, *1 dc in 2 ch sp, 1 dc in pop; rep from *to last st, 1 dc, turn.

Row 8: Ch 1, sc across. Fasten off.

Work border on each long edge of panels. Sew panels together.

Fringe: Wind A around 5½" piece of cardboard; cut all yarn strands at one end. Knot strands in every third st across both short ends of afghan. Trim. Steam lightly.

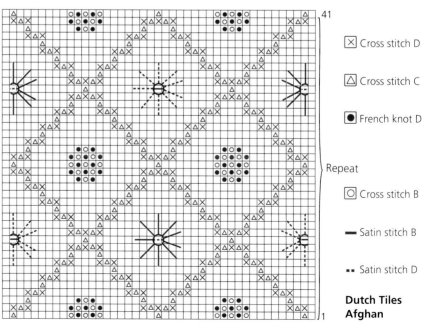

41

☒ Cross stitch D

△ Cross stitch C

⬤ French knot D

Repeat

⊡ Cross stitch B

— Satin stitch B

∙∙ Satin stitch D

Dutch Tiles Afghan

1

ANTIQUE ROSE AFGHAN
Page 113

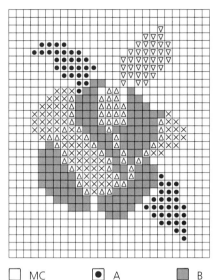

☐ MC   ⦿ A   ▨ B

△ C   ⊠ D   ▽ E

Materials: Knitting worsted-weight yarn, 25 oz Blue MC, 8 oz Pale rose B, 4 oz each of Light green A, Dark rose C, Medium rose D, and Dark green E; yarn bobbins; yarn needle; size K crochet hook or size for gauge.

Gauge: 6 sts, 7 rows = 2" in sc.

Size: Approximately 42" by 51½".

To make: Solid blocks (make 10) – With MC, ch 28.

Row 1 (right side): Sk 1 ch (does not count as st), sc across, turn – 27 sts.

Row 2: Ch 1 (does not count as st) sc across, turn. Rep row 2 30 more times. Fasten off.

Rose blocks (make 10) – Following chart for colors, work as for solid block. Along the center of each leaf in A, work a row of surface chain st in E. On each leaf in E, chain st a row in A (see page 116 Surface Chains).

To assemble: Be sure all blocks are right side up and aligned in the same direction. Alternating blocks, invisibly sew a strip of two solid and two rose blocks with solid block at left side of strip. Make two more strips the same. In same manner, sew together two more strips with rose block at left side. Being sure that blocks alternate checkerboard-style, sew strips together invisibly.

Border: Join MC at a corner of afghan with sl st. Work 498 sc evenly spaced around afghan as follows: 108 sc across top and across bottom; 138 sc along each side; 1 sc in each corner.

Round 1: With B [1 sc in corner st, *ch 4, sk 3 sc, 1 sc in each of next 2 sc; rep from * to last 3 sts before next corner, ch 4, sk 3 sc] 4 times, sl st in first sc.

Round 2: With B, sl st in 4-ch sp, working ch 3 to count as first dc of round (2 dc, ch 2, 2 dc) in each 4 ch lp and in each corner sc all round, sl st in top of first ch 3. Fasten off.

Round 3: Join D in corner 2 ch sp, [(2 sc, ch 4, 2 sc) in corner 2 ch sp, *ch 4, 2 sc in next 2 ch sp; rep from * to next corner] 4 times, sl st in first sc.

Round 4: With D, sl st in next sc and in next ch lp, working ch 3 to count as first dc of round (2 dc, ch 2, 2 dc) in each 4 ch lp all round, sl st in top of ch 3 sp. Fasten off.

Round 5: With C, rep Round 3.

Round 6: With C, rep Round 4.

Round 7: With E, rep Round 3.

Round 8: With E, rep Round 4. Fasten off.

FAN AFGHAN
Page 112

Materials: Brushed mohair, 28 oz White MC; 3 oz each Rose A, Turquoise B, Orange C, Gold D, and Yellow E. Crochet hook size I or size for gauge. 5 large yarn bobbins.

Gauge: 3 sts = 1"; 3 rows = 2".

Finished measurements (without fringe): About 50" by 68". Each square: About 9".

Square: Wind 5 yds each A, B, C, D and E on separate bobbins. (Note: Wind exact amount to avoid purchase of extra yarn.) Beg at corner, with MC ch 4.

Row 1 (wrong side): Sk 3 ch, 4 dc in next, turn – 5 dc.

Row 2: Ch 3, 1 dc in first dc (inc made), 3 dc, 2 dc in last, turn – 7 dc.

Row 3: Ch 3, 1 dc in first dc, [2 dc, 2 dc in next] twice, changing to next color on last st, turn – 10 dc.

Fan pattern:

Row 1 (right side): Ch 3, 1 dc in first dc, 1 dc, changing to B; *2 dc in next – called inc, 1 dc, changing to C **; rep from * to ** once, changing to D, then again, changing to E; turn – 15 dc in 5 colors.

Row 2: Ch 3, dc across in colors as established, turn.

Row 3: Ch 3, dc across, working inc toward center of each color, turn – 5 sts inc'd.

Rows 4 to 8: Rep Fan pat rows 2 and 3 twice more, then rep row 2 once, joining MC at end – 30 dc. Cut bobbins.

Shell pattern:

Row 1: With MC, ch 1, 3 sc, ch 1, sk 1, 1 dc, ch 1 [sk 2, 6 tr in next, sk 2, 1 dc] twice, sk 2, 6 tr in next, ch 1, sk 3, 1 dc, ch 1, sk 1, 4 sc, turn – 34 sts.

Row 2: Ch 1, sl st in back lp of first 10 sts, 1 sc, sk 2 tr, 6 tr in next, sk 2 tr, 1 tr, sk 3 tr, 6 tr in next dc, sk 2 tr, 1 sc, turn.

Row 3: Ch 1, sl st in front lp of next

4 sts, 1sc, sk 2 tr, 6 tr in next tr, sk 2 tr, 1sc. Fasten off.

Border:

Round 1: Right side facing, join MC at point of fan, 3 sc in point (corner), * work 22 sc evenly spaced to next corner, 3 sc in corner; repeat from * twice more, work 22 sc along last side, join with sl st to first sc, sl st in corner sc. Do not turn – 100 sc.

Round 2: Working ch 3 to count as first dc of round, [(5 dc in corner sc – called shell), ch 1, sk 2, {2 dc, ch 1, sk 1} 6 times, 2 dc, ch 1, sk 2], 4 times, sl st in top of 3 ch – 22 sts each side, shell in each corner. Fasten off.

Make 34 more squares, following the same color sequence, but having A in each of the 5 color positions 7 times.

Finishing: Block squares very lightly to same measurement. Arrange right side up, following chart and alternating chart rows 1 and 2 for 7 rows of 5 squares each.

Joining: Beg at side edge, holding 2 squares right sides tog and working through both lps of corresponding sts on each square at same time, join MC in center dc of shells at first corner, 1 sc in same dc, ‡ * 1 sc in next 2 dc, ch 1, sk 1-ch **; rep from * to ** to next shell, 1 sc in first 3 dc of shell; hold next 2 squares tog, 1 sc in 3rd dc of first shell; rep from ‡ across. Fasten off. Join all short rows, then join long rows in same manner, working over previous joinings at corners as follows: 1 sc in 3rd dc of corner shell at end of squares, ch 1, 1 sc in 3rd dc of corner shell on next 2 squares.

Border:

Round 1: From wrong side, join in 3rd dc of shell at one corner, working along edge * [ch 5, sk 2 dc, 1 sc in ch sp] 8 times, ch 5, 1 sc in joining between squares; rep from * around, end 1 sc in joining, turn – 45 lps on each short side, 63 lps on long sides.

Round 2: Sl st to 3rd ch on first lp, working ch 4 to count as first tr of round, [6 tr in first lp of side,* 1 dc in 3rd ch of next lp, 6 tr in 3rd ch of next lp **; rep from * to ** to next corner], 4 times, join in top of 4 ch.

Round 3: [Inserting hook between 6 tr groups at corner work 1 sc, ch 5, sk 3 tr, 1 sc, * ch 5, sk 2 tr, 1 sc in dc, ch 5, sk 3 tr, 1 sc **; rep from * to ** across one side, ch 5] 4 times, join with sl st in first sc. Fasten off.

Fringe: Wind yarn around a 5" cardboard, cut at one edge. Knot 8 strands tog in every 2nd lp around.

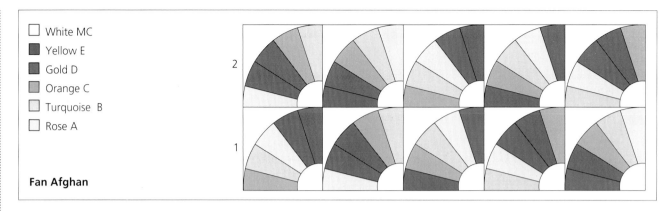

☐ White MC
■ Yellow E
■ Gold D
■ Orange C
☐ Turquoise B
☐ Rose A

Fan Afghan

KALEIDOSCOPE AFGHAN
Page 113

Materials: Knitting worsted-weight yarn – 24 oz Red MC, 8 oz Pink A, 4 oz each Burgundy B, Natural C, Light teal D, Mustard E, Cobalt F, Pale blue G, Lilac H, and Beige I; size K crochet hook or size for gauge.

Gauge: 6 sts, 7 rows = 2" in single crochet (sc).

Size: Approximately 52" x 63".

Note: Turning chain does not count as a stitch.

To make: Center: With MC, ch 118.

Row 1 (right side): Skip 1 ch, sc across, turn – 117 sc. (This is row 1 of Chart 1.)

Row 2: Ch 1, sc across, turn. Row 2 forms pattern. (Row 2 of Chart 1.) Beginning with row 1 of Chart 1, work to row 100, changing colors as indicated, then repeat rows 1 to 72. Work 2 more rows with MC – 176 rows. Fasten off.

Border: Each border strip is made up of eleven squares – 176 rows; make four strips. Following border stitch chart from row 1, ch 17 with color indicated on border color chart. Work in pat as for center, changing colors as indicated – 16 sc.

Finishing: Sew appropriate border strip to each long side edge of afghan. Sew remaining borders to top and bottom edges, easing as required. Join MC with sl st in one corner. Work 5 rounds of sc, with 3 sc in each corner. Fasten off.

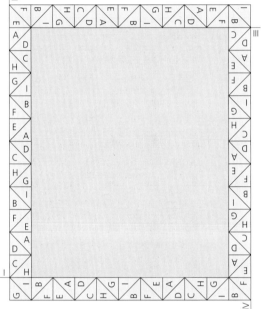

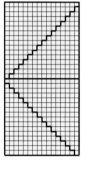

Kaleidoscope Afghan
Border Stitch Chart (above)
Border Color Chart (left)
Chart 1 (below)

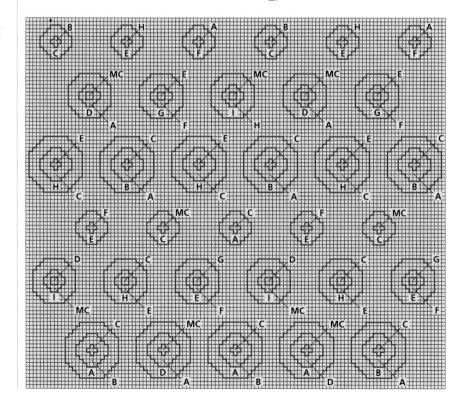

EMBROIDERY

SMOCKED EVENING BAG
Page 148

Finished size: Approximately 5" wide across smocking by 7½" long, excluding tassel.

Materials: Purple iridescent fabric, 45" wide and 16" long; strong thread to gather rows of smocking; 1 skein each of wine, peach, and red pearl cotton; fusible webbing; 1 large tassel; 1 bead; 36" thin wine colored cording; sewing thread.

Smocking: Measure 4" at one end of the fabric. Mark 4" along 45" edge of one fabric; make a line. Make 10 more lines, ½" apart, parallel to first. Mark the dots for smocking on these lines, ½" apart. Gather each row with strong thread and knot threads together in pairs (see page 146).

Smock as follows:

Row 1: 1 row of double cable stitch, in peach pearl cotton.

Rows 2, 3 and 4: 1 row of surface honeycomb stitch in wine pearl cotton.

Rows 4, 5 and 6: 1 row of trellis diamond stitch in red pearl cotton.

Rows 6, 7 and 8: 1 row of trellis diamond stitch in red pearl cotton.

Rows 8, 9 and 10: 1 row of surface honeycomb stitch in wine pearl cotton.

Row 11: 1 row of double cable stitch, in peach pearl cotton.

Remove the gathering threads, turn to wrong side and steam press.

To assemble bag: With right sides together, and matching rows of smocking carefully, stitch side edges together with a ¼" seam to form a tube of fabric. The bottom end of bag is now the end with the smallest amount of fabric below the band of smocking. Press a ½" hem to wrong side around top edge of bag, and stitch in place. Press a ¼" hem to wrong side around bottom edge of bag. Turn under this edge again by ½". Stitch in place, close to open folded edge, leaving a small opening to form a casing. Knot the end of a long piece of thread, and insert it through the casing. Pull up ends of thread to gather bottom edge of bag as tightly as possible, and tie off securely. You will have a small hole at center of gathers.

Cut four circles of fabric, each 2" in diameter. Fuse all four circles together with fusible webbing. Turn bag to right side. Place fused circle inside bag to cover hole at center bottom. Hand stitch in place.

Work a row of gathering stitches around top hem. Pull up gathers to same width as smocking. Turn under this gathered edge to wrong side of bag and stitch in place just above first row of smocking. Make a second line of stitching ¾" above first row of smocking to form a casing. Cut cording into two equal pieces. Make a small hole in casing at side seam edge, and at opposite side edge. Thread one length of cording through casing from each side of bag. Knot ends of cording. Pass a length of knotted thread through tassel. Thread on bead. Sew bead and tassel to center of fused circle at bottom of bag.

STUMPWORK SUNFLOWER
Page 150

Finished size: 2½" diameter.

Materials: One 3½" diameter flexi-hoop; 8" square of off-white fabric; small square of yellow felt; matching sewing thread; 3" square even-weave fabric; 1 skein each orange and brown embroidery floss, fabric glue, waterproof felt-tip pen; crewel needle, tapestry needle.

To make: Cut out 12 flower petals from felt. Start by positioning 6 petals evenly spaced on the center (right side) of the calico square. Sew down petal edges with small over stitches in matching thread. Arrange the remaining 6 petals on top, and sew down the edges in the same way. Work seeding (see page 129) over alternate petals, using 6 strands of orange embroidery floss. Leave each stitch loose so that it forms a raised bump on the felt. Draw a 1" diameter circle in center of evenweave fabric with a waterproof pen. Using 3 strands of orange, and 3 strands of brown embroidery floss together, work rows of turkey stitch across fabric to fill the circle (see page 169). The loops formed by the stitch may be left uncut, or they can be around circle, close to stitching. Smear glue on wrong side of circle to hold stitches in position. Leave glue to dry. Sew turkey stitch circle to center of felt petals with matching thread. Using 6 strands of orange embroidery floss, work a row of couching (see page 136) around the turkey stitch circle, and around the edge of each embroidered petal. To give the couching a raised look, pull up the laid thread with your needle to form a loop between each couching stitch instead of stitching it down flat.

Stumpwork Sunflower
Flower Petal
Template

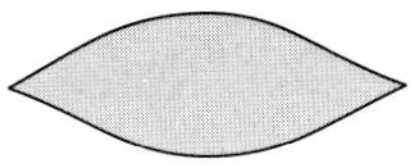

HERB SACHET
Page 150

Finished size: 5½" long by 3½" wide.

Materials: Two rectangles of calico, both 6¾" long by 4" wide; sewing thread to match calico; 2½" square red gingham; small amount of batting; strip of green gingham, 1" x 4" wide; narrow ribbon, 12" long; 1 skein each of red, dark and light green embroidery floss; embroidery needle; small amount of dried herbs.

To make: Use ¼" seams. Embroider with three strands of embroidery floss unless otherwise stated. Draw or transfer position of appliqué heart and embroidered leaf design on to right side of front sachet piece 3½" from top raw edge. Cut heart from red gingham, allowing an extra ¼" all around edges. Sew heart to front sachet and pad with batting, see page 150. Outline heart with couching (six strands red embroidery floss, stitched down with three strands light green). Embroider French knot design on padded heart in red and light green. Embroider leaf design below heart, using dark green stem stitch for stems, light green lazy daisy stitch for leaves, and red French knots for berries. Press under one long edge of green gingham strip by ¼" to wrong side. With wrong side of strip to right side of sachet, baste lower edge of strip to bottom of front sachet, matching raw edges. Hand stitch turned edge of strip to sachet front. Place sachet pieces right sides together, and stitch along side seams and lower edges. Turn right-side out. Turn ½" double hem around open end of bag, baste in position, and sew in place with a row of red and green whipstitch on right side of sachet. Fill sachet with herbs, and tie top with ribbon.

Herb Sachet
- ○ Red French knot
- ● Green French knot

NEEDLEPOINT

GIFT BOXES

Page 170

Finished sizes: Each is 4½" by 5½" or less.

Materials: (For each box) – 2 sheets 7 holes-to-the-inch plastic canvas; yarn needle; worsted-weight yarn. **Strawberry heart** – 70 yds mauve, 50 yds cream, 10 yds each dark green and pink, 8 yds red; **Beehive** – 100 yds dark gold, 8 yds each light yellow, black, brown, white, rose and light pink, 5 yds medium green; **Chickadee** – 96 yds cream, 50 yds sage green, 10 yds each light gray and medium blue, 5 yds each dark gray, black, yellow.

To make: From canvas, cut 1 top and 1 bottom, 2 sides and 2 lid bands. Chickadee box has one 54-hole and one 55-hole lid band. (Beehive – 1 side and 1 lid band). Work designs in continental tent stitch. Beehive: Work side and lid band in long stitch 4 holes high. Fill in with long stitch of varying sizes. Work design on top and bottom; complete background in continental and long stitches.

To assemble: Beehive and Chickadee – sew lid bands together at side edges, overlapping one hole. Sew band to top. In same manner, assemble bottom of box. **Strawberry** – sew lid bands together at front edges. Place this seam at lower point top; sew band to lid. Sew band seam from inside at indentation of heart. Sew side to bottom as for lid. For all boxes: Cover raw edges of box with overcast stitch. **Handle for Beehive:** Cut 1½ yd length rose yarn. Secure one end; twist other end until it begins to kink. Holding center of yarn, bring ends together. Unpin and let yarn twist around itself. Sew an end through each side of box just below lid band. Adjust cord length; knot and trim ends from inside box.

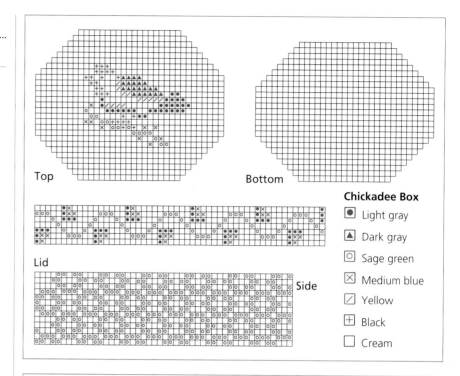

Chickadee Box

- ● Light gray
- ▲ Dark gray
- ◉ Sage green
- ⊠ Medium blue
- ⟋ Yellow
- ⊞ Black
- ☐ Cream

Top

Bottom

Lid

Side

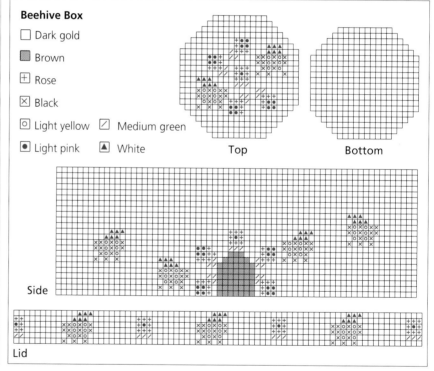

Beehive Box

- ☐ Dark gold
- ▨ Brown
- ⊞ Rose
- ⊠ Black
- ◉ Light yellow
- ⟋ Medium green
- ● Light pink
- ▲ White

Top

Bottom

Side

Lid

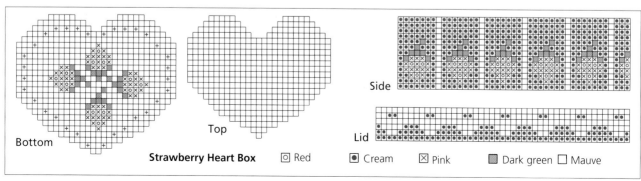

Bottom

Top

Side

Lid

Strawberry Heart Box   ◉ Red   ● Cream   ⊠ Pink   ▨ Dark green   ☐ Mauve

SURPRISE PACKAGE DOORSTOP

Page 170

Finished size: Cover to fit a brick, 8" long by 3¾" wide by 2¼" high.

Materials: Brick; 19" square piece 10 holes-to-the-inch mono canvas. Tapestry yarn skeins: 6 yellow, 5 white, 2 dark blue, 2 mid blue, 1 light blue; waterproof marker, tapestry needle, tape.

To make: Adjust size of design if necessary (see chart). Bind edges of canvas to prevent fraying. Transfer top design onto canvas. Continue ribbon and background design across side and bottom sections of canvas. Work design in tent stitch, following chart. Block finished needlepoint. Trim edges of canvas to ½". Wrap needlepoint around brick. Turn edges of canvas to wrong side. Stitch together with matching thread.

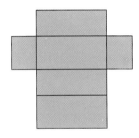

OLD WEST NEEDLEPOINT PILLOWS

Page 171

Finished sizes: Santa Fe, 11" by 14" Albuquerque, 8" by 12½".

Materials: Santa Fe – tapestry yarn skeins: 17 red, 3 each black, brown, 1 each orange, blue, green; 14" by 17" piece 12 holes-to-the-inch mono canvas; 12" by 15" black velveteen for backing.

Albuquerque – tapestry wool: 4 skeins each dark brown, beige, 3 skeins black, 2 skeins each red, blue, and 1 skein each orange, light brown; 11" by 15" piece 12 holes-to-the-inch mono canvas; 9" by 13½" black velveteen for backing.

For both pillows – tapestry needle; polyester stuffing; masking tape; waterproof marker; black sewing thread.

To make (for both): Bind edges of canvas with tape to prevent fraying. Mark horizontal and vertical centers. Beginning at center of canvas and following charts, work pillows in half cross stitch.

Note: Charts are ¼ of designs. DO NOT REPEAT horizontal and vertical center rows. Block completed needlepoint. Trim canvas ½" from design. Right sides in, with ½" seams, stitch backing to needlepoint front, leaving a 2" opening at one side for turning. Clip corners and turn right-side out. Stuff firmly with polyester stuffing and slip stitch opening.

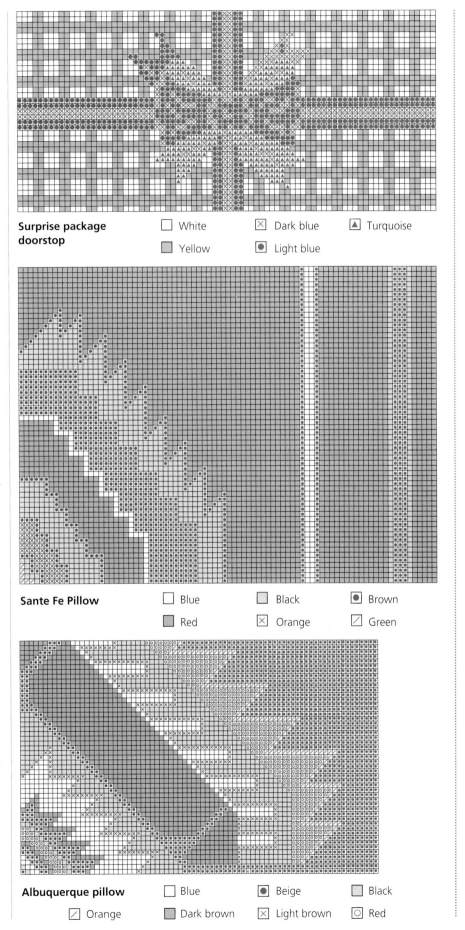

Surprise package doorstop

☐ White	☒ Dark blue	▲ Turquoise
▨ Yellow	⊙ Light blue	

Sante Fe Pillow

☐ Blue	▨ Black	⊙ Brown
▨ Red	☒ Orange	▱ Green

Albuquerque pillow

☐ Blue	⊙ Beige	▨ Black
▱ Orange	▨ Dark brown	☒ Light brown	◎ Red

FOLK-ART FLORAL

Page 171

Finished size: 18" square.

Materials: 24" square piece 5 holes-to-the-inch rug canvas; rug yarn – 100 yds khaki, 20 yds navy, 15 yds red, and 3 yds gold; 1/2 yd navy cotton fabric for pillow back; 18" navy zipper; 18" square pillow form; tapestry needle; masking tape; needlepoint marker; fabric and cotton cable cord if desired; sewing thread.

To make: Use 1/2" seams. Bind edges of canvas with masking tape. Mark an 18" square on canvas; mark center. Starting at the center and following chart, work flowers in continental tent stitch. Work two rows of navy around, inside marked edge; fill in ground with khaki. Block if necessary. Trim edges of canvas to 1/2". Cut two 10 1/4" by 19" navy back pieces. Press under 3/4" on center edges of back. Stitch one folded edge along zipper teeth; lap second edge over zipper and stitch. Trim to size of pillow top. For cording, cut bias strips 2" to 2 1/2" wide; piece to make strip long enough to go around pillow plus about 2". Right-side out, fold bias strip over cotton cord; pin to hold cord at fold. Using zipper foot, stitch close to cord. Trim seam allowance to 1/2". Matching raw edges, pin cording around right side of pillow top, clipping seam allowance at corners. Lap ends neatly and run into seam allowance. Baste close to cord. Right sides in, pin pillow top to back, leaving zipper open. Stitch. Clip corners. Turn right-side out and insert purchased pillow form.

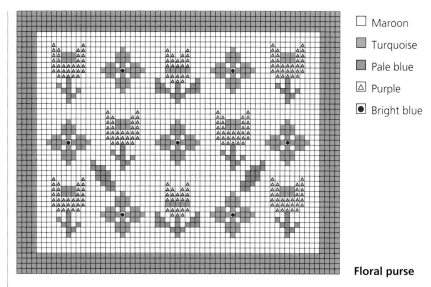

Floral purse

Maroon
Turquoise
Pale blue
Purple
Bright blue

FLORAL PURSE

Page 171

Finished size: 6 1/2" by 5".

Materials: Two pieces 10 holes-to-the-inch mono canvas, 10 1/2" x 9"; skeins tapestry yarn – 4 maroon, 3 pale blue, 1 each purple, turquoise, bright blue; piece lining fabric 7 1/2" by 11"; sewing thread to match lining; 6" zipper (optional).

To make: Front and back pieces both worked the same. Bind edges of canvas with masking tape. Mark a 5" by 6 1/2" rectangle on canvas; mark center. Starting at center, work design in continental tent stitch, following chart. Block finished pieces if necessary. Trim raw edges of canvas around needlepoint to 1/2". Turn back raw edges to wrong side.

Place front and back pieces, wrong sides together, lining up rows carefully. Hand stitch together with matching tapestry yarn down side seams and across bottom edge. Hand sew zipper to top edge of purse. Fold lining fabric in half lengthways, right sides together. Stitch side seams together with a 1/2" seam allowance. Turn right side out. Press a 1/2" hem to wrong side around open edge. Insert lining in purse. Slip stitch turned edge of lining to open edge of purse. To make cord handle; cut six 40" lengths of maroon yarn. Knot strands of yarn tightly, about 1" from the end to form a tassel. Braid strands together, and knot the ends together as before. Sew ends of cord to each side seam.

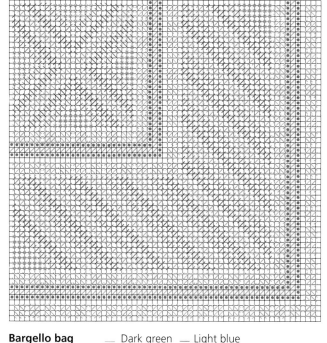

Folk-art floral ■ Red ■ Navy
□ Gold □ Khaki

Bargello bag — Dark green — Light blue
— Dark blue — Lilac

BARGELLO BAG

Page 172

Finished size: 12" square.

Materials: Tapestry yarn – 5 skeins dark green A, 4 skeins each light blue B, dark blue C, lilac D; 16" square 10 holes-to-the-inch mono needlepoint canvas; 13" square of fabric for backing; 3/8 yd fabric for lining; masking tape, tapestry needle.

To make: Bind edges of canvas with masking tape; mark center hole. Chart represents one quarter of design; rotate chart for each quarter of bag. Beginning at center, work one quarter at a time. Center design is made up of small blocks. Following chart, work center diagonal row of block in D. Work a row of C then B on either side of D. Fill blank corners of blocks with continental tent stitch – D at outer edge of center design, A on inside (continental tent stitch to be worked sloping to right). Following chart, work a row of A around center design. In continental tent stitch, work 1 row each B, D, B. Work a second row of A around. Wide border is worked in diagonal rows with continental stitch triangles at centers of bag. X's on chart represent D continental stitches. Diagonal row next to continental stitch is worked in B. Remaining diagonal rows are worked in following color sequence: C, D and B. Work this sequence 4 times. Then work 1 row each C and D at corner. Repeat sequence C, D, B 4 times then 1 row B. Work outer border as for border of center design. Block needlepoint (see page 178); trim blank canvas to 1/2". Right sides in, using 1/2" seam, stitch backing to needlepoint around 3 edges. Cut two 13" squares for lining. Right sides in, stitch lining together along 2 opposite sides; press seams open. Right sides together, slip lining over bag. Stitch around top edge. Turn lining to inside; slip stitch raw edges together. For each handle cut six 24" lengths of A. Hold together and tie one end to a stationary object. Twist strands together tightly. Grasping center, bring ends together. Release center and allow to twist. Tie ends. Sew a handle to each side of bag, having ends 6" apart.

CHRISTMAS STOCKING

Page 177

Finished size: 4 1/2" across top, 9" from top to base of heel, 7" from toe to heel.

Materials: 14" by 12" rectangle 10 holes-to-the-inch mono canvas. 12" by 10" rectangle backing fabric. 1/4 yd lining fabric, 22" wide. Matching sewing thread. Tapestry yarn: 4 skeins cream; 1 skein each of following colors: Scarlet, emerald green, dark pink, turquoise, light and dark gold, light and dark brown. Tapestry needle, tape, waterproof marker.

To make: Bind canvas edges with masking tape. Transfer design on to canvas. Work needlepoint design in continental tent stitch, following chart. Block finished needlepoint if necessary. Trim raw canvas around needlepoint to 1/2".

To finish stocking: Cut backing fabric to same size as trimmed needlepoint. Place backing and needlepoint right sides together. Clip curves. Stitch together with 1/2" seams, leaving top open. Turn right-side out. Press lightly with steam iron. Cut two lining pieces, both 1/4" larger all around edges than finished stocking. Place lining pieces right sides together. Stitch together with 1/4" seams, leaving top open. Turn right-side out. Insert lining in stocking. Fold 1/2" around top of stocking to wrong side, and 1/4" around top of lining to wrong side. Hand stitch turned (top) edges of stocking and lining together.

To make stocking loop: Cut a strip of backing fabric 6 1/2" x 2". Turn 1/4" to wrong side across both short ends. Fold long edges into center. Fold in half again, lengthways. Stitch along length of strip, close to open edges. Fold in half cross-wise, to form loop. Hand stitch ends of loop just inside top of stocking.

CHRISTMAS DECORATIONS

Page 177

Finished size: Snowflakes, circle 3" diameter; crackers – circle 3" diameter; bells – oval 4" deep by 3" wide.

Materials: All decorations worked on 14 holes-to-the-inch mono canvas in tapestry yarn. For colors of yarns, see below. Small gold-colored plastic frames to mount decorations (available from craft shops). Masking tape, waterproof pen, tapestry needle. If frames of the exact size are unavailable, check size and work slightly more or less needlepoint background to fit. **Snowflakes** – piece of canvas 7" square. 1 skein of tapestry yarn in white, and either blue or scarlet. **Crackers** – piece of canvas 7" square. 1 skein of tapestry yarn in each of the following colors: Purple, white, scarlet, green, golden yellow, light blue. **Bells** – piece of canvas 8" by 7". 1 skein of tapestry yarn in each of the following colors: Light blue, white, crimson, scarlet, dark gold, light gold.

To make: Bind canvas with masking tape to prevent fraying. Transfer design on to canvas. Work needlepoint design in continental tent stitch, following chart. Block finished needlepoint if necessary. Trim raw canvas around needlepoint to fit frames.

CHRISTMAS CARDS

Page 176

Finished size: Christmas tree, 2 1/4" by 3 1/4"; Gift box 2 1/4" by 3 1/4".

Materials: Both cards worked on 18 holes-to-the-inch petit point canvas in crewel yarn. For colors of yarns, see below. Masking tape, tapestry needle, waterproof marker. Ready bought cards for needlepoint (from craft shops), or colored cardboard to make your own cards. **Christmas tree** – piece of canvas 6 1/4" by 7 1/4". 1 skein crewel yarn in each of the following colors: Emerald green, scarlet, yellow, dark green, mauve, orange, bright pink. **Gift box** – piece of canvas 6 1/4" x 7 1/4". 1 skein crewel yarn in each of the following colors: Dark turquoise, mid-turquoise, light turquoise, cream, scarlet, emerald green, bright pink; double-sided adhesive tape.

To make: Bind canvas with tape to prevent fraying. Transfer design on to canvas. Work needlepoint design in continental tent stitch, following chart. Block finished work if necessary. Trim raw canvas around needlepoint to 1/2".

To mount: With double-sided adhesive tape, carefully stick worked needlepoint in position behind window mount.

GIFT TAGS

Page 176

Finished sizes: Approximately 2" by 2 1/4".

Materials: All tags worked on 18 holes-to-the-inch petit point canvas. For colors of crewel yarns, see below. To mount tags: Craft knife, ruler, colored cardboard, narrow ribbon, double-sided adhesive tape, adhesive for card. Masking tape, waterpoof marker, tapestry needle. **Crackers** – canvas 6" by 6 1/4". 1 skein crewel yarn in each: White, orange, bright pink, golden yellow, blue, lime green, bottle green. **Christmas tree** – canvas 6" by 6 1/4". 1 skein crewel yarn in each: Pale blue, scarlet, golden yellow, brown, dark green, mauve, bright pink, orange. **Christmas pudding** – canvas 6" by 6 1/4". 1 skein crewel yarn in each: Tan, orange, white, yellow, brown, green, red.

To make: Follow instructions for Christmas cards, below.

To mount: Allowing for border of desired width, cut piece of card twice width of finished tag. Lightly score the card at center line with craft knife.
Cut window in one half of card to size of needlepoint. Using double-sided adhesive tape, carefully stick needlepoint to back of card, behind window. Fold card along score line, and stick folded portion to border of window mount. Trim if necessary.

Christmas Pudding Gift Tag

- ☐ Dark brown
- ▨ White
- ▨ Rust brown
- ⊙ Scarlet
- ⊠ Golden yellow
- △ Light green
- ⧄ Orange

Christmas Crackers Gift Tag

- ☐ Bottle green
- ▨ White
- ☐ Bright pink
- ▨ Orange
- ⊙ Blue
- ◌ Lime green
- ⊠ Golden yellow

Christmas Tree Gift Tag

- ☐ Bright pink
- ▨ Dark green
- ▨ Orange
- ◌ Mauve
- ⊙ Scarlet
- ⊠ Golden yellow
- ⧄ Brown   ☐ Pale blue

Gift Box Card

- ☐ Cream
- ▨ Dark turqoise
- ▨ Mid turquoise
- ▼ Light turquoise
- ◌ Emerald green
- ⊙ Bright pink
- ⊠ Scarlet

Christmas Stocking

- ☐ Cream   △ Turquoise
- ▨ Scarlet   ▼ Dark brown
- ▨ Dark pink   ◌ Gold
- ⊠ Light brown   ⊙ Emerald green

246

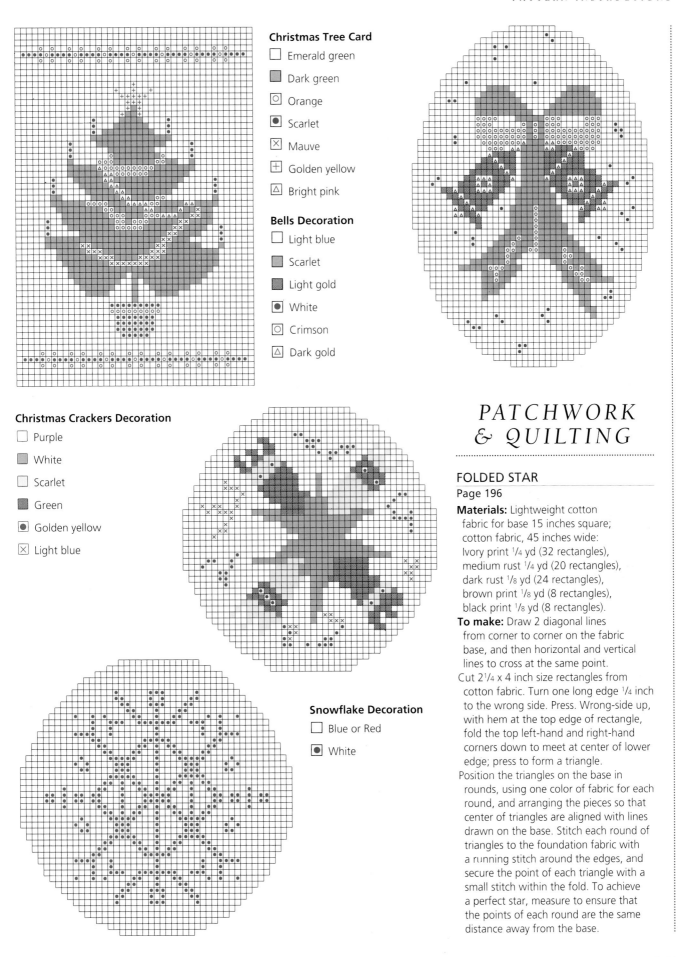

Christmas Tree Card
- ☐ Emerald green
- ▦ Dark green
- ⊙ Orange
- ● Scarlet
- ⊠ Mauve
- ⊞ Golden yellow
- △ Bright pink

Bells Decoration
- ☐ Light blue
- ▦ Scarlet
- ▦ Light gold
- ⊙ White
- ◯ Crimson
- △ Dark gold

Christmas Crackers Decoration
- ☐ Purple
- ▦ White
- ☐ Scarlet
- ▦ Green
- ⊙ Golden yellow
- ⊠ Light blue

Snowflake Decoration
- ☐ Blue or Red
- ⊙ White

PATCHWORK & QUILTING

FOLDED STAR
Page 196

Materials: Lightweight cotton fabric for base 15 inches square; cotton fabric, 45 inches wide: Ivory print 1/4 yd (32 rectangles), medium rust 1/4 yd (20 rectangles), dark rust 1/8 yd (24 rectangles), brown print 1/8 yd (8 rectangles), black print 1/8 yd (8 rectangles).

To make: Draw 2 diagonal lines from corner to corner on the fabric base, and then horizontal and vertical lines to cross at the same point. Cut 2 1/4 x 4 inch size rectangles from cotton fabric. Turn one long edge 1/4 inch to the wrong side. Press. Wrong-side up, with hem at the top edge of rectangle, fold the top left-hand and right-hand corners down to meet at center of lower edge; press to form a triangle.

Position the triangles on the base in rounds, using one color of fabric for each round, and arranging the pieces so that center of triangles are aligned with lines drawn on the base. Stitch each round of triangles to the foundation fabric with a running stitch around the edges, and secure the point of each triangle with a small stitch within the fold. To achieve a perfect star, measure to ensure that the points of each round are the same distance away from the base.

QUILTING PATTERNS
Page 208

Enlarge these patterns to use when making up your own designs.

RUGS

FRINGED MAT & PILLOW
Page 220

Finished size: About 20" by 32" (including 3" fringe).

Materials: 72 6" by 44" calico strips or ¼ yard of 44" wide fabric in the following colors: 12 assorted blues, 12 assorted yellows, 12 assorted off whites and beiges, 12 assorted greens, 12 assorted roses, 12 assorted purples, 90 feet of lacing cord. The colors in this list are given as a guide for selecting your colors. Any varied assortment of colors that you like will produce similar results.

To make: Cut or tear 6" wide braiding strips from all of the different color fabrics. Each strip should be 44" long.

Braiding: The fringed mat is made up of 24 straight braids. Three assorted color strips are braided together to make each braid. Select the colors for each braid yourself, keeping the colors varied. Any mix of colors looks good as long as the assorted shades are evenly dispersed when the braids are laced together. Fold in the long raw edges on each strip so they are about 1½" wide. Do not make a starting T. Braid straight for a distance of about 32". Hold the ends together with a safety pin. Repeat this, making twenty-four 32" braids.

Lacing: Lay the braids out in the color order that you want to have in the finished fringed mat. Work on a flat surface. Hold the first two braids next to each other and lace them together. Do not knot the cord at the end of the braids so you can adjust the length of the finished braid.

The braids that are being laced must have exactly the same number of loops so they are all the same length. As you finish lacing each one, adjust the braid length to match the previous one, tack the braiding together to prevent raveling, knot the lacing cord and cut the ends of the braids evenly to make a 3" fringe. Repeat this until all 24 braids are laced together.

Finishing: Steam the completed fringed mat lightly. Press the fabric fringe flat, tucking all the raw edges inside. The short cut ends of the fringe are left raw.

Pillow: Make a smaller version of this fringed mat and turn it into a pillow. Braid a 14" by 12" mat; add a back and stuff it with a pillow form. Slip stitch closed.

SHEEP RUG

Page 216

Finished size: 22" square.

Materials: 28"-square piece of foundation fabric; fabrics for hooking – white, dark gray, light gray, and very pale yellow for sheep; gold for bell, dark rust and light rust for bow and for border, assorted deep olive greens for background; 5" primitive-type hand hook; frame to fit.

To make: To hand hook, see pages 215–216. Enlarge design and transfer it to foundation fabric. If you wish to personalize your rug, you can add initials and/or date on the lower right and left sides.

Mount foundation fabric in a frame. Cut the strips for hooking ³/₈"-wide. Outline the sheep, the ears, the tops of the legs (but not feet or nose) with very pale yellow. Work bow with rust fabrics, using dark rust for outside of ribbon and light rust for inside. Work gold bell. Work light gray eye, edge of nose, and edge of feet. Fill in nose and feet with dark gray. Outline each scallop with dark rust. Work one row of dark rust on either side of line inside of each scallop. Work remainder of each scallop in light rust. Work outer border of rug in dark rust. Work background in various deep olive greens. For finishing, see page 224.

PATCHWORK RUG

Page 216

Finished size: 29" by 38".

Materials: ¹/₄" wide strips of wool fabric in the following colors – black A, light blue B, medium blue C, rust brown D, light gray E, dark gray F, green G, pink H, plum I, light rust J, bright rust K, sapphire L, and tan M; 37" by 46" piece of burlap; frame to fit burlap; 5" primitive-type hand hook; carpet tape; carpet thread; strong needle.

To make: Enlarge design and transfer it to burlap. To hand hook, see page 216. Follow chart for color guide. Although it is possible to hook in many directions, this rug is best handled by hooking in parallel rows, a technique that must be continued throughout for consistency. Loops should be parallel to one another and not appear twisted. For finishing, see page 224.

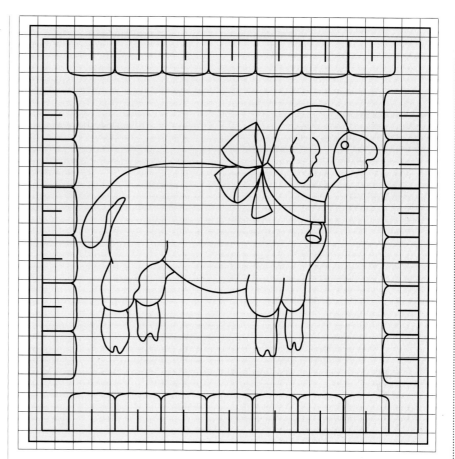

Sheep Rug

Patchwork Rug

INDEX

EMBROIDERY

PATCHWORK & QUILTING

RUGMAKING

ACKNOWLEDGMENTS

Carroll & Brown would particularly like to thank Megan Newman of William Morrow and Company, Inc., for her continual assistance, which has been invaluable during the production of this book, and the following staff/suppliers:

Photography
All original photography by Jules Selmes, assisted by Steve Head. Photographs from Good Housekeeping: Quilted leaf, page 208, Fan afghan, page 112, by Myron Miller. Log cabin quilt, page 199, four quilts, page 204, by Buck Miller.

Production Team
Lorraine Baird, Consultant; Wendy Rogers, Manager; Amanda Mackie, Assistant. Rowena Feeny, Typesetter. Text film: Disc to Print. Reproduction: Colourscan, Singapore.

Knitting
Knitters: Audur Norris, Teresa Schiff, and Denise Robertson. Knitwear detail, page 25, Tony Davey. Aran sweater, page 30, from Kilkeel Knitting Mills Ltd. Color motifs, page 54, by Sasha Kagan. Model, Helen Leigh. Knitting chart illustrations by Amy Lewis. Kaleidoscope sweater, page 5l, Log Cabin sweater, page 56, Crewel-embroidered cardigan, page 57, all designed by Stitchworx. Cardigan embroidery by Marsha Evans Moore.

Crochet
Crochet contributors: Sylvia Cosh and James Walters. Crochet worker, Pat Rhodes. Crochet chart illustrations by Amy Lewis. Sweet Heart purse, page 91, designed by Pat Higgins. Decorative doily pillow, page 109, designed by Estella Lacy for Coats & Clark. Antique roses afghan, page 112, and Kaleidoscope afghan, page 113, both designed by Stitchworx.

Embroidery
Embroidery steps and examples: Claire Slack and Deborah Gonet (surface stitches); Moyra McNeill (pulled threadwork, drawn threadwork, blackwork); Jean Hodges (smocking); Jan Eaton (stumpwork, whitework). Aida fabric by Zweigart. Dressmaker's carbon paper, embroiderer's marking pen, and all basic sewing equipment, by Prym. Antique embroideries, page 126, loaned by Meg Andrews. Samplers, page 140, by Terry Meinke, The Scarlet Letter, Ruth Ann Russell.

Needlepoint
Needlepoint steps and Christmas cracker project by Gayle Bocock. Needlepoint worker, Audur Norris. All tapestry canvas by Zweigart. Gift boxes, page 170, designed by Amy Albert Bloom. Folk Art Floral pillow, page 171, designed by Dorothy Sparling. Old West needlepoint pillows, page 171, designed by Jennifer Cass.

Patchwork & Quilting
Patchwork text copyright © Linda Seward. Patchwork and quilting worked by Lynne Edwards, Judy Hammersla, and Monica Milner. Log Cabin quilt, page 198, quilted by Helen Manzanares. Strawberries quilt, page 200, from the permanent collection of the Museum of American Folk Art (gift of Phyllis Haders). Quilts, page 204 (top left), Maggie Potter; (top right), Constance Finlayson; (bottom left), Mary Jo McCabe; (bottom right), Frances V. Dunn. Quilted leaf, page 208, designed by Paul Doe. Rotary cutter, craft knife, and cutting board from Olfa. Walking foot with seam guide attachment for sewing machine from Bernina.

Rugmaking
Rugmaking steps by Ann Davies. Sheep rug, page 216, designed by Marie Azzaro, hooked by Sandra Hoge. Patchwork rug, page 216, designed and hooked by DiFranza Designs. Braided fringed mat and pillow, page 220, designed by Shirley Botsford made with Distelfink's BraidCraft tools.